Contents at a Glance

Contents

About the Author

 **Mark Collins** wrote his first software program using Basic on the TRS-80 in 1978. As technology has evolved, so has his interest and enjoyment of this wonderful world of software. Mark's career has included many varied opportunities, including being an electrical engineer for IBM, being a system acquisition officer for the U.S. Air Force, spending 12 years designing and building world-class point-of-sale solutions, spending a two-year stint in Engand, and (most recently) providing donor management systems for two well-known nonprofit organizations. Mark has also developed a CASE tool called Omega Tool (www.TheCreativePeople.com).

About the Technical Reviewer

■ **Michael Mayberry** currently helps lead a software team for a nonprofit organization to build .NET enterprise applications. He serves as a lead architect and focuses on adopting new technologies toward solid solutions. Michael's experience includes the development of web-based extranet solutions, along with data collection and analysis applications within the auto industry. Michael moved to build CRM and BI solutions for the nonprofit industry more than seven years ago.

Acknowledgments

First of all, I want to acknowledge that anything that I have ever done that is of any value or significance was accomplished through the blessings of my Lord and Savior, Jesus Christ. This book is a visible demonstration of that fact. The challenges in a project such as this were beyond my own ability, and God's amazing grace carried me through. He is my strength, my vision, and my provider.

Next, I want to say a big "thank you" to my beautiful wife, Donna. You are an inspiration to me. You selflessly took care of our household and encouraged me to focus on this book. I could not have done it without you. You are the embodiment of a Proverbs 31 wife. I am truly blessed to be able to share my life with you.

I am also very thankful for all the people at Apress who made this book possible and for all their hard work that turned it into the finished product you see now. Through numerous rewrites and revisions you were always helpful, patient, and encouraging. Thank you!

I also want to thank Kevin Belknap, who helped me with the web application for the sample solution in the appendix. You always know how to make a site look great! Thank you for eagerly helping with this project.

Finally, I want to thank Michael Mayberry for reviewing this book. Not only did you review this book, but you also had to review several preliminary versions, which no one will probably ever see. I appreciate your heart that strives for excellence, your humility, and your selflessness.

Introduction

When I first started looking at Microsoft's Workflow Foundation (WF) I had a sense that there was something really useful there, but figuring out the right application of the technology seemed elusive. The available code samples demonstrated some specific features, but there was no roadmap to help bring it all together. So I started writing this book to help others who wanted to understand WF.

Along the way, the first beta release of WF 4.0 was made available, which was a complete departure from the previous version. So the first book based on version 3.5 was shelved, and I started writing a new book for WF 4.0. When the second Beta was released with significant changes, the book was once again rewritten. Having watched WF evolve from version 3.5 to 4.0 B1 and then 4.0 B2, and finally 4.0 RC, I can confidently say that these improvements will make your job as a workflow developer much easier.

How to Use This Book

An ancient proverb says, "Tell me and I'll forget; show me and I may not remember; involve me and I'll understand." Based on this truth, this book presents a series of workflow projects; starting with simple solutions and gradually increasing in complexity. New concepts are introduced in each chapter. In each project, I'll show you step-by-step how to implement them for yourself. I recommend that you work through each chapter in order because each chapter builds on both concepts and code that was developed in previous chapters.

As an alternative, you can download the final implementation of each chapter from www.apress.com. You can then read the book and follow along with the downloaded code. This approach is recommended for more experienced developers who are looking for a quick tutorial or perhaps an explanation of specific concepts.

In either case, once you have read the book and are starting to implement workflow in your own solutions, the sample projects provided in this book make a handy reference guide. A topical reference is provided to help you find the appropriate chapters to look at for each of the WF concepts.

Several of the projects require a SQL Server database. Just about any version will work, including the Microsoft Data Engine (MSDE) provided with Visual Studio. You will need to create the databases and configure the appropriate connection strings. You can download the database scripts from www.apress.com, which provide everything you'll need to create the schemas.

Chapter Outline

This book's projects (chapters) are grouped into five sections. In many cases, the same solution is provided in all chapters in that section, with each chapter providing new features to the project from the previous chapter.

Section 1: Basic Concepts

In the first section, you'll build three simple workflows. In Chapter 1, you'll create a workflow using the workflow designer and some of the basic built-in activities. In Chapter 2, you'll re-create the same workflow in code. This will give you an opportunity early on to see both designer workflows and coded workflows. Both types will be demonstrated throughout the book. In Chapter 3, you'll use the flowchart activity, which provides the ultimate flexibility in designing complex workflows.

Section 2: Designing Workflows

In the second section, you'll build a workflow that computes the cost of an order. Each chapter will add additional features to the project from the previous chapter. The project in Chapter 4 demonstrates how to pass data into and out of a workflow. In Chapter 5, you'll interactively execute activities based on a collection of objects. Chapter 6 will show you how to handle and throw exceptions. In Chapter 7, you'll explore the two main ways to extend the workflow activities: creating a custom activity and executing the InvokeMethod activity.

Section 3: Communication

In the third section, you'll build workflows that take advantage of the integration with the Windows Communication Foundation (WCF). The project in Chapter 8 builds a console application that communicates with other instances of the same application using WCF messages. In Chapter 9, the console app is replaced with a Windows Presentation Foundation (WPF) application, which demonstrates how the application and workflow can interact with each other. In Chapter 10, you'll host a workflow in a WCF web service. You'll also consume that service using a workflow application.

Section 4: Workflow Extensions

A key component of workflow design is the use of extensions to configure the environment in which the workflow activities operate. The project in Chapter 11, for instance, demonstrates how to use the standard SQL persistence extension. This extension allows the state of the workflow to be written to a SQL database and retrieved later, when the workflow is resumed. In Chapter 12, you'll explore ways to extend and customize the persistence operation. The project in Chapter 13 demonstrates how to track the execution of a workflow in a variety of ways. In Chapter 14, you'll use database transactions to ensure data consistency across multiple activities. In Chapter 15, you'll execute the application updates on the same database transaction used to persist the workflow state. This will guarantee that the workflow state and application data stay consistent. Finally, in Chapter 16, you'll learn how to configure extensions when the workflow is instantiated by a WorkflowServiceHost.

Section 5: Advanced Topics

Chapter 17 demonstrates how to include logic within the workflow design to handle abnormal conditions such as compensation and cancellation. In Chapter 18, you'll see how to use both built-in and custom activities to support collections of objects. The project in Chapter 19 uses the Interop activity to execute workflows and activities that were created using previous versions of WF. In Chapter 20, you'll use the Policy activity from version 3.0 in a WF 4.0 workflow.

Appendix

The Appendix describes a sample workflow that demonstrates many of the concepts presented in this book. It is designed as a review of the key concepts while providing another example of a workflow implementation. This project is not described in a step-by-step fashion. Instead, the final code can be downloaded from www.apress.com.

■ ■ ■

PART 1

Introduction

The Workflow Foundation included in .Net 4.0 (referred to as WF 4.0) represents a whole new paradigm for building workflow-based applications. It has been completely re-engineered from the ground up. In this section, you'll design some simple workflows and learn the basic concepts. In subsequent sections, you'll develop more complex solutions as you explore the capabilities provided by WF 4.0.

CHAPTER 1

Building a Simple Workflow

Let's start by building a simple workflow. Start Visual Studio (VS) 2010 and select the New Project link. Under the Installed Templates, navigate to Visual C#, Workflow and you should see that four templates have been provided. Select the Workflow Console Application, as shown in Figure 1-1. Enter the name as **Chapter01** and select a suitable location for this solution.

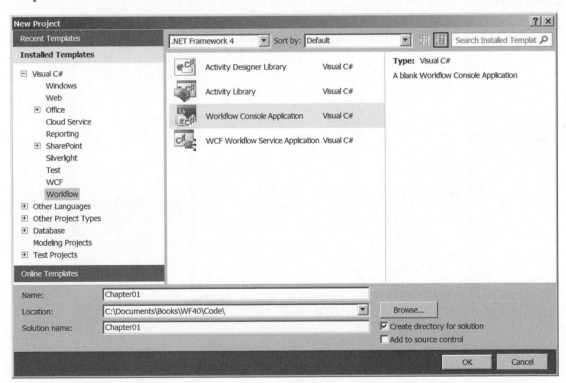

Figure 1-1. *Creating a new workflow project*

A Simple Workflow

The template generates a `Program.cs` file, which implements the console application. It also generates a `Workflow1.xaml` file, which defines the activities in your workflow. If you've worked with Windows Presentation Framework (WPF) applications, you're probably familiar with xaml, which is an XML-like syntax used for declaring programmatic elements. Instead of labels, text boxes, and grids, however, this file will contain the activity-derived elements in your workflow definition. VS 2010 provides a designer that allows you to graphically view and edit these activities.

Exploring the IDE

Figure 1-2 shows a typical layout of the Visual Studio 2010 integrated development environment (IDE). The Toolbox on the left contains the built-in and custom activities that are available to you. I have expanded some of the more common groups of activities. The Solution Explorer and the Properties window are on the right. The bottom window contains a number of tabs including the Error List and Output window.

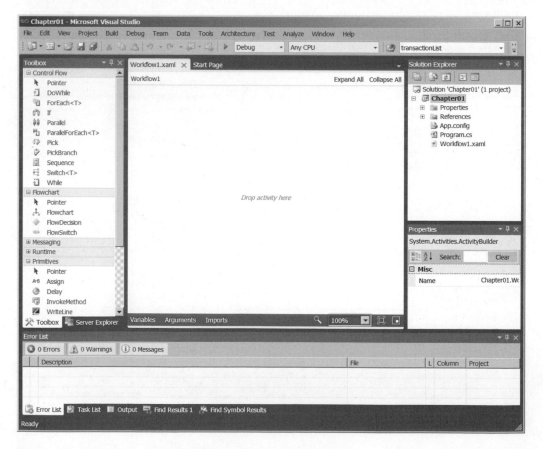

Figure 1-2. *Typical Visual Studio 2010 IDE*

The WF 4.0 designer is in the middle. At the bottom right, there are controls for zooming. Workflow designs in version 4.0 tend to be somewhat long, and this is a handy feature to see the "big picture" or to find a particular activity. There are three controls at the bottom left for displaying the variables, arguments, and imported assemblies. When you click the Variables control, a window appears to show the existing variables, as shown in Figure 1-3. To close this window, click the Variables control again.

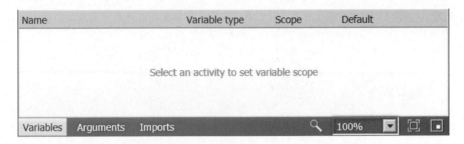

Figure 1-3. *Viewing workflow variables*

If you think of your workflow as a class, variables are the class members. You can use them to store data that must be shared between activities. You can define the scope of a variable—either the entire workflow or just a specific activity (and its children). Arguments are similar to variables, but they are intended for passing data in or out of the workflow. You can think of them as method parameters.

Figure 1-4 shows what the Arguments window looks like. Notice the Direction column; it defines whether the data is passed in to the workflow or sent out of the workflow.

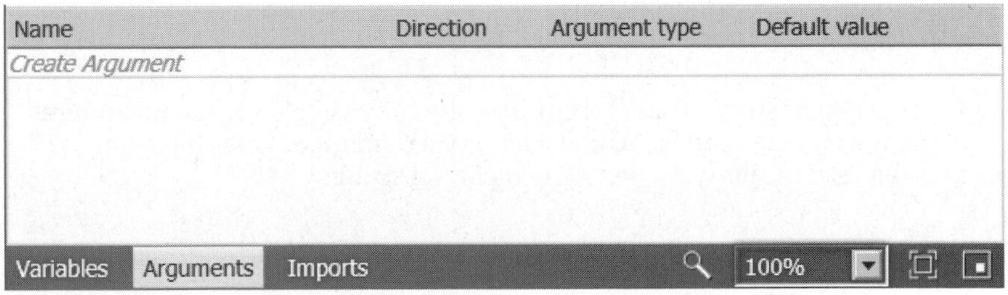

Figure 1-4. *Viewing workflow arguments*

Designing the Workflow

The initial workflow designer is empty. You will drag activities onto it to define the workflow behavior. This project will initially just display the greeting "Hello, World!" Later, you'll embellish it somewhat to discover some of the procedural activities. To start, drag a Sequence activity onto the designer. Then drag a WriteLine activity to the Sequence. The diagram should look like the one shown in Figure 1-5.

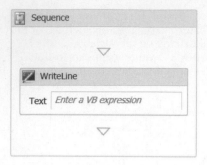

Figure 1-5. *Adding a WriteLine activity*

The Properties window is shown in Figure 1-6.

Figure 1-6. *WriteLine Properties window*

The `DisplayName` property is the text shown in the diagram. You should give this a more meaningful name because when you have many `WriteLine` activities, it will help you remember what this is for. Change this to **Hello**. Also, enter the `Text` property as the following literal string:

```
"Hello, World!"
```

The `Text` property can be any expression that results in a string. You can click the ellipses, which will display a dialog in which you can enter an expression.

You can leave the `TextWriter` property blank. By default, the text will be written to the console. You can specify a class derived from `TextWriter` (new for .Net 4.0) if you want to specify a different implementation. This will be demonstrated in Chapter 9.

Reviewing Program.cs

Open the `Program.cs` file, which will implement the console application and launch the workflow. The default implementation generated by the template is shown in Listing 1-1.

Listing 1-1. *Default Program.cs Implementation*

```
using System;
```

```
using System.Linq;
using System.Activities;
using System.Activities.Statements;

namespace Chapter01
{

    class Program
    {
        static void Main(string[] args)
        {
            WorkflowInvoker.Invoke(new Workflow1());

            Console.WriteLine("Press ENTER to exit");
            Console.ReadLine();
        }
    }
}
```

The static `WorkflowInvoker` class is used to start the workflow that is defined by the `Workflow1` class. The lines in bold are not in the default implementation:

```
Console.WriteLine("Press ENTER to exit");
Console.ReadLine();
```

I added these lines so the console app does not exit before you have a chance to see the output. You should add this code to your project.

Running the Application

Now press F5 to run the application. The result should look like this:

```
Hello, World!
Press ENTER to exit
```

Adding Procedural Elements

WF 4.0 provides a number of procedural elements such as `If`, `While`, `Assign`, `Sequence`, and so on. To demonstrate how they work, you'll enhance this greeting. First, like some old-fashioned clocks, you'll sound a number of bells to indicate the time (one bell for each hour). Open the `Workflow1.asmx` file.

Using Variables

With WF 4.0, you must declare all variables that are used by the workflow elements. You'll need two variables: one to indicate how many bells are needed and another to serve as a counter to keep track of how many bells have been sounded so far. Click the Variables button. If the Variables window looks like the one shown in Figure 1-3 (there are no variables and no way to add a variable), it means that no scope has been defined.

Click the main Sequence activity, and the Variables window should look like the one shown in Figure 1-7.

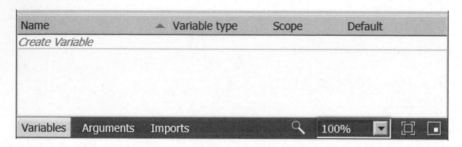

Name	▲ Variable type	Scope	Default
Create Variable			

Variables　Arguments　Imports

Figure 1-7. *Variable window with a defined scope*

Click the *Create Variable* link. Enter the name as **counter** and select Int32 as the variable type. You can leave the scope as Sequence. This means that the variable is available to the Sequence activity and all its descendants. Enter the Default as **1**. The Variables window should now look like the one shown in Figure 1-8.

Name	Variable type	Scope	Default
counter	Int32	Sequence	1
Create Variable			

Variables　Arguments　Imports

Figure 1-8. *Variable window with a new variable*

The Properties window also has these same values (see Figure 1-9). You can enter the variable's properties in the Properties window or the Variables window.

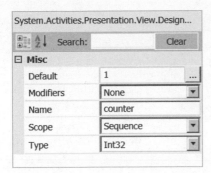

Figure 1-9. Properties window of a selected variable

Click the *Create Variable* link again. This time, use the Properties window to enter the properties. Enter the Name as **numberBells** and the Type as **Int32**. Leave the Scope as Sequence. For the Default property, click the ellipses, which will display the Expression editor, as shown in Figure 1-10.

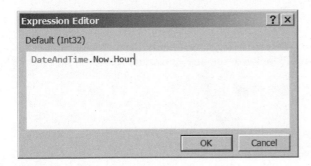

Figure 1-10. Expression editor

■ **Tip** One of the things you'll notice about WF 4.0 is that it relies a lot on expressions. Many properties can be defined using an expression. However, the form doesn't usually leave enough room to write complex expressions. To solve this, the expression editor can be used by clicking the ellipses next to any field that uses an expression. Expressions can use variables, arguments, and system functions just as you would in code.

Enter the expression DateAndTime.Now.Hour for the Default property. This will set the numberBells variable to the current hour of the day. The Variables window should now look like the one shown in Figure 1-11.

Name	Variable type	Scope	Default
counter	Int32	Sequence	1
numberBells	Int32	Sequence	DateAndTime.Now.Hour
Create Variable			

Variables   Arguments   Imports   🔍   100% ▼ 🔲 ▪

Figure 1-11. *Completed Variables window*

If

The `Hour` member of the `DateAndTime` class returns the hour based on a 24-hour clock. For example, for 2 PM, it will return 14. So you'll need to adjust for this because you should ring 2 bells, not 14. In code, you would write this as follows:

```
if (numberBells > 12)
    numberBells -= 12;
```

However, in WF 4.0, you'll need to use an `If` and an `Assign` activity to accomplish this. Drag an `If` activity just below the `Hello` activity. The diagram should look like the one shown in Figure 1-12.

Figure 1-12. *Adding an If activity*

■ **Tip** Notice the red error circles on the diagram. If you hover the mouse over them, they will display the associated warning/error. The error on the If activity lets you know that you haven't specified the Condition property. The warning on the Sequence activity simply indicates that one or more child activities have an error.

In the Properties window, change the DisplayName to **Adjust for PM**. The If activity consists of three elements. The Condition specifies the logic that is evaluated. It should resolve to a Boolean (true or false) value. Then contains the activities that are executed when the Condition is true, and Else contains the activities that are executed when the Condition is false. You do not have to specify both Then and Else; only one is required. If no activity is defined, then no activities are executed. Enter the Condition as **numberBells > 12**.

Assign

Drag an Assign activity to the Then section. The Assign activity allows you to assign a value to a variable or an argument. The activity should look like the one shown in Figure 1-13.

Figure 1-13. *Defining an Assign activity*

Both the To and Value properties accept an expression. You can either enter the expression directly in the box provided or click the ellipses to use the Expression editor. For the To property, enter **numberBells**. For the Value property, enter **numberBells – 12**. The Properties window should look like the one shown in Figure 1-14.

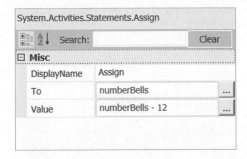

Figure 1-14. *Assign activity Properties window*

Many activities are *compound activities*, meaning that they can contain other activities. The If activity is a good example of this. As you design more complex workflows, you will be navigating through several layers in the workflow design.

While

Now you'll add a While activity to sound the bells. Drag a While activity just below "Adjust for PM". Set the DisplayName to **Sound Bells**. The diagram should look like the one shown in Figure 1-15.

Figure 1-15. *Defining a While activity*

In a While activity, the activity in the Body section is executed as long as the Condition is true. The Condition is evaluated first and then, if true, the activities are executed. This is repeated until the Condition is false.

■ **Note** The DoWhile activity is identical to While, except that the activities are executed first and then the Condition is evaluated. This ensures that the activities are executed at least once. With a While activity, if the Condition is initially false, the activities in the Body section will never be executed.

Enter the Condition as **counter <= numberBells**. Drag a Sequence activity to the Body section. Set the DisplayName of the Sequence activity to **Sound Bell**. The diagram should look like the one shown in Figure 1-16.

Figure 1-16. *A While activity that contains a sequence*

Sequence

You'll drag three activities onto the "Sound Bell" Sequence. In this exercise, you won't actually sound a bell. Instead, you will write a line of text to the console that will count the bells (as if they were actually sounding). Drag a WriteLine activity to the "Sound Bell" activity. In the Text property, enter the following:

```
counter.ToString()
```

This will display the current value of the counter to the console. Then drag an Assign activity just below the WriteLine activity. For the To property, enter **counter**; in the Value property, enter **counter + 1**. This simply increments the counter.

Delay

Finally, drag a Delay activity just below the Assign activity. A Delay activity pauses a workflow for a specified period of time. The only property of a Delay activity is the Duration, which indicates how long to pause. This should be specified as a TimeSpan class. Enter the following expression:

```
TimeSpan.FromSeconds(1)
```

The diagram should look like the one shown in Figure 1-17.

Figure 1-17. *Completed sequence diagram*

More Embellishments

Click the Collapse link on the top-right corner of the "Sound Bells" While activity. The workflow diagram should look like the one shown in Figure 1-18.

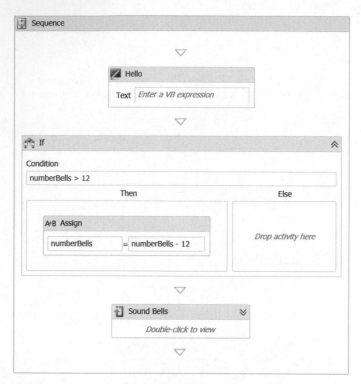

Figure 1-18. *Collapsed While activity*

Drag a WriteLine activity just below the Sound Bells activity. Change the DisplayName to **Display Time**; for the Text property, enter the following expression:

```
"The time is: " + DateAndTime.Now.ToString()
```

Drag an If activity just below "Display Time" and set the DisplayName to **Greeting**. For the Condition, enter the following expression:

```
DateAndTime.Now.Hour >= 18
```

Drag a WriteLine activity to both the Then and Else sections. For the Then section, enter the Text as **"Good Evening"**; for the Else section, enter the Text as **"Good Day"**. The "Greeting" activity should look like the one shown in Figure 1-19.

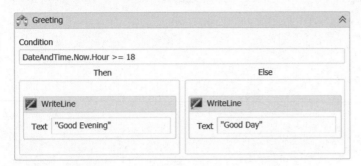

Figure 1-19. *Greeting activity*

Running the Application

Press F5 to run the application. Depending on the time of day, your results will be similar to this:

```
Hello, World!
1
2
The time is: 10/28/2009 2:26:02 PM
Good Day
Press ENTER to exit
```

Navigating the Designer

Even with this fairly simple workflow, you can see that it will be difficult to display the entire diagram. Fortunately, the designer has some useful features to help you work on large workflows. At the top-right corner of the designer, click the Collapse All link. The diagram should look similar to the one shown in Figure 1-20.

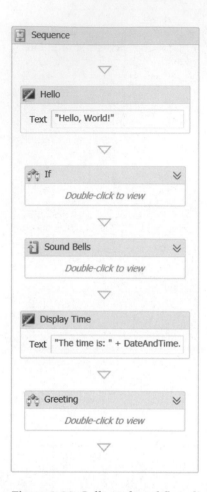

Figure 1-20. Collapsed workflow diagram

This gives you a quick way to see the top-level activities. Now click the Expand All link. This expands all the activities, but now you can see only part of the diagram. Click the Overview control at the bottom-right corner of the designer, which displays a window that shows the entire diagram. The yellow box indicates the viewable area. You can drag this around, which will pan the main window to the desired area. Close the overview window and click the Fit to screen control. This will zoom in as far as possible and still keep the entire diagram visible. Depending on your monitor size, this may be a little difficult to read. The drop-down control will allow you to change the zoom level. Finally, if you click the magnifying class, the zoom will return to the default 100 percent level.

Double-click the "Sound Bell" activity. This will display only that activity (and its child activities). To help you know where you are in the overall workflow, a navigation bar is displayed like the one shown in Figure 1-21.

Workflow1 > Sequence > Sound Bells > Sound Bell

Figure 1-21. *Designer navigation bar*

You can click any of the links on this navigation bar to display that level within the workflow design. Click the Workflow1 link to display the top-level workflow.

Looking a Bit Deeper

Let's take a brief look at what you just implemented. First, I mentioned earlier that the workflow was defined by an .xaml file. So far, you have been using the designer to graphically define the workflow. Now you'll see what the designer actually generated for that design. In the Solution Explorer, right-click the Sequence1.xaml file and choose Code View. You might get a warning that the file is already open. Just click Yes to let it close the existing designer window. The .xaml code is shown in Listing 1-2.

Listing 1-2. *Sequence1.xaml source code*

```
<p:Activity mc:Ignorable="" x:Class="Chapter01.Sequence1"
  xmlns="http://schemas.microsoft.com/netfx/2009/xaml/activities/design"
  xmlns:__Sequence1="clr-namespace:Chapter01;"
  xmlns:mc="http://schemas.openxmlformats.org/markup-compatibility/2006"
  xmlns:p="http://schemas.microsoft.com/netfx/2009/xaml/activities"
  xmlns:sad="clr-namespace:System.Activities.Debugger;assembly=System.Activities"
  xmlns:x="http://schemas.microsoft.com/winfx/2006/xaml">
  <p:Sequence sad:XamlDebuggerXmlReader.FileName=
    "C:\Documents\Books\WF40\Code\Chapter01\Chapter01\Sequence1.xaml">
<p:Sequence.Variables>
      <p:Variable x:TypeArguments="x:Int32" Default="[1]" Name="counter" />
      <p:Variable x:TypeArguments="x:Int32" Default="[DateTime.Now.Hour]"
        Name="numberBells" />
    </p:Sequence.Variables>
<p:WriteLine DisplayName="Hello">["Hello, World!"]</p:WriteLine>
<p:If Condition="[numberBells &gt; 12]" DisplayName="Adjust for PM">
      <p:If.Then>
        <p:Assign>
          <p:Assign.To>
            <p:OutArgument x:TypeArguments="x:Int32">[numberBells]</p:OutArgument>
          </p:Assign.To>
          <p:Assign.Value>
            <p:InArgument x:TypeArguments="x:Int32">[numberBells - 12]
              </p:InArgument>
          </p:Assign.Value>
        </p:Assign>
```

```
            </p:If.Then>
          </p:If>
  <p:While Condition="[counter &lt;= numberBells]" DisplayName="Sound Bells">
          <p:Sequence DisplayName="Sound Bell">
            <p:WriteLine>[counter.ToString()]</p:WriteLine>
            <p:Assign>
              <p:Assign.To>
                <p:OutArgument x:TypeArguments="x:Int32">[counter]</p:OutArgument>
              </p:Assign.To>
              <p:Assign.Value>
                <p:InArgument x:TypeArguments="x:Int32">[counter + 1]</p:InArgument>
              </p:Assign.Value>
            </p:Assign>
            <p:Delay>[TimeSpan.FromSeconds(1)]</p:Delay>
          </p:Sequence>
        </p:While>
  <p:WriteLine DisplayName="Display Time">
          ["The time is: " + DateTime.Now.ToString()]</p:WriteLine>
  <p:If Condition="[DateTime.Now.Hour &gt;= 18]" DisplayName="Greeting">
          <p:If.Else>
            <p:WriteLine>["Good Day"]</p:WriteLine>
          </p:If.Else>
          <p:If.Then>
            <p:WriteLine>["Good Evening"]</p:WriteLine>
          </p:If.Then>
        </p:If>
      </p:Sequence>
    </p:Activity>


  <Activity mc:Ignorable="sap" x:Class="Chapter01.Workflow1"
    mva:VisualBasic.Settings=
      "Assembly references and imported namespaces serialized as XML namespaces"
    xmlns="http://schemas.microsoft.com/netfx/2009/xaml/activities"
    xmlns:mc="http://schemas.openxmlformats.org/markup-compatibility/2006"
    xmlns:mv="clr-namespace:Microsoft.VisualBasic;assembly=Microsoft.VisualBasic,
      Version=10.0.0.0, Culture=neutral, PublicKeyToken=b03f5f7f11d50a3a"
    xmlns:mv1="clr-namespace:Microsoft.VisualBasic;assembly=System"
    xmlns:mva="clr-namespace:Microsoft.VisualBasic.Activities;
      assembly=System.Activities"
    xmlns:s="clr-namespace:System;assembly=mscorlib, Version=4.0.0.0,
      Culture=neutral, PublicKeyToken=b77a5c561934e089"
    xmlns:s1="clr-namespace:System;assembly=mscorlib"
    xmlns:s2="clr-namespace:System;assembly=System"
```

```
  xmlns:s3="clr-namespace:System;assembly=System.Xml"
  xmlns:s4="clr-namespace:System;assembly=System.Core"
  xmlns:sa="clr-namespace:System.Activities;assembly=System.Activities,
    Version=4.0.0.0, Culture=neutral, PublicKeyToken=31bf3856ad364e35"
  xmlns:sad="clr-namespace:System.Activities.Debugger;assembly=System.Activities"
  xmlns:sap="http://schemas.microsoft.com/netfx/2009/xaml/activities/presentation"
  xmlns:scg="clr-namespace:System.Collections.Generic;assembly=System"
  xmlns:scg1="clr-namespace:System.Collections.Generic;
    assembly=System.ServiceModel"
  xmlns:scg2="clr-namespace:System.Collections.Generic;assembly=System.Core"
  xmlns:scg3="clr-namespace:System.Collections.Generic;assembly=mscorlib"
  xmlns:sd="clr-namespace:System.Data;assembly=System.Data"
  xmlns:sd1="clr-namespace:System.Data;assembly=System.Data.DataSetExtensions"
  xmlns:sl="clr-namespace:System.Linq;assembly=System.Core"
  xmlns:st="clr-namespace:System.Text;assembly=mscorlib"
  xmlns:x="http://schemas.microsoft.com/winfx/2006/xaml">
  <sap:WorkflowViewStateService.ViewState>
    <scg3:Dictionary x:TypeArguments="x:String, x:Object">
      <x:Boolean x:Key="ShouldExpandAll">False</x:Boolean>
      <x:Boolean x:Key="ShouldCollapseAll">True</x:Boolean>
    </scg3:Dictionary>
  </sap:WorkflowViewStateService.ViewState>
  <Sequence sad:XamlDebuggerXmlReader.FileName=
    "C:\Documents\Books\WF40\Code\Chapter01\Chapter01\Workflow1.xaml"
    sap:VirtualizedContainerService.HintSize="233.6,552">
<Sequence.Variables>
      <Variable x:TypeArguments="x:Int32" Default="1" Name="counter" />
      <Variable x:TypeArguments="x:Int32" Default="[DateAndTime.Now.Hour]"
        Name="numberBells" />
    </Sequence.Variables>
    <sap:WorkflowViewStateService.ViewState>
      <scg3:Dictionary x:TypeArguments="x:String, x:Object">
        <x:Boolean x:Key="IsExpanded">True</x:Boolean>
      </scg3:Dictionary>
    </sap:WorkflowViewStateService.ViewState>
<WriteLine DisplayName="Hello"
      sap:VirtualizedContainerService.HintSize="211.2,59.2"
      Text="Hello, World!" />
<If Condition="[numberBells &gt; 12]"
      sap:VirtualizedContainerService.HintSize="211.2,49.6">
      <sap:WorkflowViewStateService.ViewState>
        <scg3:Dictionary x:TypeArguments="x:String, x:Object">
          <x:Boolean x:Key="IsExpanded">True</x:Boolean>
```

```
          <x:Boolean x:Key="IsPinned">False</x:Boolean>
        </scg3:Dictionary>
      </sap:WorkflowViewStateService.ViewState>
      <If.Then>
        <Assign sap:VirtualizedContainerService.HintSize="289.6,100.8">
          <Assign.To>
            <OutArgument x:TypeArguments="x:Int32">[numberBells]</OutArgument>
          </Assign.To>
          <Assign.Value>
            <InArgument x:TypeArguments="x:Int32">[numberBells - 12]</InArgument>
          </Assign.Value>
        </Assign>
      </If.Then>
    </If>
<While DisplayName="Sound Bells"
      sap:VirtualizedContainerService.HintSize="211.2,49.6">
      <sap:WorkflowViewStateService.ViewState>
        <scg3:Dictionary x:TypeArguments="x:String, x:Object">
          <x:Boolean x:Key="IsExpanded">False</x:Boolean>
          <x:Boolean x:Key="IsPinned">False</x:Boolean>
        </scg3:Dictionary>
      </sap:WorkflowViewStateService.ViewState>
      <While.Condition>[counter &lt;= numberBells]</While.Condition>
      <Sequence DisplayName="Sound Bell"
        sap:VirtualizedContainerService.HintSize="438.4,100.8">
        <sap:WorkflowViewStateService.ViewState>
          <scg3:Dictionary x:TypeArguments="x:String, x:Object">
            <x:Boolean x:Key="IsExpanded">True</x:Boolean>
          </scg3:Dictionary>
        </sap:WorkflowViewStateService.ViewState>
        <WriteLine sap:VirtualizedContainerService.HintSize="243.2,59.2"
          Text="[counter.ToString()]" />
        <Assign sap:VirtualizedContainerService.HintSize="243.2,57.6">
          <Assign.To>
            <OutArgument x:TypeArguments="x:Int32">[counter]</OutArgument>
          </Assign.To>
          <Assign.Value>
            <InArgument x:TypeArguments="x:Int32">[counter + 1]</InArgument>
          </Assign.Value>
        </Assign>
        <Delay Duration="[TimeSpan.FromSeconds(1)]"
          sap:VirtualizedContainerService.HintSize="243.2,22.4" />
      </Sequence>
```

```xml
            </While>
<WriteLine DisplayName="Display Time"
        sap:VirtualizedContainerService.HintSize="211.2,59.2"
        Text="[&quot;The time is: &quot; + DateAndTime.Now.ToString()]" />
<If Condition="[DateAndTime.Now.Hour &gt;= 18]" DisplayName="Greeting"
        sap:VirtualizedContainerService.HintSize="211.2,49.6">
        <sap:WorkflowViewStateService.ViewState>
          <scg3:Dictionary x:TypeArguments="x:String, x:Object">
            <x:Boolean x:Key="IsExpanded">False</x:Boolean>
            <x:Boolean x:Key="IsPinned">False</x:Boolean>
          </scg3:Dictionary>
        </sap:WorkflowViewStateService.ViewState>
        <If.Then>
          <WriteLine sap:VirtualizedContainerService.HintSize="219.2,100.8"
            Text="Good Evening" />
        </If.Then>
        <If.Else>
          <WriteLine sap:VirtualizedContainerService.HintSize="219.2,100.8"
            Text="Good Day" />
        </If.Else>
      </If>
    </Sequence>
  </Activity>
```

I made some lines bold to help you find the top-level activities. First, the Variables section defines the two variables you created. Then there's a WriteLine activity named "Hello" and an If activity named "Adjust for PM". This is followed by a While activity named "Sound Bells", a WriteLine activity named "Display Time", and an If activity named "Greeting".

One key point that I want you to see is that there is no executable code here. This file is just a nested collection of properties. For example, to increment the counter, you would normally expect to see a line of code like this:

```
counter = counter + 1;
```

Instead you have an Assign class with a counter expression and a counter + 1 expression. The actual execution that makes the assignment of counter = counter + 1 is performed by the Assign activity. Code is executed only in the Activity classes, and there is no code execution in the workflow definition.

Differences from Previous Versions

If you have used previous versions of Workflow Foundation (version 3.0 or 3.5), you might be wondering what happened here. WF 4.0 is a complete departure from previous versions of Workflow. Your previous Workflow applications will run just fine under .Net 4.0 because the previous set of activities and services were carried forward with minimal changes. WF 4.0, however, is a completely new design. The activities and services from WF 4.0 are not interchangeable with previous versions. So you can design, implement, and maintain workflows using the WF 3.5 approach. Or you can choose to use the WF 4.0 paradigm; either will work fine. But you cannot switch back and forth, except for a few scenarios that are described later in this book.

In WF 3.5, there was a code class and a designer class. The code class contained the implementation for the CodeActivity objects. It also contained the definition of the class members and the event handler code. In WF 4.0, there is no code class. Probably the most notable effect of this is that there is no CodeActivity object in WF 4.0. To compensate for this, WF 4.0 provides activities to accomplish some of the common tasks previously performed by CodeActivity objects. WriteLine and Assign are two such activities. If the built-in activities are not sufficient, you can create a custom activity to perform the task you would have used a CodeActivity for.

Another key difference is the explicit use of variables and arguments. Again, because there is no code file, you can't simply add class members as you would with normal class development. Instead, you have to define these using the "Workflow way."

Finally, you may have noticed when looking at the Program.cs file that there is no WorkflowRuntime class. Previously, you would have created the WorkflowRuntime class and then called its CreateWorkflow() method. With WF 4.0, the code simply calls this:

```
WorkflowInvoker.Invoke(new Workflow1());
```

Throughout this document, you will undoubtedly notice other differences. For example, there is no longer a state machine workflow. I won't point these out because the purpose of this book is not to illustrate the differences. However, I did want to note some of the obvious changes just in case, like me, you had to scratch your head for a few minutes when looking at WF 4.0 for the first time.

CHAPTER 2

■ ■ ■

Coded Workflows

In Chapter 1, you implemented a fairly simple workflow using the workflow designer. Now you'll implement the same workflow using code instead. Any workflow can be implemented in code or with the designer; the choice is simply a matter of preference. However, implementing a workflow in code will help you gain a better sense of how workflow works.

Creating a Console Application

To start, create a simple console application (do not use a workflow template), as shown in Figure 2-1.

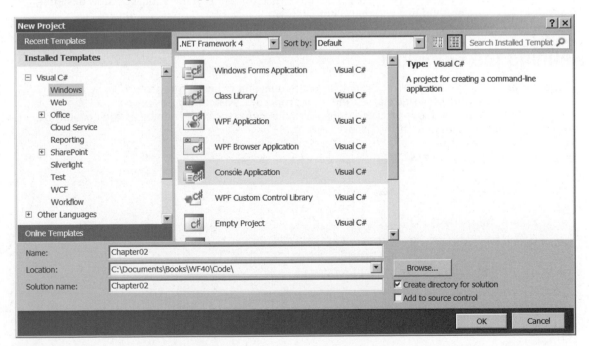

Figure 2-1. *Creating a console application*

Add a reference to System.Activities. This will enable you to use the workflow activities in your application. Then replace the set of namespaces in your Program.cs file with the following:

```
using System;
using System.Activities;
using System.Activities.Statements;
using System.Activities.Expressions;
```

To implement the main() function, enter the following code:

```
WorkflowInvoker.Invoke(CreateWorkflow());

Console.WriteLine("Press ENTER to exit");
Console.ReadLine();
```

Note that this is identical to the main() implementation from Chapter 1. If you want, you can simply copy and paste from your previous application. There is one difference, however. The following line calls CreateWorkflow() instead of new Workflow1():

```
WorkflowInvoker.Invoke(CreateWorkflow());
```

Workflow1 was defined in the Workflow1.xaml file, which was generated by the workflow designer. CreateWorkflow() is a method that you'll implement now.

Defining the Workflow

As I mentioned in the last chapter, a *workflow* is just a collection of nested properties. To be more accurate, it is a collection of nested classes and their properties. To simplify this process, I'll show you the implementation to enter, one level at a time. I'll explain what the code is doing as you go. Start by adding the following method to the Program.cs file:

```
static Activity CreateWorkflow()
{
    Variable<int> numberBells = new Variable<int>()
    {
        Name = "numberBells",
        Default = DateTime.Now.Hour
    };
    Variable<int> counter = new Variable<int>()
    {
        Name = "counter",
        Default = 1
    };
```

```
    return new Sequence()
    {
    };
}
```

The `CreateWorkflow()` method first creates two `Variable<T>` template classes of type int, called `numberBells` and `counter`. These are the variables used by the various activities.

The `CreateWorkflow()` method is declared to return an `Activity`, which is what the `WorkflowInvoker` class is expecting. It actually returns an anonymous instance of the Sequence class. The `Activity` class is the base class from which all workflow activities are derived, including Sequence. So the compiler returns the Sequence instance as its base class, `Activity`.

Implementing Level 1

So far, you have defined an empty Sequence activity. This is roughly equivalent to creating a new workflow that has a Sequence with no activities. Now, define the activities on this Sequence by replacing the call to `return new Sequence()` with the code shown in Listing 2-1.

Listing 2-1. *Definition of the Sequence Activity*

```
return new Sequence()
{
    DisplayName = "Main Sequence",
    Variables = { numberBells, counter },
    Activities =
    {
        new WriteLine()
        {
            DisplayName = "Hello",
            Text = "Hello, World!"
        },
        new If()
        {
            DisplayName = "Adjust for PM"
            // Code to be added here in Level 2
        },
        new While()
        {
            DisplayName = "Sound Bells"
            // Code to be added here in Level 2
        },
        new WriteLine()
        {
            DisplayName = "Display Time",
```

```
            Text = "The time is: " + DateTime.Now.ToString()
        },
        new If()
        {
            DisplayName = "Greeting"
            // Code to be added here in Level 2
        }
    }
};
```

■ **Note** This implementation relies heavily on creating anonymous class instances. Classes such as Sequence, WriteLine, and If are instantiated but never named. This approach is similar to the technique called *functional construction*, which is used to build XML trees. If it seems strange to you, you might want to review some of the documentation on functional construction on MSDN.

This code first defines the DisplayName and associates the Variable objects with this activity. It then initializes the Activities member as a collection of activities. Specifically, it creates the activities shown in Table 2-1.

Table 2-1. *Activities*

Type	DisplayName
WriteLine	"Hello"
If	"Adjust for PM"
While	"Sound Bells"
WriteLine	"Display Time"
If	"Greeting"

For the WriteLine activities, the Text property is defined. For the remaining activities, the implementation of these will be defined in the next level.

Implementing Level 2

For the first If activity, enter the following code:

```
DisplayName = "Adjust for PM",
```

```
// Code to be added here in Level 2
Condition = ExpressionServices.Convert<bool>
    (env => numberBells.Get(env) > 12),
Then = new Assign<int>()
{
    DisplayName = "Adjust Bells"
    // Code to be added here in Level 3
}
```

This code defines the Condition and the Then properties (there is no Else branch). The Assign activity will be implemented in the next level. The definition of the Condition property, however, probably needs some explanation.

Expressions

The static Convert<T>() method of the ExpressionServices class is used to create an InArgument<T> class, which is what the Condition property is expecting. These classes and methods use the generic type (<T>) so they can be used for any data type. In this case, we need to use type bool because the Condition property of an If activity is expecting only true or false.

The expression is implemented by a lambda expression (similar to that used by LINQ syntax) to extract the data from the workflow environment. In a lambda expression, the => is referred to as the lambda operator. Parameters to the left are input parameters, and the actual expression is defined on the right side of the lambda operator. The value of env is supplied by the runtime when it tries to evaluate the Condition.

The workflow is actually stateless; it doesn't store any data elements. The Variable classes are simply data definitions. To get the actual data from a Variable class, you'll use its Get() method. This requires a token of sorts, which is an ActivityContext class. This is used to differentiate the values for this particular workflow instance from others that might be running concurrently. The value returned from Get(env) is then compared to see whether it's greater than 12.

Enter the following code for the While activity:

```
DisplayName = "Sound Bells",
// Code to be added here in Level 2
Condition = ExpressionServices.Convert<bool>
    (env => counter.Get(env) <= numberBells.Get(env)),
Body = new Sequence()
{
    DisplayName = "Sound Bell"
    // Code to be added here in Level 3
}
```

The Condition property on the While activity is identical to the If activity. It also uses the ExpressionServices class to create an InArgument<T> class, also of type bool. In this case, it is evaluating whether count <= numberBells. For both of these variables, it uses the Get(env) method to obtain the actual value.

For the second If activity (named "Greeting"), enter the following code:

27

```
DisplayName = "Greeting",
// Code to be added here in Level 2
Condition = ExpressionServices.Convert<bool>
    (env => DateTime.Now.Hour >= 18),
Then = new WriteLine() { Text = "Good Evening" },
Else = new WriteLine() { Text = "Good Day" }
```

For this Condition, the env input parameter is not used, but it must still be declared in the expression. The logic uses the current time to see whether it is past 6:00 PM. For both the Then and Else properties, a WriteLine activity is created. One says "Good Evening"; the other says "Good Day".

Implementing Level 3

For the first If activity (named "Adjust for PM"), you created a blank Assign activity in the Then property. Enter the following for its implementation:

```
DisplayName = "Adjust Bells",
// Code to be added here in Level 3
To = new OutArgument<int>(numberBells),
Value = new InArgument<int>(env => numberBells.Get(env) - 12)
```

Assign Activity

The Assign class is a generic, so it can support any data type. In this case, it is assigning integer values, so it was created as Assign<int>. The To and Value properties also use template classes and should be created with the same type (<int>). The To property is an OutArgument class, which takes a Variable class in its constructor. The Value property uses an InArgument class. You used this before for the If and While Condition property. For its constructor, it uses a lambda expression just as you did for the Condition property.

Sequence

In the While activity, you created an empty Sequence for the Execute property. This defines the sequence of activities that will be executed every time the while loop is iterated. Enter the following to populate the Activities property:

```
DisplayName = "Sound Bell",
// Code to be added here in Level 3
Activities =
{
    new WriteLine()
    {
        Text = new InArgument<string>(env => counter.Get(env).ToString())
    },
```

```
new Assign<int>()
{
    DisplayName = "Increment Counter",
    To = new OutArgument<int>(counter),
    Value = new InArgument<int>(env => counter.Get(env) + 1)
},
new Delay()
{
    Duration = TimeSpan.FromSeconds(1)
}
}
```

This code adds three activities to this Sequence:

- A WriteLine activity to display the counter
- An Assign activity to increment the counter
- A Delay activity to force a short pause between iterations

For this WriteLine activity, the Text property is not a literal string as the other ones were. In this case, the value to be displayed is defined as an expression. The Text property is expecting a string, so it creates an InArgument<string> class. By now, you're probably getting used to these lambda expressions. The Get(env) method of the Variable class provides the current value as an integer. The ToString() method converts it to a string.

For the Delay activity, the Duration property is passed as a TimeSpan class, which is created by the FromSeconds() static method.

Running the Application

Press F5 to run the application. Depending on the time of day, your results should look something like this:

```
Hello, World!
1
2
3
4
5
6
7
The time is: 10/5/2009 7:02:41 PM
Good Evening
Press ENTER to exit
```

The complete implementation of Program.cs is included in Listing 2-2.

Listing 2-2. *Complete Solution Implementation (Program.cs)*

```
using System;
using System.Activities;
using System.Activities.Statements;
using System.Activities.Expressions;

namespace Chapter02
{
    class Program
    {
        static void Main(string[] args)
        {
            WorkflowInvoker.Invoke(CreateWorkflow());

            Console.WriteLine("Press ENTER to exit");
            Console.ReadLine();
        }

        static Activity CreateWorkflow()
        {
            Variable<int> numberBells = new Variable<int>()
            {
                Name = "numberBells",
                Default = DateTime.Now.Hour
            };
            Variable<int> counter = new Variable<int>()
            {
                Name = "counter",
                Default = 1
            };

            return new Sequence()
            {
                DisplayName = "Main Sequence",
                Variables = { numberBells, counter },
                Activities =
                {
                    new WriteLine()
                    {
                        DisplayName = "Hello",
```

```
        Text = "Hello, World!"
    },
    new If()
    {
        DisplayName = "Adjust for PM",
        // Code to be added here in Level 2
        Condition = ExpressionServices.Convert<bool>
            (env => numberBells.Get(env) > 12),
        Then = new Assign<int>()
        {
            DisplayName = "Adjust Bells",
            // Code to be added here in Level 3
            To = new OutArgument<int>(numberBells),
            Value = new InArgument<int>
                (env => numberBells.Get(env) - 12)
        }
    },
    new While()
    {
        DisplayName = "Sound Bells",
        // Code to be added here in Level 2
        Condition = ExpressionServices.Convert<bool>
            (env => counter.Get(env) <= numberBells.Get(env)),
        Body = new Sequence()
        {
            DisplayName = "Sound Bell",
            // Code to be added here in Level 3
            Activities =
            {
                new WriteLine()
                {
                    Text = new InArgument<string>
                        (env => counter.Get(env).ToString())
                },
                new Assign<int>()
                {
                    DisplayName = "Increment Counter",
                    To = new OutArgument<int>(counter),
                    Value = new InArgument<int>
                        (env => counter.Get(env) + 1)
                },
                new Delay()
                {
```

```
                            Duration = TimeSpan.FromSeconds(1)
                        }
                    }
                }
            },
            new WriteLine()
            {
                DisplayName = "Display Time",
                Text = "The time is: " + DateTime.Now.ToString()
            },
            new If()
            {
                DisplayName = "Greeting",
                // Code to be added here in Level 2
                Condition = ExpressionServices.Convert<bool>
                    (env => DateTime.Now.Hour >= 16),
                Then = new WriteLine() { Text = "Good Evening" },
                Else = new WriteLine() { Text = "Good Day" }
            }
        }
    };
}
}
}
```

Review

Some of the sample projects throughout this book will use the designer, whereas others will use a coded workflow. Using the designer will probably be initially easier than coded workflows. However, as you become more familiar with workflows, you might find that coded workflows are faster to write. The end result is the same, and either approach works fine.

CHAPTER 3

■■■

Flowchart Workflow

In this chapter, you'll create a workflow that uses the Flowchart activity. As its name suggests, a Flowchart activity works just like a flowchart; activities are connected together by decision trees. Using a Sequence activity, the child activities are executed in top-down (sequential) order. However, in a Flowchart activity, the child activities can be executed in any order, based on the decision branches.

Creating a Flowchart Workflow

Start by creating a new project/solution. Choose the Workflow Console Application template, as shown in Figure 3-1.

Figure 3-1. *Creating a flowchart workflow project*

Designing the Flowchart

Drag a Flowchart activity to the designer. The initial workflow diagram will be similar to the one shown in Figure 3-2. The green circle represents the starting node of your flowchart, and the empty space beneath it is where you will add the activities that make up your workflow.

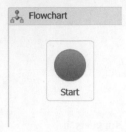

Figure 3-2. Initial flowchart diagram

The primary difference between a Flowchart activity and a Sequence activity is in how the child activities are connected. Recall from Chapter 1 that when you added activities to a Sequence, they were always executed in top-down order. You could control the order by rearranging the activities, but they were always aligned vertically and spaced evenly, and the arrows between the activities were drawn for you automatically. With a Flowchart activity, you can place the activities anywhere on the palette. And more importantly, you have to draw the arrows. But herein lies the power of the Flowchart activity; you can draw a connection back to a previous activity.

In this application, you will display an appropriate greeting based on the time of day. Start by displaying a standard greeting of "Hello, World!" To do this, drag a WriteLine activity below the green circle. Set the DisplayName to **Hello** and the Text property to **"Hello, World!"**.

Defining Connections

Roll the mouse over the green circle, and four gray connection points should appear (see Figure 3-3).

Figure 3-3. Finding the beginning connection points

Click one of these connection points and, holding the mouse button down, drag the mouse over the "Hello" activity until you see its connection points appear, as shown in Figure 3-4.

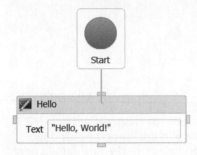

Figure 3-4. *Finding the ending connection points*

You don't have to select a connection point. As soon as you see the points appear, you'll know that the object has been selected. Let the mouse button up, and the two activities will be connected (see Figure 3-5).

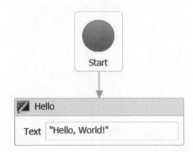

Figure 3-5. *Completed connection*

That's how you establish the connections between two activities. Hover over the predecessor until you see the connection points, click one, drag the mouse to the successor until you see its connection points, and let the mouse button up.

FlowDecision

Drag a FlowDecision activity below the "Hello" activity. The FlowDecision activity looks like a yellow diamond, much like a decision symbol in a normal flowchart diagram. In the Properties window, enter the *condition* as DateTime.Now.Hour >= 12. If you hover the mouse over the FlowDecision activity, you should see the connection points, as shown in Figure 3-6.

Figure 3-6. *FlowDecision activity*

There is a connection point on the left for the True branch and a connection point on the right for the False branch. The Condition is also displayed. Notice the small yellow triangle at the top-right corner. If you click it, the Condition property remains displayed, even when the mouse is not hovered over the activity. You can change the text for the True and False branches. In the Properties window, enter **Morning** for the FalseLabel property and **Afternoon** for the TrueLabel property. You should now see Morning and Afternoon when you hover the mouse over this activity.

First, connect the "Hello" activity to the FlowDecision activity by selecting a connection point on the "Hello" activity and dragging it to the FlowDecision. Then drag a WriteLine activity to the right of the FlowDecision. Set the DisplayName to **Morning** and the Text to **"Good Morning"**. Then hover over the FlowDecision and click the Morning connection point. Drag the mouse over the "Morning" activity until you see its connection points and let the mouse up. Your diagram should look like the one shown in Figure 3-7.

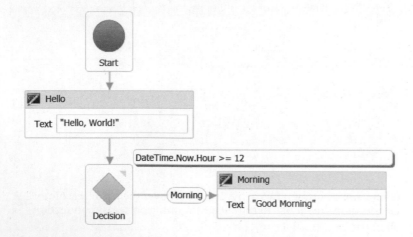

Figure 3-7. *Connecting the Morning branch*

■ **Note** The DisplayName property is not available on a FlowDecision activity. However, with the ability to display the Condition and to edit the True and False branches, the purpose of the activity should be evident in the diagram.

Drag another FlowDecision to the left of the first one. Set the Condition as **DateTime.Now.Hour >= 18**. Connect the Afternoon branch of the first FlowDecision to the new activity. Set the FalseLabel to **Afternoon** and the TrueLabel to **Evening**. Drag two WriteLine activities onto the workflow and name them **Afternoon** and **Evening**, and set the Text as **"Good Afternoon"** and **"Good Evening"**, respectively. Connect the Evening branch of the second FlowDecision to "Evening" and the Afternoon branch to "Afternoon". Your flowchart should look like the one shown in Figure 3-8.

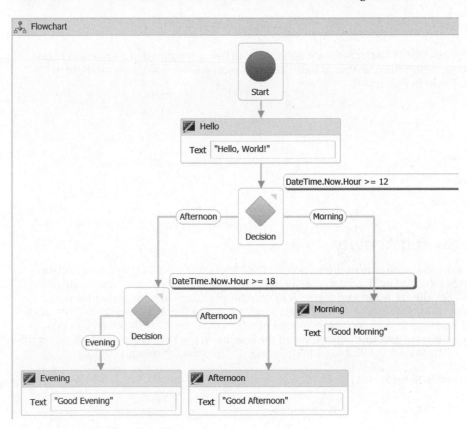

Figure 3-8. *Completed flowchart*

Running the Application

Before running the application, open the Program.cs file. This code is identical to the file generated in Chapter 1. Add the following code after the call to WorkflowInvoker class:

```
Console.WriteLine("Press ENTER to exit");
Console.ReadLine();
```

This keeps the console app from exiting before you can read the results. Press F5. Depending on the time of day, your results should be similar to the following:

```
Hello, World!
Good Evening
Press ENTER to exit
```

Flow Switch

A FlowSwitch activity works like a FlowDecision except instead of being restricted to a True and False branch, you can define an unlimited number of branches. It is analogous to a switch statement in C#. A FlowSwitch activity is shown in Figure 3-9.

Figure 3-9. *A FlowSwitch activity*

Adding a FlowSwitch Activity

Drag a FlowSwitch activity to the bottom of the workflow. The FlowSwitch activity is a template class (notice the <T> in the toolbox) so you'll need to specify the data type. It will default to Int32, which it what you'll need. Just click the OK button on the Select Types prompt. Draw a connection from the "Morning", "Afternoon", and "Evening" activities to the FlowSwitch activity. A FlowSwitch activity has a single property called Expression, which resolves to a set of values that define the branches. In this project, you'll display a different greeting depending on the season. In the Properties window, select the Expression property and then click the ellipses. Enter the following in the Expression editor:

```
CInt(((DateTime.Now.Month Mod 12) + 1) / 4)
```

■ **Note** The syntax of this expression might be surprising. All expressions in WF 4.0 use the Visual Basic syntax. Expressions are not compiled; they are evaluated by the workflow activities. So the syntax of the expressions is independent of the programming language used by the application. By convention, the VB syntax is used. To help you remember this, the Expression properties display the text "Enter a VB expression".

This expression approximates the season based on the current date. If the month is December, January, or February, the expression evaluates to 0. Similarly March, April, and May evaluate to 1. You will now create four branches; one for each season.

■ **Tip** When you hover the mouse over a `FlowSwitch` activity, the `Expression` will be displayed as shown in Figure 3-10. Just as with the `FlowDecision` activity, you can click on the yellow triangle and the `Expression` will remain displayed.

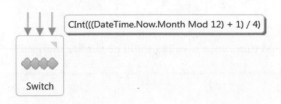

Figure 3-10. *Displaying the FlowSwitch expression*

Adding the FlowStep Activities

Each branch of a `FlowSwitch` activity is called a `FlowStep`. Although there is no `FlowStep` activity in the Toolbox, and you don't explicitly add these branches to the workflow, they are created internally as you draw connections from the `FlowSwitch` activity. Drag five `WriteLine` activities onto your workflow near the `FlowSwitch` activity. Set the `DisplayName` on each of these to **Winter**, **Spring**, **Summer**, **Autumn**, and **Default**. Draw a connection from the `FlowSwitch` to each of the `WriteLine` activities.

Click one of the connections. In the Properties window, you'll enter the `Case` value that determines when this case should be executed. For "Winter", the value should be **1**; for "Spring", it should be **2**, and so on. For the "Default" activity, leave the `Case` value blank and check the `IsDefaultCase` check box.

Your workflow should look like the one shown in Figure 3-11.

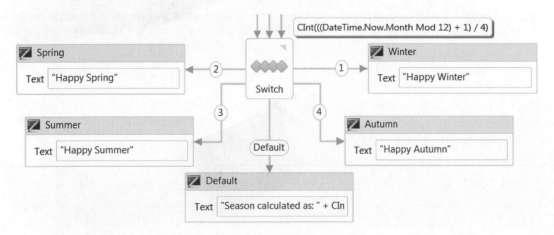

Figure 3-11. *FlowSwitch connections*

Enter an appropriate Text property on each of the WriteLine activities, such as **"Happy Summer"**. The "Default" activity should never be executed because you have defined a branch for each possible value of the Expression. However, it is useful to have it here in case there are problems with the Expression or any of the Case values. For the Text property on the "Default" activity, use the following:

```
"Season calculated as: " + CInt(((DateTime.Now.Month Mod 12) + 1) / 4).ToString()
```

Running the Application

Press F5 to run the application. Depending on the date and time, your results should be similar to these:

```
Hello, World!
Good Evening
Happy Summer!
Press ENTER to exit
```

Parallel

Before leaving this project, let me demonstrate the Parallel activity, which allows you to define a number of activity sequences that run in parallel. For this project, each of the branches will display a piece of information. The order that they are displayed is not important, so instead of executing them sequentially, you'll put them in a Parallel activity and execute them simultaneously.

Adding a Parallel Activity

Drag a Parallel activity to the bottom of your workflow. Draw a connection from each of the WriteLine activities to the Parallel activity. Your workflow should look like the one shown in Figure 3-12.

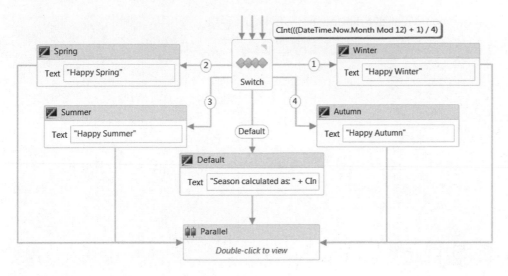

Figure 3-12. *Adding a Parallel activity*

Adding the Branches

Double-click the Parallel activity and drag three WriteLine activities onto it. One of these activities will display the date; another will display the time; and another will display the day of the week. Enter one of these expressions for the Text property on each of the WriteLine activities:

```
"Time: " + DateTime.Now.TimeOfDay.ToString()
"Date: " + DateTime.Now.Date.ToShortDateString()
"Today is: " + DateTime.Now.ToString("dddd")
```

The diagram should look like the one shown in Figure 3-13.

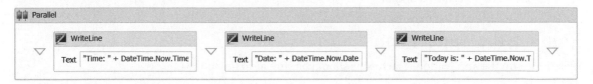

Figure 3-13. *Defining Parallel branches*

───

■ **Tip** The Parallel activity allows only a single activity in each branch. For this project, it works fine. However, if you need multiple activities in each branch, use a Sequence activity. Then you can add any number of activities onto it.

───

The final workflow should look like the one shown in Figure 3-14.

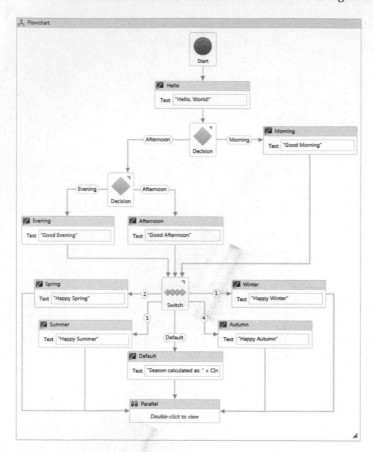

Figure 3-14. *Final flowchart workflow*

Running the Application

Press F5 to run the application. The results should be similar to the following:

```
Hello, World!
Good Evening
Happy Summer!
Time: 22:01:36.0594175
Date: 8/5/2009
Today is: Wednesday
Press ENTER to exit
```

PART 2

■ ■ ■

Designing Workflows

So far, you have used the basic procedural and flowchart elements to design some simple workflows. In this section, you will learn some useful techniques that will help you build more complex workflows. You'll build a workflow that computes the total amount of an order. Each chapter will build upon the previous chapter and demonstrate new concepts along the way.

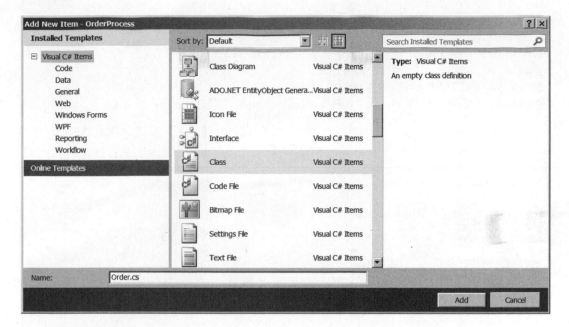

Figure 4-3. Defining a new class

The Solution Explorer should look like the one shown in Figure 4-4.

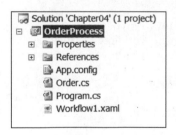

Figure 4-4. Solution Explorer

Enter the definition of the Order class, as shown in Listing 4-1.

Listing 4-1. *Order class*

```csharp
using System;
using System.Collections.Generic;

namespace OrderProcess
{
```

```
public class OrderItem
{
    public int OrderItemID { get; set; }
    public int Quantity { get; set; }
    public string ItemCode { get; set; }
    public string Description { get; set; }
}

public class Order
{
    public Order()
    {
        Items = new List<OrderItem>();
    }

    public int OrderID { get; set; }
    public string Description { get; set; }
    public decimal TotalWeight { get; set; }
    public string ShippingMethod { get; set; }

    public List<OrderItem> Items { get; set; }
}
}
```

The Order class contains a few public members (OrderID, Description, TotalWeight, and ShippingMethod) plus a collection of OrderItem classes. These are the details the workflow will need to determine the cost of the order. Build the solution by pressing F6. This will compile the Order class so it will be available for the next step.

Implementing the Workflow

The solution template created a workflow file named Workflow1.xaml. In the Solution Explorer, right-click the Workflow1.xaml file and choose Rename, as shown in Figure 4-5. Change the name to **OrderWF.xaml**.

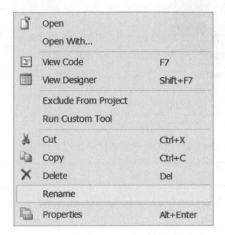

Figure 4-5. *Renaming the workflow file*

You will also need to open the `OrderWF.xaml` in code view. In the first line, change the `Class` attribute to this:

```
x:Class="OrderProcess.OrderWF"
```

Defining the Arguments

Open the `OrderWF.xaml` file (in design mode). You will now define the arguments into and out of the workflow. Click the Argument button at the bottom left of the workflow designer. An empty collection of arguments should be displayed, as shown in Figure 4-6.

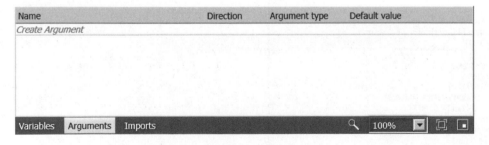

Figure 4-6. *The initial (empty) Arguments list*

■ **Tip** You might recall from Chapter 1 that variables had a specified scope. They could be defined for the entire workflow or for a specific activity (and its descendants). Arguments, however, are by definition, for the entire workflow because they define data passed to and from the workflow. Therefore, there is no Scope property when defining an argument.

Click the *Create Argument* link. Enter the Name as **OrderInfo**. The Direction should be In. Click the ArgumentType and expand the drop-down menu, shown in Figure 4-7.

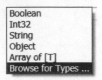

Figure 4-7. *The ArgumentType drop-down menu*

Select the last entry (Browse for Types). This will display the dialog shown in Figure 4-8.

Figure 4-8. *Selecting the Order class for the ArgumentType*

Expand the OrderProcess assembly, select the Order class, and click OK.

■ **Caution** If the OrderProcess assembly is not shown or does not contain the Order class, you have to build the solution first. Click the Cancel button and press F6 to build the solution. Then set up the ArgumentType.

Click the *Create Argument* link again to create another argument. Enter the Name as **TotalAmount**, the Direction should be **Out**, and the ArgumentType should be **Decimal**. The Decimal type is not in the drop-down list so you need to browse for the type (as you did for the first argument). The Decimal type can be found in the mscorlib assembly in the System namespace.

■ **Tip** You don't have to browse through the assemblies and namespaces to find the type you're looking for. You can just type the namespace and the type at the top of the dialog. For example, to select the Decimal type, just type **System.Decimal**. Actually, you don't even need to specify the namespace. If you start typing **Decimal**, just like IntelliSense, the types matching your input will appear.

Designing the Workflow

Now you're ready to define the activities that will process the order that is passed in. Start by dragging a Sequence activity to the workflow diagram. Then drag a WriteLine activity onto the Sequence. Set the Text property to **"Order Received"**. Drag an Assign activity below the WriteLine activity. Set the DisplayName to **Initialize Total**. For the To property, enter **TotalAmount**, and for the Value property enter **0**. The Properties window is shown in Figure 4-9.

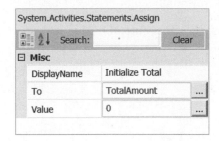

Figure 4-9. The Assign activity's Properties window

This activity simply initializes TotalAmount to 0.

Switch Activity

The Switch activity works like a switch statement in C#. It allows you to execute a sequence of activities based on the expression being evaluated. You will use the Switch activity to evaluate the ShippingMethod to determine the appropriate handling charge. In the Toolbox, the Switch activity is listed as Switch<T>.

This means it is defined as a template class and can operate on different data types. Drag a `Switch` activity onto the workflow below the `Assign` activity. You should see the dialog box shown in Figure 4-10, which requires you to specify the data type. The `ShippingMethod` is a string, so select the String type.

Figure 4-10. *Dialog prompting for the specific data type*

Click OK. In the Properties window, set the `DisplayName` to **Handling Charges**. The activity should look like the one shown in Figure 4-11.

Figure 4-11. *The initial Switch activity diagram*

A `Switch` activity has an `Expression` property, a default case, and any number of user-specified cases. Enter the expression as **OrderInfo.ShippingMethod**. Click the *Add new case* link at the bottom of the diagram. Enter the case value as **NextDay**. Click the *Add new case* link again and enter the value as **2ndDay**. The diagram should look like the one shown in Figure 4-12.

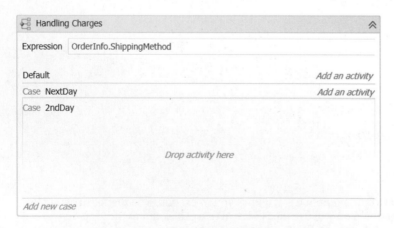

Figure 4-12. *Switch activity with cases defined*

The designer shows all the defined cases with one of them expanded so you can see the activity associated with that case. You can click one of the *Add an activity* links to expand a collapsed case.

Expression Activities

So far, you have defined the NextDay and 2ndDay cases plus the default case, which is used when the ShippingMethod value is not one of the defined cases. Now you'll need to specify the activity (or sequence of activities) that are to be executed for each case. For this project, you'll use the Add activity.

■ **Tip** The System.Activities.Expressions namespace contains a number of activities that you can use in your workflow, including Add, Subtract, Multiply, and Divide. It also includes activities such as Equal, GreaterThan, And, and Or that are used by the built-in activities to evaluate expressions. You can use them directly in your workflow.

Unfortunately, the Add activity is not in the toolbox. You'll need to enter this by editing the .xaml code. Save the project. In the Solution Explorer, right-click OrderWF.xaml and choose View Code. It will prompt you to close the existing designer window; just click Yes. The Switch activity is defined by the following code:

```
<Switch x:TypeArguments="x:String" DisplayName="Handling Charges"
  Expression="[OrderInfo.ShippingMethod]">
  sap:VirtualizedContainerService.HintSize="473.6,257.6">
  <x:Null x:Key="NextDay" />
  <x:Null x:Key="2ndDay" />
</Switch>
```

Notice the x:Null attribute on the NextDay and 2ndDay cases. This indicates that no activity has been defined for these cases. Replace these two lines of code with the following:

```
<Add x:TypeArguments="s:Decimal, s:Decimal, s:Decimal" x:Key="NextDay"
  DisplayName="Add 15" Left="[TotalAmount]" Result="[TotalAmount]"
  Right="[15.0D]" />
<Add x:TypeArguments="s:Decimal, s:Decimal, s:Decimal" x:Key="2ndDay"
  DisplayName="Add 10" Left="[TotalAmount]" Result="[TotalAmount]"
  Right="[10.0D]" />
```

Then add the following code just before the previous code to define the default case:

```
<Switch.Default>
  <p:Add x:TypeArguments="s:Decimal, s:Decimal, s:Decimal" DisplayName="Add 5"
    Left="[TotalAmount]" Result="[TotalAmount]" Right="[5.0D]" />
</Switch.Default>
```

The Add activity has three properties: Left, Right, and Result. The value of the Right property is added to the Left, and the sum is stored in the Result property. The Left and Result properties are set to the TotalAmount argument. The Right property is specified as a static value, which is different in each case.

The complete definition of the Switch activity is shown in Listing 4-2.

Listing 4-2. *Definition of the Switch activity*

```
<Switch x:TypeArguments="x:String" DisplayName="Handling Charges"
  Expression="[OrderInfo.ShippingMethod]">
  sap:VirtualizedContainerService.HintSize="473.6,257.6">
  <Switch.Default>
    <Add x:TypeArguments="s:Decimal, s:Decimal, s:Decimal" DisplayName="Add 5"
      Left="[TotalAmount]" Result="[TotalAmount]" Right="[5.0D]" />
  </Switch.Default>
  <Add x:TypeArguments="s:Decimal, s:Decimal, s:Decimal" x:Key="NextDay"
    DisplayName="Add 15" Left="[TotalAmount]" Result="[TotalAmount]"
    Right="[15.0D]" />
  <Add x:TypeArguments="s:Decimal, s:Decimal, s:Decimal" x:Key="2ndDay"
    DisplayName="Add 10" Left="[TotalAmount]" Result="[TotalAmount]"
    Right="[10.0D]" />
</Switch>
```

Save the project, and from the Solution Explorer right-click the OrderWF.xaml file and choose View Designer. The Switch activity should look like the one shown in Figure 4-13.

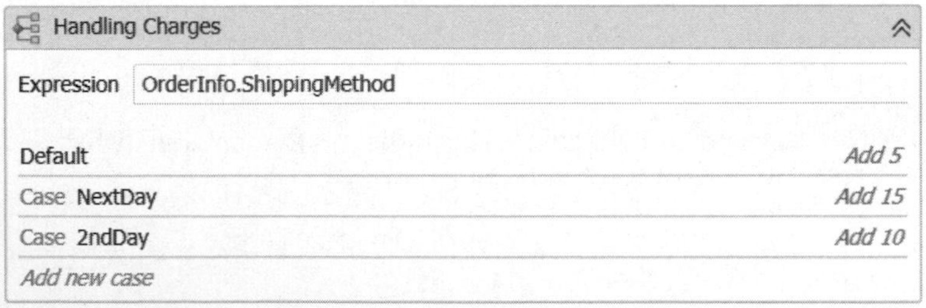

Handling Charges	⌃
Expression	OrderInfo.ShippingMethod
Default	Add 5
Case NextDay	Add 15
Case 2ndDay	Add 10
Add new case	

Figure 4-13. *Completed Switch activity*

When the ShippingMethod is NextDay, $15 is added to the TotalAmount; for 2ndDay, $10 is added. For all other shipping methods, the default case adds $5. The diagram displays all the case values (including the default case) and the DisplayName of the activity that is executed for that case value. If you click any of these cases, the Switch activity is expanded to show the case activity (see Figure 4-14).

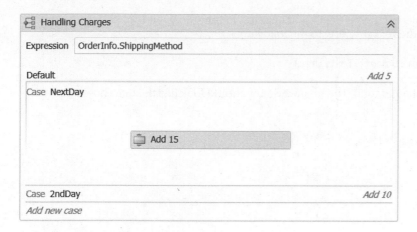

Figure 4-14. Expanded Switch activity

Click the Add activity, and its properties will be shown in the Properties window (see Figure 4-15). You can update the properties here, if necessary.

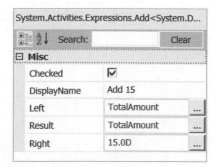

Figure 4-15. Add activity Properties window

■ **Caution** The decimal value is entered as **15.0D**; this is the correct format for specifying Decimal constants in Visual Basic. If you try to use the C# notation (**15.0m**) you will get a validation error. This is just another reminder that expressions are entered using VB syntax.

Drag another Assign activity below the Switch activity and set the DisplayName to **Freight Charges**. For the To property, enter **TotalAmount**. For the Value property, enter the following:

```
TotalAmount + (OrderInfo.TotalWeight * 0.50D)
```

This formula will add $.50 per pound for the freight charges. Finally, drag another `WriteLine` activity after "Freight Charges" and set the `Text` property to the following:

```
"The total amount is: $" + TotalAmount.ToString()
```

This displays the calculated order total. The final workflow should look like the one shown in Figure 4-16.

Figure 4-16. *Final workflow diagram*

Invoking the Workflow

In this project, the console application will invoke the workflow synchronously and display the results when it completes. Replace the generated implementation of `Program.cs` using the code shown in Listing 4-3.

Listing 4-3. *Implementation of Program.cs*

```
using System;
using System.Activities;
using System.Activities.Statements;
using System.Collections.Generic;

namespace OrderProcess
{

    class Program
    {
        static void Main(string[] args)
        {
            Order myOrder = new Order
            {
                OrderID = 1,
                Description = "Need some stuff",
                ShippingMethod = "2ndDay",
                TotalWeight = 100
            };

            // create dictionary with input arguments for the workflow
            IDictionary<string, object> input = new Dictionary<string, object>
            {
                { "OrderInfo" , myOrder }
            };

            // execute the workflow
            IDictionary<string, object> output
                = WorkflowInvoker.Invoke(new OrderWF(), input);

            // Get the TotalAmount returned by the workflow
            decimal total = (decimal)output["TotalAmount"];
            Console.WriteLine("Workflow returned ${0} for my order total", total);

            Console.WriteLine("Press ENTER to exit");
            Console.ReadLine();
        }
    }
}
```

This code creates an Order class and populates it with some test data. It then creates a Dictionary object and stores the Order object in the dictionary. It calls the static Invoke() method of the WorkflowInvoker class, passing in the Dictionary object. The Invoke() method creates and executes a workflow instance on the application's thread.

Passing the data in a Dictionary object allows for multiple parameters to be passed. It's important to ensure that the dictionary key (in this case, OrderInfo) matches the name of the argument defined in the workflow and the type of object in the dictionary matches the specified ArgumentType in the workflow.

The Invoke() method returns a Dictionary object, which contains all the workflow arguments with the Out or In/Out Direction. The TotalAmount argument is extracted from the dictionary and written to the console.

Running the Application

Press F5 to run the application. The results should look like these:

```
Order Received
The total amount is: $60
Workflow returned $60 for my order total
Press ENTER to exit
```

To verify that this total is correct, you can calculate it manually. The ShippingMethod was 2ndDay, which adds a $10 charge. The TotalWeight was set to 100, and the freight charges were computed as $.50 per pound, for a total of $50. The combination of these two is $60.

■ ■ ■

CHAPTER 5

Replicated Activities

In Chapter 4, you created a workflow that calculates the order total of an order passed in as an argument. So far, it includes only the handling and freight charges. In this chapter, you'll add logic to add the cost of each of the order items. To do that, you'll need to perform a sequence of activities for each of the items.

Reusing the Chapter 4 Project

Start Visual Studio 2010 and create a new project. Choose the Blank Solution template, as shown in Figure 5-1. Enter the solution name as **Chapter05**.

Figure 5-1. *Creating a blank solution*

Next, copy the OrderProcess subfolder from the Chapter04 folder to the Chapter05 folder, as shown in Figure 5-2.

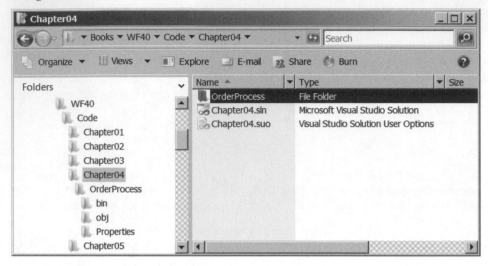

Figure 5-2. *Copying the project from Chapter 4*

In the Solution Explorer, right-click the Chapter05 solution and choose Add ➤ Existing Project, as shown in Figure 5-3.

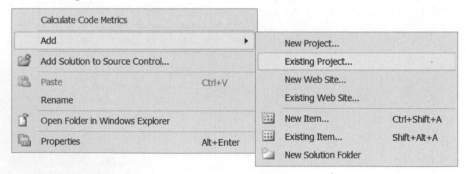

Figure 5-3. *Adding an existing project to this solution*

The Add Existing Project dialog shown in Figure 5-4 will display. Select the OrderProcess.csproj file from the Chapter05\OrderProcess folder.

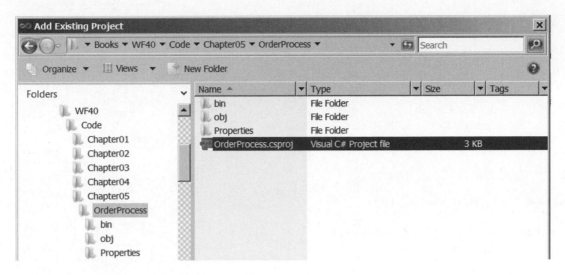

Figure 5-4. *Selecting the existing project*

When you click the Open button, the project is loaded into this solution. The Solution Explorer should look like the one shown in Figure 5-5.

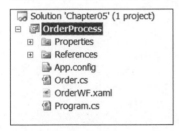

Figure 5-5. *Initial Solution Explorer view*

Adding OrderItem Processing

Now you're ready to add the step that calculates the cost of the order items.

ForEach Activity

The ForEach activity executes an activity (or a sequence of activities) for each item in a collection. This is exactly what you need for this project.

Open the OrderWF.xaml file in the design view. Drag a ForEach<T> activity just below the "Initialize Total" activity. Change the DisplayName to **Accumulate Order Items**. The activity may be collapsed. If it is, click the expand link at the top-right corner of the activity. The diagram should look like the one shown in Figure 5-6.

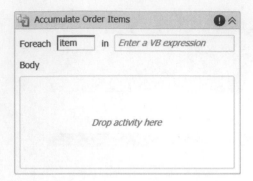

Figure 5-6. *The initial ForEach activity*

In the Expression field, enter the following:

OrderInfo.Items

The <T> in the activity name indicates that this is a generic class, and you'll need to define the type that is contained in the collection. Look in the Properties window and you'll see that the default type is Int32. You may have also noticed the red circle indicating that there is an error (see Figure 5-7). This is letting you know the Expression you entered (OrderInfo.Items) does not contain a collection of integers.

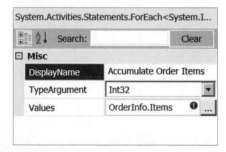

Figure 5-7. *The ForEach Properties window*

OrderInfo.Items is a collection of OrderItem objects from the Order that was passed in to the workflow. In the TypeArgument drop-down list, select Browse for Types. In the dialog box, expand the OrderProcess assembly and select the OrderItem class, as shown in Figure 5-8.

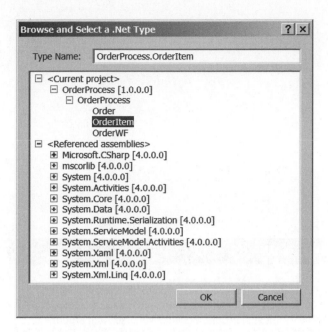

Figure 5-8. *Selecting the OrderItem class*

For this project, you'll simply charge a fixed amount for all items. In a real scenario, you would probably look up the item properties from a database. For now, however, drag an `Assign` activity onto the `ForEach` activity.

■ **Tip** You can drag only a single activity onto the `ForEach` activity. If you need more than one, just drag a `Sequence` activity onto it. Then you can add any number of activities onto the `Sequence` activity.

For the `To` property, enter **TotalAmount**; for the `Value` property, enter this:

```
TotalAmount + (item.Quantity * 10.0D)
```

This adds $10 for every item included in the order. The diagram should look like the one shown in Figure 5-9.

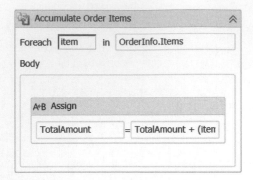

Figure 5-9. Completed ForEach activity

Replicator in WF 3.5

If you've used previous versions of WF, you might recognize this feature. In WF 3.5, it was provided by the `Replicator` activity. The version 4.0 implementation is much more intuitive. One of the most significant improvements is that the built-in activities can access your instance data. Because variables and arguments are managed by the workflow runtime in version 4.0, the built-in activities can access them.

In this project, for example, the `Assign` activity could reference the `item.Quantity` property. In previous versions, you had to create a custom activity and write code to copy the instance data to the custom activity.

Drag a `WriteLine` activity just below "Accumulate Order Items". For the `DisplayName,` enter **Display Item Total** and for Text property, enter the following:

```
"The item total is: $" + TotalAmount.ToString()
```

This will display the total of the order items before the workflow adds in the handling and freight charges. The complete workflow should look like the one shown in Figure 5-10.

Figure 5-10. *Complete workflow diagram*

■ **Tip** I used the Collapse All link at the top right of the workflow designer to see all the activities and still be able to read the diagram. Notice that the "Accumulate Order Items" and "Handling Charges" activities have the Expand link at the top right. You can use these links to selectively expand each activity.

Adding Order Items

Before you can test this new feature, you'll need to modify the application to add some OrderItem objects to the Order class. Open the Program.cs file. Add the following code just after the Order class is created:

```
// Add some OrderItem objects
myOrder.Items.Add(new OrderItem
{
    OrderItemID = 1,
    Quantity = 1,
    ItemCode = "12345",
    Description = "Widget"
});

myOrder.Items.Add(new OrderItem
{
    OrderItemID = 2,
    Quantity = 3,
    ItemCode = "12346",
    Description = "Gadget"
});

myOrder.Items.Add(new OrderItem
{
    OrderItemID = 3,
    Quantity = 2,
    ItemCode = "12347",
    Description = "Super Widget"
});
```

Running the Application

Press F5 to run the application. Your results should look like the following:

```
Order Received
The item total is: $60
The total amount is: $120
Workflow returned $120 for my order total
Press ENTER to exit
```

The first OrderItem had a quantity of 1, the second was 3, and the third was 2. So there are a total of 6 items, and at $10 each, the item total should be $60. As was explained in the previous chapter, the handling and freight charges is also $60. So the $120 order total is the correct amount.

The complete listing for the Program.cs class is shown in Listing 5-1.

Listing 5-1. *Implementation of Program.cs*

```
using System;
```

```csharp
using System.Activities;
using System.Activities.Statements;
using System.Collections.Generic;

namespace OrderProcess
{
    class Program
    {
        static void Main(string[] args)
        {
            Order myOrder = new Order
            {
                OrderID = 1,
                Description = "Need some stuff",
                ShippingMethod = "2ndDay",
                TotalWeight = 100
            };

            // Add some OrderItem objects
            myOrder.Items.Add(new OrderItem
            {
                OrderItemID = 1,
                Quantity = 1,
                ItemCode = "12345",
                Description = "Widget"
            });

            myOrder.Items.Add(new OrderItem
            {
                OrderItemID = 2,
                Quantity = 3,
                ItemCode = "12346",
                Description = "Gadget"
            });

            myOrder.Items.Add(new OrderItem
            {
                OrderItemID = 3,
                Quantity = 2,
                ItemCode = "12347",
                Description = "Super Widget"
            });
```

```
// create dictionary with input arguments for the workflow
IDictionary<string, object> input = new Dictionary<string, object>
{
    { "OrderInfo" , myOrder }
};

// execute the workflow
IDictionary<string, object> output
    = WorkflowInvoker.Invoke(new OrderWF(), input);

// Get the TotalAmount returned by the workflow
decimal total = (decimal)output["TotalAmount"];
Console.WriteLine("Workflow returned ${0} for my order total", total);

Console.WriteLine("Press ENTER to exit");
Console.ReadLine();
        }
    }
}
```

ParallelForEach Activity

Instead of the ForEach activity, you could have used the ParallelForEach activity. They are configured in exactly the same way. The only difference is in how the activities are executed.

As its name suggests, the ParallelForEach activity executes the child activities simultaneously, whereas the ForEach activity executes them sequentially. For this project, it really makes no difference which one you use. For more complex activity sequences, running them in parallel might be more appropriate. For example, if you were to send a message and wait for a response, you might want to run them in parallel so the wait time is not compounded.

To test this, delete the ForEach activity and drag a ParallelForEach activity in its place. Configure it just as you did the ForEach activity. Then run the application and verify that you get the same results.

CHAPTER 6

■ ■ ■

Exception Handling

In this chapter, you'll add logic to verify that each of the order items is in stock. To do that, you'll iterate through each of the order items in the same way as you did in the previous chapter. If an item is out of stock, you'll throw an exception, which will be caught by your workflow.

Reusing the Chapter 5 Project

Start Visual Studio 2010 and create a new project. Choose the Blank Solution template, as shown in Figure 6-1. Enter the solution name as **Chapter06**.

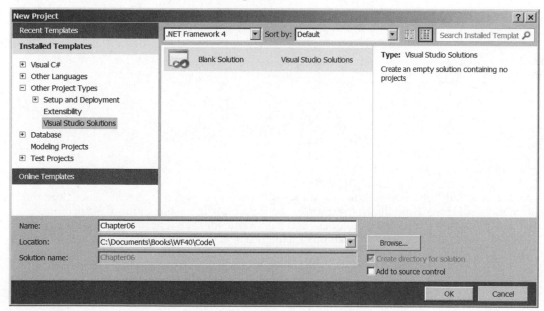

Figure 6-1. *Creating a blank solution*

Next, copy the OrderProcess subfolder from the Chapter05 folder to the Chapter06 folder. In the Solution Explorer, right-click the Chapter06 solution and choose Add ➤ Existing Project. The Add Existing Project dialog will display. Select the `OrderProcess.csproj` file from the Chapter06\OrderProcess folder. (This is the same procedure you used in the last chapter to copy the project from Chapter 4.)

Adding the Check Stock Activity

Now you'll add logic to see whether there is sufficient stock for this order.

TryCatch Activity

Open the `OrderWF.xaml` file in design view. Drag a `TryCatch` activity onto your workflow just above the "Handling Charges" activity. Change the `DisplayName` to **Check Stock** and click the expand link at the top right. The designer diagram should look like the one shown in Figure 6-2.

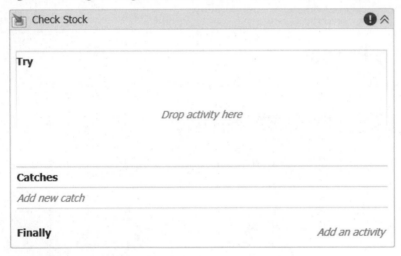

Figure 6-2. *An initial TryCatch activity*

The `TryCatch` activity has three sections. In the Try section, you'll place a sequence of activities that could potentially generate exceptions. In the Catches section, you'll define one or more `Catch` objects. Each `Catch` object handles a specific exception, so you'll need one for each type of exception that could occur. The Finally section is optional. You can put a sequence of activities here that are executed after the Try activities (and any `Catch` objects that may be invoked by an exception).

Defining an Exception

You will now define the exception that should be thrown when an item is out of stock. Open the `Order.cs` file and add the following code to define the `OutOfStockException` class. It should be added after the definition of the Order class but inside the OrderProcess namespace. The complete implementation of Order.cs is shown in Listing 6-1.

```
//-----------------------------------------------
// Define the exception to be thrown if an item
// is out of stock
//-----------------------------------------------
public class OutOfStockExccption : Exception
{
    public OutOfStockException()
        : base()
    {
    }

    public OutOfStockException(string message)
        : base(message)
    {
    }
}
```

Now press F6 to build the application.

Listing 6-1. Complete Order.cs file

```
using System;
using System.Collections.Generic;

namespace OrderProcess
{
    public class OrderItem
    {
        public int OrderItemID { get; set; }
        public int Quantity { get; set; }
        public string ItemCode { get; set; }
        public string Description { get; set; }
    }

    public class Order
    {
        public Order()
        {
            Items = new List<OrderItem>();
        }
```

```
        public int OrderID { get; set; }
        public string Description { get; set; }
        public decimal TotalWeight { get; set; }
        public string ShippingMethod { get; set; }

        public List<OrderItem> Items { get; set; }
    }


    //---------------------------------------------
    // Define the exception to be thrown if an item
    // is out of stock
    //---------------------------------------------
    public class OutOfStockException : Exception
    {
        public OutOfStockException()
            : base()
        {
        }

        public OutOfStockException(string message)
            : base(message)
        {
        }
    }
}
```

ForEach Activity

Drag a ForEach activity to the Try section and set the DisplayName to **Check Each Item**. Click the expand link. In the Expression field, enter the following:

OrderInfo.Items

This defines the property that contains the collection of items to be iterated and acted upon. (Refer to Chapter 5 for more information about the ForEach activity.) In the Properties window, for the TypeArgument property, select Browse for Types and then select the OrderItem class from the OrderProcess assembly (as you did in Chapter 5).

If Activity

Drag an If activity onto the Try section, click the expand link, and set the DisplayName to **If Out of Stock**. The diagram should look like the one shown in Figure 6-3.

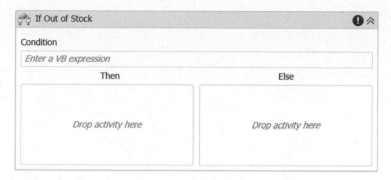

Figure 6-3. *The "If Out of Stock" activity*

In the `Condition` property, enter the following expression:

```
item.ItemCode = "12346"
```

■ **Note** In a real application, you would check the existing stock availability from a database. In this example, the out-of-stock condition is hard-coded based on the `ItemCode` to simplify the sample project.

Throw Activity

Drag a `Throw` activity in the Then section. In the Properties window, there are only two properties: `DisplayName` and `Exception`. For the `Exception` property, enter the following expression:

```
New OrderProcess.OutOfStockException("Item Code: " + item.ItemCode)
```

This creates a new `OutOfStockException` and specifies the message text that indicates which item is out of stock. The "If Out of Stock" activity should look like the one shown in Figure 6-4.

73

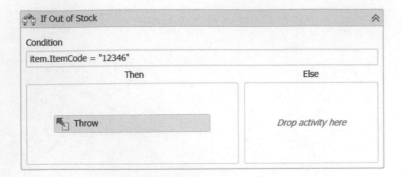

Figure 6-4. *Final If activity diagram*

Catch Activity

The "Check Stock" activity should look like the one shown in Figure 6-5.

Figure 6-5. *Partially completed TryCatch activity*

Click the *Add new catch* link. A drop-down will appear, listing the common exceptions. Choose Browse for Types and select the OutOfStockException from the OrderProcess assembly, as shown in Figure 6-6.

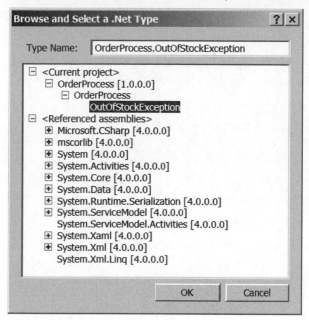

Figure 6-6. *Selecting the OutOfStockException*

The diagram should now look like the one shown in Figure 6-7.

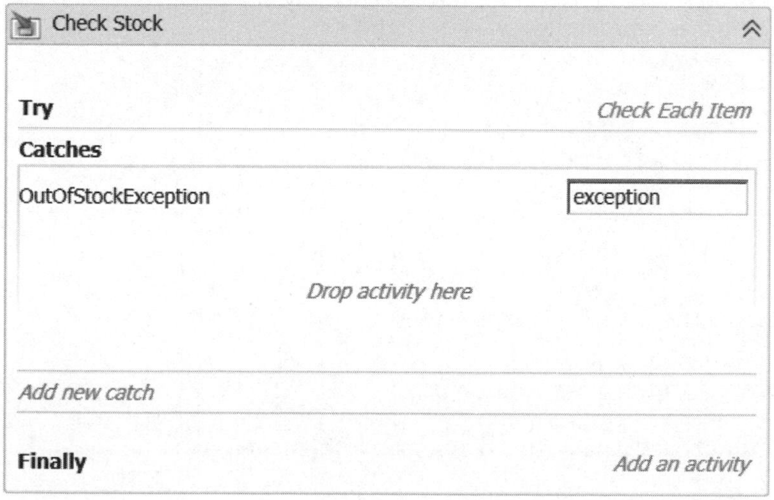

Figure 6-7. *A partially completed Catch activity*

For each exception that you'll catch, you'll need to define the activity(ies) that should be executed to handle the exception. For this project, you'll write a line to the console indicating which item is out of stock. Drag a WriteLine activity to the Catches section and enter the following for the Text property:

```
"Item is out of stock - " + exception.Message
```

This code gets the message from the Exception, which contains the ItemCode of the out-of-stock item. Collapse the "Check Stock" activity and then expand it. The final "Check Stock" activity is shown in Figure 6-8.

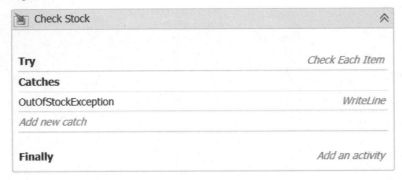

Figure 6-8. *The final "Check Stock" activity diagram*

The default expanded view of a TryCatch activity looks like Figure 6-8. Each of the sections (Try, Catches, and Finally) are summarized. In the Try section it tells you that there is an activity named "Check Each Item". The Catches section lists the exceptions that are handled; in this case, there is only one—OutOfStockException and it is handled by a WriteLine activity. Because there is no activity defined for the Finally section, there is an *Add an activity* link instead. You can click any of these links (*Check Each Item*, *WriteLine*, or *Add an activity*), and that section will be expanded.

Running the Application

Now you're ready to run the application. Press F5. The results should look similar to these:

```
Order Received
The item total is: $60
Item is out of stock - Item Code: 12346
The total amount is: $120
Workflow returned $120 for my order total
Press ENTER to exit
```

Exceptions

Just as with other exception handling that you may be familiar with, workflow exceptions bubble up the hierarchy until they are caught. They can be re-thrown, which will cause them to continue up the chain until caught again.

It is important to choose where to place the exception handling. For example, you could put your entire workflow in the Try section of a TryCatch activity. Although this is a simple way to ensure all exceptions are caught, it may not give you the ability to actually "handle" the exception. Let me explain.

When an exception is thrown, if not caught by the parent activity, the parent activity is aborted and the remaining child activities are not executed. In this project, for example, the exception was thrown by the Then branch of the If activity. The TryCatch was around the ForEach activity. Because the exception was not caught earlier, when it bubbled up to the ForEach activity, the ForEach activity stopped iterating any more items. This means that once an OutOfStockException is thrown, the workflow stops checking any more items. That was how I intended for it to work. The requirement was to verify that we had all the items needed to fulfill the order. So as soon as an out-of-stock item was found, we could stop checking.

The following pseudocode illustrates how this works:

```
Sequence
{
    CheckStock (Try)
    {
        Check Each Item (ForEach)
        {
            If Out of Stock (If)
            {
                Throw Exception (Then)
            }
        }
    }
    Catch
    {
    }

    Remaining Activities
}
```

When an exception is thrown, the execution will proceed directly to the Catch sequence. The workflow then continues from there. With this design, it would execute the activities to calculate the handling and freight charges. However, if you wanted it to keep checking the stock on the remaining items, you would need to put the TryCatch activity around the If activity. That would handle the exception before it reached the ForEach activity, as shown in the following pseudocode:

```
Sequence
{
    Check Each Item (ForEach)
```

```
    {
        (Try)
        {
            If Out of Stock (If)
            {
                Throw Exception (Then)
            }
        }
        Catch
        {
        }
    }
}
```

Because the Catch sequence is still inside the ForEach activity, once the Catch is executed, the workflow would proceed to the next item in the ForEach activity after the Catch executes. If however, you wanted the whole process to stop and not continue to process the order, you would want to put the TryCatch around the main workflow sequence, as illustrated in this final pseudocode:

```
(Try)
{
    Sequence
    {
        Check Each Item
        {
            If Out of Stock
            {
                Throw Exception
            }
        }

        Remaining Activities
    }
}
Catch
{
}
```

Because the Catch sequence is outside the main sequence, the workflow is completed after the Catch is executed.

CHAPTER 7

■■■

Extending the Built-In Activities

In this chapter, you'll start with the project from Chapter 6 and refine the order pricing rules. In the process, I'll demonstrate two techniques for extending the built-in activities: creating custom activities and using the InvokeMethod activity.

Reusing the Chapter 6 Project

Start Visual Studio 2010 and create a new project. Choose the Blank Solution template, as shown in Figure 7-1. Enter the solution name as **Chapter07**.

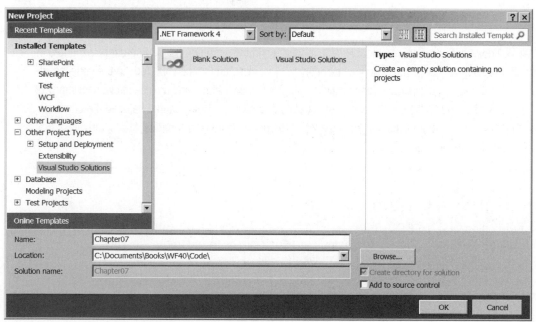

Figure 7-1. Creating a blank solution

Copy the OrderProcess subfolder from the Chapter06 folder to the Chapter07 folder. In the Solution Explorer, right-click the Chapter07 solution and choose Add ➤ Existing Project. This will display the Add Existing Project dialog. Select the `OrderProcess.csproj` file from the Chapter07\OrderProcess folder.

Using Custom Activities

The current project uses a fixed price of $10 for all items. You can refine it by creating a custom activity that will "look up" the price of an item using the `ItemCode` property. Open the `Order.cs` file and add the following class definition. This class defines the item properties that will be returned by the custom activity:

```
//---------------------------------------------
// Define the structure returned by the
// LookupItem custom activity
//---------------------------------------------
public class ItemInfo
{
    public string ItemCode { get; set; }
    public string Description { get; set; }
    public decimal Price { get; set; }
}
```

■ **Note** WF 4.0 does not allow any executable code in your workflow definition. All code must be executed in an activity. In previous versions, you could use a `CodeActivity` class and place your code in the code-beside class. With WF 4.0, the `CodeActivity` class is now an abstract class that is used as a base class for many of the built-in activities (and available as a base class for custom activities). But it cannot be used directly in a workflow. In WF 4.0, you will find yourself writing a lot of custom activities. Fortunately, that's fairly easy to accomplish (as you'll see in this chapter).

Implementing a Custom Activity

In the Solution Explorer, right-click the OrderProcess project and choose Add ➤ New Item. In the Add New Item dialog, select the Code Activity template, which can be found in the Workflow category. Enter the class name as **LookupItem.cs**, as shown in Figure 7-2.

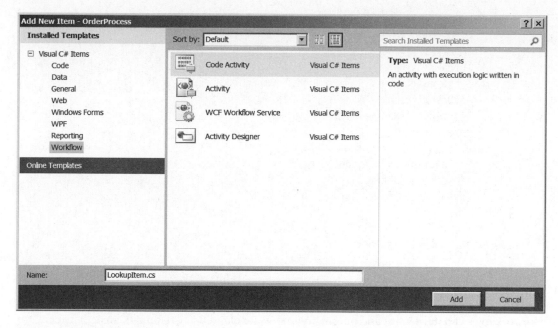

Figure 7-2. *Creating a custom activity*

The implementation of this class is shown in Listing 7-1.

Listing 7-1. *LookupItem Class*

```csharp
using System;
using System.Activities;

namespace OrderProcess
{
    public sealed class LookupItem : CodeActivity
    {
        public InArgument<string> ItemCode { get; set; }
        public OutArgument<ItemInfo> Item { get; set; }

        protected override void Execute(CodeActivityContext context)
        {
            ItemInfo i = new ItemInfo();
            i.ItemCode = context.GetValue<string>(ItemCode);

            switch (i.ItemCode)
            {
```

81

```
            case "12345":
                i.Description = "Widget";
                i.Price = (decimal)10.0;
                break;
            case "12346":
                i.Description = "Gadget";
                i.Price = (decimal)15.0;
                break;
            case "12347":
                i.Description = "Super Gadget";
                i.Price = (decimal)25.0;
                break;
        }

        context.SetValue(this.Item, i);
    }
  }
}
```

Just as workflows can have input and output arguments (explained in Chapter 4), an activity can also have input and output arguments. In fact, the properties you have been setting for the built-in classes (such as the Text property on a WriteLine activity) are activity arguments. Your custom activity (LookupItem) takes an ItemCode as an input argument and returns the ItemInfo class as an output argument.

The LookupItem class is derived from the CodeActivity base class and overrides the Execute method. This method creates an ItemInfo class and stores the ItemCode in it. Notice that it has to use the context.GetValue() method to obtain the value of ItemCode because the argument data is maintained by the workflow itself. The CodeActivityContext is provided to the Execute() method when it is called.

The Execute() method then specifies the Description and Price properties based on the ItemCode. (In a real application, you would look them up in a database.) Finally, it calls the context.SetValue() method to store the ItemInfo class in the output argument.

Press F6 to rebuild the application.

Using the LookupItem Activity

Open the OrderWF.xaml file in design mode. Notice that the LookupItem activity has been added to the Toolbox (see Figure 7-3).

Figure 7-3. The LookupItem activity has been added to the Toolbox

Expand the "Accumulate Order Items" activity, if necessary. The diagram should look like the one shown in Figure 7-4.

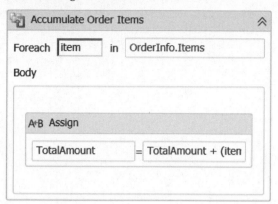

Figure 7-4. *The initial design of the Accumulate Order Items activity*

This simply enumerates each of the order items and executes an Assign activity, which adds $10 for each item to the OrderTotal. Select the Assign activity and click the Delete key to remove this activity. In its place, drag a Sequence activity onto the Body section. Set its DisplayName to **Lookup Item** and expand it. Drag a LookupItem activity onto this the "Lookup Item" Sequence. Notice that the Properties window (shown in Figure 7-5) contains the ItemCode and Item arguments that you defined for this activity. The DisplayName argument was defined in the base CodeActivity class.

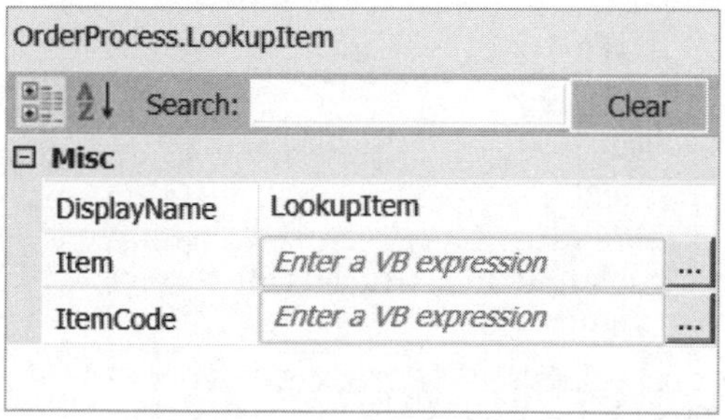

Figure 7-5. *The Properties window of the LookupItem activity*

For the ItemCode property, enter the following expression:

```
item.ItemCode
```

You have to define a variable to store the ItemInfo class that is returned. Click the Variables button on the bottom left of the designer. Click the *Create Variable* link. Enter **ItemDetails** for the Name. For the Variable type field, open the drop-down list and select Browse for Types.

The dialog shown in Figure 7-6 will display. Expand the OrderProcess assembly, select the ItemInfo class, and click OK.

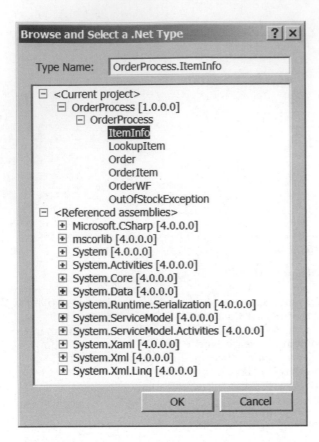

Figure 7-6. *Selecting the class that defines the variable type*

The Scope should default to the current Sequence activity ("Lookup Item"), which is the correct scope. The variable definition should look like the one shown in Figure 7-7.

Name	▼ Variable type	Scope	Default
ItemDetails	ItemInfo	Lookup Item	*Enter a VB expression*
Create Variable			

| Variables | Arguments | Imports | | 🔍 | 100% ▼ | 🔲 🔳 |

Figure 7-7. *The definition for the ItemDetails variable*

Now select the LookupItem activity and specify the Item property as **ItemDetails**. This will take the ItemInfo class returned by the custom activity and store it in the ItemDetails variable. Drag an Assign activity just below the LookupItem activity. For the To property, enter **TotalAmount**. For the Value property, enter **TotalAmount + (item.Quantity * ItemDetails.Price)**.

This expression takes the Price property from the ItemInfo class, multiplies it by the Quantity, and adds the result to the TotalAmount variable. The "Accumulate Order Items" activity should look like the one shown in Figure 7-8.

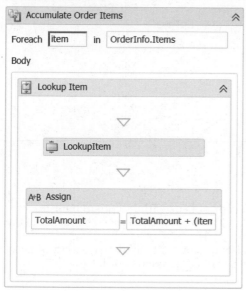

Figure 7-8. *The final Accumulate Order Items activity*

Running the Application

Press F5 to run the application. Your results should be similar to these:

```
Order Received
The item total is: $105
Item is out of stock - Item Code: 12346
The total amount is: $165
Workflow returned $165 for my order total
Press ENTER to exit
```

You can verify that the item total of $105 is correct by computing it manually.

Table 7-1. Order Item Price Calculation

ItemCode	Quantity	Price	Ext. Price
12345	1	$10	$10
12346	3	$15	$45
12347	2	$25	$50
Total			$105

InvokeMethod Activity

The InvokeMethod activity is another useful way to implement code outside of the standard built-in activities. You can use this activity to invoke a method of a class. The class does not need to be part of the workflow or use any of the workflow base classes.

In this project, you will implement a class to calculate a discount amount based on a variety of rules. This class will be invoked by the workflow to compute the discount of the specified order.

Creating a Discount Class

In the Solution Explorer, right-click the OrderProcess project and choose Add ➤ Class. Enter the class name as **OrderDiscount.cs**. The implementation of this class is shown in Listing 7-2.

Listing 7-2. OrderDiscount class

```
using System;
using System.Collections.Generic;

namespace OrderProcess
{
    public static class OrderDiscount
    {
        public static decimal ComputeDiscount(Order o, decimal total)
        {
            // Count the number of items ordered
            int count = 0;
            foreach (OrderItem i in o.Items)
            {
                count += i.Quantity;
            }
```

```
        // Determine the discount percentage
        decimal pct = 0;
        if (total > 500)
            pct = (decimal)0.20;
        if (total > 200)
            pct = (decimal)0.15;
        if (total > 100)
            pct = (decimal)0.10;

        // Calculate the discount amount
        decimal discount = total * pct;

        // Subtract a dollar for every item ordered
        discount -= (decimal)count;

        // Make sure it's not less than zero
        if (discount < 0)
            discount = 0;

        Console.WriteLine("Discount computed: ${0}", discount.ToString());
        return discount;
    }
  }
}
```

The ComputeDiscount() method takes two parameters: an Order class and the item total. It returns the discount amount that is applicable to this order. The discount logic I used is somewhat arbitrary and not really important for our purposes. It first determines the discount percentage based on the total amount of the order. It then subtracts $1 for every item ordered.

Press F6 to rebuild the application.

Using the InvokeMethod Activity

Now you'll use the InvokeMethod activity to execute the ComputeDiscount() method. Drag an InvokeMethod activity onto your workflow just before the "Check Stock" activity. Enter the DisplayName property as **Calculate Discount**.

Specifying the Target Object

The TargetType property specifies the class that contains the method that is to be invoked. In the drop-down list, select Browse for Types. In the dialog that appears, expand the OrderProcess assembly and select the OrderDiscount class, as shown in Figure 7-9.

Figure 7-9. *Selecting the OrderDiscount class*

■ **Tip** You can use two methods to specify the object that contains the method to be invoked. If the method is in a static class, you can simply specify the TargetType property, as we did in this project. If the class is not static, you have to define the specific instance of that object. The best way to do that is to define a variable of that class type. Then in the TargetObject property, specify that variable name. If there are multiple instances, and you need to control which instance is used, you can set the variable through either an Assign activity or a custom activity prior to executing the InvokeMethod activity. If you specify the TargetObject property, you don't have to specify the TargetType property.

For the MethodName property, enter **ComputeDiscount**.

Specifying the Parameters

If you hover the mouse over the error indicator next to the "Calculate Discount" activity, you'll see an error message similar to the one shown in Figure 7-10.

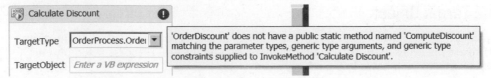

Figure 7-10. *InvokeMethod error message*

This message is displayed because you have not defined the parameters yet. In the Properties window, select the Parameters property and click the ellipsis. The Parameters dialog shown in Figure 7-11 will display.

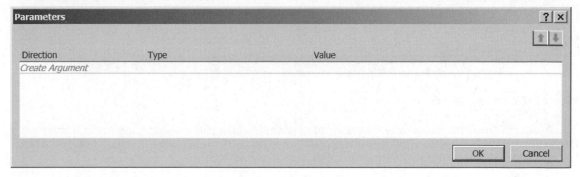

Figure 7-11. *An empty Parameters collection*

This dialog is very similar to the Arguments control used for setting up input and output arguments for the workflow. Click the *Create Argument* link. The Direction should be In. To select the Order class for the Type property, you might have to select Browse for Types and then choose the Order class from the OrderProcess assembly. The Value should be **OrderInfo**. It will use the existing OrderInfo variable, which is a reference to the Order class being processed.

Click the *Create Argument* link again to add the second parameter. The Direction is In, the Type is Decimal, and the Value should be **TotalAmount**. The completed collection should look like the one shown in Figure 7-12.

Direction	Type	Value
In	Order	OrderInfo
In	Decimal	TotalAmount
Create Argument		

Figure 7-12. *The completed Parameters collection*

Specifying the Result

The ComputeDiscount() method returns the discount amount as a decimal. Now you need to create a variable to store the result that is returned. Click the Variables control at the bottom of the designer. Click the *Create Variable* link. Enter the Name as **Discount**, the Variable type should be **Decimal**, and the Scope should be Sequence. The variable list should look like the one shown in Figure 7-13.

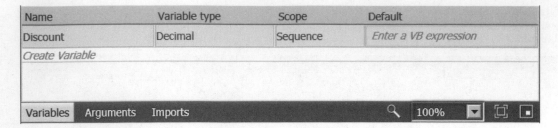

Figure 7-13. *Adding a Discount variable*

Select the InvokeMethod activity. In the Properties window, select the Result property and enter **Discount**. This will cause the results returned by the method to be stored in the Discount variable. The completed Properties window should look like the one shown in Figure 7-14.

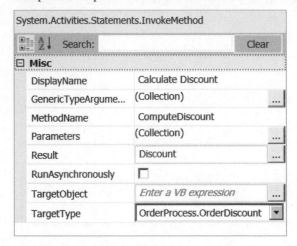

Figure 7-14. *The completed Properties window*

The "Calculate Discount" activity will look like the one shown in Figure 7-15.

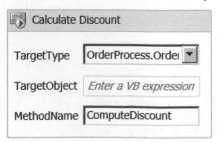

Figure 7-15. *The Calculate Discount activity*

Adding the Discount

The last step is to subtract the discount from the current order total. To do this, drag an Assign activity to the workflow just below the "Calculate Discount" activity. For the To property, enter **TotalAmount**. For the Value property, enter **TotalAmount – Discount**.

The workflow diagram is too large to display here, but the three activities between "Accumulate Order Items" and "Check Stock" are shown in Figure 7-16. This part of your workflow should look similar.

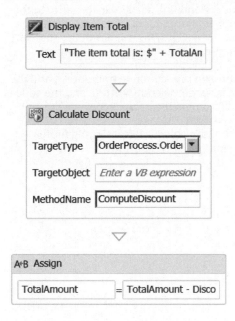

Figure 7-16. *Partial workflow diagram*

Running the Application

Press F5 to run the application. Your results should be similar to the following:

```
Order Received
The item total is: $105
Discount computed: $4.5
Item is out of stock - Item Code: 12346
The total amount is: $160.5
Workflow returned $160.5 for my order total
Press ENTER to exit
```

To confirm the discount of $4.50 is correct, calculate it manually. The item total is $105, which qualifies for a 10 percent discount, which is $10.50. There are a total of 6 items, so $6 is subtracted. The net discount is $4.50.

Summary

WF 4.0 can be used in a number of very different scenarios, and subsequent chapters will explore some of them. Before we leave this section, however, I want you to understand this particular scenario. In the last four chapters, you built a workflow that takes a data structure as an input, performs some complex processing on it, and returns a value back to the application that invoked it. This might not be what you would intuitively think of as a typical use of WF. There are no long-running processes or any human interaction; it's simply a collection of computational steps.

However, using this approach, each of the various steps is broken into concrete operations, and the whole process can be viewed in a graphic representation. There is very little code written, and the code is extremely modularized. For example, you could implement a different method for calculating the discount; you simply have to modify the InvokeMethod and change the MethodName.

In these last four chapters, you also used some of the basic building blocks for designing more complex workflows. Features such as passing arguments and using custom classes will be used throughout the rest of this book.

■ ■ ■

PART 3

Communication

One of the important aspects of many workflow solutions is the communication that occurs between applications, between clients and servers, and between the workflow and the host application. In this section, you'll learn how to use workflow activities to simplify and coordinate the various communication scenarios. For the sample application, you will build a solution used by a public library to request a book to be transferred from another branch. The same application will both send a request to another branch as well as respond to requests from other branches.

CHAPTER 8

■ ■ ■

Send and Receive

The primary activities used for communication are the Send and Receive activities (and their variations SendReply and ReceiveReply). These activities use the Windows Communication Foundation (WCF) to transmit and listen for messages. In this chapter, you'll build a simple console application that uses workflow to communicate with another copy of the same application.

Creating the Project

Start by creating a new project using the Console Application template, as shown in Figure 8-1.

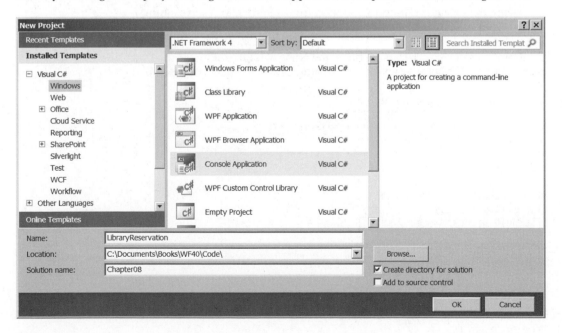

Figure 8-1. Creating a new console application

This is a standard console application, not a workflow console application. Use **LibraryReservation** as the project name and **Chapter08** as the solution. In the Solution Explorer, right-click the LibraryReservation project and choose Add Reference. From the .NET tab, add the following references:

- `System.Activities`
- `System.Configuration`
- `System.ServiceModel`
- `System.ServiceModel.Activities`

Define the Messages

You will start by creating the classes that will define the messages between the applications. In the Solution Explorer, right-click the LibraryReservation project and choose Add ➤ Class. Enter the name as **Reservation.cs**. In the `Reservation.cs` file, add the following namespaces:

```
using System.Runtime.Serialization;
using System.ServiceModel;
```

You will define three classes in this file:

- `Branch`: Defines the data elements for a library branch location.
- `ReservationRequest`: Defines a request from a branch to reserve a title.
- `ReservationResponse`: Defines the response sent back to the requesting branch.

The definition of the `Branch` class is shown in Listing 8-1. Enter it inside the `LibraryReference` namespace. (Remove the blank `Reservation` class that was generated by the template.)

Listing 8-1. *Branch Class Implementation*

```
/**************************************************/
// Define the Branch data structure
/**************************************************/
public class Branch
{
    public String BranchName { get; set;}
    public String Address { get; set; }
    public Guid BranchID { get; set; }

    #region Constructors
    public Branch()
    {
    }

    public Branch(String name, String address)
    {
        BranchName = name;
        Address = address;
```

```
        BranchID = Guid.NewGuid();
    }

    public Branch(String name, String address, Guid id)
    {
        BranchName = name;
        Address = address;
        BranchID = id;
    }

    public Branch(String name, String address, String id)
    {
        BranchName = name;
        Address = address;
        BranchID = new Guid(id);
    }
    #endregion Constructors
}
```

The Branch class has three members to store the branch name, network address, and unique identifier. Several constructors are provided for ease of use. I added the region markers around the constructors so they can be collapsed to make the code more readable.

Now add the definition of the ReservationRequest class, as shown in Listing 8-2.

Listing 8-2. *ReservationRequest Class Implementation*

```
/***************************************************/
// Define the request message, ReservationRequest
/***************************************************/
[MessageContract(IsWrapped = false)]
public class ReservationRequest
{
    private String _ISBN;
    private String _Title;
    private String _Author;
    private Guid _RequestID;
    private Branch _Requester;
    private Guid _InstanceID;

    #region Constructors
    public ReservationRequest()
    {
    }

    public ReservationRequest(String title, String author, String isbn,
        Branch requestor)
    {
        _Title = title;
        _Author = author;
        _ISBN = isbn;
        _Requester = requestor;
```

```csharp
        _RequestID = Guid.NewGuid();
    }

    public ReservationRequest(String title, String author, String isbn,
        Branch requestor, Guid id)
    {
        _Title = title;
        _Author = author;
        _ISBN = isbn;
        _Requester = requestor;
        _RequestID = id;
    }
    #endregion Constructors

    #region Public Properties
    [MessageBodyMember]
    public String Title
    {
        get { return _Title; }
        set { _Title = value; }
    }

    [MessageBodyMember]
    public String ISBN
    {
        get { return _ISBN; }
        set { _ISBN = value; }
    }

    [MessageBodyMember]
    public String Author
    {
        get { return _Author; }
        set { _Author = value; }
    }

    [MessageBodyMember]
    public Guid RequestID
    {
        get { return _RequestID; }
        set { _RequestID = value; }
    }

    [MessageBodyMember]
    public Branch Requester
    {
        get { return _Requester; }
        set { _Requester = value; }
    }

    [MessageBodyMember]
```

```
public Guid InstanceID
{
    get { return _InstanceID; }
    set { _InstanceID = value; }
}
#endregion Public Properties
}
```

The ReservationRequest class contains the ISBN, Title, and Author members for defining the book that is being requested. It also includes a Branch class that represents the branch that is requesting the book.

MessageContract

Because the ReservationRequest class will be used to define the outgoing message, the MessageContract attribute indicates that this class will be included in a SOAP envelope. When using SOAP, messages are sent using an XML-like markup language. This allows for greater platform interoperability between clients and servers. SOAP is a standard protocol supported by WCF.

There is also a MessageBodyMember attribute on each of the public properties. This is needed by the WCF layer to properly format the SOAP message.

Now enter the implementation for the ReservationResponse class, as shown in Listing 8-3.

Listing 8-3. Implementation of the ReservationResponse class

```
/*****************************************************/
// Define the request message, ReservationResponse
/*****************************************************/
[MessageContract(IsWrapped = false)]
public class ReservationResponse
{
    private bool _Reserved;
    private Branch _Provider;
    private Guid _RequestID;

    #region Constructors
    public ReservationResponse()
    {
    }

    public ReservationResponse(ReservationRequest request, bool reserved,
        Branch provider)
    {
        _RequestID = request.RequestID;
        _Reserved = reserved;
        _Provider = provider;
    }
    #endregion Constructors

    #region Public Properties
```

```
[MessageBodyMember]
public bool Reserved
{
    get { return _Reserved; }
    set { _Reserved = value; }
}

[MessageBodyMember]
public Branch Provider
{
    get { return _Provider; }
    set { _Provider = value; }
}

[MessageBodyMember]
public Guid RequestID
{
    get { return _RequestID; }
    set { _RequestID = value; }
}
#endregion Public Properties
}
```

The ReservationResponse class includes a Boolean member (Reserved) that indicates whether the book was available to be reserved. It also contains a Branch class that represents the branch that fulfilled the request.

ServiceContract

To define a WCF endpoint, there are three pieces of information that must be specified: binding, address, and contract. The *binding* indicates the protocol that is used (such as HTTP, TCP, and so on). The *address* indicates where the endpoint can be found, and the type of address used will depend on the binding. For example, with HTTP binding, you would specify a URL. For TCP, the address would be a server name or an IP address.

The *contract* is specified by a ServiceContract, which is an interface that defines the methods that are available at the endpoint. So far, you have defined the messages, which will be passed as parameters in the service methods. Now add the interface definition shown in Listing 8-4 to the same Reservation.cs file.

Listing 8-4. *Definition of the Service Contract*

```
/***********************************************/
// Define the service contract, ILibraryReservation
// which consists of two methods, RequestBook() and
// RespondToRequest()
/***********************************************/
[ServiceContract]
public interface ILibraryReservation
{
```

```
[OperationContract]
void RequestBook(ReservationRequest request);
[OperationContract]
void RespondToRequest(ReservationResponse response);
}
```

The RequestBook() method will be called by the client to send a ReservationRequest message to the server. Likewise, the RespondToRequest() method will send a ReservationResponse message back to the client.

Press F6 to build the project and fix any compiler errors.

Application Configuration

As I mentioned earlier, you will run multiple copies of this application, each one representing a different branch location. To make that work, the branch details will be stored in a configuration file. Each copy of the application will have its own configuration file that contains its specific attributes.

In the Solution Explorer, right-click the LibraryReservation project and choose Add ➤ New Item. In the New Item dialog, select the Application Configuration File template, which can be found in the General group. You can use the default name of App.config for the file name. See Figure 8-2.

Figure 8-2. *Adding an application configuration file*

Enter the configuration details using the example shown in Listing 8-5.

Listing 8-5. Setting Up the app.config file

```xml
<?xml version="1.0" encoding="utf-8" ?>
<configuration>
  <appSettings>
    <add key="Branch Name" value="Central Library"/>
    <add key="ID" value="{43E6DADD-4751-4056-8BB7-7459B5C361AB}"/>
    <add key="Address" value="8000"/>
    <add key="Request Address" value="8730"/>
  </appSettings>
</configuration>
```

The `appSettings` section has values for the `Branch Name`, `ID` (a unique identifier) and `Address` (which defines the port number that this application will be listening on). The `Request Address` defines the port number that requests will be sent to. There is nothing special about the port numbers used, and you are free to use other ports if you wish.

Defining the Workflows

The next step is to define the client and server workflows. They will communicate with each other using the `Send` and `Receive` activities. In this project, you'll use a coded workflow instead of using the designer to generate an `.xaml` file. You might want to refer to Chapter 2, in which I explained how coded workflows are used.

In the Solution Explorer, right-click the LibraryReservation project and choose Add ➤ Class. Enter the name as **ReservationWF.cs**. Add the following namespaces to this file:

```
using System.Activities;
using System.Activities.Statements;
using System.ServiceModel.Activities;
using System.ServiceModel;
```

Client–SendRequest

First, you'll define the workflow used to send a request to another branch. Replace the `ReservationWF` class that was generated by the template with the code shown in Listing 8-6.

Listing 8-6. Initial Implementation of the SendRequest Class

```csharp
public sealed class SendRequest : Activity
{
    // Define the input and output arguments
    public InArgument<string> Title { get; set; }
    public InArgument<string> Author { get; set; }
    public InArgument<string> ISBN { get; set; }
    public OutArgument<ReservationResponse> Response { get; set; }

    public SendRequest()
```

```
    {
        // Define the variables used by this workflow
        Variable<ReservationRequest> request =
            new Variable<ReservationRequest> { Name = "request" };
        Variable<string> requestAddress =
            new Variable<string> { Name = "RequestAddress" };

        // Define the Send activity
        Send submitRequest = new Send
        {
            ServiceContractName = "ILibraryReservation",
            EndpointAddress = new InArgument<Uri>
                (env => new Uri("http://localhost:" + requestAddress.Get(env) +
                    "/LibraryReservation")),
            Endpoint = new Endpoint
            {
                Binding = new BasicHttpBinding()
            },
            OperationName = "RequestBook",
            Content = SendContent.Create
                (new InArgument<ReservationRequest>(request))
        };

        // Define the SendRequest workflow

    }
}
```

This workflow has three input arguments (Title, Author, and ISBN) that define the book being requested. It also has an output argument (Response), which is the response message you defined earlier (ReservationResponse class).

The constructor also defines some local variables. They are not passed in or out of the workflow; they are used internally by the workflow activities. The request variable contains the outgoing message, which is a ReservationRequest class. The requestAddress variable will hold the port number assigned to the other branch that will receive the request.

■ **Tip** In the coded workflow that you created in Chapter 2, all the activities were created inline as anonymous classes. This works well in most cases. The Send activity is created here as a named class because it will need to be referenced by the ReceiveReply activity. This is really no different from the arguments and variables that you created. They are created as named classes so you can reference them later.

Send Activity

The submitRequest instance is defined as a Send activity. The Send activity uses WCF to send a message to the specified endpoint. You probably recognized the three pieces of information needed to specify an endpoint:

- ServiceContractName specified as ILibraryReservation

- EndpointAddress specified as a URL with a variable port number

- Binding specified with the BasicHttpBinding class

In addition, there are a few more properties that must be defined. OperationName indicates the specific method of the service contract that should be called at the destination when the message is received. The Content property stores a reference to the message (a ReservationRequest class) that is to be sent.

Custom Activity—CreateRequest

You will now create a custom activity that will build the request message from the arguments passed in to the workflow. In the Solution Explorer, right click the LibraryReservation project and choose Add ➤ Class. Enter the class name as **CreateRequest.cs**. The implementation of this class is shown in Listing 8-7.

Listing 8-7. Implementation of CreateRequest

```
using System;
using System.Activities;
using System.Configuration;

namespace LibraryReservation
{
    /****************************************************/
    // This custom activity creates a ReservationRequest
    // class using the input parameters (Title, Author and
    // ISBN).  This is provided in the Request output
    // parameter.  It also returns the network address of
    // the branch that the request should be sent to.
    /****************************************************/
    public sealed class CreateRequest : CodeActivity
    {
        public InArgument<string> Title { get; set; }
        public InArgument<string> Author { get; set; }
        public InArgument<string> ISBN { get; set; }
        public OutArgument<ReservationRequest> Request { get; set; }
        public OutArgument<string> RequestAddress { get; set; }

        protected override void Execute(CodeActivityContext context)
        {
            // Open the config file and get the Request Address
            Configuration config = ConfigurationManager
                .OpenExeConfiguration(ConfigurationUserLevel.None);
```

```
        AppSettingsSection app =
            (AppSettingsSection)config.GetSection("appSettings");

        // Create a ReservationRequest class and populate
        // it with the input arguments
        ReservationRequest r = new ReservationRequest
            (
                Title.Get(context),
                Author.Get(context),
                ISBN.Get(context),
                new Branch
                {
                    BranchName = app.Settings["Branch Name"].Value,
                    BranchID = new Guid(app.Settings["ID"].Value),
                    Address = app.Settings["Address"].Value
                }
            );

        // Store the request in the OutArgument
        Request.Set(context, r);

        // Store the address in the OutArgument
        RequestAddress.Set(context, app.Settings["Request Address"].Value);
    }
  }
}
```

The Execute() method first opens the application configuration file to determine the branch details that are needed to format the request. It then creates a ReservationRequest class using one of the constructors you provided. The Branch class, which is one of the constructor parameters, is created as an anonymous class by specifying the BranchName, BranchID, and Address properties. The ReservationRequest class is then stored in the Request output parameter.

The Request Address in the configuration file contains the address (port number) of the branch that will be receiving the request. It is stored in the RequestAddress output argument because it will be needed by the workflow.

Go back to the ReservationWF.cs file. Add the workflow definition shown in Listing 8-8. This should go where the placeholder is (// Define the SendRequest workflow).

Listing 8-8. *Completed Implementation of the SendRequest workflow*

```
// Define the SendRequest workflow
this.Implementation = () => new Sequence
{
    DisplayName = "SendRequest",
    Variables = { request, requestAddress},
    Activities =
    {
        new CreateRequest
        {
```

```
                Title = new InArgument<string>(env => Title.Get(env)),
                Author = new InArgument<string>(env => Author.Get(env)),
                ISBN = new InArgument<string>(env => ISBN.Get(env)),
                Request = new OutArgument<ReservationRequest>
                    (env => request.Get(env)),
                RequestAddress = new OutArgument<string>
                    (env => requestAddress.Get(env))
            },
        new CorrelationScope
        {
            Body = new Sequence
            {
                Activities =
                {
                    submitRequest,
                    new WriteLine
                    {
                        Text = new InArgument<string>
                            (env => "Request sent; waiting for response"),
                    },
                    new ReceiveReply
                    {
                        Request = submitRequest,
                        Content = ReceiveContent.Create
                            (new OutArgument<ReservationResponse>
                                (env => Response.Get(env)))
                    }
                }
            }
        },
        new WriteLine
        {
            Text = new InArgument<string>
                (env => "Response received from " +
                    Response.Get(env).Provider.BranchName),
        },
    }
};
```

The Implementation property of an activity class (referred to as this.Implementation) contains the child activity. In this case, it is defined as a Sequence activity that consists of a number of child activities. The variables used by these activities must be declared. They are the request and requestAddressvariables that were defined in the constructor.

The first activity is the custom CreateRequest activity that you just implemented. Notice that as you're specifying the properties, Intellisense knows the input and output arguments that you defined in your class. The Title, Author, and ISBN arguments are set to the input arguments of the workflow. The Request and RequestAddress output arguments are stored in the workflow variables.

A CorrelationScope activity is added next, which contains a sequence of activities. Specifically, it contains the Send and the ReceiveReply activities. By placing them inside a CorrelationScope activity, the workflow will correlate the response message with the correct workflow instance. A WriteLine activity is added after the Send activity to indicate that the request has been sent.

ReceiveReply Activity

The ReceiveReply activity must be associated with a Send activity. It listens for the response to the message that was sent by the Send activity. To implement this, the Request property is set to the named instance of the Send activity (submitRequest).

The Content property defines where the response message (a ReservationResponse class) is stored. This is set to the Response output argument of the workflow. It will then be available to the host application when the workflow completes.

Server–ProcessRequest

Now you'll define the workflow that is executed to process a request from another branch. In the ReservationWF.cs file, add the class definition shown in Listing 8-9.

Listing 8-9. Initial Implementation of ProcessRequest

```
public sealed class ProcessRequest : Activity
{
    public ProcessRequest()
    {
        // Define the variables used by this workflow
        Variable<ReservationRequest> request =
            new Variable<ReservationRequest> { Name = "request" };
        Variable<ReservationResponse> response =
            new Variable<ReservationResponse> { Name = "response" };
        Variable<bool> reserved = new Variable<bool> { Name = "reserved" };
        Variable<CorrelationHandle> requestHandle =
            new Variable<CorrelationHandle> { Name = "RequestHandle" };

        // Create a Receive activity
        Receive receiveRequest = new Receive
        {
            ServiceContractName = "ILibraryReservation",
            OperationName = "RequestBook",
            CanCreateInstance = true,
            Content = ReceiveContent.Create
                (new OutArgument<ReservationRequest>(request)),
            CorrelatesWith = requestHandle
        };

        // Define the ProcessRequest workflow
    }
}
```

This workflow does not have any input or output arguments. There are four variables that are defined. The request variable stores the incoming message (a ReservationRequest class), and the response variable stores the outgoing response (a ReservationResponse class). The reserved variable indicates whether the title could be reserved or not. The requestHandle is used to correlate the response to the incoming request.

Receive Activity

A named instance of a `Receive` activity (`receiveRequest`) is then defined. You don't need to specify the binding or address on the receiving end of a WCF message, but you do need to define the service contract. The `ServiceContractName` indicates that the `ILibraryReservation` service contract should be used, and the `OperationName` property specifies the `RequestBook()` method.

`CanCreateInstance` is set to true because when this activity is executed, it will create a new workflow instance. It requires that this activity must be the first one in the workflow. The `Content` property will contain the incoming message and is configured to store it in the request variable. The `CorrelatesWith` property uses the `requestHandle` variable.

Custom Activity—CreateResponse

Before defining the workflow activities, you'll need a custom activity to create the `ReservationResponse` class. In the Solution Explorer, right click the LibraryReservation project and choose Add ➤ Class. Enter the class name as **CreateResponse.cs**. The implementation of this class is shown in Listing 8-10.

Listing 8-10. *Implementation of CreateResponse*

```
using System;
using System.Activities;
using System.Configuration;

namespace LibraryReservation
{
    /****************************************************/
    // This custom activity creates a ReservationResponse
    // class.  The original request is provided as an
    // InArgument as well as a boolean to indicate if the
    // request was satisfied or not.  The class is provided
    // in the Response OutArgument.
    /****************************************************/
    public sealed class CreateResponse : CodeActivity
    {
        public InArgument<ReservationRequest> Request { get; set; }
        public InArgument<bool> Reserved { get; set; }
        public OutArgument<ReservationResponse> Response { get; set; }

        protected override void Execute(CodeActivityContext context)
        {
            // Open the config file
            Configuration config = ConfigurationManager
                .OpenExeConfiguration(ConfigurationUserLevel.None);
            AppSettingsSection app =
                (AppSettingsSection)config.GetSection("appSettings");

            // Create the ReservationResponse class and populate it
            ReservationResponse r = new ReservationResponse
                (
```

```
                        Request.Get(context),
                        Reserved.Get(context),
                        new Branch
                        {
                            BranchName = app.Settings["Branch Name"].Value,
                            BranchID = new Guid(app.Settings["ID"].Value),
                            Address = app.Settings["Address"].Value
                        }
                );

            // Store the Response in the OutArgument
            Response.Set(context, r);
        }
    }
}
```

The `CreateResponse` activity is very much like the `CreateRequest` activity. It first opens the application configuration file to get the branch details. A `ReservationResponse` class is then created using one of the supplied constructors and then stored in the `Response` output argument.

Go back to the `ReservationWF.cs` class and enter the workflow definition, as shown in Listing 8-11. There is a placeholder (`// Define the ProcessRequest workflow`) that indicates where it should go.

Listing 8-11. Completed Implementation of ProcessRequest Workflow

```
// Define the ProcessRequest workflow
this.Implementation = () => new Sequence
{
    DisplayName = "ProcessRequest",
    Variables = { request, response, reserved, requestHandle },
    Activities =
    {
        receiveRequest,
        new WriteLine
        {
            Text = new InArgument<string>(
                env => "Got request from: " +
                request.Get(env).Requester.BranchName),
        },
        new WriteLine
        {
            Text = new InArgument<string>(env => "Requesting: " +
                request.Get(env).Title),
        },
        new Assign
        {
            To = new OutArgument<Boolean>(reserved),
            Value = new InArgument<Boolean>(env => true)
        },
        new Delay
        {
            Duration = TimeSpan.FromSeconds(2)
```

```
            },
            new CreateResponse
            {
                Request = new InArgument<ReservationRequest>(env => request.Get(env)),
                Response = new OutArgument<ReservationResponse>
                    (env => response.Get(env)),
                Reserved = new InArgument<bool>(env => reserved.Get(env)),
            },
            new WriteLine
            {
                Text = new InArgument<string>(env => "Sending response to: " +
                    request.Get(env).Requester.BranchName),
            },
            new SendReply
            {
                Request = receiveRequest,
                Content = SendContent.Create
                    (new InArgument<ReservationResponse>(response))
            }
        }
    }
};
```

The four variables defined in the constructor are declared in the body of the workflow. As expected, the Receive activity (receiveRequest) is the first activity in the workflow. It is followed by two WriteLine activities: the first displays the name of the branch that is making the request, and the second shows the title that is being requested.

The Assign activity simply sets the reserved variable to true. In this example, we will assume that the title was available. The Delay activity will pause the workflow for two seconds, simulating some processing that would normally occur to check their inventory. The custom CreateResponse activity is then executed to create the ReservationResponse class, which will be stored in the response variable. A final WriteLine activity indicates that the response is being sent.

SendReply Activity

A SendReply activity must be associated with a Receive activity. This is done by specifying the Request property as a reference to the Receive activity (receiveRequest). The Content property defines the message that will be sent back to the requester. This is set to the response variable.

Your workflows are now complete. The final implementation of ReservationWF.cs is provided in Listing 8-12.

Listing 8-12. *Complete Implementation of ReservationWF.cs*

```
using System;
using System.Collections.Generic;
using System.Linq;
using System.Text;

using System.Activities;
using System.Activities.Statements;
using System.ServiceModel.Activities;
```

```csharp
using System.ServiceModel;

namespace LibraryReservation
{
    /*****************************************************/
    // This file contains the definition of two workflows:
    //
    // SendRequest initiates a new request
    // ProcessRequest handles incoming requests
    //
    /*****************************************************/
    public sealed class SendRequest : Activity
    {
        // Define the input and output arguments
        public InArgument<string> Title { get; set; }
        public InArgument<string> Author { get; set; }
        public InArgument<string> ISBN { get; set; }
        public OutArgument<ReservationResponse> Response { get; set; }

        public SendRequest()
        {
            // Define the variables used by this workflow
            Variable<ReservationRequest> request =
                new Variable<ReservationRequest> { Name = "request" };
            Variable<string> requestAddress =
                new Variable<string> { Name = "RequestAddress" };

            // Define the Send activity
            Send submitRequest = new Send
            {
                ServiceContractName = "ILibraryReservation",
                EndpointAddress = new InArgument<Uri>
                    (env => new Uri("http://localhost:" + requestAddress.Get(env) +
                    "/LibraryReservation")),
                Endpoint = new Endpoint
                {
                    Binding = new BasicHttpBinding()
                },
                OperationName = "RequestBook",
                Content = SendContent.Create
                    (new InArgument<ReservationRequest>(request)),
            };

            // Define the SendRequest workflow
            this.Implementation = () => new Sequence
            {
                DisplayName = "SendRequest",
                Variables = { request, requestAddress},
                Activities =
                {
                    new CreateRequest
                    {
```

```
                    Title = new InArgument<string>(env => Title.Get(env)),
                    Author = new InArgument<string>(env => Author.Get(env)),
                    ISBN = new InArgument<string>(env => ISBN.Get(env)),
                    Request = new OutArgument<ReservationRequest>
                        (env => request.Get(env)),
                    RequestAddress = new OutArgument<string>
                        (env => requestAddress.Get(env))
                },
                new CorrelationScope
                {
                    Body = new Sequence
                    {
                        Activities =
                        {
                            submitRequest,
                            new WriteLine
                            {
                                Text = new InArgument<string>
                                    (env => "Request sent; waiting for response"),
                            },
                            new ReceiveReply
                            {
                                Request = submitRequest,
                                Content = ReceiveContent.Create
                                    (new OutArgument<ReservationResponse>
                                        (env => Response.Get(env)))
                            }
                        }
                    }
                },
                new WriteLine
                {
                    Text = new InArgument<string>
                        (env => "Response received from " +
                         Response.Get(env).Provider.BranchName),
                },
            }
        };
    }
}

public sealed class ProcessRequest : Activity
{
    public ProcessRequest()
    {
        // Define the variables used by this workflow
        Variable<ReservationRequest> request =
            new Variable<ReservationRequest> { Name = "request" };
        Variable<ReservationResponse> response =
            new Variable<ReservationResponse> { Name = "response" };
        Variable<bool> reserved = new Variable<bool> { Name = "reserved" };
```

```
Variable<CorrelationHandle> requestHandle =
    new Variable<CorrelationHandle> { Name = "RequestHandle" };

// Create a Receive activity
Receive receiveRequest = new Receive
{
    ServiceContractName = "ILibraryReservation",
    OperationName = "RequestBook",
    CanCreateInstance = true,
    Content = ReceiveContent.Create
        (new OutArgument<ReservationRequest>(request)),
    CorrelatesWith = requestHandle
};

// Define the ProcessRequest workflow
this.Implementation = () => new Sequence
{
    DisplayName = "ProcessRequest",
    Variables = { request, response, reserved, requestHandle },
    Activities =
    {
        receiveRequest,
        new WriteLine
        {
            Text = new InArgument<string>(
                env => "Got request from: " +
                request.Get(env).Requester.BranchName),
        },
        new WriteLine
        {
            Text = new InArgument<string>(env => "Requesting: " +
                request.Get(env).Title),
        },
        new Assign
        {
            To = new OutArgument<Boolean>(reserved),
            Value = new InArgument<Boolean>(env => true)
        },
        new Delay
        {
            Duration = TimeSpan.FromSeconds(2)
        },
        new CreateResponse
        {
            Request = new InArgument<ReservationRequest>
                (env => request.Get(env)),
            Response = new OutArgument<ReservationResponse>
                (env => response.Get(env)),
            Reserved = new InArgument<bool>(env => reserved.Get(env)),
        },
        new WriteLine
```

```
                    {
                        Text = new InArgument<string>
                            (env => "Sending response to: " +
                            request.Get(env).Requester.BranchName),
                    },
                    new SendReply
                    {
                        Request = receiveRequest,
                        Content = SendContent.Create
                            (new InArgument<ReservationResponse>(response))
                    }
                }
            };
        }
    }
}
```

Implementing the Application

The last step of building this solution is to implement the host application. You'll use the console application (`Program.cs`) that was generated by the template. The application both initiates and processes requests, so you'll need to supply the logic for both. First, you'll set up the application to listen for and process incoming requests. Then you'll initiate a new request that is sent to another application instance.

Add the following namespaces to the `Program.cs` file:

```
using System.ServiceModel;
using System.ServiceModel.Activities;
using System.ServiceModel.Activities.Description;
using System.ServiceModel.Description;
using System.Activities;
using System.Xml.Linq;
using System.Configuration;
```

WorkflowServiceHost

If you have used WCF before, you may be familiar with the `ServiceHost` class, which is used to listen for incoming messages. WF 4.0 provides a `WorkflowServiceHost` class that implements a `ServiceHost` but initiates a workflow when a message is received.

Enter the code in Listing 8-13 as the implementation of the `main()` function of the `Program` class.

Listing 8-13. *Partial Implementation on the main() Function*

```
// Open the config file and get the name for this branch
// and its network address
Configuration config = ConfigurationManager
    .OpenExeConfiguration(ConfigurationUserLevel.None);
AppSettingsSection app =
```

```
    (AppSettingsSection)config.GetSection("appSettings");

string adr = app.Settings["Address"].Value;
Console.WriteLine(app.Settings["Branch Name"].Value);

// Create a service to handle incoming requests
WorkflowService service = new WorkflowService
{
    Name = "LibraryReservation",
    Body = new ProcessRequest(),
    Endpoints =
    {
        new Endpoint
        {
            ServiceContractName="ILibraryReservation",
            AddressUri = new Uri("http://localhost:" + adr +
                "/LibraryReservation"),
            Binding = new BasicHttpBinding(),
        }
    }
};

// Create a WorkflowServiceHost that listens for incoming messages
System.ServiceModel.Activities.WorkflowServiceHost wsh =
    new System.ServiceModel.Activities.WorkflowServiceHost(service);

wsh.Open();
```

This code first opens the application configuration file and retrieves the Address setting, which specifies the port number that the application will listen on. It also gets the branch name, which is displayed in the console window. Because you'll have multiple applications running, this will help you keep track of which one is which.

Service

It then creates a WorkflowService class . For the Body property, it uses a new instance of the ProcessRequest class that defines the workflow used to process incoming requests.

Endpoint

The Service class also defines the endpoint using the ILibraryReservation service contract, a URI that includes the variable port number and the BasicHttpBinding class.

Finally, a WorkflowServiceHost class is instantiated using the defined service class. It is then opened by calling its Open() method. At this point, the application is listening for incoming messages. When one is received, an instance of the ProcessRequest workflow is started to handle the request.

115

WorkflowInvoker

Now you'll need to add code to initiate a request. Enter the code shown in Listing 8-14 just after the call to wsh.Open().

Listing 8-14. *Remaining Implementation of the main() Function*

```
Console.WriteLine
    ("Waiting for requests, press ENTER to send a request.");
Console.ReadLine();

// Create dictionary with input arguments for the workflow
IDictionary<string, object> input = new Dictionary<string, object>
{
    { "Title" , "Gone with the Wind" },
    { "Author", "Margaret Mitchell" },
    { "ISBN", "9781416548898" }
};

// Invoke the SendRequest workflow
IDictionary<string, object> output =
    WorkflowInvoker.Invoke(new SendRequest(), input);
ReservationResponse resp = (ReservationResponse)output["Response"];

// Display the response
Console.WriteLine("Response received from the {0} branch",
    resp.Provider.BranchName);

Console.WriteLine();
Console.WriteLine("Press ENTER to exit");
Console.ReadLine();

// Close the WorkflowServiceHost
wsh.Close();
```

This code waits for the user to press the Enter key, which will give you time to get multiple copies running and listening for incoming messages. The remaining code should be familiar because it is very similar to the code you wrote in Chapters 4–7. You first create a Dictionary to hold the input arguments. It then uses the Invoke() method of the WorkflowInvoker class to start a new instance of the SendRequest workflow.

The Response output argument is then extracted from the Dictionary that is returned when the workflow completes. The name of the branch that responded to the request is displayed in the console.

Finally, the WorkflowServiceHost is closed before the application exits. The complete implementation of Program.cs is provided in Listing 8-15.

Listing 8-15. *Complete Implementation of Program.cs*

```
using System;
using System.Collections.Generic;
using System.Linq;
using System.Text;
```

```csharp
using System.ServiceModel;
using System.ServiceModel.Activities;
using System.ServiceModel.Activities.Description;
using System.ServiceModel.Description;
using System.Activities;
using System.Xml.Linq;
using System.Configuration;

namespace LibraryReservation
{
    class Program
    {
        static void Main(string[] args)
        {
            // Open the config file and get the name for this branch
            // and its network address
            Configuration config = ConfigurationManager
                .OpenExeConfiguration(ConfigurationUserLevel.None);
            AppSettingsSection app =
                (AppSettingsSection)config.GetSection("appSettings");

            string adr = app.Settings["Address"].Value;
            Console.WriteLine(app.Settings["Branch Name"].Value);

            // Create a service to handle incoming requests
            WorkflowService service = new WorkflowService
            {
                Name = "LibraryReservation",
                Body = new ProcessRequest(),
                Endpoints =
                {
                    new Endpoint
                    {
                        ServiceContractName="ILibraryReservation",
                        AddressUri = new Uri("http://localhost:" + adr +
                            "/LibraryReservation"),
                        Binding = new BasicHttpBinding(),
                    }
                }
            };

            // Create a WorkflowServiceHost that listens for incoming messages
            System.ServiceModel.Activities.WorkflowServiceHost wsh =
                new System.ServiceModel.Activities.WorkflowServiceHost(service);

            wsh.Open();

            Console.WriteLine
                ("Waiting for requests, press ENTER to send a request.");
            Console.ReadLine();
```

```
// Create dictionary with input arguments for the workflow
IDictionary<string, object> input = new Dictionary<string, object>
{
    { "Title" , "Gone with the Wind" },
    { "Author", "Margaret Mitchell" },
    { "ISBN", "9781416548898" }
};

// Invoke the SendRequest workflow
IDictionary<string, object> output =
    WorkflowInvoker.Invoke(new SendRequest(), input);
ReservationResponse resp = (ReservationResponse)output["Response"];

// Display the response
Console.WriteLine("Response received from the {0} branch",
    resp.Provider.BranchName);

Console.WriteLine();
Console.WriteLine("Press ENTER to exit");
Console.ReadLine();

// Close the WorkflowServiceHost
wsh.Close();
        }
    }
}
```

Running the Application

Press F6 to rebuild the application. You have to start two instances of this application, and they need to have different configuration files so you can specify different port numbers for each.

Configuring a Library Branch

Open Windows Explorer and navigate to your code directory. Add a Branch subfolder, as shown in Figure 8-3.

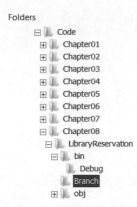

Figure 8-3. *Creating a new branch folder*

Then copy (not move) the files highlighted in Figure 8-4 from the Debug folder to the Branch folder.

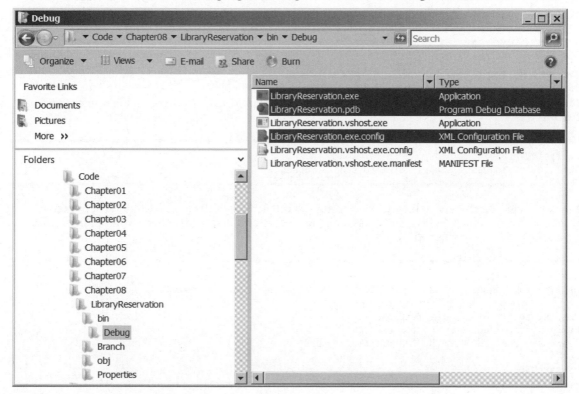

Figure 8-4. *Copying the application*

In the Branch folder, open the `LibraryReservation.exe.config` file. You can open it with any text editor. If you right-click this file and select Open With, you should have an option for Visual Studio 2010. Change the settings to the match the following:

```xml
<?xml version="1.0" encoding="utf-8" ?>
<configuration>
  <appSettings>
    <add key="Branch Name" value="Southwest Regional"/>
    <add key="ID" value="{CA62F4ED-FACF-4835-8468-16CAAC298F4C}"/>
    <add key="Address" value="8730"/>
    <add key="Request Address" value="8000"/>
  </appSettings>
</configuration>
```

Notice that the port numbers for the `Address` and `Request Address` are reversed from the configuration file in the main application folder. Double-click the `.exe` file; a console window should appear with the following text:

```
Southwest Regional
Waiting for requests, press ENTER to send a request.
```

Expected Results

From Visual Studio, press F5 to start the application. This should start another console window with the following text:

```
Central Library
Waiting for requests, press ENTER to send a request.
```

You might need to move the windows around so you can see both console windows at the same time. Select one of the windows and press the Enter key. After a couple of seconds, you should see the following text on that window:

```
Southwest Regional
Waiting for requests, press ENTER to send a request.

Request sent; waiting for response
Response received from Central Library
Response received from the Central Library branch

Press ENTER to exit
```

In the other window you should see the following:

```
Central Library
Waiting for requests, press ENTER to send a request.
Got request from: Southwest Regional
Requesting: Gone with the Wind
Sending response to: Southwest Regional
```

Select the other window and press the Enter key. In that window, you should see the following:

```
Central Library
Waiting for requests, press ENTER to send a request.
Got request from: Southwest Regional
Requesting: Gone with the Wind
Sending response to: Southwest Regional

Request sent; waiting for response
Response received from Southwest Regional
Response received from the Southwest Regional branch

Press ENTER to exit
```

In the other window you should see the following:

```
Southwest Regional
Waiting for requests, press ENTER to send a request.

Request sent; waiting for response
Response received from Central Library
Response received from the Central Library branch

Press ENTER to exit
Got request from: Central Library
Requesting: Gone with the Wind
Sending response to: Central Library
```

You can press Enter in both windows to close the applications.

Allowing Port Access

Because of the enhanced security in Windows Vista and Windows 7, your application might generate an exception that indicates you do not have access to the specified port. If you have this situation, the easiest way to resolve it is to run the application with administrator privileges. For example, when starting Visual Studio from the Start menu or desktop icon, right-click the menu or icon and choose "Run as administrator", as shown in Figure 8-5.

Figure 8-5. Running with Administrator privileges

When starting the branch application, you can right-click the `.exe` file and also choose "Run as administrator".

Another option is to grant your Windows login access to the desired ports. To do that, start a command window (you must start it with administrator privileges) and execute the following command:

```
netsh http add urlacl url=http://+:8000/ user=Domain\UserName
```

Instead of 8000, you can enter whatever port you plan to use. You need to run this command for each port that you want to grant access to. Replace Domain\UserName with the actual login that you use. Wherever possible, in the sample projects I will use only 8000 and 8730 to minimize the number of ports you'll need access to. Although this might be a little more trouble to set up, you have to do it only once and it will save you time in the long run.

CHAPTER 9

■ ■ ■

Communicating with the Host Application

In this chapter, you'll build a solution similar to the one from Chapter 8, except that you'll replace the console application with a Windows Presentation Foundation (WPF) application. In the projects you've built so far, the host simply invoked the workflow and displayed the results upon completion. With this project you'll need a lot more communication between the workflow and the host application. Fortunately, WF 4.0 provides the features you'll need to accomplish this.

Creating a WPF Project

Open VS 2010 and create a new project using the WPF Application template, as shown in Figure 9-1. For the project name, use **LibraryReservation**, and the solution should be **Chapter09**.

Figure 9-1. Creating a WPF application

123

In the Solution Explorer, right-click the LibraryReservation project and choose Add Reference. From the .NET tab, add the following references:

- `System.Activities`

- `System.Configuration`

- `System.ServiceModel`

- `System.ServiceModel.Activities`

The template generates a window file named `Window1.xaml`. In the Solution Explorer, rename it to **Reservations.xaml**. The `App.xaml` file defines the startup window; it is currently set to `Window1`. Open this file and change the setting to the following:

```
StartupUri="Reservations.xaml"
```

Reusing the Classes from Chapter 8

Some of the classes from the Chapter 8 project can be reused in this project. Open Windows Explorer; copy (not move) the files highlighted in Figure 9-2 from the LibraryReservation folder in the Chapter08 solution to the same folder in the Chapter09 solution.

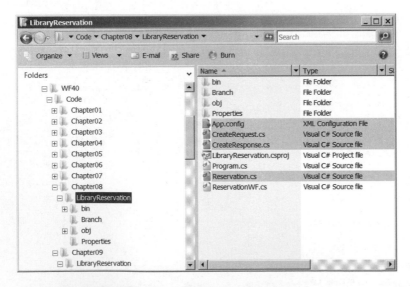

Figure 9-2. *Copying files from the Chapter 8 project*

Back in Visual Studio, in the Solution Explorer, right-click the LibraryReservation project and choose Add, Existing Item. In the Add Existing Item dialog, navigate to the Chapter09/LibraryReservation folder. Select All Files (*.*) at the bottom right of the dialog. Select the same files that you just copied (see Figure 9-3) and click the Add button.

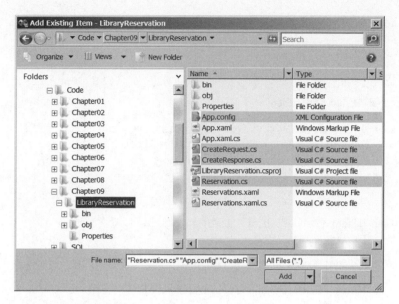

Figure 9-3. *Adding existing items to the project*

The Solution Explorer should look like the one shown in Figure 9-4.

Figure 9-4. *The Solution Explorer with the copied classes*

Defining the Window Form

Open the Reservations.xaml file and select the XAML tab. Replace the generated code with the code shown in Listing 9-1.

Listing 9-1. *Reservations.xaml Implementation*

```
<Window x:Class="LibraryReservation.MainWindow"
    xmlns="http://schemas.microsoft.com/winfx/2006/xaml/presentation"
    xmlns:x="http://schemas.microsoft.com/winfx/2006/xaml"
    Title="Reservations" Height="480" Width="650"
    Loaded="Window_Loaded" Unloaded="Window_Unloaded">
<Grid>
    <Label Height="40" HorizontalAlignment="Left" Margin="12,0,0,0"
     Name="lblBranch" FontSize="24" VerticalAlignment="Top" Width="276"
     FontStretch="Expanded">Library Branch</Label>
    <ListView x:Name="requestList" Margin="12,42,12,5" Height="150"
     VerticalAlignment="Top" ItemsSource="{Binding}">
        <ListView.View>
            <GridView>
                <GridViewColumn Header="Request List" Width="610">
                    <GridViewColumn.CellTemplate>
                        <DataTemplate>
                            <StackPanel Orientation="Horizontal">
                                <TextBlock
                                  Text="{Binding Requester.BranchName}"
                                  Width="100"/>
                                <TextBlock Text="{Binding Author}" Width="95"/>
                                <TextBlock Text="{Binding Title}" Width="180"/>
                                <TextBlock Text="{Binding ISBN}" Width="90"/>
                                <Button Content="Reserve"
                                  Tag="{Binding InstanceID}"
                                  Click="Reserve" Width="65"/>
                                <Button Content="Cancel"
                                  Tag="{Binding InstanceID}"
                                  Click="Cancel" Width="60"/>
                            </StackPanel>
                        </DataTemplate>
                    </GridViewColumn.CellTemplate>
                </GridViewColumn>
            </GridView>
        </ListView.View>
    </ListView>
    <Label Height="30" Margin="45,25,0,210" Name="label5"
     VerticalAlignment="Bottom" HorizontalAlignment="Left" Width="60"
     HorizontalContentAlignment="Right">Author:</Label>
    <Label Height="30" Margin="45,25,0,180" Name="label2"
     VerticalAlignment="Bottom" HorizontalAlignment="Left" Width="60"
     HorizontalContentAlignment="Right">Title:</Label>
    <Label Height="30" Margin="45,25,0,150" Name="label3"
     VerticalAlignment="Bottom" HorizontalAlignment="Left" Width="60"
     HorizontalContentAlignment="Right">ISBN:</Label>
    <TextBox Height="25" Margin="102,0,0,210" Name="txtAuthor"
     VerticalAlignment="Bottom" HorizontalAlignment="Left" Width="200" />
    <TextBox Height="25" Margin="102,25,0,180" Name="txtTitle"
     VerticalAlignment="Bottom" HorizontalAlignment="Left" Width="300" />
```

```
        <TextBox Height="25" Margin="102,25,0,150" Name="txtISBN"
         VerticalAlignment="Bottom" HorizontalAlignment="Left" Width="100" />
        <Button Height="23" Margin="250,25,12,150" Name="btnRequest"
         VerticalAlignment="Bottom" HorizontalAlignment="Left" Width="98"
         Click="btnRequest_Click">Send Request</Button>
        <Label Height="27" HorizontalAlignment="Left" Margin="15,0,0,137"
         Name="label4" VerticalAlignment="Bottom" Width="76">Event Log</Label>
        <ListBox Margin="12,0,12,12" Name="lstEvents" Height="130"
         VerticalAlignment="Bottom" FontStretch="Condensed" FontSize="10" />
    </Grid>
</Window>
```

Then select the Design tab. The form should look like the one shown in Figure 9-5.

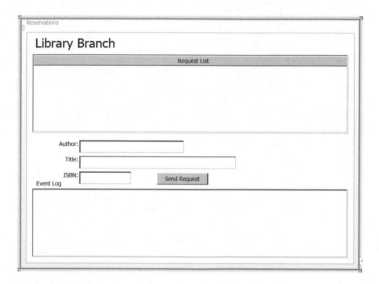

Figure 9-5. *The application window in design view*

The Request List is at the top of the form and will display all the incoming requests that need to be acted on. To send a request to another branch, use the fields in the middle of the form to specify the Author, Title, and ISBN; then click the Send Request button. The Event Log at the bottom will display messages from the workflow similar to the way the console app does.

Implementing a TextWriter

For the WriteLine activities that you have used so far, you have not set the TextWriter property. If no TextWriter is specified, the default behavior is to write the specified text to the console. Now you will implement a TextWriter class that will add this text to the Event Log at the bottom of your application form.

Providing a Static Application Reference

First, you'll create a static class that will provide access to the application window. From the Solution Explorer, right-click the LibraryReservation project and choose Add, Class. For the class name, enter **ApplicationInterface.cs**. The implementation for this class is shown in Listing 9-2.

Listing 9-2. Implementation of the ApplicationInterface Class

```
using System;
using System.Windows.Controls;
using System.Activities;
namespace LibraryReservation
{
    public static class ApplicationInterface
    {
        public static MainWindow _app { get; set; }

        public static void AddEvent(String status)
        {
            if (_app != null)
            {
                new ListBoxTextWriter(_app.GetEventListBox()).WriteLine(status);
            }
        }
    }
}
```

The ApplicationInterface class has a static reference (_app) to the application window (the MainWindow class). The static AddEvent() method instantiates a ListBoxTextWriter class, which you'll implement later, and calls its WriteLine() method.

Now open the Reservations.xaml.cs file and add the following namespaces:

```
using System.ServiceModel;
using System.ServiceModel.Activities;
using System.ServiceModel.Activities.Description;
using System.ServiceModel.Description;
using System.ServiceModel.Channels;
using System.Activities;
using System.Xml.Linq;
using System.Configuration;
```

Add the following code to the constructor:

```
ApplicationInterface._app = this;
```

This will initialize the _app reference in the ApplicationInterface class. Because it is a static class, there will be only a single instance, and this instance will now have a reference to the MainWindow class.

Add the following methods in the Reservations.xaml.cs file:

```
public ListBox GetEventListBox()
{
    return this.lstEvents;
}

private void AddEvent(string szText)
{
    lstEvents.Items.Add(szText);
}
```

The GetEventListBox() method returns a reference to the actual ListBox control that will display these events. This method is used by the ApplicationInterface class. The AddEvent() method is used by the application when it needs to add an event.

Implementing ListBoxTextWriter

From the Solution Explorer, right-click the LibraryReservation project and choose Add, Class. Enter **ListBoxTextWriter.cs** for the class name. The implementation of this class is shown in Listing 9-3.

Listing 9-3. Implementation of ListBoxTextWriter

```
using System;
using System.Collections.Generic;
using System.Linq;
using System.Text;
using System.IO;
using System.Windows.Controls;

namespace LibraryReservation
{
    public class ListBoxTextWriter : TextWriter
    {
        const string textClosed = "This TextWriter must be opened before use";

        private Encoding _encoding;
        private bool _isOpen = false;
        private ListBox _listBox;

        public ListBoxTextWriter()
        {
            // Get the static list box
            _listBox = ApplicationInterface._app.GetEventListBox();
            if (_listBox != null)
                _isOpen = true;
        }

        public ListBoxTextWriter(ListBox listBox)
        {
            this._listBox = listBox;
            this._isOpen = true;
```

```csharp
        }

        public override Encoding Encoding
        {
            get
            {
                if (_encoding == null)
                {
                    _encoding = new UnicodeEncoding(false, false);
                }
                return _encoding;
            }
        }

        public override void Close()
        {
            this.Dispose(true);
        }

        protected override void Dispose(bool disposing)
        {
            this._isOpen = false;
            base.Dispose(disposing);
        }

        public override void Write(char value)
        {
            if (!this._isOpen)
                throw new ApplicationException(textClosed); ;

            this._listBox.Dispatcher.BeginInvoke
                (new Action(() => this._listBox.Items.Add(value.ToString())));
        }

        public override void Write(string value)
        {
            if (!this._isOpen)
                throw new ApplicationException(textClosed); ;

            if (value != null)
                this._listBox.Dispatcher.BeginInvoke
                    (new Action(() => this._listBox.Items.Add(value)));
        }

        public override void Write(char[] buffer, int index, int count)
        {
            String toAdd = "";

            if (!this._isOpen)
                throw new ApplicationException(textClosed); ;
```

```
            if (buffer == null || index < 0 || count < 0)
                throw new ArgumentOutOfRangeException("buffer");

            if ((buffer.Length - index) < count)
                throw new ArgumentException("The buffer is too small");

            for (int i = 0; i < count; i++)
                toAdd += buffer[i];

            this._listBox.Dispatcher.BeginInvoke
                (new Action(() => this._listBox.Items.Add(toAdd)));
        }
    }
}
```

The ListBoxTextWriter class is derived from the abstract TextWriter class and provides an implementation of the Write() method that adds the string to a ListBox control. (You'll implement three overloaded Write() methods to allow it to be passed in as a char, a string, or a char[] array.)

The default constructor uses the static ApplicationInterface class to get the lstEvents control of the MainWindow. It also provides a constructor into which the ListBox can be passed. This constructor is used by the AddEvent() method of the ApplicationInterface class.

The ListBox Add() method is executed on the application's thread. It does this by using the BeginInvoke() method of the Dispatcher associated with the lstEvents control. This enables the method to work even when called from different threads.

Because the ListBoxTextWriter class is derived from TextWriter, you can specify it as the TextWriter property on any WriteLine activity. And because of the static ApplicationInterface class, the ListBoxTextWriter class can access the lstEvents control even from outside of the application.

So now you have three ways to add text to the lstEvents control:

- From inside the application, use the local AddEvent() method.

- From outside the application, use the AddEvent() method of the ApplicationInterface class.

- From a WriteLine activity, set the TextWriter property to ListBoxTextWriter.

Implementing the Workflows

The overall logic and message flow is illustrated in Figure 9-6. I will explain some of the elements in this diagram later, but I wanted to give you the basic concept before getting into the details.

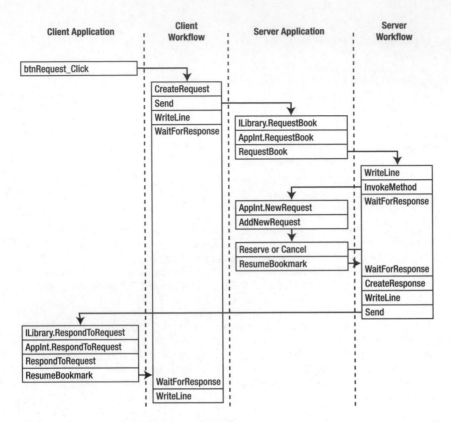

Figure 9-6. *Overall logic and message flow*

This is quite a bit different from the workflows used in the previous chapter. The most notable difference is that there are no Receive activities. Instead, the application will listen for the incoming messages and then invoke (or resume) the workflow.

Listening for Messages

In Figure 9-6, the server application receives a message, and the associated element in the diagram is labeled ILibrary.RequestBook. Likewise, the client application receives a message and that element is labeled ILibrary.RespondToRequest. These are the methods in the service contract that you implemented in Chapter 8. (To save space in the diagram, I abbreviated ILibraryReservation to just ILibrary.)

Open the Reservation.cs file, and you should see the following interface definition:

```
[ServiceContract]
public interface ILibraryReservation
{
    [OperationContract]
    void RequestBook(ReservationRequest request);
```

```
    [OperationContract]
    void RespondToRequest(ReservationResponse response);
}
```

You'll need to make a minor change to this contract. Modify the OperationContract attribute to add the (IsOneWay = true) qualifier, as illustrated in the following code snippet:

```
[ServiceContract]
public interface ILibraryReservation
{
    [OperationContract(IsOneWay = true)]
    void RequestBook(ReservationRequest request);

    [OperationContract(IsOneWay = true)]
    void RespondToRequest(ReservationResponse response);
}
```

The message is being sent by the workflow, but the response is received by the ServiceHost within the application. So this is not technically a two-way conversation. There are messages going in both directions, but because the sending and receiving endpoints are different, WCF treats this as separate one-way messages.

Implementing the Service Contract

This service contract only *defines* the available methods; it does not provide the implementation for them. In Chapter 8, the workflow provided the implementation. For this project, you must provide it. In the Solution Explorer, right-click the LibraryReservation project and choose Add, Class. For the class name, enter **ClientService.cs**. The implementation for this class is shown in Listing 9-4.

Listing 9-4. Implementation of the ClientService Class

```
using System;
using System.ServiceModel;

namespace LibraryReservation
{
    public class ClientService : ILibraryReservation
    {
        public void RequestBook(ReservationRequest request)
        {
            ApplicationInterface.RequestBook(request);
        }

        public void RespondToRequest(ReservationResponse response)
        {
            ApplicationInterface.RespondToRequest(response);
        }
    }
}
```

133

This implementation takes advantage of the static `ApplicationInterface` class that you already created. Each method simply calls the corresponding method in the `ApplicationInterface` class. Open the `ApplicationInterface.cs` file and add the following methods to this class:

```
public static void RequestBook(ReservationRequest request)
{
    if (_app != null)
        _app.RequestBook(request);
}

public static void RespondToRequest(ReservationResponse response)
{
    if (_app != null)
        _app.RespondToRequest(response);
}
```

These methods, in turn, call the corresponding method in the application using the static reference. You will need to implement these methods in the `Reservation.xaml.cs` file, but we'll come back to that later.

Implementing a ServiceHost

The application needs to implement a `ServiceHost` to listen for incoming messages. Open the `Reservation.xaml.cs` file and add the following class member:

```
private ServiceHost _sh;
```

This should go just before the constructor. The first part of this file should look like this:

```
public partial class MainWindow : Window
{
    private ServiceHost _sh;

    public MainWindow()
    {
        InitializeComponent();

        ApplicationInterface._app = this;
    }
```

You will start the `ServiceHost` when the window is loaded and close it when the window is unloaded. Add the methods shown in Listing 9-5 to the `MainWindow` class to implement the `Loaded` and `Unloaded` event handlers.

Listing 9-5. *The Loaded and Unloaded Event Handlers*

```
private void Window_Loaded(object sender, RoutedEventArgs e)
{
```

```
    // Open the config file and get the name for this branch
    // and its network address
    Configuration config = ConfigurationManager
        .OpenExeConfiguration(ConfigurationUserLevel.None);
    AppSettingsSection app =
        (AppSettingsSection)config.GetSection("appSettings");
    string adr = app.Settings["Address"].Value;

    // Display the Branch name on the form
    lblBranch.Content = app.Settings["Branch Name"].Value;

    // Create the ServiceHost
    _sh = new ServiceHost(typeof(ClientService));

    // Add the Endpoint
    string szAddress = "http://localhost:" + adr + "/ClientService";
    System.ServiceModel.Channels.Binding bBinding = new BasicHttpBinding();
    _sh.AddServiceEndpoint(typeof(ILibraryReservation), bBinding, szAddress);

    // Open the ServiceHost to listen for messages
    _sh.Open();
}

private void Window_Unloaded(object sender, RoutedEventArgs e)
{
    // Terminate the service host
    _sh.Close();
}
```

The Loaded event handler opens the configuration file and puts the branch name in the lblBranch control so the form will display the local branch name. It then creates a ServiceHost passing the ClientService class that you just created as its implementation. It then configures an Endpoint for this ServiceHost using the familiar address, binding, and contract trio. The Unloaded event handler simply closes the ServiceHost so it will no longer listen for messages.

Bookmarks

Bookmarks allow you to suspend a workflow instance and save a marker so the instance can be resumed exactly where it left off. They are designed to receive data upon resumption. In this project, for example, when a request is received, the application will display the request and wait for the user to see whether the item is available. The user then responds with a yes or no, and the workflow is resumed, passing in this answer.

A bookmark is generally created in a custom activity. In this project, you'll create a generic activity that can be reused wherever a bookmark is required. In the Solution Explorer, right-click the LibraryReservation project and choose Add ➤ Class. Enter **WaitForInput.cs** as the class name. The implementation for this class is shown in Listing 9-6.

Listing 9-6. Implementation of the WaitForInput Class

```
using System;
using System.Activities;

namespace LibraryReservation
{
    public sealed class WaitForInput<T> : NativeActivity<T>
    {
        public WaitForInput()
            : base()
        {
        }

        public string BookmarkName { get; set; }
        public OutArgument<T> Input { get; set; }

        protected override void Execute(NativeActivityContext context)
        {
            context.CreateBookmark(BookmarkName,
                new BookmarkCallback(this.Continue));
        }

        void Continue(NativeActivityContext context, Bookmark bookmark,
            object obj)
        {
            Input.Set(context, (T)obj);
        }

        protected override bool CanInduceIdle { get { return true; } }
    }
}
```

This custom activity uses the NativeActivity base class (instead of CodeActivity) because this gives it access to the NativeActivityContext, which is required when creating a bookmark. It also uses the template version (note the <T> in the class name). The Input argument represents the data that is passed into the workflow when it is resumed. By using the template version, this activity can be reused with any data type.

The Execute() method calls the CreateBookmark() method of the NativeActivityContext, specifying the bookmark name and a reference to the callback method named Continue(). When the workflow is resumed, this callback method is executed. Notice that the callback method receives an object as the third parameter. This is the data provided by the application. It is stored in the Input argument, making it available to the workflow.

Activities that use bookmarks must override the CanInduceIdle property to return true. This allows the workflow to enter the Idle state while waiting for the bookmark to resume.

Implementing the SendRequest Workflow

Now you're ready to implement the workflows. From the Solution Explorer, right-click the LibraryReservation project and choose Add ➤ Class. For the class name, enter **ReservationWF.cs**. The implementation for the SendRequest workflow is shown in Listing 9-7.

Listing 9-7. *Implementation of the SendRequest Workflow*

```
using System;
using System.Activities;
using System.Activities.Statements;
using System.ServiceModel.Activities;
using System.ServiceModel;
using System.ServiceModel.Channels;
using System.Runtime.Serialization;
using System.Xml.Linq using System.IO;


namespace LibraryReservation
{
    /****************************************************/
    // This file contains the definition of two workflows:
    //
    // SendRequest initiates a new request
    // ProcessRequest handles incoming requests
    //
    /****************************************************/
    public sealed class SendRequest : Activity
    {
        // Define the input and output arguments
        public InArgument<string> Title { get; set; }
        public InArgument<string> Author { get; set; }
        public InArgument<string> ISBN { get; set; } public InArgument<TextWriter> Writer {
            get; set; }
        public OutArgument<ReservationResponse> Response { get; set; }

        public SendRequest()
        {
            // Define the variables used by this workflow
            Variable<ReservationRequest> request =
                new Variable<ReservationRequest> { Name = "request" };
            Variable<string> requestAddress =
                new Variable<string> { Name = "RequestAddress" };
            Variable<bool> reserved = new Variable<bool> { Name = "Reserved" };

            // Define the SendRequest workflow
            this.Implementation = () => new Sequence
            {
                DisplayName = "SendRequest",
                Variables = { request, requestAddress, reserved },
                Activities =
```

```
            {
                new CreateRequest
                {
                    Title = new InArgument<string>(env => Title.Get(env)),
                    Author = new InArgument<string>(env => Author.Get(env)),
                    ISBN = new InArgument<string>(env => ISBN.Get(env)),
                    Request = new OutArgument<ReservationRequest>
                        (env => request.Get(env)),
                    RequestAddress = new OutArgument<string>
                        (env => requestAddress.Get(env))
                },
                new Send
                {
                    OperationName = "RequestBook",
                    ServiceContractName = "ILibraryReservation",
                    Content = SendContent.Create
                        (new InArgument<ReservationRequest>(request)),
                    EndpointAddress = new InArgument<Uri>
                        (env => new Uri("http://localhost:" +
                        requestAddress.Get(env) + "/ClientService")),
                    Endpoint = new Endpoint
                    {
                        Binding = new BasicHttpBinding()
                    },
                },
                new WriteLine
                {
                    Text = new InArgument<string>
                        (env => "Request sent; waiting for response"),
                    TextWriter = new InArgument<TextWriter>
                        (env => Writer.Get(env))
                },
                new WaitForInput<ReservationResponse>
                {
                    BookmarkName = "GetResponse",
                    Input = new OutArgument<ReservationResponse>
                        (env => Response.Get(env))
                },
                new WriteLine
                {
                    Text = new InArgument<string>
                        (env => "Response received from " +
                        Response.Get(env).Provider.BranchName + " [" +
                        Response.Get(env).Reserved.ToString() + "]"),
                    TextWriter = new InArgument<TextWriter>
                        (env => Writer.Get(env))
                },
            }
        };
    }
}
```

```
    // Add the ProcessRequest workflow here
}
```

Much of this workflow is identical to the one you implemented in Chapter 8, so I won't explain it in detail. (Refer to the previous chapter if you need some review.) I will point out the differences, however. Notice that each of the WriteLine activities has an extra property:

```
TextWriter = new ListBoxTextWriter()
```

This indicates that the new ListBoxTextWriter class that you implemented should be used when displaying this text. It will cause this text to be displayed in the lstEvents control.

The other difference is that the custom WaitForInput activity is used instead of a Receive activity. The application will be receiving the response message directly. When the response is received, the application will resume the workflow, passing in the ReservationResponse class. Notice that the custom activity is defined as WaitForInput<ReservationResponse>, indicating that the data passed in will be a ReservationResponse class.

Implementing the ProcessRequest Workflow

The ProcessRequest workflow definition is shown in Listing 9-8. Add this code to the ReservationWF.cs file.

Listing 9-8. *Implementation of the ProcessRequuest Workflow*

```csharp
public sealed class ProcessRequest : Activity
{
    public InArgument<ReservationRequest> request { get; set; } public
        InArgument<TextWriter> Writer { get; set; }

    public ProcessRequest()
    {
        // Define the variables used by this workflow
        Variable<ReservationResponse> response =
            new Variable<ReservationResponse> { Name = "response" };
        Variable<bool> reserved = new Variable<bool> { Name = "Reserved" };
        Variable<string> address = new Variable<string> { Name = "Address" };

        // Define the ProcessRequest workflow
        this.Implementation = () => new Sequence
        {
            DisplayName = "ProcessRequest",
            Variables = { response, reserved, address },
            Activities =
            {
                new WriteLine
                {
                    Text = new InArgument<string>(env => "Got request from: " +
                        request.Get(env).Requester.BranchName),
                    TextWriter = new InArgument<TextWriter>
                        (env => Writer.Get(env))
                },
```

```
            new InvokeMethod
            {
                TargetType = typeof(ApplicationInterface),
                MethodName = "NewRequest",
                Parameters =
                {
                    new InArgument<ReservationRequest>(env => request.Get(env))
                }
            },
            new WaitForInput<bool>
            {
                BookmarkName = "GetResponse",
                Input = new OutArgument<bool>(env => reserved.Get(env))
            },
            new CreateResponse
            {
                Request = new InArgument<ReservationRequest>
                    (env => request.Get(env)),
                Reserved = new InArgument<bool>(env => reserved.Get(env)),
                Response = new OutArgument<ReservationResponse>
                    (env => response.Get(env))
            },
            new WriteLine
            {
                Text = new InArgument<string>(env => "Sending response to: " +
                    request.Get(env).Requester.BranchName),
                TextWriter = new InArgument<TextWriter>
                    (env => Writer.Get(env))
            },
            new Send
            {
                OperationName = "RespondToRequest",
                ServiceContractName = "ILibraryReservation",
                EndpointAddress = new InArgument<Uri>(
                    env => new Uri("http://localhost:" +
                    request.Get(env).Requester.Address + "/ClientService")),
                Endpoint = new Endpoint
                {
                    Binding = new BasicHttpBinding()
                },
                Content = SendContent.Create
                    (new InArgument<ReservationResponse>(response))
            }
        }
    };
    }
}
```

This workflow is different from the version implemented in Chapter 8. Instead of starting with a Receive activity to get the incoming request, the ReservationRequest is passed in to the workflow using an input argument. The WriteLine activity that follows it acknowledges the incoming request.

You used an InvokeMethod activity in Chapter 7 to call a method to compute the order discount. Now you'll use it to send data to the application. The ApplicationInterface class comes in really handy for this purpose. It enables the workflow to make a call into the application. The InvokeMethod activity calls the NewRequest() method of the ApplicationInterface class passing in the ReservationRequest class. Open the ApplicationInterface.cs file and add the following method, which simply calls the AddNewRequest() method in the application:

```
public static void NewRequest(ReservationRequest request)
{
    if (_app != null)
        _app.AddNewRequest(request);
}
```

The next activity is the custom WaitForInput activity that you used in the SendRequest workflow. This time, it is expecting a bool input to indicate whether the title was reserved. The CreateResponse and WriteLine activities are the same as was used in Chapter 8.

In Chapter 8, you used a SendReply activity because it was associated with the initial Receive activity. In this project, because there is no Receive activity, you'll use a Send activity. Notice that the EndpointAddress is set up using the address (port number) provided in the input request.

Implementing the Application

The last step is to implement the application. There are several event handlers that must be implemented as well as the methods invoked by the static ApplicationInterface class.

Maintaining Workflow Instances

The application has to keep track of the workflow instances so it can resume the correct instance. You can accomplish this fairly easily by using a Dictionary object. Open the Reservations.xaml.cs file and add the following class members just below the ServiceHost member:

```
private IDictionary<Guid, WorkflowApplication> _incomingRequests;
private IDictionary<Guid, WorkflowApplication> _outgoingRequests;
```

These use the workflow's instance ID as the dictionary key and the WorkflowApplication object as the value. Because the application handles both the SendRequest and ProcessRequest workflows, you'll need two Dictionary objects. Add the following code to the constructor to initialize these objects:

```
_incomingRequests = new Dictionary<Guid, WorkflowApplication>();
_outgoingRequests = new Dictionary<Guid, WorkflowApplication>();
```

There is also one small change that you'll need to make to the custom CreateRequest activity. The workflow instance ID must be used as the RequestID field of the ReservationRequest class. The application will use this when resuming the workflow. Open the CreateRequest.cs file and modify the call that creates the ReservationRequest class to use the alternate constructor that takes a fifth parameter for the RequestID. Add the line in bold from the following code snippet:

```
// Create a ReservationRequest class and populate
// it with the input arguments
```

```
ReservationRequest r = new ReservationRequest
    (
        Title.Get(context),
        Author.Get(context),
        ISBN.Get(context),
        new Branch
        {
            BranchName = app.Settings["Branch Name"].Value,
            BranchID = new Guid(app.Settings["ID"].Value),
            Address = app.Settings["Address"].Value
        },
        context.WorkflowInstanceId
    );
```

Event Handlers

To create a new request, the user will fill in the Author, Title, and ISBN; then click the Send Request button. The implementation of the button's Click event is shown in Listing 9-9.

Listing 9-9. Implementing the Click Event

```
private void btnRequest_Click(object sender, RoutedEventArgs e)
{
    // Setup a dictionary object for passing parameters
    Dictionary<string, object> parameters = new Dictionary<string, object>();
    parameters.Add("Author", txtAuthor.Text);
    parameters.Add("Title", txtTitle.Text);
    parameters.Add("ISBN", txtISBN.Text);
    parameters.Add("Writer", new ListBoxTextWriter(lstEvents));

    WorkflowApplication i =
        new WorkflowApplication(new SendRequest(), parameters);
    _outgoingRequests.Add(i.Id, i);
    i.Run();
}
```

The first part of this method should look familiar. It uses a Dictionary object to store the input arguments, which will be passed in to the workflow. It then creates a WorkflowApplication. The parameters passed to the WorkflowApplication constructor are the following:

The definition of the workflows

The Dictionary object containing the input arguments

The WorkflowApplication is then added to the _outgoingRequests collection. Finally, the instance is started by calling it's Run() method.

■ **Tip** In previous projects, you used the `Invoke()` method of the `WorkflowInvoker` class to start a `WorkflowApplication`. This approach starts the workflow synchronously; the workflow will execute on the caller's thread. This means that the application will be blocked until the workflow becomes idle. That's not what you want in this project. You want to start the workflow on its own thread while the application can continue to respond to events (and incoming messages). Using the `Run()` method accomplishes this.

In the form's Request List, there will be Reserve and Cancel buttons, which the users will use to indicate whether the item was available. Listing 9-10 shows the implementation of event handlers for these buttons. Add these methods to the Reservations class.

***Listing 9-10.** Implementing the Reserve and Cancel Buttons*

```
// Handle the Reserve button click event
private void Reserve(object sender, RoutedEventArgs e)
{
    // Get the instanceID from the Tag property
    FrameworkElement fe = (FrameworkElement)sender;
    Guid id = (Guid)fe.Tag;
    ResumeBookmark(id, true);
}

// Handle the Cancel button click event
private void Cancel(object sender, RoutedEventArgs e)
{
    // Get the instanceID from the Tag property
    FrameworkElement fe = (FrameworkElement)sender;
    Guid id = (Guid)fe.Tag;
    ResumeBookmark(id, false);
}

private void ResumeBookmark(Guid id, bool bReserved)
{
    WorkflowApplication i = _incomingRequests[id];
    try
    {
        i.ResumeBookmark("GetResponse", bReserved);
    }
    catch (Exception e)
    {
        AddEvent(e.Message);
    }
}
```

These event handlers obtain the workflow's instance ID from the Tag property of the Button control. They then call the `ResumeBookmark()` method, passing in either `true` or `false`, depending on which Button was clicked. The `ResumeBookmark()` method retrieves the `WorkflowApplication` from the `_incomingRequests` collection and calls its `ResumeBookmark()` method. This is passed the bookmark name and the value to be passed in when the instance is resumed.

143

ApplicationInterface Methods

You defined three methods in the `ApplicationInterface` class. Now you'll provide the implementation for these methods in the `MainWindow` class. The implementation for these methods is shown in Listing 9-11.

Listing 9-11. *Implementing the Method Calls by the ApplicationInterface Class*

```
public void RequestBook(ReservationRequest request)
{
    // Setup a dictionary object for passing parameters
    Dictionary<string, object> parameters = new Dictionary<string, object>();
    parameters.Add("request", request);
    parameters.Add("Writer", new ListBoxTextWriter(lstEvents));

    WorkflowApplication i =
        new WorkflowApplication(new ProcessRequest(), parameters);

    request.InstanceID = i.Id;
    _incomingRequests.Add(i.Id, i);
    i.Run();
}

public void RespondToRequest(ReservationResponse response)
{
    Guid id = response.RequestID;

    WorkflowApplication i = _outgoingRequests[id];
    try
    {
        i.ResumeBookmark("GetResponse", response);
    }
    catch (Exception e2)
    {
        AddEvent(e2.Message);
    }
}

public void AddNewRequest(ReservationRequest request)
{
    this.requestList.Dispatcher.BeginInvoke
        (new Action(() => this.requestList.Items.Add(request)));
}
```

The `RequestBook()` method is similar to the `btnRequest_Click()` method. It is called when an incoming message is received by the `ServiceHost` and the `RequestBook` method of the service contract is specified. It builds a `Dictionary` object to store the single input argument, creates the `WorkflowApplication`, adds it to the `_incomingRequests` collection, and then starts the workflow.

The `RespondToRequest()` method is also called when a message is received by the `ServiceHost`. It is called when the `RespondToRequest` method is specified. This happens when the other branch is sending back a response to the original request. It gets the `WorkflowApplication` from the `_outgoingRequests` collection and resumes the bookmark passing in the `ReservationResponse` class.

The AddNewRequest() method is called by the ProcessRequest workflow when a new message is received. This is done through the InvokeMethod activity. It simply adds an entry to the RequestList ListView control. Because this will be called on the workflow's thread, the Dispatcher class is used to execute the Add() method using the main window's thread.

The complete implementation of Reservations.xaml.cs is shown in Listing 9-12.

Listing 9-12. *Final Implementation of Reservations.xaml.cs*

```
using System;
using System.Collections.Generic;
using System.Linq;
using System.Text;
using System.Windows;
using System.Windows.Controls;
using System.Windows.Data;
using System.Windows.Documents;
using System.Windows.Input;
using System.Windows.Media;
using System.Windows.Media.Imaging;
using System.Windows.Navigation;
using System.Windows.Shapes;

using System.ServiceModel;
using System.ServiceModel.Activities;
using System.ServiceModel.Activities.Description;
using System.ServiceModel.Description;
using System.ServiceModel.Channels;
using System.Activities;
using System.Xml.Linq;
using System.Configuration;

namespace LibraryReservation
{
    /// <summary>
    /// Interaction logic for MainWindow.xaml
    /// </summary>
    public partial class MainWindow : Window
    {
        private ServiceHost _sh;
        private IDictionary<Guid, WorkflowApplication> _incomingRequests;
        private IDictionary<Guid, WorkflowApplication> _outgoingRequests;

        public MainWindow()
        {
            InitializeComponent();

            ApplicationInterface._app = this;

            _incomingRequests = new Dictionary<Guid, WorkflowApplication>();
            _outgoingRequests = new Dictionary<Guid, WorkflowApplication>();
        }
```

```csharp
private void Window_Loaded(object sender, RoutedEventArgs e)
{
    // Open the config file and get the name for this branch
    // and its network address
    Configuration config = ConfigurationManager
        .OpenExeConfiguration(ConfigurationUserLevel.None);
    AppSettingsSection app =
        (AppSettingsSection)config.GetSection("appSettings");
    string adr = app.Settings["Address"].Value;

    // Display the Branch name on the form
    lblBranch.Content = app.Settings["Branch Name"].Value;

    // Create the ServiceHost
    _sh = new ServiceHost(typeof(ClientService));

    // Add the Endpoint
    string szAddress = "http://localhost:" + adr + "/ClientService";
    System.ServiceModel.Channels.Binding bBinding = new BasicHttpBinding();
    _sh.AddServiceEndpoint(typeof(ILibraryReservation),
        bBinding, szAddress);

    // Open the ServiceHost to listen for messages
    _sh.Open();
}

private void Window_Unloaded(object sender, RoutedEventArgs e)
{
    // Terminate the service host
    _sh.Close();
}

private void btnRequest_Click(object sender, RoutedEventArgs e)
{
    // Setup a dictionary object for passing parameters
    Dictionary<string, object> parameters =
        new Dictionary<string, object>();
    parameters.Add("Author", txtAuthor.Text);
    parameters.Add("Title", txtTitle.Text);
    parameters.Add("ISBN", txtISBN.Text);

    WorkflowApplication i =
        new WorkflowApplication(new SendRequest(), parameters);

    _outgoingRequests.Add(i.Id, i);
    i.Run();
}

// Handle the Reserve button click event
private void Reserve(object sender, RoutedEventArgs e)
{
```

```
    // Get the instanceID from the Tag property
    FrameworkElement fe = (FrameworkElement)sender;
    Guid id = (Guid)fe.Tag;
    ResumeBookmark(id, true);
}

// Handle the Cancel button click event
private void Cancel(object sender, RoutedEventArgs e)
{
    // Get the instanceID from the Tag property
    FrameworkElement fe = (FrameworkElement)sender;
    Guid id = (Guid)fe.Tag;
    ResumeBookmark(id, false);
}

private void ResumeBookmark(Guid id, bool bReserved)
{
    WorkflowApplication i = _incomingRequests[id];
    try
    {
        i.ResumeBookmark("GetResponse", bReserved);
    }
    catch (Exception e)
    {
        AddEvent(e.Message);
    }
}

public void RequestBook(ReservationRequest request)
{
    // Setup a dictionary object for passing parameters
    Dictionary<string, object> parameters =
        new Dictionary<string, object>();
    parameters.Add("request", request);

    WorkflowApplication i =
        new WorkflowApplication(new ProcessRequest(), parameters);

    request.InstanceID = i.Id;
    _incomingRequests.Add(i.Id, i);
    i.Run();
}

public void RespondToRequest(ReservationResponse response)
{
    Guid id = response.RequestID;
    WorkflowApplication i = _outgoingRequests[id];
    try
    {
        i.ResumeBookmark("GetResponse", response);
    }
    catch (Exception e2)
```

147

```
        {
            AddEvent(e2.Message);
        }
    }

    public void AddNewRequest(ReservationRequest request)
    {
        this.requestList.Dispatcher.BeginInvoke
            (new Action(() => this.requestList.Items.Add(request)));
    }

    public ListBox GetEventListBox()
    {
        return this.lstEvents;
    }

    private void AddEvent(string szText)
    {
        lstEvents.Items.Add(szText);
    }
    }
}
```

Running the Application

As with the solution from the last chapter, you'll need to run multiple copies of the application; each with its own version of the configuration file. First, press F6 to rebuild the solution and fix any compiler issues. Create a new folder under the LibraryReservation folder called Branch. Then copy (not move) the files highlighted in Figure 9-7 to the Branch folder.

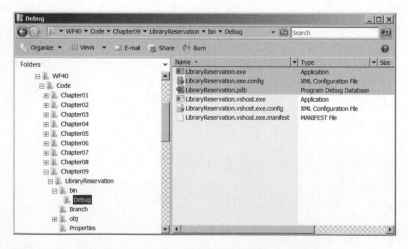

Figure 9-7. *Copying the executable files to the Branch folder*

Open the `LibraryReservation.exe.config` file (from the Branch subfolder) and edit the contents to match the following:

```xml
<?xml version="1.0" encoding="utf-8" ?>
<configuration>
  <appSettings>
    <add key="Branch Name" value="Southwest Regional"/>
    <add key="ID" value="{CA62F4ED-FACF-4835-8468-16CAAC298F4C}"/>
    <add key="Address" value="8730"/>
    <add key="Request Address" value="8000"/>
  </appSettings>
</configuration>
```

■ **Note** If you see any access denied errors, you might need to run the application with administrator privileges. For more information, refer to the note at the end of Chapter 8.

Double-click the `LibraryReservation.exe` file (in the Branch folder). The application should look like the one shown in Figure 9-8.

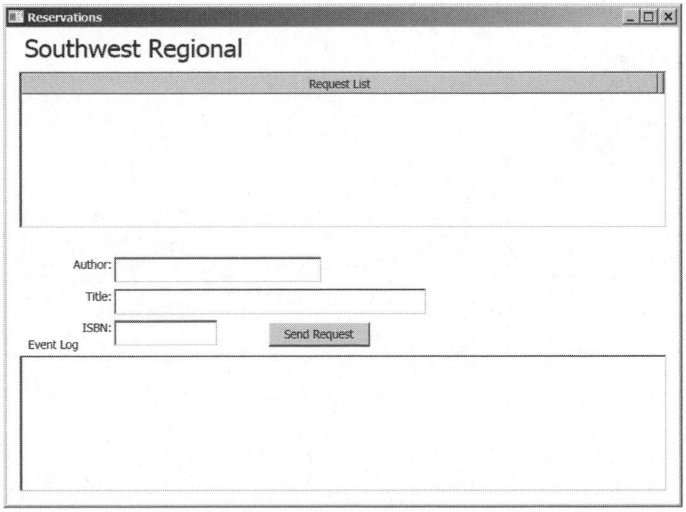

Figure 9-8. *The initial application window*

From Visual Studio, press F5 to debug the application. A similar window should display, but the label should say Central Library. Rearrange the windows so you can see both applications at the same time. In one of the applications, enter an Author, Title, and ISBN and then click the Send Request button. You should see the request added to the Request List in the other application. Click the Reserve button in the other application. You should see a message added to the Event Log, indicating that a response was received. Your windows should look similar to the ones shown in Figures 9-9 and 9-10.

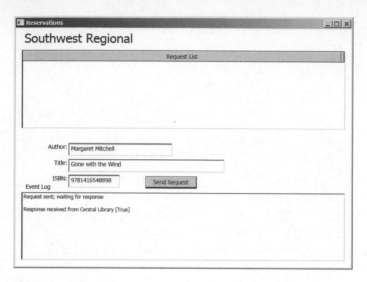

Figure 9-9. Sending a request from the Southwest Regional library

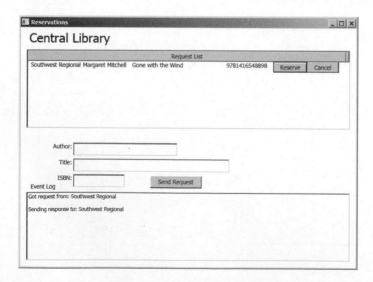

Figure 9-10. Processing a request by the Central Library

Try sending several requests from both windows. Also try the Cancel button and verify that the response message in the Event Log (in the other application) says [False].

CHAPTER 10

■ ■ ■

Web Services

Workflows can be hosted in a web service, which provides an ideal way to expose workflow solutions to non-workflow clients such as web applications. A web service receives a request, performs some appropriate processing, and returns a response. This naturally translates to the Receive and Send activities you used in the last two chapters. Because these activities are integrated with the Windows Communication Foundation (WCF), you can easily create WCF services.

Creating a Workflow Service

Start Visual Studio 2010 and create a new project using the WCF Workflow Service Application template. Enter the project name as **BookInventory** and the solution as **Chapter10**, as shown in Figure 10-1.

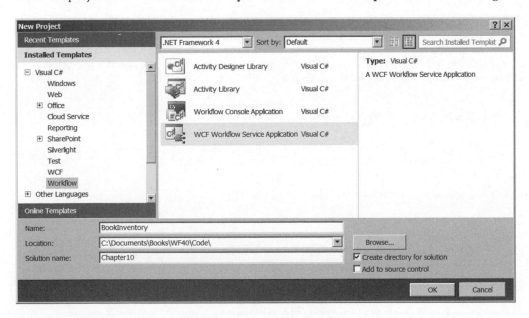

Figure 10-1. *Creating a WCF Workflow Service Application*

The template creates an initial workflow Sequence that contains a Receive and SendReply activity, as shown in Figure 10-2.

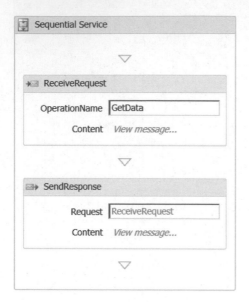

Figure 10-2. *The initial workflow sequence*

You will first configure these activities to define the service contract that they will satisfy. Then you'll add the workflow processing that will take place between the Receive and SendReply activities.

The template generated this initial workflow in a file named Service1.xamlx. From the Solution Explorer, rename this file to **BookInventory.xaml**. The service you will create looks up the specified book and returns the status of each copy that the library owns.

Defining the Service Contract

In the Solution Explorer, right-click the BookInventory project and choose Add ➤ Class. Enter the class name as **BookInfo.cs**. The implementation for this file is shown in Listing 10-1.

Listing 10-1. *Service contract definition: BookInfo.cs*

```
using System;
using System.Collections.Generic;
using System.Runtime.Serialization;
using System.ServiceModel;

namespace BookInventory
{
    /**************************************************/
    // Define the service contract, IBookInventory
```

```
// which consists of a single method, LookupBook()
/****************************************************/
[ServiceContract]
public interface IBookInventory
{
    [OperationContract]
    BookInfoList LookupBook(BookSearch request);
}

/****************************************************/
// Define the request message, BookSearch
/****************************************************/
[MessageContract(IsWrapped = false)]
public class BookSearch
{
    private String _ISBN;
    private String _Title;
    private String _Author;

    public BookSearch()
    {
    }

    public BookSearch(String title, String author, String isbn)
    {
        _Title = title;
        _Author = author;
        _ISBN = isbn;
    }

    #region Public Properties
    [MessageBodyMember]
    public String Title
    {
        get { return _Title; }
        set { _Title = value; }
    }

    [MessageBodyMember]
    public String Author
    {
        get { return _Author; }
        set { _Author = value; }
    }

    [MessageBodyMember]
    public String ISBN
    {
        get { return _ISBN; }
        set { _ISBN = value; }
    }
}
```

```
    #endregion Public Properties
}

/***************************************************/
// Define the BookInfo class
/***************************************************/
[MessageContract(IsWrapped = false)]
public class BookInfo
{
    private Guid _InventoryID;
    private String _ISBN;
    private String _Title;
    private String _Author;
    private String _Status;

    public BookInfo()
    {
    }

    public BookInfo(String title, String author, String isbn,
        String status)
    {
        _Title = title;
        _Author = author;
        _ISBN = isbn;
        _Status = status;
        _InventoryID = Guid.NewGuid();
    }

    #region Public Properties
    [MessageBodyMember]
    public Guid InventoryID
    {
        get { return _InventoryID; }
        set { _InventoryID = value; }
    }

    [MessageBodyMember]
    public String Title
    {
        get { return _Title; }
        set { _Title = value; }
    }

    [MessageBodyMember]
    public String Author
    {
        get { return _Author; }
        set { _Author = value; }
    }
```

```csharp
    [MessageBodyMember]
    public String ISBN
    {
        get { return _ISBN; }
        set { _ISBN = value; }
    }

    [MessageBodyMember]
    public String status
    {
        get { return _Status; }
        set { _Status = value; }
    }
    #endregion Public Properties
}


/*****************************************************/
// Define the response message, BookInfoList, which
// is a list of BookInfo classes
/*****************************************************/
[MessageContract(IsWrapped = false)]
public class BookInfoList
{
    private List<BookInfo> _BookList;

    public BookInfoList()
    {
        _BookList = new List<BookInfo>();
    }

    [MessageBodyMember]
    public List<BookInfo> BookList
    {
        get { return _BookList; }
    }
}
}
```

The service contract, IBookInventory, contains a single method called LookupBook(). It is passed a BookSearch class that has various properties that can be used to find the desired book, such as Author and Title. It returns a BookInfoList class, which contains a collection of BookInfo classes. You can refer to Chapter 8, in which I explain the use of the ServiceContract, MessageContract, and MessageBodyMember attributes.

Press F6 to build the solution.

Configuring Receive and SendReply

Open the BookInventory.xamlx file and select the "ReceiveRequest" activity. In the Properties window, the ServiceContract property has a default value of {http://tempuri.org/}IService. Change the IService to **IBookInventory**. Enter the OperationName as **LookupBook**.

From the workflow designer, click the Variables control at the bottom left. You'll notice that the template created a couple of variables for you. The handle variable is used to correlate the response with the same instance that sent the request. The data variable was set up as the data being passed in. Select the data variable and press the Delete key to remove it. Create two new variables. For the first one, enter the Name as **search**; for the Variable type, select Browse for Types. In the dialog that appears, expand the BookInventory assembly and choose the BookSearch class (see Figure 10-3).

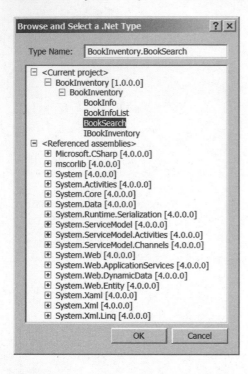

Figure 10-3. *Selecting the BookSearch data type*

For the second variable, enter the Name as **result**. For the Variable type property, choose Browse for Types and then select the BookInfoList class. The variable list should look like the one shown in Figure 10-4.

Name	Variable type	Scope	Default
handle	CorrelationHandle	Sequential Service	*Handle cannot be initialized*
search	BookSearch	Sequential Service	*Enter a VB expression*
result	BookInfoList	Sequential Service	*Enter a VB expression*
Create Variable			

| Variables | Imports | | 🔍 | 100% | ▼ | ⬜ | ◾ |

Figure 10-4. *Variables defined for the workflow*

On the workflow designer, the "ReceiveRequest" activity has a *View message* link for the Content property. Click it to display the dialog that is used to define the incoming message. (You can also click the ellipses next to the Content property in the Properties window.) The input can be defined in two ways: a message or a collection of parameters. I will explain the parameter approach later in this chapter. For now, make sure that the Message radio button is selected.

For the Message data property, enter **search**. It specifies that the incoming message should be stored in the search variable. For the Message type, select BookInventory.BookSearch. The dialog should look like the one shown in Figure 10-5.

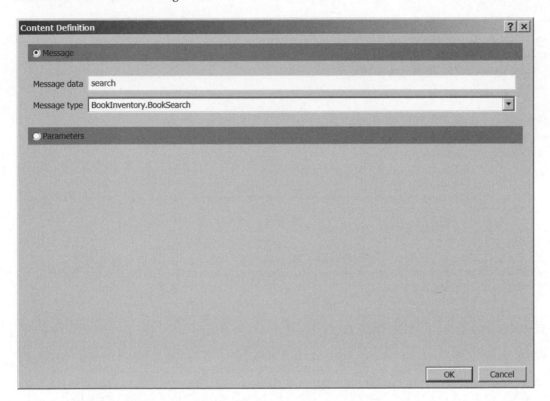

Figure 10-5. *Specifying the incoming message*

The Properties window should look like the one shown in Figure 10-6.

Figure 10-6. *The Receive activity Properties window*

Select the "SendResponse" activity and click its *View message* link. Again, make sure that the Message radio button is selected. For the Message data property, enter **result**; for the Message type property, select the **BookInfoList** class.

Creating the PerformLookup Activity

For this project, you'll create a custom activity to perform the "lookup." Actually, it will simply return some hard-coded data. In a real solution, it would probably execute a query against a database to retrieve the requested data. From the Solution Explorer, right-click the BookInventory project and choose Add ➤ New Item. In the Add New Item dialog, select the Code Activity template from the Workflow category. Enter the Name as **PerformLookup.cs** as shown in Figure 10-7.

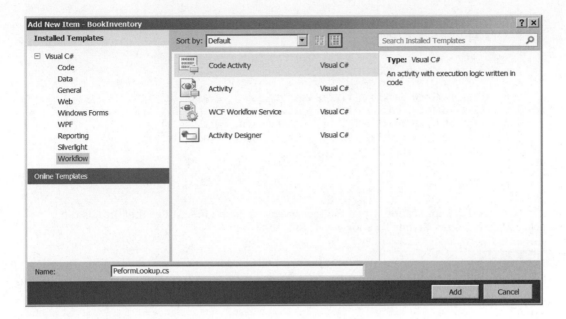

Figure 10-7. *Creating a custom activity*

Enter the implementation of the PerformLookup activity, as shown in Listing 10-2.

Listing 10-2. *Implementation of the PerformLookup activity*

```csharp
using System;
using System.Collections.Generic;
using System.Linq;
using System.Text;
using System.Activities;

namespace BookInventory
{
    /***************************************************/
    // This custom activity creates a BookInfoList class
    // which is a collection of BookInfo classes.  It uses
    // the input parameters (BookSearch class) to "lookup"
    // the matching items. The BookInfoList class is
    // returned in the output parameter.
    /***************************************************/
    public sealed class PerformLookup : CodeActivity
    {
        public InArgument<BookSearch> Search { get; set; }
        public OutArgument<BookInfoList> BookList { get; set; }

        protected override void Execute(CodeActivityContext context)
        {
```

```
        string author = Search.Get(context).Author;
        string title = Search.Get(context).Title;
        string isbn = Search.Get(context).ISBN;

        BookInfoList l = new BookInfoList();

        l.BookList.Add(new BookInfo(title, author, isbn, "Available"));
        l.BookList.Add(new BookInfo(title, author, isbn, "CheckedOut"));
        l.BookList.Add(new BookInfo(title, author, isbn, "Missing"));
        l.BookList.Add(new BookInfo(title, author, isbn, "Available"));
        BookList.Set(context, l);
    }
  }
}
```

Press F6 to rebuild the application. Open the `BookInventory.xamlx` file. Notice that the custom `PerformLookup` activity is now in your Toolbox (see Figure 10-8).

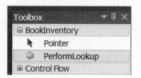

Figure 10-8. *Toolbox with custom PerformLookup activity*

Drag a `PerformLookup` activity between the "ReceiveRequest" and "SendResponse" activities. The workflow should look like the one shown in Figure 10-9.

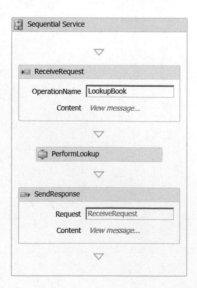

Figure 10-9. *Completed service workflow*

Select the PerformLookup activity. In the Properties window, for the BookList property enter **result**; for the Search property, enter **search**.

Testing the Service

Press F5 to debug the service. Because this is a web service, Visual Studio automatically starts the WCF Test Client. This is a very handy utility. It loads the web service and discovers the methods that are provided. They are listed in the left pane, as shown in Figure 10-10.

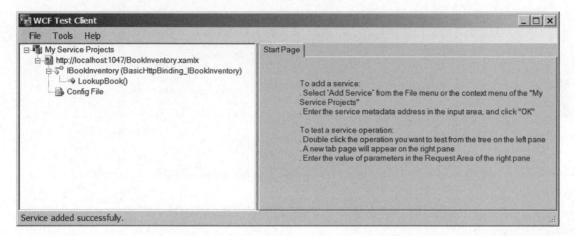

Figure 10-10. *The initial WCF Test Client window*

Double-click the LookupBook() method and the upper portion of the right pane will provide a place for you to enter the contents of the incoming message. This is able to handle even complex messages containing collections of classes and properties. Enter an author, ISBN number, and title; then click the Invoke button. You should see results similar to the ones shown in Figure 10-11.

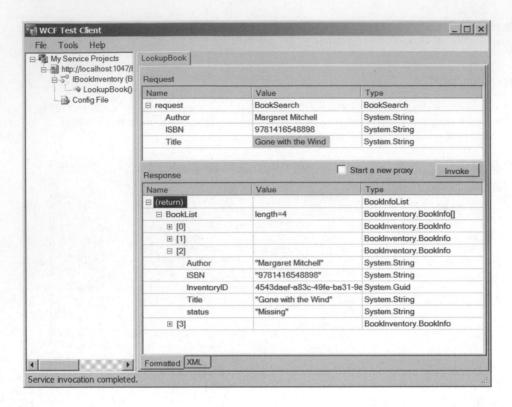

Figure10-11. *WCF Test Client showing service results*

The service returned four BookInfo classes. In Figure 10-11, the third record is expanded to show an example of the data returned. This particular item has a status of Missing.

■ **Caution** If the .xamlx file is the current file in Visual Studio when you press F5, the WCF Test Client is launched, as demonstrated here. However, if you have some other file as the current file, when you press F5, you will probably see a web page displayed that shows a directory listing of the current folder. If that happens, just close the web page, which will stop the debugger. Then select the .xamlx file and press F5 again.

Using Parameters

In the previous project, the input into the web service was specified as a class with a MessageContract attribute. This is the typical way of calling WCF services. However, instead of creating a single message class that contains all the input data, you can pass them as individual parameters to the workflow services. To demonstrate this, you'll create a second identical service that uses parameters instead of messages.

Creating a Second Service

From the Solution Explorer, right-click the BookInventory project and choose Add ➤ New Item. In the Add New Item dialog, select the WCF Workflow Service template, which is found in the Workflow category, as shown in Figure 10-12. For the Name, enter **BookInventory2.xamlx**.

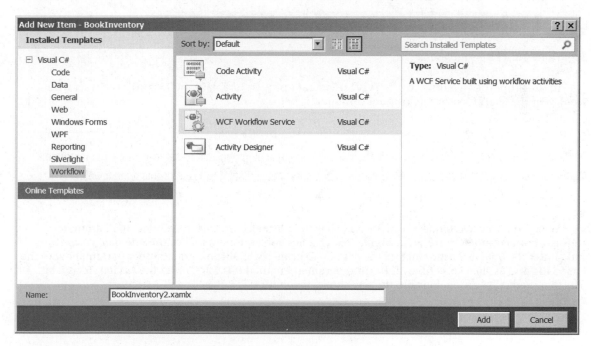

Figure 10-12. *Creating a WCF Workflow Service*

In the workflow designer, click the Variables control at the bottom left. The same two initial variables are created as they were with the first service. Delete the data variable and create a new variable named result. For the Variable type, select ArrayOf<T>. A dialog will appear to select the type represented by <T>. In the drop-down list, select Browse for Types; then select the BookInfo class from the BookInventory assembly. Add three more String variables named author, title, and isbn. The variable list should look like the one shown in Figure 10-13.

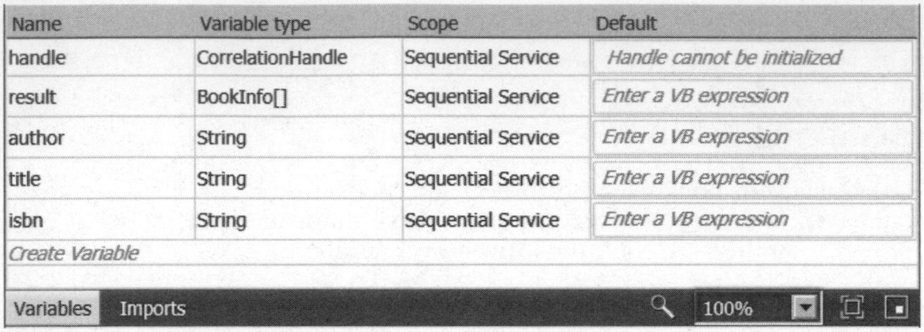

Name	Variable type	Scope	Default
handle	CorrelationHandle	Sequential Service	*Handle cannot be initialized*
result	BookInfo[]	Sequential Service	*Enter a VB expression*
author	String	Sequential Service	*Enter a VB expression*
title	String	Sequential Service	*Enter a VB expression*
isbn	String	Sequential Service	*Enter a VB expression*
Create Variable			

Variables Imports   🔍 100% ▼ 🔲 ■

Figure 10-13. *The variables list*

In the Properties window, for the ServiceContract property, replace the IService contract with **Book**. For the OperationName, enter **LookupBook2**.

■ **Caution** In the first service you created, the CanCreateInstance property was set to true by the template. With the second one, however, it is set to false. Make sure that you set it to true for this one as well.

Select the "ReceiveRequest" activity and click the Content link. This time, select the Parameters radio button. Parameters are set up similar to variables and arguments. Click the *Add new parameter* link. Enter the Name as **Author** and set the Assign To property to **author**. Add another parameter with the Name **Title** and Assign To as **title**. Add a third parameter named **ISBN** and enter the Assign To as **isbn**. The completed list should look like the one shown in Figure 10-14.

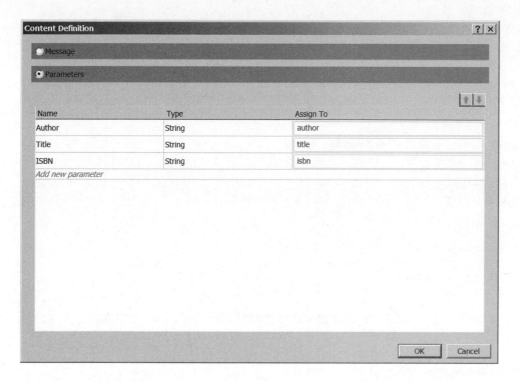

Figure 10-14. *The ReceiveRequest parameter list*

Click the Content link of the "SendResponse" activity. Select the Parameters radio button and click the *Add new parameter* link. Enter the Name as **Result**; for Type, select BookInventory.BookInfo[] from the drop-down list. (This type is in the drop-down list because you just used it to define the result variable.) The dialog should look like the one shown in Figure 10-15.

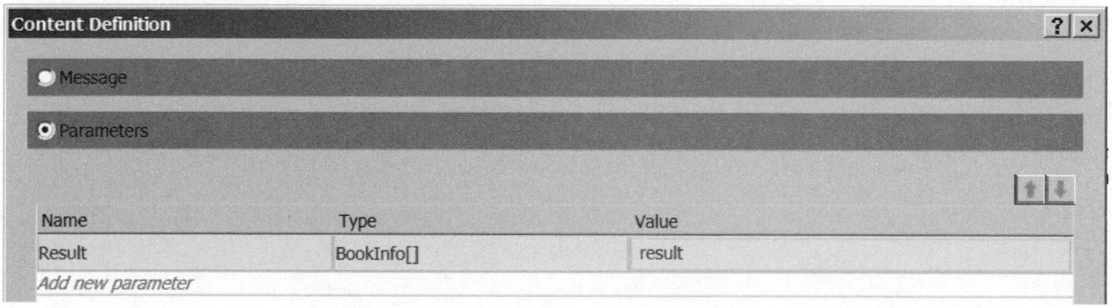

Name	Type	Value
Result	BookInfo[]	result
Add new parameter		

Figure 10-15. *The SendResponse parameter list*

Creating a Modified PerformLookup Activity

The custom PerformLookup activity that you created for the first service takes a BookSearch class as the input argument and returns a BookInfoList class. Now you'll need to create a different custom activity that uses the separate parameters. From the Solution Explorer, right-click the BookInventory project and select Add ➤ New Item. Select the Code Activity template and enter the Name as **PerformLookup2.cs**. The implementation for this activity is shown in Listing 10-3.

Listing 10-3. *Implementation of PerformLookup2*

```csharp
using System;
using System.Collections.Generic;
using System.Activities;

namespace BookInventory
{
    /****************************************************/
    // This custom activity creates a BookInfo array and
    // uses the input parameters to "lookup" the matching
    // items. The BookInfo array is returned in the output
    // parameter.
    /****************************************************/
    public sealed class PerformLookup2 : CodeActivity
    {
        public InArgument<String> Title { get; set; }
        public InArgument<String> Author { get; set; }
        public InArgument<String> ISBN { get; set; }
        public OutArgument<BookInfo[]> BookList { get; set; }

        protected override void Execute(CodeActivityContext context)
        {
            string author = Author.Get(context);
            string title = Title.Get(context);
            string isbn = ISBN.Get(context);

            BookInfo[] l = new BookInfo[4];

            l[0] = new BookInfo(title, author, isbn, "Available");
            l[1] = new BookInfo(title, author, isbn, "CheckedOut");
            l[2] = new BookInfo(title, author, isbn, "Missing");
            l[3] = new BookInfo(title, author, isbn, "Available");
            BookList.Set(context, l);
        }
    }
}
```

This code works just like the first one, except that the input arguments are passed individually, and the results are returned in an array instead of a class. Press F6 to rebuild the solution.

Select the BookInventory2.xamlx file and drag a PerformLookup2 activity from the Toolbox between the "ReceiveRequest" and "SendResponse" activities. In the Properties window, enter the appropriate values, as shown in Figure 10-16.

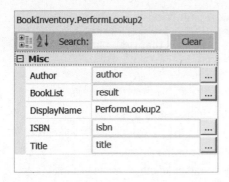

Figure 10-16. *Properties window of the PerformLookup2 activity*

Testing the Service

Make sure that the BookInventory2.xamlx file is the current file in Visual Studio and press F5 to debug. The WCF Test Client should start just like with the first service. Double-click the LookupBook2() method, enter the request details, and click the Invoke button. Your results should look similar to what is shown in Figure 10-17.

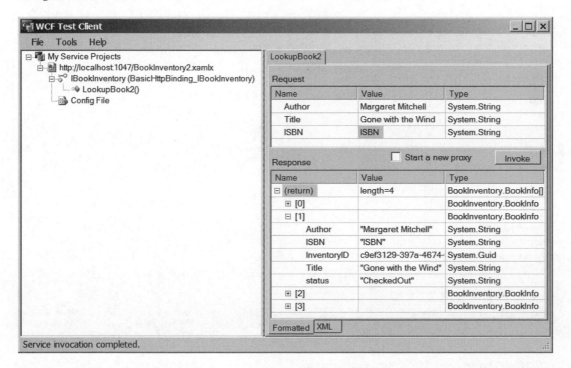

Figure 10-17. *WCF Test Client*

The format is slightly different from the first service, but it basically functions the same way. In the figure, I expanded the second record to show that this particular copy is checked out. For the second service, you did not create a service contract; you just defined the parameters that were passed in and returned by the service. The service contract is automatically generated.

■ **Caution** When defining the `Receive`/`SendReply` pair, you have the option to use either messages or parameters. However, you cannot mix the two options. If you use parameters for the `Receive` activity, you cannot use a message for the `SendReply` activity. Also, when using parameters, the types must *not* have the `MessageContract` attribute. If you violate either of these rules, you will get a rather lengthy runtime exception that basically tells you what I just said.

Creating a Client Workflow

Now you'll create client workflow that will invoke the web service. From the Solution Explorer, right-click the Chapter10 solution and choose Add ➤ New Project. Select the Workflow Console Application template; for the project name, enter **BookLookup**, as shown in Figure 10-18.

Figure 10-18. Adding a workflow console application

From the Solution Explorer, right-click the BookLookup project and choose Add Service Reference. The dialog shown in Figure 10-19 will appear.

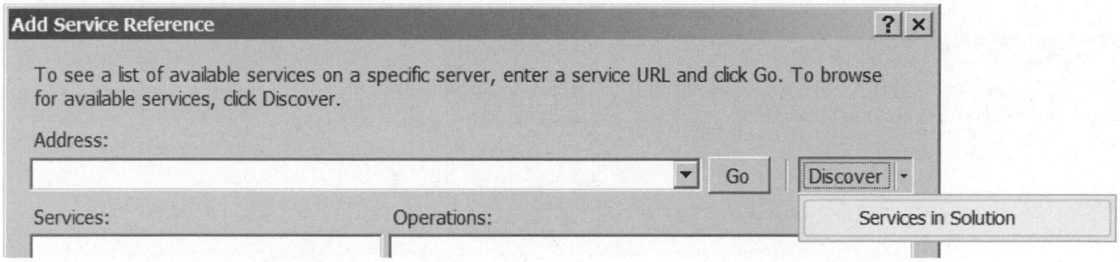

Figure 10-19. *Finding the available services*

Click the Discover drop-down link and choose Services in Solution. The dialog shown in Figure 10-20 will list the two services you created in the BookInventory project.

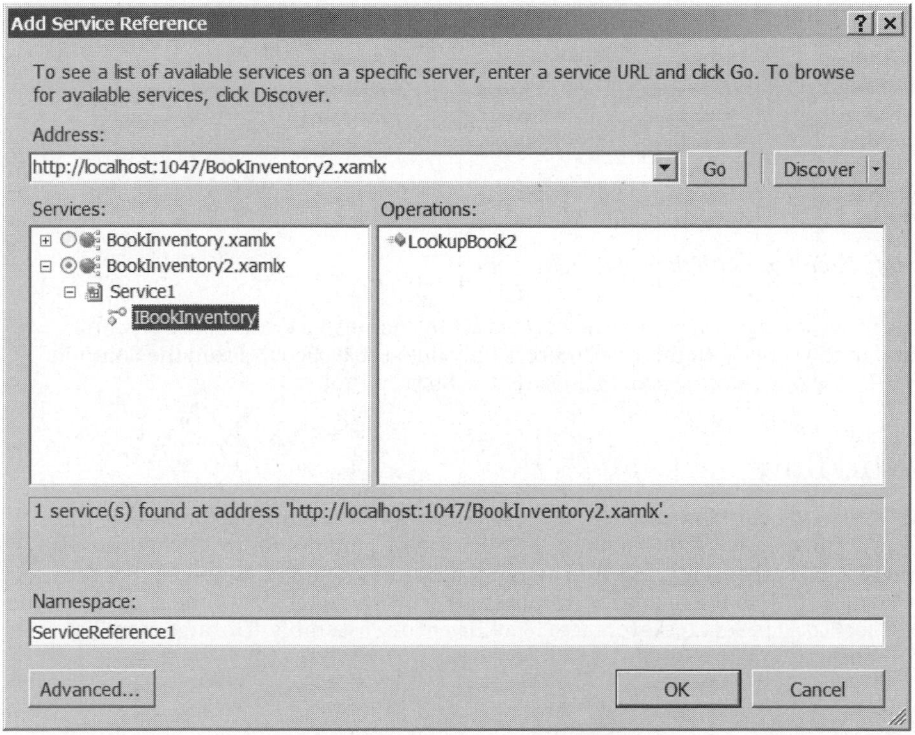

Figure 10-20. *Selecting the desired service*

You can expand these services to see the methods provided in each. Select the second one (BookInventory2.xamlx) and click OK. After a few seconds, you should see the dialog shown in Figure 10-21.

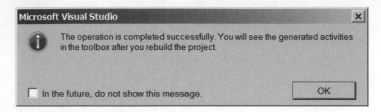

Figure 10-21. *Operation completed dialog*

This lets you know that a reference to the service has been added to the project. Press F6 to rebuild the solution. The Window1.xaml file should be displayed; if not, open it. The top portion of the Toolbox should look like Figure 10-22.

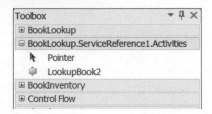

Figure 10-22. *The updated Toolbox, with the service wrapper*

In the Toolbox, the BookLookup.ServiceReference1.Activities namespace contains a custom activity for each method in the service. In this case, there is only one: LookupBook2. From the Solution Explorer, right-click the BookLookup project and choose Set as Startup Project.

Defining the Workflow

Drag a LookupBook2 activity to the workflow. Now you'll need to set up the arguments for passing the search criteria into the workflow and to return the results. Click the Arguments control. Add three String input arguments named Title, Author, and ISBN. Add an output argument named **BookList**. For the Argument type, select Array Of[T]. In the dialog that appears, select Browse for Types and then select the BookInfo class from the BookLookup.ServiceReference1.BookInventory assembly. The argument list should look like the one shown in Figure 10-23.

Name	Direction	Argument type	Default value
Title	In	String	*Enter a VB expression*
Author	In	String	*Enter a VB expression*
ISBN	In	String	*Enter a VB expression*
BookList	Out	BookInfo[]	*Default value not supported*
Create Argument			

Variables	**Arguments**	Imports		🔍	100%	▼	🗗	▣

Figure 10-23. *The workflow arguments*

Select the "LookupBook2" activity; in the Properties window, enter the property values as shown in Figure 10-24.

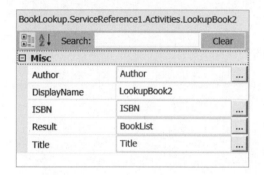

Figure 10-24. *LookupBook2 properties*

Implementing the Host Application

Open the `Program.cs` file in the LookupBook project. The implementation for this file is shown in Listing 10-4.

Listing 10-4. *Implementation of Program.cs*

```csharp
using System;
using System.Linq;
using System.Activities;
using System.Activities.Statements;
using System.Collections.Generic;
using BookLookup.ServiceReference1;

namespace BookLookup
{
    class Program
    {
```

```
static void Main(string[] args)
{
    // create dictionary with input arguments for the workflow
    IDictionary<string, object> input = new Dictionary<string, object>
    {
        { "Author" , "Margaret Mitchell" },
        { "Title" , "Gone with the Wind" },
        { "ISBN" , "1234567890123" }
    };

    // execute the workflow
    IDictionary<string, object> output =
        WorkflowInvoker.Invoke(new Workflow1(), input);

    BookInfo[] l = output["BookList"] as BookInfo[];
    if (l != null)
    {
        foreach (BookInfo i in l)
        {
            Console.WriteLine("{0}: {1}, {2}",
                i.Title, i.status, i.InventoryID);
        }
    }
    else
        Console.WriteLine("No items were found");

    Console.WriteLine("Press ENTER to exit");
    Console.ReadLine();
}
}
}
```

This code passes in the Author, Title, and ISBN arguments through a Dictionary object (as in Chapter 4). The workflow returns an array of BookInfo objects. This code displays the contents of this array.

Running the Application

Press F5 to run the application. Your results should be similar to these:

```
Gone with the Wind: Available, 58ab51cd-2796-4b32-a7be-21170f1e922b
Gone with the Wind: CheckedOut, 64406a94-a6ef-45a7-8373-066f5f991134
Gone with the Wind: Missing, a37186ec-faa7-4e6b-8226-484f17075998
Gone with the Wind: Available, e34d39e5-aafa-4fd3-8000-664809b7e98d
Press ENTER to exit
```

Using Pick

WF 4.0 provides an activity called Pick, which has multiple branches (called PickBranch). Each branch contains a Trigger property and an Action property. Each of them executes an activity (or a sequence of activities). When the Pick activity is executed, all the Trigger activities are started. As soon as one of these activities completes, its corresponding Action is executed, and all other branches are cancelled.

This is useful for determining the appropriate action based on some event. For example, you could use a Receive activity for the Trigger. Each branch could have a Receive activity that is waiting for a different message. Based on which message is received, the corresponding action is taken. For this project, you will use a Pick activity to provide a timeout feature to your workflow.

■ **Tip** If you are familiar with the previous versions of workflow, this is roughly equivalent to the Listen activity.

Open the Window1.xaml file, right-click the "LookupBook2" activity, and select Cut. Drag a Pick activity onto the workflow. Right-click the Trigger section of the first branch and choose Paste. Drag a Delay activity to the Trigger section of the second branch. Set its Duration property to **TimeSpan.FromSeconds(5)**. Drag a WriteLine activity to each of the Action sections and set their Text properties to **"The service completed"** and **"The service timed-out"**. The workflow should look like the one shown in Figure 10-25.

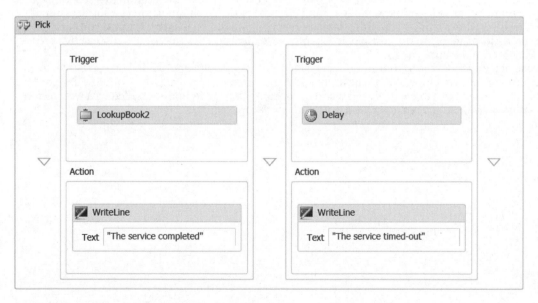

Figure 10-25. *Workflow with timeout logic*

Press F5 to run the application. The results should be identical to the last time you ran it except for the added message ("The service completed"). To test the timeout feature, open the BookInventory2.xamlx file. Drag a Delay activity before the "SendResponse" activity and set its Duration property to **TimeSpan.FromSeconds(7)**. Press F5 to run the application. This time, after a five-second delay, the results should look like these:

```
The service timed-out
No items were found
Press ENTER to exit
```

Review

Workflows are often distributed across multiple applications and even different servers, so communication is an important part of workflow design. In the sample project, for example, different library branches communicate with each other to request an item to be transferred. The Send and Receive activities (and their counterparts, ReceiveReply and SendReply) provide a convenient way to send and receive messages. These activities rely on WCF to transmit the messages and therefore can use a number of protocols such as HTTP or TCP. However, the host application can also receive WCF messages directly as was demonstrated in Chapter 9.

Although workflow activities do not have a user interface, they often need to communicate with a host application, either to update the application or to request input from the user. In this section, you used a Bookmark to pause a workflow while waiting for user input. The application can easily resume the workflow from where it left off after the data has been provided. You have used the WriteLine activity since Chapter 1 to write text to the console. In Chapter 9, you learned how to use this same activity to write to a list box on the application.

The use of web services is becoming an increasingly popular design approach. You can either start with a service contract or simply define the input and output parameters using the workflow designer. Workflow can be used both to create services and to consume them. Methods provided by a web service become a custom activity that you can drop onto your workflow.

PART 4

■■■

Workflow Extensions

Using Persistence, Tracking and Transactions

In this section you'll explore some of the standard Workflow extensions used for persisting and tracking your workflow activities. You'll also write some custom extensions and discover the benefit of using extensions in simplifying your solutions. WF 4.0 also allows you to use database transactions across activities and even applications to ensure your application data is updated consistently.

All of these projects will require a SQL Server database. Just about any version will work including the Microsoft Data Engine (MSDE 2000). You can download a `SQL.zip` file from `www.apress.com` that contains a folder for each of these chapters. There are database scripts inside these folders that you will use to create the database schema needed by the applications. The instructions in each chapter will explain how to use this scripts.

The sample projects will build a solution to enter and manage sales leads. Leads can be entered and later assigned to a sales agent. The agent can then update the lead when the follow-up has been completed. Each chapter will add more features to the solution and demonstrate new WF concepts in the process.

CHAPTER 11

SQL Persistence

In this chapter, you'll build a simple WPF application that is used to enter sales leads. The leads will be persisted to a SQL database, and any existing leads will be loaded from the database when the application is restarted.

Creating the Application

Start by creating a Windows Presentation Foundation (WPF) project as shown in Figure 11-1. For the project name, enter **LeadGenerator**, and for the solution enter **Chapter11**.

Figure 11-1. *Creating a WPF application project*

Renaming the Window

The template will generate a window form named `MainWindow.xaml`. Rename this file to **AddLead.xaml**.
Open the `App.xaml` file and change the `StartupUri` attribute as follows:

```
StartupUri="AddLead.xaml"
```

Then open the `AddLead.xaml.cs` file and modify the class as follows (the modified lines are in bold):

```
namespace LeadGenerator
{
    /// <summary>
    /// Interaction logic for AddLead.xaml
    /// </summary>
    public partial class AddLead : Window
    {
        public AddLead()
        {
            InitializeComponent();
        }
    }
}
```

In the Solution Explorer, right-click the LeadGenerator project and choose Add Reference. From the
.NET tab, add the following references:

- `System.Activities`

- `System.Activities.DurableInstancing`

- `System.Configuration`

- `System.Data.Linq`

- `System.Runtime.DurableInstancing`

- `System.ServiceModel`

- `System.ServiceModel.Activities`

Defining the Window Form

Open the `AddLead.xaml` file. Click the XAML tab and enter the code shown in Listing 11-1.

Listing 11-1. Implementation of AddLead.xaml

```
<Window x:Class="LeadGenerator.AddLead"
 xmlns="http://schemas.microsoft.com/winfx/2006/xaml/presentation"
 xmlns:x="http://schemas.microsoft.com/winfx/2006/xaml"
```

```
Title="Lead Generator" Height="518" Width="547"
Loaded="Window_Loaded">
    <Grid MinWidth="300" MinHeight="100" Width="514">
        <Label Height="30" Margin="5,10,10,10" Name="lblName"
         VerticalAlignment="Top" HorizontalAlignment="Left" Width="90"
         HorizontalContentAlignment="Right">Contact Name:</Label>
        <Label Height="30" Margin="270,10,10,10" Name="lblPhone"
         VerticalAlignment="Top" HorizontalAlignment="Left" Width="90"
         HorizontalContentAlignment="Right">Phone Number:</Label>
        <Label Height="30" Margin="5,40,10,10" Name="lblInterest"
         VerticalAlignment="Top" HorizontalAlignment="Left" Width="90"
         HorizontalContentAlignment="Right">Interested in:</Label>
        <Label Height="30" Margin="5,70,10,10" Name="lblNotes"
         VerticalAlignment="Top" HorizontalAlignment="Left" Width="90"
         HorizontalContentAlignment="Right" Content="Notes:"></Label>
        <Label Height="30" Margin="430,70,10,10" Name="lblRating"
         VerticalAlignment="Top" HorizontalAlignment="Left" Width="20"
         HorizontalContentAlignment="Right" Content="$"></Label>
        <TextBox Height="25" Margin="100,10,10,10" Name="txtName"
         VerticalAlignment="Top" HorizontalAlignment="Left" Width="170" />
        <TextBox Height="25" Margin="365,10,10,10" Name="txtPhone"
         VerticalAlignment="Top" HorizontalAlignment="Left" Width="100" />
        <TextBox Height="25" Margin="100,40,10,10" Name="txtInterest"
         VerticalAlignment="Top" HorizontalAlignment="Left" Width="300" />
        <TextBox Height="45" Margin="100,70,10,10" Name="txtNotes"
         VerticalAlignment="Top" HorizontalAlignment="Left" Width="300"
         VerticalScrollBarVisibility="Auto" AcceptsReturn="True" />
        <TextBox Height="25" Margin="450,70,10,10" Name="txtRating"
         VerticalAlignment="Top" HorizontalAlignment="Left" Width="30" />
        <Button Height="23" Margin="410,40,10,10" Name="btnLead"
         VerticalAlignment="Top" HorizontalAlignment="Left" Width="70"
         Click="btnAddLead_Click">Add Lead</Button>

        <ListView x:Name="lstLeads" Margin="10,125,10,10" Height="145"
         VerticalAlignment="Top" ItemsSource="{Binding}"
         HorizontalContentAlignment="Center"
         SelectionChanged="lstLeads_SelectionChanged" >
            <ListView.View>
                <GridView>
                    <GridViewColumn Header="Current Leads" Width="480">
                        <GridViewColumn.CellTemplate>
                            <DataTemplate>
                                <StackPanel Orientation="Horizontal">
                                    <TextBlock Text="{Binding ContactName}"
                                     Width="110"/>
                                    <TextBlock Text="{Binding ContactPhone}"
                                     Width="70"/>
                                    <TextBlock Text="{Binding Interests}"
                                     Width="130"/>
                                    <TextBlock Text="{Binding Status}"
                                     Width="70"/>
```

```
                          <TextBlock Text="{Binding AssignedTo}"
                             Width="100"/>
                       </StackPanel>
                    </DataTemplate>
                 </GridViewColumn.CellTemplate>
              </GridViewColumn>
           </GridView>
        </ListView.View>
    </ListView>
    <Label Height="37" HorizontalAlignment="Stretch" Margin="10,272,5,10"
     Name="lblSelectedNotes" VerticalAlignment="Top" Visibility="Hidden" />

    <Label Height="30" Margin="10,0,0,140" Name="lblAgent"
     VerticalAlignment="Bottom" HorizontalAlignment="Left" Width="40"
     HorizontalContentAlignment="Left" Visibility="Hidden">Agent:</Label>
    <TextBox Height="25" Margin="60,0,0,140" Name="txtAgent"
     VerticalAlignment="Bottom" HorizontalAlignment="Left" Width="190"
     Visibility="Hidden" />
    <Button Height="25" Margin="270,0,0,140" Name="btnAssign"
     VerticalAlignment="Bottom" HorizontalAlignment="Left" Width="90"
     Click="btnAssign_Click" Visibility="Hidden">Assign Agent</Button>

    <Label Height="27" HorizontalAlignment="Left" Margin="10,0,0,110"
     Name="lblEvent" VerticalAlignment="Bottom" Width="76">Event Log</Label>
    <ListBox Margin="12,0,5,12" Name="lstEvents" Height="100"
     VerticalAlignment="Bottom" FontStretch="Condensed" FontSize="10" />
    </Grid>
</Window>
```

Then select the Design tab. The form should look like the one shown in Figure 11-2.

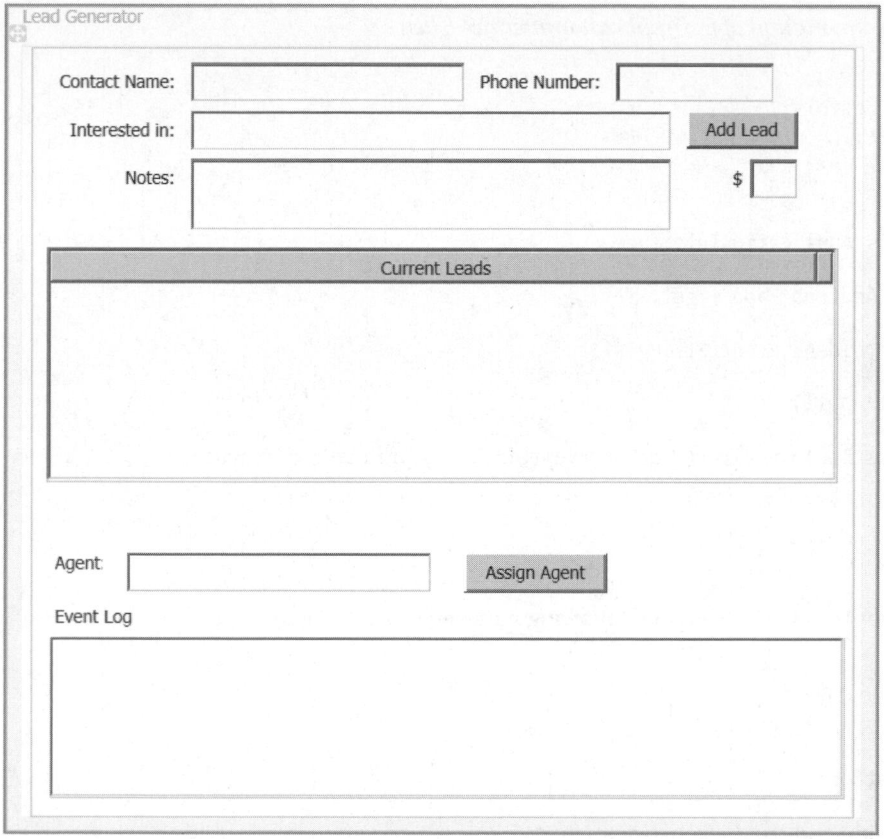

Figure 11-2. *Design of the window form*

Implementing a TextWriter

In Chapter 9, you implemented a `ListBoxTextWriter` class that was used by the `WriteLine` activities to display messages in the application. You will use the same approach in this project. First, you'll need a static class to provide access into the application. In the Solution Explorer, right-click the LeadGenerator project and choose Add ➤ Class. Enter the class name as **ApplicationInterface.cs**. The implementation for this class is shown in Listing 11-2.

■ **Note** I won't elaborate here about the `ApplicationInterface` or `ListBoxTextWriter` classes. You might want to refer to Chapter 9 if you have any questions.

Listing 11-2. *Initial Implementation of the ApplicationInterface Class*

```csharp
using System;
using System.Windows.Controls;
using System.Activities;

namespace LeadGenerator
{
    public static class ApplicationInterface
    {
        public static AddLead _app { get; set; }

        public static void AddEvent(String status)
        {
            if (_app != null)
            {
                new ListBoxTextWriter(_app.GetEventListBox()).WriteLine(status);
            }
        }
    }
}
```

Open the AddLead.xaml.cs file and add the following namespaces:

```csharp
using System.Activities;
using System.Activities.DurableInstancing;
using System.Runtime.Persistence;
using System.Data.Linq;
using System.Configuration;
```

Then add the following code to the constructor:

```csharp
ApplicationInterface._app = this;
```

Add the following methods to the AddLead.xaml.cs class:

```csharp
// Add a line of text to the Event Log
private void AddEvent(string szText)
{
    lstEvents.Items.Add(szText);
}

public ListBox GetEventListBox()
{
    return this.lstEvents;
}
```

In the Solution Explorer, right-click the LeadGenerator project and choose Add ➤ Class. For the class name, enter **ListBoxTextWriter.cs**. The implementation of this class is shown in Listing 11-3.

■ **Tip** The implementation of the ListBoxTextWriter class is identical to the one you implemented in Chapter 9. You can copy the ListBoxTextWriter.cs file from the Chapter09 folder to the Chapter11 folder. From the Solution Explorer, right-click the LeadGenerator project and choose Add ➤ Existing Item and select this file. You will need to change the namespace from LibraryReservation to LeadGenerator.

Listing 11-3. Implementation of ListBoxTextWriter

```
using System;
using System.Text;
using System.IO;
using System.Windows.Controls;

namespace LeadGenerator
{
    public class ListBoxTextWriter : TextWriter
    {
        const string textClosed = "This TextWriter must be opened before use";

        private Encoding _encoding;
        private bool _isOpen = false;
        private ListBox _listBox;

        public ListBoxTextWriter()
        {
            // Get the static list box
            _listBox = ApplicationInterface._app.GetEventListBox();
            if (_listBox != null)
                _isOpen = true;
        }

        public ListBoxTextWriter(ListBox listBox)
        {
            this._listBox = listBox;
            this._isOpen = true;
        }

        public override Encoding Encoding
        {
            get
            {
                if (_encoding == null)
                {
                    _encoding = new UnicodeEncoding(false, false);
                }
                return _encoding;
            }
        }
    }
```

```
public override void Close()
{
    this.Dispose(true);
}

protected override void Dispose(bool disposing)
{
    this._isOpen = false;
    base.Dispose(disposing);
}

public override void Write(char value)
{
    if (!this._isOpen)
        throw new ApplicationException(textClosed); ;

    this._listBox.Dispatcher.BeginInvoke
        (new Action(() => this._listBox.Items.Add(value.ToString())));
}

public override void Write(string value)
{
    if (!this._isOpen)
        throw new ApplicationException(textClosed); ;

    if (value != null)
        this._listBox.Dispatcher.BeginInvoke
            (new Action(() => this._listBox.Items.Add(value)));
}

public override void Write(char[] buffer, int index, int count)
{
    String toAdd = "";

    if (!this._isOpen)
        throw new ApplicationException(textClosed); ;

    if (buffer == null || index < 0 || count < 0)
        throw new ArgumentOutOfRangeException("buffer");

    if ((buffer.Length - index) < count)
        throw new ArgumentException("The buffer is too small");

    for (int i = 0; i < count; i++)
        toAdd += buffer[i];

    this._listBox.Dispatcher.BeginInvoke
        (new Action(() => this._listBox.Items.Add(toAdd)));
}
}
}
```

Setting Up the Database

If you haven't already, download the SQL.zip file, which can be found on this book's page at http://www.apress.com. Unzip it to your local disk. This file contains a folder for each chapter with the files you'll need to configure the database.

Creating a Database

Create a database named Chapter11. You can use whatever SQL tools you're familiar with or you can use Visual Studio. To use Visual Studio, in the Server Explorer, right-click Data Connections and choose Create New SQL Server Database. The dialog shown in Figure 11-3 will display.

Figure 11-3. *Creating a new database*

Enter **localhost** for the server name (or whatever is appropriate for your environment) and **Chapter11** for the database name, and then click OK.

Installing the Schema

Once you have a database created, you'll need to create the tables and stored procedures used by the persistence service. To do this, you'll execute the scripts provided in the SQL.zip file. From the File menu, choose Open ➤ File as shown in Figure 11-4.

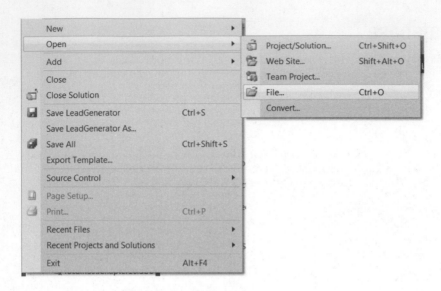

Figure 11-4. Opening the database script

Navigate to the Chapter11Data\Create Scripts folder where you have downloaded and unzipped the SQL.zip file and open the SqlWorkflowInstanceStoreSchema.sql file. Then connect to the database by right-clicking anywhere on this file and choosing Connection ➤ Connect as shown in Figure 11-5.

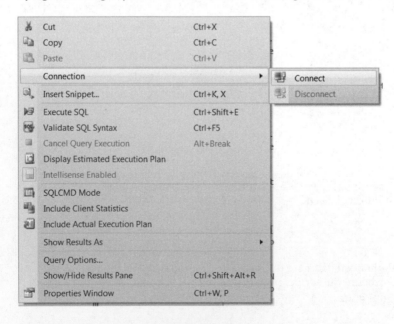

Figure 11-5. Connecting to the database

The dialog shown in Figure 11-6 will be displayed. Enter the appropriate information to connect to the database that you just created.

Figure 11-6. Entering your credentials

After you have connected, make sure you change the database to `Chapter11` using the dropdown near the top of the page (it will probably default to the `master` database, depending on your permissions). Finally, execute this script by right-clicking anywhere on the file and choosing Execute SQL as shown in Figure 11-7.

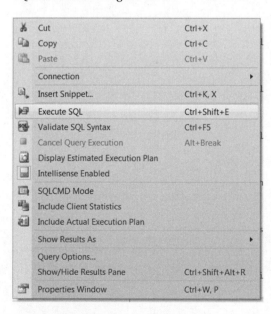

Figure 11-7. Executing the script

Repeat this process to run the SqlWorkflowInstanceStoreLogic.sql script.

■ **Caution** It's important that you run these scripts in this order. If you run the logic script first, it will fail because the tables don't exist yet.

In the same way, run the Lead.sql script to create the Lead table, which is used by the application.

Creating the LINQ to SQL Classes

LINQ to SQL

To access the Lead table, you'll use LINQ to SQL, which is a relatively new technology that was introduced by Microsoft with C# version 3.0. In fact, all the database work for the remainder of this book will use LINQ instead of the more traditional approach of datasets and stored procedures.

If this is a bit foreign to you, you might want to read *Pro LINQ in C# 2008*, by Joseph C. Rattz, Jr. This book does an excellent job of introducing the world of LINQ and provides a thorough review of the technology. This is not necessary, however, and I'll explain what you'll need to know to work through these projects. I think you'll find it very easy to use.

Now you'll need to provide the LINQ classes that will allow you to access this table. Right-click the LeadGenerator project and choose Add ➤ New Item. In the Add New Item dialog (see Figure 11-8), select the LINQ to SQL Classes template, which can be found in the Data category. Enter **LeadData.dbml** for the file name and click Add.

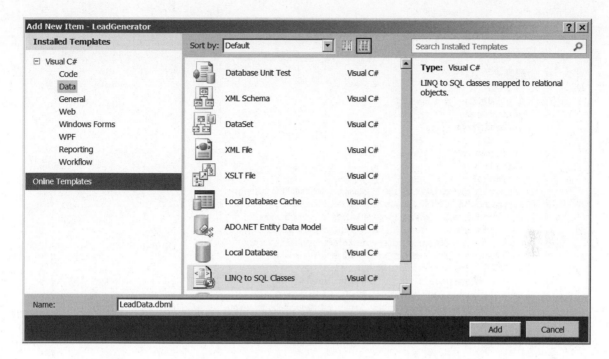

Figure 11-8. Adding the LINQ to SQL classes

The Object Relational Designer (O/R Designer) will display. In the Server Explorer, expand the localhost.Chapter11.dbo data connection and then expand the Tables node. This will list the existing tables in the Chapter11 database. In addition to the Lead table, there are several tables used by the standard SQLWorkflowInstanceStore, which will be explained later in this chapter. You can expand the Lead table to see the columns included (see Figure 11-9).

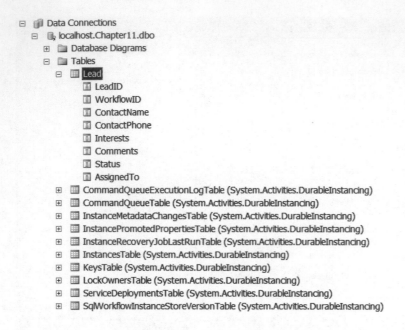

Figure 11-9. Enumerating the tables in the Chapter11 database

Drag the Lead table to the O/R Designer. The designer should look like the one shown in Figure 11-10.

Figure 11-10. Object Relational Designer with the Lead table included

The O/R Designer generates a number of files. You can see them listed in the Solution Explorer (see Figure 11-11).

Figure 11-11. *Files generated by the O/R Designer*

In particular, you might want to look at the LeadData.designer.cs class, which contains a class derived from DataContext called LeadDataDataContext. You will use this class to connect to the database and also to commit your updates. This file also contains a class for each table with the same name as the table. For this project, there is only one class, named Lead. This class contains members for each of the columns in the Lead table. If you look at the code, you'll find that there is a lot of extra "stuff" that LINQ uses to map the class to the table and to provide extensions for you to modify the LINQ functionality. You will not need to modify this file; the default implementation works just fine for our purposes.

Designing the Workflow

You will need two custom activities for this workflow that are similar to the activities you implemented in Chapter 9. In the Solution Explorer, right-click the LeadGenerator project; choose Add ➤ New Folder; and enter the folder name as **Activities**.

Custom CreateLead Activity

The CreateLead activity will take several input arguments and create a Lead class, which is returned as an output argument. This is just like you did with the CreateReservation or CreateResponse activities in Chapter 8. CreateLead, however, will also insert a record into the Lead table. The connection string that it will use will be passed in as another input argument.

From the Solution Explorer, right-click the Activities folder and choose Add ➤ New Item. Select the Code Activity template from the Workflow category. Enter the name as **CreateLead.cs**. The implementation is shown in Listing 11-4.

Listing 11-4. Implementation of the CreateLead Activity

```
using System;
using System.Activities;

namespace LeadGenerator
{
    /***************************************************/
    // This custom activity creates a Lead class using
    // the input parameters (ContactName, ContactPhone,
    // Interests and Notes).  A Lead record is inserted
    // into the database and then this is returned in
    // the Lead output parameter.
    /***************************************************/
    public sealed class CreateLead : CodeActivity
    {
        public InArgument<string> ContactName { get; set; }
        public InArgument<string> ContactPhone { get; set; }
        public InArgument<string> Interests { get; set; }
        public InArgument<string> Notes { get; set; }
        public InArgument<string> ConnectionString { get; set; }
        public OutArgument<Lead> Lead { get; set; }

        protected override void Execute(CodeActivityContext context)
        {
            // Create a Lead class and populate it with the input arguments
            Lead l = new Lead();
            l.ContactName = ContactName.Get(context);
            l.ContactPhone = ContactPhone.Get(context);
            l.Interests = Interests.Get(context);
            l.Comments = Notes.Get(context);
            l.WorkflowID = context.WorkflowInstanceId;
            l.Status = "Open";

            // Insert a record into the Lead table
            LeadDataDataContext dc =
                new LeadDataDataContext(ConnectionString.Get(context));
            dc.Leads.InsertOnSubmit(l);
            dc.SubmitChanges();

            // Store the request in the OutArgument
            Lead.Set(context, l);
        }
    }
}
```

The Execute() method creates a Lead class and sets its properties using the input arguments. It then creates a LeadDataDataContext class, which was generated by the O/R Designer. The connection string is passed in to the constructor. The instance of the Lead class is provided to the data context class using the InsertOnSubmit() method. Finally, the SubmitChanges() method is called, which will cause the record to be inserted into the database.

Custom WaitForInput Activity

The WaitForInput activity is identical to the one you implemented in Chapter 9. You can copy this file from the Chapter09\LibraryReservation folder to the Chapter11\LeadGenerator\Activities folder. Then from the Solution Explorer, right-click the Activities folder and choose Add, Existing Item. Navigate to the Activities folder and select the WaitForInput.cs file. You will need to change the namespace from LibraryReservation to LeadGenerator. The complete implementation is shown in Listing 11-5.

Listing 11-5. *Implementation of the WaitForInput Activity*

```
using System;
using System.Activities;

namespace LeadGenerator
{
    public sealed class WaitForInput<T> : NativeActivity<T>
    {
        public WaitForInput()
            : base()
        {
        }

        public string BookmarkName { get; set; }
        public OutArgument<T> Input { get; set; }

        protected override void Execute(ActivityExecutionContext context)
        {
            context.CreateNamedBookmark(BookmarkName,
                new BookmarkCallback(this.Continue));
        }

        void Continue(ActivityExecutionContext context, Bookmark bookmark,
            object obj)
        {
            Input.Set(context, (T)obj);
        }

        protected override bool CanInduceIdle { get { return true; } }
    }
}
```

Defining the Workflow Activities

Now you're ready to define the actual workflow. From the Solution Explorer, right-click the LeadGenerator project and choose Add ➤ Class. For the class name, enter **LeadGeneratorWF.cs**. The implementation is shown in Listing 11-6.

Listing 11-6. Implementation of LeadGeneratorWF.cs

```
using System;
using System.Activities;
using System.Activities.Statements;
using System.IO;

namespace LeadGenerator
{
    /****************************************************/
    // This file contains the definition of the EnterLead
    // workflow
    /****************************************************/
    public sealed class EnterLead : Activity
    {
        // Define the input and output arguments
        public InArgument<string> ContactName { get; set; }
        public InArgument<string> ContactPhone { get; set; }
        public InArgument<string> Interests { get; set; }
        public InArgument<string> Notes { get; set; }
        public InArgument<string> ConnectionString { get; set; }
        public InArgument<int> Rating { get; set; }
        public InArgument<TextWriter> Writer { get; set; }

        public EnterLead()
        {
            // Define the variables used by this workflow
            Variable<Lead> lead = new Variable<Lead> { Name = "lead" };

            // Define the SendRequest workflow
            this.Implementation = () => new Sequence
            {
                DisplayName = "EnterLead",
                Variables = { lead },
                Activities =
                {
                    new CreateLead
                    {
                        ContactName = new InArgument<string>
                            (env => ContactName.Get(env)),
                        ContactPhone = new InArgument<string>
                            (env => ContactPhone.Get(env)),
                        Interests = new InArgument<string>
                            (env => Interests.Get(env)),
                        Notes = new InArgument<string>(env => Notes.Get(env)),
                        ConnectionString = new InArgument<string>
                            (env => ConnectionString.Get(env)),
                        Lead = new OutArgument<Lead>(env => lead.Get(env)),
                    },
                    new WriteLine
                    {
```

```
                    Text = new InArgument<string>
                        (env => "Lead received [" + Rating.Get(env).ToString()
                        + "]; waiting for assignment"),
                    TextWriter = new InArgument<TextWriter>
                        (env => Writer.Get(env))
                },
                new InvokeMethod
                {
                    TargetType = typeof(ApplicationInterface),
                    MethodName = "NewLead",
                    Parameters =
                    {
                        new InArgument<Lead>(env => lead.Get(env))
                    }
                },
                new WaitForInput<Lead>
                {
                    BookmarkName = "GetAssignment",
                    Input = new OutArgument<Lead>(env => lead.Get(env))
                },
                new WriteLine
                {
                    Text = new InArgument<string>
                        (env => "Lead assigned [" + Rating.Get(env).ToString()
                        + "] to " + lead.Get(env).AssignedTo),
                    TextWriter = new InArgument<TextWriter>
                        (env => Writer.Get(env))
                }
            }
        };
    }
}
}
```

The EnterLead workflow takes a number of input arguments that define the sales lead including contact info, interests, and notes. It also includes a rating that is a subjective evaluation of the potential revenue from this lead. The first activity, CreateLead, takes these arguments and creates a Lead class. It also inserts a record into the database. The WriteLine activity acknowledges that the Lead has been created. The InvokeMethod activity uses the static ApplicationInterface class to call into the application. It calls the NewLead() method, which will add an item to the ListView control. The WaitForInput activity creates a bookmark and waits for the application to resume the workflow. The final WriteLine activity acknowledges that the lead has been assigned to an agent.

Implementing the Application

Now you'll implement the application. This will be very similar to the application you created in Chapter 9.

Application Configuration File

Visual Studio automatically created an app.config file that contains the connection string. Open the app.config file and change the Name attribute to **LeadGenerator**. The file should look like this (the modified line is shown in bold):

```xml
<?xml version="1.0" encoding="utf-8" ?>
<configuration>
  <configSections>
  </configSections>
  <connectionStrings>
    <add name="LeadGenerator"
      connectionString=
        "Data Source=localhost;Initial Catalog=Chapter11;Integrated Security=True"
        providerName="System.Data.SqlClient" />
  </connectionStrings>
</configuration>
```

Open the AddLead.xaml.cs file and add the following class member, which will be used to hold the connection string:

```
private string _connectionString = "";
```

Add the following method to handle the Loaded event. This code reads the app.config file and obtains the connection string:

```
private void Window_Loaded(object sender, RoutedEventArgs e)
{
    // Open the config file and get the connection string
    Configuration config =
        ConfigurationManager.OpenExeConfiguration
            (ConfigurationUserLevel.None);
    ConnectionStringsSection css =
        (ConnectionStringsSection)config.GetSection("connectionStrings");
    _connectionString =
        css.ConnectionStrings["LeadGenerator"].ConnectionString;
}
```

Configuring the Persistence Provider Factory

In the AddLead.xaml.cs file, add the following class member. This is a reference to the InstanceStore class that will be used to persist and load the workflow instances:

```
private InstanceStore _instanceStore;
```

Then add the following code to the Loaded event handler; it configures the store:

```
_instanceStore = new SqlWorkflowInstanceStore(_connectionString);
InstanceView view = _instanceStore.Execute
    (_instanceStore.CreateInstanceHandle(),
```

```
    new CreateWorkflowOwnerCommand(),
    TimeSpan.FromSeconds(30));
_instanceStore.DefaultInstanceOwner = view.InstanceOwner;
```

InstanceStore is an abstract class from which all persistence providers are derived. In this project, you will use the SqlWorkflowInstanceStore class, which uses a SQL Server database. An instance of the concrete class (SqlWorkflowInstanceStore) is created, passing the connection string in the constructor. The parameters to the Execute() method are a handle (provided by InstanceStore), a command, and a timeout value. It returns an InstanceView class, which is roughly analogous to a connection handle.

Creating Leads

To create a new lead, the user will fill in the fields on the form and then click the Add Lead button. Add a method to implement the event handler when the Add Lead button is clicked using the code shown in Listing 11-7.

Listing 11-7. *Implementation of the btnAddLead_Click Event Handler*

```
private void btnAddLead_Click(object sender, RoutedEventArgs e)
{
    // Setup a dictionary object for passing parameters
    Dictionary<string, object> parameters =
        new Dictionary<string, object>();
    parameters.Add("ContactName", txtName.Text);
    parameters.Add("ContactPhone", txtPhone.Text);
    parameters.Add("Interests", txtInterest.Text);
    parameters.Add("Notes", txtNotes.Text);
    parameters.Add("ConnectionString", _connectionString);
    parameters.Add("Rating", int.Parse(txtRating.Text));
    parameters.Add("Writer", new ListBoxTextWriter(lstEvents));

    WorkflowApplication i = new WorkflowApplication
        (new EnterLead(), parameters);

    // Setup persistence
    i.InstanceStore = _instanceStore;
    i.PersistableIdle = (waiea) => PersistableIdleAction.Unload;

    i.Run();
}
```

This code creates a Dictionary object and stores data in it for all the input arguments. It then creates a WorkflowInstance. The constructor takes two parameters:

- workflow definition—an instance of the EnterLead class

- Dictionary object containing the input arguments

The code then configures the workflow instance to be persisted. First, it sets the InstanceStore property using the reference created in the Loaded event handler. It then provides an event handler for the PersistableIdle event, which tells the instance to unload itself from memory. It is persisted to the database prior to being unloaded.

■ **Tip** The syntax for the PersistableIdle event handler might seem strange. In the next chapter, you will implement other event handlers, and I will explain this syntax. For now, just take it on faith that this is handling the PersistableIdle event.

Finally, the btnAddLead_Click() method calls the instance's Run() method, which starts the workflow asynchronously. The workflow uses the InvokeMethod activity to tell the application about the lead that has just been created. It does this by calling the NewLead() method in the static ApplicationInterface class. Now you will implement this. Open the ApplicationInterface.cs file and add the following method:

```
public static void NewLead(Lead l)
{
    if (_app != null)
        _app.AddNewLead(l);
}
```

This calls the AddNewLead() method in the application. Open the AddLead.xaml.cs file and add the AddNewLead() method as follows:

```
public void AddNewLead(Lead l)
{
    this.lstLeads.Dispatcher.BeginInvoke
        (new Action(() => this.lstLeads.Items.Add(l)));
}
```

The code simply adds this Lead to the lstLeads ListView control. It uses the Dispatcher object to invoke this method using the window's thread.

Assigning Leads

The ListView control displays all the leads that have been entered. The user can click any one of these leads, and more information is displayed about that lead. Specifically, the notes are displayed along with the agent that it has been assigned to. If not yet assigned, a text box and button are displayed to allow the user to assign the lead to an agent.

To allow this dynamic display, add the method shown in Listing 11-8. It implements the SelectionChanged event handler.

Listing 11-8. Implementation of the SelectionChanged event

```
private void lstLeads_SelectionChanged(object sender, RoutedEventArgs e)
{
```

```
if (lstLeads.SelectedIndex >= 0)
{
    Lead l = (Lead)lstLeads.Items[lstLeads.SelectedIndex];
    lblSelectedNotes.Content = l.Comments;
    lblSelectedNotes.Visibility = Visibility.Visible;
    if (l.Status == "Open")
    {
        lblAgent.Visibility = Visibility.Visible;
        txtAgent.Visibility = Visibility.Visible;
        btnAssign.Visibility = Visibility.Visible;
    }
    else
    {
        lblAgent.Visibility = Visibility.Hidden;
        txtAgent.Visibility = Visibility.Hidden;
        btnAssign.Visibility = Visibility.Hidden;
    }
}
else
{
    lblSelectedNotes.Content = "";
    lblSelectedNotes.Visibility = Visibility.Hidden;
    lblAgent.Visibility = Visibility.Hidden;
    txtAgent.Visibility = Visibility.Hidden;
    btnAssign.Visibility = Visibility.Hidden;
}
}
```

To enable a user to assign a lead to a sales agent, add an event handler for the Assign Agent button, as shown in Listing 11-9.

Listing 11-9. *Implementation of the btnAssign_Click event Handler*

```
private void btnAssign_Click(object sender, RoutedEventArgs e)
{
    if (lstLeads.SelectedIndex >= 0)
    {
        Lead l = (Lead)lstLeads.Items[lstLeads.SelectedIndex];
        Guid id = l.WorkflowID;

        LeadDataDataContext dc = new LeadDataDataContext(_connectionString);
        dc.Refresh(RefreshMode.OverwriteCurrentValues, dc.Leads);
        l = dc.Leads.SingleOrDefault<Lead>(x => x.WorkflowID == id);
        if (l != null)
        {
            l.AssignedTo = txtAgent.Text;
            l.Status = "Assigned";
            dc.SubmitChanges();
```

```
        // Clear the input
        txtAgent.Text = "";
    }

    // Update the grid
    lstLeads.Items[lstLeads.SelectedIndex] = l;
    lstLeads.Items.Refresh();

    WorkflowApplication i = new WorkflowApplication(new EnterLead());
    i.InstanceStore = _instanceStore;
    i.PersistableIdle = (waiea) => PersistableIdleAction.Unload;
    i.Load(id);

    try
    {
        i.ResumeBookmark("GetAssignment", l);
    }
    catch (Exception e2)
    {
        AddEvent(e2.Message);
    }
    }
}
```

This code gets the WorkflowID from the selected Lead object. It uses the LINQ classes to retrieve this Lead from the database. It updates the AssignedTo property, changes the Status to Assigned, and writes the updates to the database. It then refreshes the lstLeads control so it will display the updated information.

Finally, it creates a workflow instance. It is then configured for persistence, as in the btnAddLead_Click() method. The Load() method retrieves the workflow from the database. The workflow is then resumed using the GetAssignment bookmark.

Loading Existing Leads

Finally, add the following method to retrieve any existing leads and add them to the ListView control:

```
private void LoadExistingLeads()
{
    LeadDataDataContext dc = new LeadDataDataContext(_connectionString);
    dc.Refresh(RefreshMode.OverwriteCurrentValues, dc.Leads);
    IEnumerable<Lead> q = dc.Leads
        .Where<Lead>(x => x.Status == "Open" || x.Status == "Assigned");
    foreach (Lead l in q)
    {
        AddNewLead(l);
    }
}
```

This code uses LINQ to query the database for all leads in the Open or Assigned status. For each Lead returned, the AddNewLead() method is called to add the Lead to the lstLeads control. Add the following code to the Loaded event (it calls the LoadExistingLeads() method when the application is started):

```
LoadExistingLeads();
```

The complete implementation of AddLead.xaml.cs is shown in Listing 11-10.

Listing 11-10. *Complete Implementation of AddLead.xaml.cs*

```
using System;
using System.Collections.Generic;
using System.Linq;
using System.Text;
using System.Windows;
using System.Windows.Controls;
using System.Windows.Data;
using System.Windows.Documents;
using System.Windows.Input;
using System.Windows.Media;
using System.Windows.Media.Imaging;
using System.Windows.Navigation;
using System.Windows.Shapes;

using System.Activities;
using System.Activities.DurableInstancing;
using System.Runtime.Persistence;
using System.Data.Linq;
using System.Configuration;

namespace LeadGenerator
{
    /// <summary>
    /// Interaction logic for AddLead.xaml
    /// </summary>
    public partial class AddLead : Window
    {
        private string _connectionString = "";
        private InstanceStore _instanceStore;

        public AddLead()
        {
            InitializeComponent();

            ApplicationInterface._app = this;
        }

        // Add a line of text to the Event Log
        private void AddEvent(string szText)
        {
```

```
        lstEvents.Items.Add(szText);
    }

    public ListBox GetEventListBox()
    {
        return this.lstEvents;
    }

    private void Window_Loaded(object sender, RoutedEventArgs e)
    {
        // Open the config file and get the connection string
        Configuration config =
            ConfigurationManager.OpenExeConfiguration
                (ConfigurationUserLevel.None);
        ConnectionStringsSection css =
            (ConnectionStringsSection)config.GetSection("connectionStrings");
        _connectionString =
            css.ConnectionStrings["LeadGenerator"].ConnectionString;

        _instanceStore = new SqlWorkflowInstanceStore(_connectionString);
        InstanceView view = _instanceStore.Execute
            (_instanceStore.CreateInstanceHandle(),
            new CreateWorkflowOwnerCommand(),
            TimeSpan.FromSeconds(30));
        _instanceStore.DefaultInstanceOwner = view.InstanceOwner;

        LoadExistingLeads();
    }

    private void btnAddLead_Click(object sender, RoutedEventArgs e)
    {
        // Setup a dictionary object for passing parameters
        Dictionary<string, object> parameters =
            new Dictionary<string, object>();
        parameters.Add("ContactName", txtName.Text);
        parameters.Add("ContactPhone", txtPhone.Text);
        parameters.Add("Interests", txtInterest.Text);
        parameters.Add("Notes", txtNotes.Text);
        parameters.Add("ConnectionString", _connectionString);
        parameters.Add("Rating", int.Parse(txtRating.Text));

        WorkflowApplication i = new WorkflowApplication
            (new EnterLead(), parameters);

        // Setup persistence
        i.InstanceStore = _instanceStore;
        i.PersistableIdle = (waiea) => PersistableIdleAction.Unload;

        i.Run();
    }
```

```csharp
public void AddNewLead(Lead l)
{
    this.lstLeads.Dispatcher.BeginInvoke
        (new Action(() => this.lstLeads.Items.Add(l)));
}

private void lstLeads_SelectionChanged(object sender, RoutedEventArgs e)
{
    if (lstLeads.SelectedIndex >= 0)
    {
        Lead l = (Lead)lstLeads.Items[lstLeads.SelectedIndex];
        lblSelectedNotes.Content = l.Comments;
        lblSelectedNotes.Visibility = Visibility.Visible;
        if (l.Status == "Open")
        {
            lblAgent.Visibility = Visibility.Visible;
            txtAgent.Visibility = Visibility.Visible;
            btnAssign.Visibility = Visibility.Visible;
        }
        else
        {
            lblAgent.Visibility = Visibility.Hidden;
            txtAgent.Visibility = Visibility.Hidden;
            btnAssign.Visibility = Visibility.Hidden;
        }
    }
    else
    {
        lblSelectedNotes.Content = "";
        lblSelectedNotes.Visibility = Visibility.Hidden;
        lblAgent.Visibility = Visibility.Hidden;
        txtAgent.Visibility = Visibility.Hidden;
        btnAssign.Visibility = Visibility.Hidden;
    }
}

private void btnAssign_Click(object sender, RoutedEventArgs e)
{
    if (lstLeads.SelectedIndex >= 0)
    {
        Lead l = (Lead)lstLeads.Items[lstLeads.SelectedIndex];
        Guid id = l.WorkflowID;

        LeadDataDataContext dc = new LeadDataDataContext(_connectionString);
        dc.Refresh(RefreshMode.OverwriteCurrentValues, dc.Leads);
        l = dc.Leads.SingleOrDefault<Lead>(x => x.WorkflowID == id);
        if (l != null)
        {
            l.AssignedTo = txtAgent.Text;
            l.Status = "Assigned";
            dc.SubmitChanges();
```

```
                // Clear the input
                txtAgent.Text = "";
            }

            // Update the grid
            lstLeads.Items[lstLeads.SelectedIndex] = l;
            lstLeads.Items.Refresh();

            WorkflowApplication i = new WorkflowApplication(new EnterLead());
            i.InstanceStore = _instanceStore;
            i.PersistableIdle = (waiea) => PersistableIdleAction.Unload;
            i.Load(id);

            try
            {
                i.ResumeBookmark("GetAssignment", l);
            }
            catch (Exception e2)
            {
                AddEvent(e2.Message);
            }
        }
    }

    private void LoadExistingLeads()
    {
        LeadDataDataContext dc = new LeadDataDataContext(_connectionString);
        dc.Refresh(RefreshMode.OverwriteCurrentValues, dc.Leads);
        IEnumerable<Lead> q = dc.Leads
            .Where<Lead>(x => x.Status == "Open" || x.Status == "Assigned");
        foreach (Lead l in q)
        {
            AddNewLead(l);
        }
    }
}
}
```

Running the Application

Press F5 to run the application. Enter a few leads (but do not assign them yet). Select one of the leads so its details will be displayed. The form should look similar to the one shown in Figure 11-12.

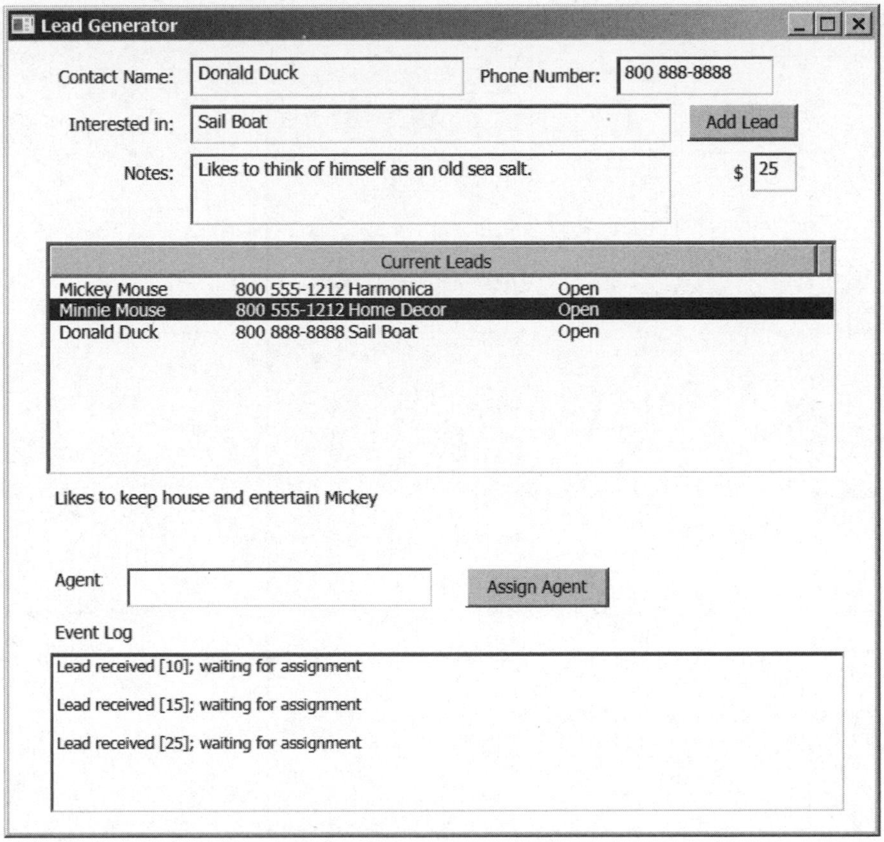

Figure 11-12. *Application with unassigned leads*

Close the application and press F5 to restart it. The leads should be redisplayed on the form. Select one of the leads, enter an agent's name, and click the Assign Agent button. The window should look like the one shown in Figure 11-13.

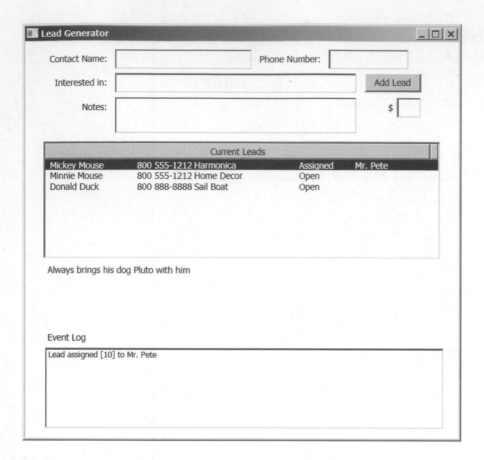

Figure 11-13. *Restarted application with some leads assigned*

Digging a Bit Deeper

So now you've implemented SQL persistence. Let's look at how this works. The instance state information is stored in the InstancesTable. Open the contents of this table using the Server Explorer. It should be similar to the contents shown in Figure 11-14.

	Id	CreationTime	LastUpdated	BlockingBookmarks	ExecutionStatus
	cbe761ca-9992-4...	11/15/2009 ...	11/15/2009 ...	[GetAssignment: WaitForInput<Lead>]	Idle
	30b35ad4-52fa-4...	11/15/2009 ...	11/15/2009 ...	[GetAssignment: WaitForInput<Lead>]	Idle
▶*	*NULL*	*NULL*	*NULL*	*NULL*	*NULL*

Figure 11-14. *Contents of the InstanceData table*

Notice that there are only two records in the table. When an agent (Mr. Pete) was assigned to Mickey Mouse, the workflow instance completed and was removed from this table. The InstancesTable only contains records for active workflow instances.

Persisting Arguments and Variables

When the workflow instance is persisted, all the state information about what activities have been executed is stored. In addition, all the arguments and variables that you have defined in your workflow are persisted as well. To demonstrate this, I purposely did not include the rating information in the Lead table. You can check the Lead table and verify that this column is not there. However, when the workflow is loaded, the rating information has been restored. When the lead is assigned to an agent, the WriteLine activity includes the rating in the output string, so you can verify that it is the same as you originally entered.

Workflow Foundation Overview (Tear Out)

This section provides a brief overview of the Workflow Foundation (WF). It is designed to give you the big picture in a concise form. This material is covered throughout the book in more detail.

Workflow Architecture

As shown in Figure TO-1, the `WorkflowApplication` class is the core of the workflow architecture and represents a single workflow instance. Separate `WorkflowApplication` objects are created for each instance. For example, in a workflow that processes work requests, a new instance is needed for each request. Each request (instance) works its way through the defined activities independently of other instances.

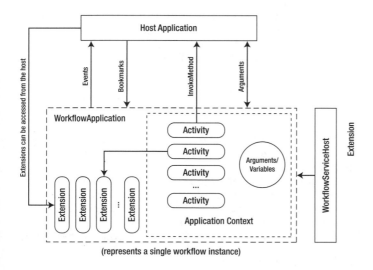

Figure TO-1. Workflow architecture

Activities

A `WorkflowApplication` executes a collection of activities. Much of workflow development revolves around defining the activities that are to be executed. WF provides a fairly large set of built-in activities, and custom activities can be easily added. WF provides a tool called workflow designer that allows you to graphically design the activities of your workflow.

These activities execute within an application context, which maintains the state for that instance. A key feature of WF 4.0 is the explicit definition of arguments and variables. Arguments are used just like variables, except they can be passed into and out of the workflow. When a workflow is persisted to a durable store such as a database, the current value of the arguments and variables is also saved. The activities are stateless; they access the arguments and variables through the application context.

Activities can be executed conditionally based on rules that you define, so each instance might not necessarily take the same path though those activities. Although there might be multiple instances executing simultaneously, they do not interact with each other. From a workflow perspective, each instance is unaware that other instances exist. There is no mechanism within the workflow to communicate with other instances.

Extensions

Although activities are executed in some defined progression, extensions provide services to all the activities. Extensions can be accessed by both the host and the activities. Extensions are generally created and configured by the host and added to the `WorkflowApplication`. The activities can then access the configured extensions as appropriate.

A special extension, called `InstanceStore`, is used to persist the current state of the workflow and to retrieve it when needed. This feature, combined with the statelessness of the activities, makes WF scale extremely well. A `WorkflowApplication` is created to process a workflow instance, and then the state is persisted and the `WorkflowApplication` disposed of. Only active instances consume system resources.

Another special extension is used for tracking workflow activity. Tracking extensions register with the application context to receive trackable events. Tracking extensions perform different actions with these events based on the specific extension.

You can also write your own custom extensions. You should use extensions when the actions are needed by multiple activities.

Host

The `WorkflowApplication` must be executed within a host application. You can host the runtime in your own custom application. Many of the sample solutions in this book use a console application or a Windows Presentation Foundation (WPF) application to start the `WorkflowApplication`. The host creates the `WorkflowApplication`, creates and configures the extensions, and then starts the workflow.

In some cases, the workflow must be started in response to an event, such as receiving a request. This is the case, for example, in web services. In this situation, you'll use a `WorkflowServiceHost`, which listens for WCF messages and launches a new `WorkflowApplication` to process it. The `WorkflowServiceHost` must be set up initially so it knows what extensions to create and how to configure them.

The host can communicate with the workflow in several ways:

- Arguments can be passed in to the workflow and returned back to the host when the workflow completes.

- The host can handle events that are generated by the workflow, such as the Idle and Completed events.

- The host can access the extensions, which provides a convenient method for passing data to all activities (such as a connection string).

- The workflow can use the InvokeMethod activity to call methods in the host application.

- The host application can resume a workflow, passing data through the bookmark.

Topical Reference

This book demonstrates how to use WF by working through a series of sample projects; starting with fairly simple solutions and gradually increasing complexity. Along the way, specific topics are introduced and explained. The following provides a topical outline of the WF concepts presented in this book. If you are looking for information on a specific topic, it will show you the chapters to start with. The index at the back of the book will give a more thorough listing of every place the topic is mentioned.

Built-in Activities

Topic   Chapter(s)

AddToCollection   18
Assign   1
ClearCollection   18
CompensableActivity   17
Compensate   17
Confirm   17
CorrelationScope   8
Delay   1
DoWhile   1
ExistsInCollection   18
Expressions   4
Flowchart   3
FlowDecision   3
FlowStep   3
FlowSwitch   3
ForEach<T>   5
If   1
Interop   19
InvokeMethod   7
Parallel   3, 17
ParallelForEach<T>   5
Persist   16

Pick   10
PolicyActivity (3.0)   20
Receive   8
ReceiveReply   8
RemoveFromCollection   18
Rethrow   17
Send   8
SendReply   8
Sequence   1
Switch   4
Throw   6
TransactionScope   14
TryCatch   6, 17
While   1
WriteLine   1

Techniques

Topic   Chapter(s)

Accessing Extensions from an Activity   12
Accessing Extensions from the Host   12

Tools

CHAPTER 12

■ ■ ■

Extensions

In the previous chapter, you used a workflow extension to persist the workflow instance to a database. In this chapter, I'll explain what extensions are and how to use them. You will also develop some custom extensions.

Setting Up the Solution

You will start with the project that you developed in Chapter 11 and then add some new features. Start by creating a blank solution, as shown in Figure 12-1. For the solution name, enter **Chapter12**.

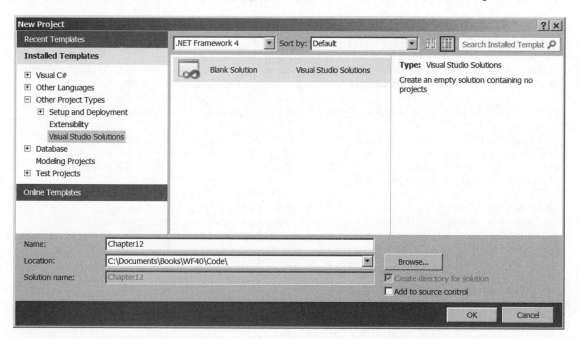

Figure 12-1. Creating a blank solution

Copy Solution from Chapter 11

From Windows Explorer, copy the LeadGenerator folder from the Chapter11 folder to the Chapter12 folder. Back in Visual Studio, from the Solution Explorer, right-click the Chapter12 solution and choose Add ➤ Existing Project. Select the LeadGenerator project that you just copied to the Chapter12 folder.

Setting Up the Database

Create a Chapter12 database and run the following scripts to initialize the database schema:

- SqlWorkflowInstanceStoreSchema.sql
- SqlWorkflowInstanceStoreLogic.sql
- Lead.sql

■ **Tip** Refer to Chapter 11 if you have questions about setting up the database. There are more detailed instructions in Chapter 11, and the steps are identical in both projects.

Open the app.config file and change the connectionString attribute to use the Chapter12 database.

Implementing SetupInstance

Generally, in a client application such as this one, the application that hosts the workflow is responsible for creating and starting the WorkflowApplication class. Before the instance is started, the extensions (such as the instance store) need to be configured, and the event handlers are added. When the workflow becomes idle, the state information is persisted, and the instance of the WorkflowApplication class is destroyed.

When the workflow is reloaded, a new instance of the WorkflowApplication class must be created and configured all over again. Notice that the PersistableIdle event handler was added in two places: when the workflow is first started in the btnAddLead_Click event handler and when the workflow is reloaded in the btnAssign_Click event handler.

Because you will be adding more extensions and event handlers, it will simplify development to put this code into a method that can be called from both places. Then, as you add more extensions and event handlers, you need to make the change in only one place. Add the following method to the AddLead.xaml.cs file:

```
private void SetupInstance(WorkflowApplication i)
{
    // Setup the instance store
    i.InstanceStore = _instanceStore;

    // Setup the PersistableIdle event handler
    i.PersistableIdle = (waiea) => PersistableIdleAction.Unload;
}
```

In the btnAddLead_Click() method, replace the code that adds the PersistableIdle event handler with a call to the new SetupInstance() method, as shown in the following code snippet (the modified line is shown in bold):

```
WorkflowApplication i = new WorkflowApplication
    (new EnterLead(), parameters);

SetupInstance(i);

i.Run();
```

Finally, in the btnAssign_Click() method, replace the PersistableIdle event handler code as shown in this code snippet:

```
// Reload the workflow instance
WorkflowApplication i = new WorkflowApplication(new EnterLead());

SetupInstance(i);
i.Load(id);
```

Running the Application

At this point, it is good practice to run the application to make sure that the database is set up correctly and the application is running properly. It should work just like the solution from the previous chapter.

Extensions

Extensions allow you to add configurable behavior to a workflow solution. The activities that you include in your workflow define the steps that are performed, while the extensions provide the operating environment that these activities are executed in. In our solution, for example, the persistence extension is not aware of what activities are executed; the extension however, provides the ability to persist those activities (whatever they might be) to a durable store.

There are two key aspects of extensions that make then extremely useful. First, as was inferred earlier, they are configurable. For example, the persistence provider that was used (SqlWorkflowInstanceStore) was designed to use a SQL Server database. Without changing the application or the workflow definition, it could be replaced with a custom extension that uses an Oracle database, or perhaps an XML file, or whatever is appropriate for the environment.

The second aspect of extensions is that they can be accessed both from the application as well as the workflow activities. This provides a convenient tool for sharing information between the application and the workflow, as you'll see shortly.

Implementing a Simple Extension

In the Solution Explorer, right-click the LeadGenerator project and choose Add ➤ New Folder. Enter the folder name as **Extensions**. You'll be adding your custom extensions here. The first extension will be used to store the connection string. Instead of passing the connection string as an input argument, any activity that needs the connection string can access it from this extension.

First, you'll define the extension. In the Solution Explorer, right-click the Extensions folder and choose Add ➤ Class. Enter the class name as **DBExtension.cs**. The implementation of this class is shown in Listing 12-1.

Listing 12-1. Implementation of the DBExtension Class

```
using System;

namespace LeadGenerator
{
    public class DBExtension
    {
        private string _connectionString = "";

        public DBExtension(string connectionString)
        {
            _connectionString = connectionString;
        }

        public string ConnectionString { get { return _connectionString; } }
    }
}
```

This class simply defines a private member that holds the connection string. The value of this string is passed in the class constructor. A public property is provided for accessing this string.

Configuring the Extension

Open the AddLead.xaml.cs file and add the following class member. This will store a reference to this custom extension:

```
private DBExtension _dbExtension;
```

Then add the following code to the Loaded event handler. This instantiates the DBExtension class, passing in the connection string:

```
// Create the DBExtension
_dbExtension = new DBExtension(_connectionString);
```

Finally, in the SetupInstance() method, add the following code to add this extension to the workflow instance:

```
// Setup the connection string
i.Extensions.Add(_dbExtension);
```

Using the Extension in an Activity

Open the CreateLead.cs file, which is in the Activities folder. Remove the input argument used to pass in the connection string. Add the following code to the Execute() method to get the new DBExtension:

```
// Get the connection string
DBExtension ext = context.GetExtension<DBExtension>();
if (ext == null)
    throw new InvalidProgramException("No connection string available");
```

Change the call to the LeadDataDataContext constructor to pass ext.ConnectionString instead of the connection string argument. The complete implementation of the CreateLead activity is shown in Listing 12-2.

Listing 12-2. *Implementation of the CreateLead Activity*

```
using System;
using System.Activities;

namespace LeadGenerator
{
    /*****************************************************/
    // This custom activity creates a Lead class using
    // the input parameters (ContactName, ContactPhone,
    // Interests and Notes).  A Lead record is inserted
    // into the database and then this is returned in
    // the Lead output parameter.
    /*****************************************************/
    public sealed class CreateLead : CodeActivity
    {
        public InArgument<string> ContactName { get; set; }
        public InArgument<string> ContactPhone { get; set; }
        public InArgument<string> Interests { get; set; }
        public InArgument<string> Notes { get; set; }
        public OutArgument<Lead> Lead { get; set; }

        protected override void Execute(CodeActivityContext context)
        {
            // Create a Lead class and populate it with the input arguments
            Lead l = new Lead();
            l.ContactName = ContactName.Get(context);
            l.ContactPhone = ContactPhone.Get(context);
            l.Interests = Interests.Get(context);
            l.Comments = Notes.Get(context);
            l.WorkflowID = context.WorkflowInstanceId;
            l.Status = "Open";

            // Get the connection string
            DBExtension ext = context.GetExtension<DBExtension>();
            if (ext == null)
```

```
        throw new InvalidProgramException("No connection string available");

    // Insert a record into the Lead table
    LeadDataDataContext dc = new LeadDataDataContext(ext.ConnectionString);
    dc.Leads.InsertOnSubmit(l);
    dc.SubmitChanges();

    // Store the request in the OutArgument
    Lead.Set(context, l);
    }
  }
}
```

Updating the Application

Now open the LeadGeneratorWF.cs class and remove the ConnectionString argument. You'll also need to delete the code that passes this to the CreateLead activity. In the code snippet shown in Listing 12-3, the lines to be deleted are in bold.

Listing 12-3. Code Snippet from EnterLead

```
public sealed class EnterLead : Activity
    {
        // Define the input and output arguments
        public InArgument<string> ContactName { get; set; }
        public InArgument<string> ContactPhone { get; set; }
        public InArgument<string> Interests { get; set; }
        public InArgument<string> Notes { get; set; }
        public InArgument<string> ConnectionString { get; set; }
        public InArgument<int> Rating { get; set; }

        public EnterLead()
        {
            // Define the variables used by this workflow
            Variable<Lead> lead = new Variable<Lead> { Name = "lead" };

            // Define the SendRequest workflow
            this.Body = () => new Sequence
            {
                DisplayName = "EnterLead",
                Variables = { lead },
                Activities =
                {
                    new CreateLead
                    {
                        ContactName = new InArgument<string>
                            (env => ContactName.Get(env)),
                        ContactPhone = new InArgument<string>
```

```
                          (env => ContactPhone.Get(env)),
                    Interests = new InArgument<string>
                          (env => Interests.Get(env)),
                    Notes = new InArgument<string>(env => Notes.Get(env)),
                    ConnectionString = new InArgument<string>
                          (env => ConnectionString.Get(env)),
                    Lead = new OutArgument<Lead>(env => lead.Get(env)),
                },
```

Finally, in the AddLead.xaml.cs file, in the btnAddLead_Click() method, remove the following line that adds the connection string to the Dictionary object:

```
parameters.Add("ConnectionString", _connectionString);
```

Run the application to make sure everything still works correctly. As you modify this application in subsequent chapters, you'll create other custom activities that will need to access the database. With this simple extension, you now have a convenient way of providing it to any activity that needs it.

Participating in Persistence

The next custom extension that you'll develop will be designed to participate in the persistence process. You'll create an extension called CommentExtension, which allows the workflow to log comments throughout the processing of the workflow.

Creating the Extension

In the Solution Explorer, right-click the Extensions folder and choose Add ➤ Class. Enter the class name as **CommentExtension.cs**. The implementation of this class is shown in Listing 12-4.

Listing 12-4. *Implementation of CommentExtension.cs*

```
using System;
using System.Activities.Persistence;
using System.Collections.Generic;
using System.Xml.Linq;

namespace LeadGenerator
{
    public class CommentExtension : PersistenceParticipant
    {
        private string _comments = "";

        public string Comments { get { return _comments; } }

        internal void AddComment(string s)
        {
            if (_comments.Length > 1)
                _comments += "\r\n";
```

```
            this._comments += s;
        }

        protected override void CollectValues
            (out IDictionary<XName, object> readWriteValues,
             out IDictionary<XName, object> writeOnlyValues)
        {
            readWriteValues = new Dictionary<XName, object>(1)
            {
                { "Comment", this._comments }
            };
            writeOnlyValues = null;
        }

        protected override void PublishValues
            (IDictionary<XName, object> readWriteValues)
        {
            object loadedData;
            if (readWriteValues.TryGetValue("Comment", out loadedData))
            {
                this._comments = (string)loadedData;
            }
        }
    }
}
```

This first part of this class is fairly straightforward. It has a single private class member to store the comment and a public method to return the comment. The `AddComment()` method is used to append the input string to the existing comment adding a carriage return/line feed to separate the comments.

PersistenceParticipant

The remaining methods are needed so this class can override the `PersistenceParticipant` methods. These methods will be called by the `WorkflowApplication` when it is being persisted or loaded.

When the instance is being persisted, the `CollectValues()` method is called to obtain a `Dictionary` object that contains the data that the extension wants persisted. When the workflow is loaded from the database, this object is then provided back to this extension in the `PublishValues()` method. In this class, the `CollectValues()` method returns a `Dictionary` with a single entry; the `_comments` string. When it is passed to the `PublishValues()` method, it is extracted from the `Dictionary` and stored in the `_comments` member.

AddComment Activity

You will now create a custom activity that will allow you to use the new `CommentExtension` from within the workflow. From the Solution Explorer, right-click the Activities folder and choose Add ➤ Class. Enter the class name as **AddComment.cs**. The implementation for this activity is shown in Listing 12-5.

Listing 12-5. *Implementation of the AddComment Activity*

```
using System.Activities;
using System.ComponentModel;

namespace LeadGenerator
{
    public sealed class AddComment : CodeActivity
    {
        public InArgument<string> Comment { get; set; }
        public OutArgument<string> Comments { get; set; }

        protected override void CacheMetadata(CodeActivityMetadata metadata)
        {
            base.CacheMetadata(metadata);
            metadata.AddDefaultExtensionProvider(() => new CommentExtension());
        }

        protected override void Execute(CodeActivityContext context)
        {
            CommentExtension ext = context.GetExtension<CommentExtension>();
            ext.AddComment(Comment.Get(context));

            Comments.Set(context, ext.Comments);
        }
    }

    public sealed class GetComments : CodeActivity
    {
        public OutArgument<string> Comments { get; set; }

        protected override void CacheMetadata(CodeActivityMetadata metadata)
        {
            base.CacheMetadata(metadata);
            metadata.AddDefaultExtensionProvider(() => new CommentExtension());
        }

        protected override void Execute(CodeActivityContext context)
        {
            CommentExtension ext = context.GetExtension<CommentExtension>();
            Comments.Set(context, ext.Comments);
        }
    }
}
```

This activity takes an input argument, which is the comment being added, and an output argument, which is the current comment that includes all previous comments.

This activity overrides the CacheMetadata method. This implementation adds the CommentExtension to the collection of default extensions. This will ensure that the CommentExtension is added to the workflow (if it doesn't already exist) when the AddComment activity is executed.

The `Execute()` method for this activity gets the `CommentExtension` and calls its `AddComment()` method passing in the input comment argument. The complete comment string is then stored in the output argument.

GetComments Activity

This file also implements the `GetComments` activity, which works just like the `AddComment` activity except it returns only the existing comment without adding one.

Modifying the Workflow

Open the `LeadGeneratorWF.cs` file and add the following activity definition just after the `InvokeMethod` activity:

```
new AddComment
{
    Comment = new InArgument<string>(env => "Lead has been created")
},
```

Add the following activity definition just after the `WaitForInput` activity:

```
new AddComment
{
    Comment = new InArgument<string>(env => "Lead is being assigned")
},
```

Accessing the Extension from the Application

Open the `AddLead.xaml.cs` file and add the following code to the `SetupInstance()` method:

```
// Display the accumulated comments
i.Completed = (wacea) =>
{
    // Get the CommentExtension
    IEnumerable<CommentExtension> q =
        wacea.GetInstanceExtensions<CommentExtension>();

    // Add the comments to the event log
    if (q.Count() > 0)
    {
        string comments = "Comments: \r\n" +
            q.First<CommentExtension>().Comments;
        this.lstEvents.Dispatcher.BeginInvoke
            (new Action(() => this.lstEvents.Items.Add(comments)));
    }

    this.lstEvents.Dispatcher.BeginInvoke
        (new Action(() => this.lstEvents.Items.Add
```

```
                ("\r\nThe workflow has completed")));
};
```

This code implements a handler for the `Completed` event. This event is raised when a workflow instance completes. The code gets the `CommentExtension` from the `WorkflowInstance` and then adds an event to the `lstEvents` control using the `Comments` property of the extension. This is done on the window's thread by using the `Dispatcher` object.

■ **Note** In this scenario, the extension was created by a workflow activity. It was then accessed by the application when the instance was completed to extract any data stored by the workflow activities. The first extension you developed worked just the opposite. The application created the extension, storing data in it. The workflow activities then accessed the extension to get the data provided by the application. These two examples demonstrate both the usefulness and flexibility of workflow extensions.

Event Handler Syntax

As I promised in the previous chapter, let me explain the syntax used to implement the workflow event handlers. If you hover the mouse over the `Completed` property, the specific property prototype is displayed, as shown in Figure 12-2.

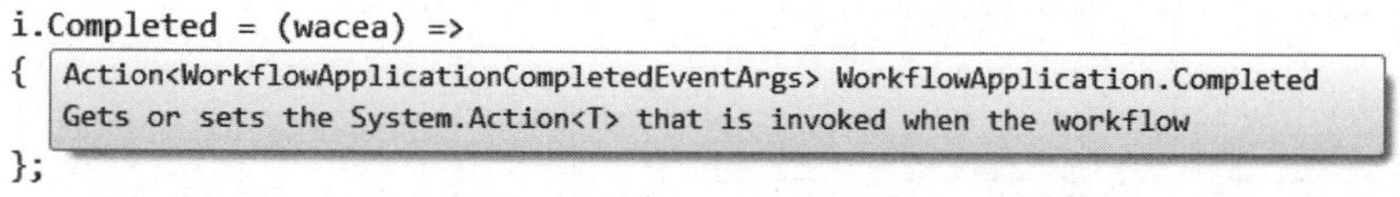

```
i.Completed = (wacea) =>
{   Action<WorkflowApplicationCompletedEventArgs> WorkflowApplication.Completed
    Gets or sets the System.Action<T> that is invoked when the workflow
};
```

Figure 12-2. Definition of the event handler

You can see that this property in an `Action<T>` class, `<T>` in this case, is a `WorkflowApplicationCompletedEventArgs` class. Here is the definition of the `Action<T>` class:

```
public delegate void Action<T>(T obj)
```

This may look a bit more familiar. This is a delegate function that has no return value and accepts a single parameter of type `<T>`, which is a `WorkflowApplicationCompletedEventArgs` class. In more traditional syntax, the `Completed` property is looking for a delegate function with the following prototype:

```
void f(WorkflowApplicationCompletedEventArgs x)
```

The lambda expression is simply shorthand for declaring a function for this delegate. The input parameter (declared as `wacea`) was not used. If you wanted to display the termination message, for example, you could access it with the following code:

```
wacea.TerminationException.Message
```

Let's go back to the `PersistableIdle` event handler. The code used to define this was this:

```
i.PersistableIdle = (waiea) => PersistableIdleAction.Unload;
```

In this case, the delegate function expects a return type of `PersistableIdleAction`. Because there is no code being executed, you can simply provide the return value (`PersistableIdleAction.Unload`). If you want to execute some code in this event handler, the syntax would be the following:

```
i.PersistableIdle = (waiea) =>
{
    // Do something
    return PersistableIdleAction.Unload;
}
```

Running the Application

Press F5 to start the application. Create a lead, but don't assign it. Close the application. Press F5 to start the application again. The lead you previously entered should be in the list. Select it and assign an agent. The window should look like the one shown n Figure 12-3.

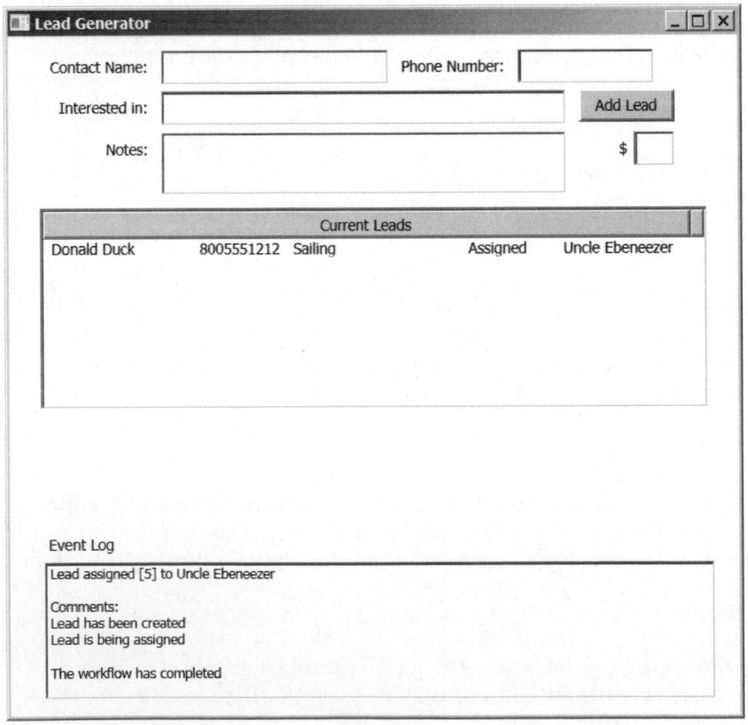

Figure 12-3. *Sample application window*

Notice the comments in the Event Log. The first one, "Lead has been created", was added before the application was closed. It was restored from the persistent store when the application was restarted.

The complete implementation of AddLead.xaml.cs is shown in Listing 12-6.

Listing 12-6. *Complete implementation of AddLead.xaml.cs*

```
using System;
using System.Collections.Generic;
using System.Linq;
using System.Text;
using System.Windows;
using System.Windows.Controls;
using System.Windows.Data;
using System.Windows.Documents;
using System.Windows.Input;
using System.Windows.Media;
using System.Windows.Media.Imaging;
using System.Windows.Navigation;
using System.Windows.Shapes;

using System.Activities;
using System.Activities.DurableInstancing;
using System.Runtime.DurableInstancing;
using System.Data.Linq;
using System.Configuration;

namespace LeadGenerator
{
    /// <summary>
    /// Interaction logic for AddLead.xaml
    /// </summary>
    public partial class AddLead : Window
    {
        private string _connectionString = "";
        private InstanceStore _instanceStore;
        private DBExtension _dbExtension;

        public AddLead()
        {
            InitializeComponent();

            ApplicationInterface._app = this;
        }

        // Add a line of text to the Event Log
        private void AddEvent(string szText)
        {
            lstEvents.Items.Add(szText);
        }
```

```
public ListBox GetEventListBox()
{
    return this.lstEvents;
}

private void Window_Loaded(object sender, RoutedEventArgs e)
{
    // Open the config file and get the connection string
    Configuration config =
        ConfigurationManager.OpenExeConfiguration
            (ConfigurationUserLevel.None);
    ConnectionStringsSection css =
        (ConnectionStringsSection)config.GetSection("connectionStrings");
    _connectionString =
        css.ConnectionStrings["LeadGenerator"].ConnectionString;

    _instanceStore = new SqlWorkflowInstanceStore(_connectionString);
    InstanceView view = _instanceStore.Execute
        (_instanceStore.CreateInstanceHandle(),
        new CreateWorkflowOwnerCommand(),
        TimeSpan.FromSeconds(30));
    _instanceStore.DefaultInstanceOwner = view.InstanceOwner;

    // Create the DBExtension
    _dbExtension = new DBExtension(_connectionString);

    LoadExistingLeads();
}

private void btnAddLead_Click(object sender, RoutedEventArgs e)
{
    // Setup a dictionary object for passing parameters
    Dictionary<string, object> parameters =
        new Dictionary<string, object>();
    parameters.Add("ContactName", txtName.Text);
    parameters.Add("ContactPhone", txtPhone.Text);
    parameters.Add("Interests", txtInterest.Text);
    parameters.Add("Notes", txtNotes.Text);
    parameters.Add("Rating", int.Parse(txtRating.Text));
    parameters.Add("Writer", new ListBoxTextWriter(lstEvents));


    WorkflowApplication i = new WorkflowApplication
        (new EnterLead(), parameters);

    // Setup persistence
    SetupInstance(i);

    i.Run();
}
```

```
public void AddNewLead(Lead l)
{
    this.lstLeads.Dispatcher.BeginInvoke
        (new Action(() => this.lstLeads.Items.Add(l)));
}

private void lstLeads_SelectionChanged(object sender, RoutedEventArgs e)
{
    if (lstLeads.SelectedIndex >= 0)
    {
        Lead l = (Lead)lstLeads.Items[lstLeads.SelectedIndex];
        lblSelectedNotes.Content = l.Comments;
        lblSelectedNotes.Visibility = Visibility.Visible;
        if (l.Status == "Open")
        {
            lblAgent.Visibility = Visibility.Visible;
            txtAgent.Visibility = Visibility.Visible;
            btnAssign.Visibility = Visibility.Visible;
        }
        else
        {
            lblAgent.Visibility = Visibility.Hidden;
            txtAgent.Visibility = Visibility.Hidden;
            btnAssign.Visibility = Visibility.Hidden;
        }
    }
    else
    {
        lblSelectedNotes.Content = "";
        lblSelectedNotes.Visibility = Visibility.Hidden;
        lblAgent.Visibility = Visibility.Hidden;
        txtAgent.Visibility = Visibility.Hidden;
        btnAssign.Visibility = Visibility.Hidden;
    }
}

private void btnAssign_Click(object sender, RoutedEventArgs e)
{
    if (lstLeads.SelectedIndex >= 0)
    {
        Lead l = (Lead)lstLeads.Items[lstLeads.SelectedIndex];
        Guid id = l.WorkflowID;

        LeadDataDataContext dc = new LeadDataDataContext(_connectionString);
        dc.Refresh(RefreshMode.OverwriteCurrentValues, dc.Leads);
        l = dc.Leads.SingleOrDefault<Lead>(x => x.WorkflowID == id);
        if (l != null)
        {
            l.AssignedTo = txtAgent.Text;
            l.Status = "Assigned";
            dc.SubmitChanges();
```

```
            // Clear the input
            txtAgent.Text = "";
        }

        // Update the grid
        lstLeads.Items[lstLeads.SelectedIndex] = l;
        lstLeads.Items.Refresh();

        WorkflowApplication i = new WorkflowApplication(new EnterLead());

        SetupInstance(i);
        i.Load(id);

        try
        {
            i.ResumeBookmark("GetAssignment", l);
        }
        catch (Exception e2)
        {
            AddEvent(e2.Message);
        }
    }
}

private void LoadExistingLeads()
{
    LeadDataDataContext dc = new LeadDataDataContext(_connectionString);
    dc.Refresh(RefreshMode.OverwriteCurrentValues, dc.Leads);
    IEnumerable<Lead> q = dc.Leads
        .Where<Lead>(x => x.Status == "Open" || x.Status == "Assigned");
    foreach (Lead l in q)
    {
        AddNewLead(l);
    }
}

private void SetupInstance(WorkflowApplication i)
{
    // Setup the instance store
    i.InstanceStore = _instanceStore;

    // Setup the PersistableIdle event handler
    i.PersistableIdle = (waiea) => PersistableIdleAction.Unload;

    // Setup the connection string
    i.Extensions.Add(_dbExtension);

    // Display the accumulated comments
    i.Completed = (wacea) =>
    {
```

```
        // Get the CommentExtension
        IEnumerable<CommentExtension> q =
            wacea.GetInstanceExtensions<CommentExtension>();

        // Add the comments to the event log
        if (q.Count() > 0)
        {
            string comments = "Comments: \r\n" +
                q.First<CommentExtension>().Comments;
            this.lstEvents.Dispatcher.BeginInvoke
                (new Action(() => this.lstEvents.Items.Add(comments)));
        }
        this.lstEvents.Dispatcher.BeginInvoke
            (new Action(() => this.lstEvents.Items.Add
                ("\r\nThe workflow has completed")));
    };
  }
 }
}
```

The complete implementation of LeadGeneratorWF.cs is shown in Listing 12-7.

Listing 12-7. Complete implementation of LeadGeneratorWF.cs

```
using System;
using System.Activities;
using System.Activities.Statements;
using System.IO;

namespace LeadGenerator
{
    /****************************************************/
    // This file contains the definition of the EnterLead
    // workflow
    /****************************************************/
    public sealed class EnterLead : Activity
    {
        // Define the input and output arguments
        public InArgument<string> ContactName { get; set; }
        public InArgument<string> ContactPhone { get; set; }
        public InArgument<string> Interests { get; set; }
        public InArgument<string> Notes { get; set; }
        public InArgument<int> Rating { get; set; }
        public InArgument<TextWriter> Writer { get; set; }


        public EnterLead()
        {
            // Define the variables used by this workflow
            Variable<Lead> lead = new Variable<Lead> { Name = "lead" };
```

225

```
// Define the SendRequest workflow
this.Implementation = () => new Sequence
{
    DisplayName = "EnterLead",
    Variables = { lead },
    Activities =
    {
        new CreateLead
        {
            ContactName = new InArgument<string>
                (env => ContactName.Get(env)),
            ContactPhone = new InArgument<string>
                (env => ContactPhone.Get(env)),
            Interests = new InArgument<string>
                (env => Interests.Get(env)),
            Notes = new InArgument<string>(env => Notes.Get(env)),
            Lead = new OutArgument<Lead>(env => lead.Get(env)),
        },
        new WriteLine
        {
            Text = new InArgument<string>
                (env => "Lead received [" + Rating.Get(env).ToString()
                + "]; waiting for assignment"),
            TextWriter = new InArgument<TextWriter>
                (env => Writer.Get(env))
        },
        new InvokeMethod
        {
            TargetType = typeof(ApplicationInterface),
            MethodName = "NewLead",
            Parameters =
            {
                new InArgument<Lead>(env => lead.Get(env))
            }
        },
        new AddComment
        {
            Comment = new InArgument<string>
                (env => "Lead has been created")
        },
        new WaitForInput<Lead>
        {
            BookmarkName = "GetAssignment",
            Input = new OutArgument<Lead>(env => lead.Get(env))
        },
        new AddComment
        {
            Comment = new InArgument<string>
                (env => "Lead is being assigned")
```

```
                },
                new WriteLine
                {
                    Text = new InArgument<string>
                        (env => "Lead assigned [" + Rating.Get(env).ToString()
                         + "] to " + lead.Get(env).AssignedTo),
                    TextWriter = new InArgument<TextWriter>
                        (env => Writer.Get(env))
                }
            }
        };
    }
}
}
```

CHAPTER 13

Tracking

In this chapter, you'll use extensions to track events as your workflow executes the defined activities. This is useful for monitoring a workflow's execution and for triggering external processing. It is also helpful for leaving an audit trail for future diagnostics.

Setting Up the Solution

You will start with the project that you developed in Chapter 12. Start by creating a blank solution as shown in Figure 13-1. For the solution name, enter **Chapter13**.

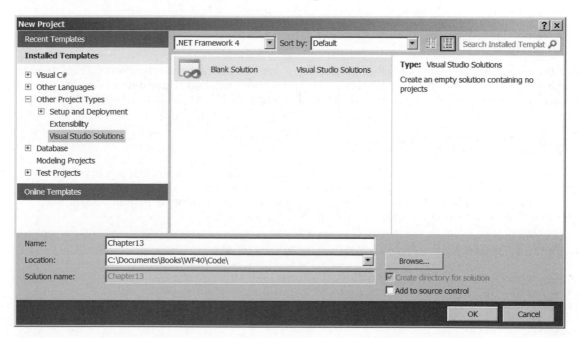

Figure 13-1. Creating a blank solution

Copy Solution from Chapter 12

From Windows Explorer, copy the LeadGenerator folder from the Chapter12 folder to the Chapter13 folder. Back in Visual Studio, from the Solution Explorer, right-click the Chapter13 solution and choose Add ➤ Existing Project. Select the LeadGenerator project that you just copied to the Chapter13 folder.

Setting Up the Database

Create a Chapter13 database and run the following scripts to initialize the database schema:

- SqlWorkflowInstanceStoreSchema.sql
- SqlWorkflowInstanceStoreLogic.sql
- Lead.sql

Open the app.config file and change the connectionString attribute to use the Chapter13 database.

■ **Tip** You might be familiar with the tracking mechanism provided by previous versions of WF. In version 3.0 and 3.5, tracking was implemented by writing the events to a database, which could then be queried by the application or an external monitoring utility. The tracking provided in version 4.0 is designed with a whole new approach.

Tracking Participants

In WF 4.0, tracking is accomplished through tracking participants, which are extensions that are derived from the TrackingParticipant abstract class. In this project, you will build three different tracking participants that should give you a sense of the flexibility provided in the tracking architecture.

ListBoxTrackingParticipant

The first tracking participant will write the tracking records to the same list box that you have been using for the WriteLine activities. In the Solution Explorer, right-click the Extension folder in the LeadGenerator project and choose Add ➤ Class. For the class name, enter **ListBoxTrackingParticipant.cs**. The implementation for this class is shown in Listing 13-1.

Listing 13-1. Implementation of the ListBoxTrackingParticipant class

```
using System;
using System.Activities.Tracking;
using System.Windows.Controls;
using System.Collections.Generic;
using System.Text;
```

```
namespace LeadGenerator
{
    public class ListBoxTrackingParticipant : TrackingParticipant
    {
        private ListBox _eventLog;
        private const String participantName = "ListBoxTrackingParticipant";

        public ListBoxTrackingParticipant(ListBox listBox)
        {
            _eventLog = listBox;
        }

        private void AddEvent(String msg)
        {
            if (_eventLog != null)
                _eventLog.Dispatcher.BeginInvoke
                    (new Action(() => _eventLog.Items.Add(msg)));
        }

        protected override void Track(TrackingRecord record, TimeSpan timeout)
        {
            // Log header information
            AddEvent(String.Format("Type: {0}  Level: {1}, RecordNumber: {2}",
                record.GetType().Name, record.Level, record.RecordNumber));

            // If this is a instance record
            WorkflowInstanceRecord instance = record as WorkflowInstanceRecord;
            if (instance != null)
            {
                AddEvent(String.Format(" InstanceID: {0} State: {1}",
                    instance.InstanceId, instance.State));
            }

            // If this is a bookmark record
            BookmarkResumptionRecord bookmark = record as BookmarkResumptionRecord;
            if (bookmark != null)
            {
                AddEvent(String.Format(" Bookmark {0} resumed",
                    bookmark.BookmarkName));
            }

            // If this is an activity record
            ActivityStateRecord activity = record as ActivityStateRecord;
            if (activity != null)
            {
                IDictionary<String, object> variables = activity.Variables;
                StringBuilder s = new StringBuilder();

                if (variables.Count > 0)
                {
                    s.AppendLine(" Variables:");
```

```
                foreach (KeyValuePair<string, object> v in variables)
                {
                    s.AppendLine(String.Format("    {0} Value: [{1}]",
                        v.Key, v.Value));
                }
            }
            AddEvent(String.Format(" Activity: {0} State: {1} {2}",
                activity.Activity.Name, activity.State, s.ToString()));
        }

        // If this is a user record
        CustomTrackingRecord user = record as CustomTrackingRecord;
        if ((user != null) && (user.Data.Count > 0))
        {
            AddEvent(String.Format(" User Data: {0}", user.Name));
            foreach (string data in user.Data.Keys)
            {
                AddEvent(String.Format("   {0} : {1}", data, user.Data[data]));
            }
        }
    }
  }
}
```

The ListBoxTrackingParticipant class is derived from the abstract TrackingParticipant class. It overrides the Track() method, which is where most of the work is done. When a *trackable* event occurs, the workflow instance will enumerate all the extensions and will call the Track() method in any that are derived from the TrackingParticipant base class. I'll explain what a trackable event is later in this chapter.

The ListBoxTrackingParticipant class has a private member, _eventLog, which is a reference to a ListBox control. This is passed in the class constructor. There is also an AddEvent() method that adds a string to the ListBox using the window's main thread. This allows the tracking logic that runs in the workflow's thread to safely access the application controls.

Overriding the Track() Method

A TrackingRecord is passed into the Track() method. This is an abstract class; the actual instance passed in will be one of the following classes, which are derived from the TrackingRecord class:

- WorkflowInstanceRecord contains data about the workflow instance.

- BookmarkResumptionRecord contains data about the bookmark being resumed.

- ActivityStateRecord contains data about a specific activity.

- CustomTrackingRecord contains user-defined data.

■ **Caution** The second parameter is a TimeSpan object that specifies how long the caller will wait before aborting this call to the Track() method. When implementing a tracking participant, you should never perform any long-running operations. While the Track() method is executing, it is blocking the workflow from executing activities. The workflow instance expects the Track() method to return quickly and will abort it if it thinks it is taking too long. The default timeout is 30 seconds.

The Track() method first logs some generic information. It then determines what type of tracking record it has received. It does this by essentially casting the parameter to one of the derived types. If the cast was successful, it uses the derived type to log type-specific information. The pertinent information is obtained, formatted, and written to the ListBox.

Configuring a Tracking Participant

Open the AddLead.xaml.cs file and add the following namespace:
using System.Activities.Tracking;

Add the following class member to hold a reference to the tracking participant. It should go just before the AddLead() constructor:

private ListBoxTrackingParticipant _tracking;

Add the following code to the Loaded event handler. This calls a method that you will implement to set up the tracking participant.

```
// Set up the tracking participants
CreateTrackingParticipant();
```

Then add the following code to the SetupInstance() method, which will register the extension with the WorkflowInstance class:

```
// Set up tracking
i.Extensions.Add(_tracking);
```

Finally, the implementation for the CreateTrackingParticipant() method is shown in Listing 13-2. Add this method to the AddLead class.

Listing 13-2. Implementation of the CreateTrackingParticipant method

```
private void CreateTrackingParticipant()
{
    _tracking = new ListBoxTrackingParticipant(this.lstEvents)
    {
        TrackingProfile = new TrackingProfile()
        {
```

233

```
            Name = "ListBoxTrackingProfile",
            Queries =
            {
                // For instance data, only track the started and completed events
                new WorkflowInstanceQuery()
                {
                    States = { WorkflowInstanceStates.Started,
                               WorkflowInstanceStates.Completed },
                },

                // For bookmark data, only track the GetAssignment event
                new BookmarkResumptionQuery()
                {
                    Name = "GetAssignment"
                },

                // For activity data, track all states of the InvokeMethod
                new ActivityStateQuery()
                {
                    ActivityName = "InvokeMethod",
                    States = { "*" },
                },

                // For User data, track all events
                new CustomTrackingQuery()
                {
                    Name = "*",
                    ActivityName = "*"
                }
            }
        }
    };
}
```

The CreateTrackingParticipant() method creates a ListBoxTrackingParticipant class passing the lstEvent control to the constructor. The rest of the code builds a TrackingProfile class.

Configuring a Tracking Profile

A TrackingProfile defines a collection of *queries* that specify which events are to be tracked by the associated tracking participant. These queries are used to determine if an event is *trackable*. The queries are stored in the Queries property, which is a collection of classes derived from the abstract TrackingQuery class. There are four derived classes that correspond to the four types of tracking records:

- WorkflowInstanceQuery
- BookmarkResumptionQuery
- ActivityStateQuery
- CustomTrackingQuery

■ **Note** In Listing 13-2, there is one of each type of query. That was done to demonstrate each type. You don't have to have a query for each type. You can have any number of queries of each type, including none.

WorkflowInstanceQuery

A WorkflowInstanceQuery is used to define the workflow instance events that should be tracked. These are the process states that occur at the instance level such as Started, Completed, Unloaded, and so on. When entering the desired states, type **WorkflowInstanceStates**; the complete list of possible events will appear as shown in Figure 13-2.

Figure 13-2. List of workflow instance states

This tracking profile will record only the Started and Completed events.

BookmarkResumptionQuery

In a BookmarkResumptionQuery, you specify the name of the bookmark that you want to track whenever it is resumed. You can specify only a single bookmark in a query. If you want to track multiple bookmarks, you should create multiple queries—one for each bookmark. You could enter an asterisk (*) for the Name property to specify that all bookmarks should be tracked.

ActivityStateQuery

An ActivityStateQuery class specifies both the Name of the activity and the State collection (events) that should be tracked. You can specify an asterisk (*) for either, which indicates that all activities and/or states should be tracked.

CustomTrackingQuery

The CustomTrackingQuery specifies the ActivityName, which indicates the activity that generated the CustomTrackingRecord and the Name property, which indicates the name given to the CustomTrackingRecord. You can specify an asterisk for either (or both) as the example, above does. When both are set to *, it indicates that all user events should be tracked.

CustomTrackingRecord

Now you will modify the workflow to generate a custom tracking event. Open the CreateLead.cs file and add the following namespace:

```
using System.Activities.Tracking;
```

Then add the following code to the Execute() method:

```
// Add a custom track record
CustomTrackingRecord userRecord = new CustomTrackingRecord("New Lead")
{
    Data =
    {
        {"Name", l.ContactName},
        {"Phone", l.ContactPhone}
    }
};

// Emit the custom tracking record
context.Track(userRecord);
```

This code creates a new CustomTrackingRecord class, passing the name "New Lead" in the constructor. It then defines some data elements. Finally, it calls the Track() method of the CodeActivityContext class, which will forward this record to any tracking participant that has a TrackingProfile with a query that matches this record.

■ **Tip** If you want to track only this specific record, in the TrackingProfile, add a CustomTrackingQuery where the ActivityName is **CreateLead** and the Name is **New Lead**.

The complete implementation of CreateLead.cs is shown in Listing 13-3.

Listing 13-3. *Complete Implementation of CreateLead.cs*

```
using System;
using System.Activities;
using System.Configuration;
using System.Activities.Tracking;
```

```
namespace LeadGenerator
{
    /**************************************************/
    // This custom activity creates a Lead class using
    // the input parameters (ContactName, ContactPhone,
    // Interests and Notes).  A Lead record is inserted
    // into the database and then this is returned in
    // the Lead output parameter.
    /**************************************************/
    public sealed class CreateLead : CodeActivity
    {
        public InArgument<string> ContactName { get; set; }
        public InArgument<string> ContactPhone { get; set; }
        public InArgument<string> Interests { get; set; }
        public InArgument<string> Notes { get; set; }
        public InArgument<string> ConnectionString { get; set; }
        public OutArgument<Lead> Lead { get; set; }

        protected override void Execute(CodeActivityContext context)
        {
            // Create a Lead class and populate it with the input arguments
            Lead l = new Lead();
            l.ContactName = ContactName.Get(context);
            l.ContactPhone = ContactPhone.Get(context);
            l.Interests = Interests.Get(context);
            l.Comments = Notes.Get(context);
            l.WorkflowID = context.WorkflowInstanceId;
            l.Status = "Open";

            // Get the connection string
            DBExtension ext = context.GetExtension<DBExtension>();
            if (ext == null)
                throw new InvalidProgramException("No connection string available");

            // Insert a record into the Lead table
            LeadDataDataContext dc = new LeadDataDataContext(ext.ConnectionString);
            dc.Leads.InsertOnSubmit(l);
            dc.SubmitChanges();

            // Store the request in the OutArgument
            Lead.Set(context, l);

            // Add a custom track record
            CustomTrackingRecord userRecord = new CustomTrackingRecord("New Lead")
            {
                Data =
                {
                    {"Name", l.ContactName},
                    {"Phone", l.ContactPhone}
                }
            };
```

```
            // Emit the custom tracking record
            context.Track(userRecord);
        }
    }
}
```

Running the Application

Press F5 to run the application. Enter a lead and then select it and assign an agent. A portion of the event log is shown in Figure 13-3. You can scroll through the ListBox and view all the events listed. All the tracking events start with Type:, and the type-specific data is found on subsequent lines and indented.

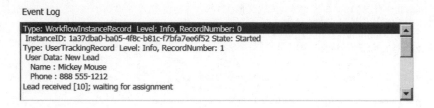

Figure 13-3. *Sample tracking events*

Event Tracing for Windows (ETW)

The next tracking participant that you'll add writes the tracking events to the standard Windows Event Log. WF 4.0 provides an EtwTrackingParticipant class that provides this capability.

Setting Up the Extension

Open the AddLead.xaml.cs file and add the following class member:

private EtwTrackingParticipant _etwTracking;

This stores a reference to the tracking participant. Add the following code to the Loaded event handler. It calls a method that you'll implement shortly, which creates an instance of the tracking participant:

CreateETWTrackingParticipant();

Add the following code to the SetupInstance() method that adds this participant as an extension to the workflow instance:

i.Extensions.Add(_etwTracking);

Configuring the TrackingProfile

Finally, add the following method to the AddLead class. This creates the EtwTrackingParticipant class and configures the TrackingProfile:

```
private void CreateETWTrackingParticipant()
{
    _etwTracking = new EtwTrackingParticipant()
    {
        TrackingProfile = new TrackingProfile()
        {
            Name = "EtwTrackingProfile",
            Queries =
            {
                new CustomTrackingQuery()
                {
                 Name = "*",
                 ActivityName = "*"
                }
            }
        }
    };
}
```

■ **Tip** To keep things simple, this participant tracks only the custom events. You can modify this code to track additional events if you want. The previous TrackingProfile that you configured tracked all four types of events, and I explained how to configure each of the corresponding queries. You could also copy and paste the code from the previous sample. If you had multiple tracking participants and you wanted each of them to track the same events, you could create a named instance of a TrackingProfile class and then reference the same instance for each of the participants.

Running the Application

Press F5 to run the application and enter a lead and close the application. Now run the Event Viewer application, which is usually under the Administrative Tools start menu. (You can usually find it in the Administrative Tools section of the Control Panel as well.) In the Event Viewer, open the Applications and Services Logs and then navigate to the Microsoft, Application Server-Applications, Analytic entry (see Figure 13-4).

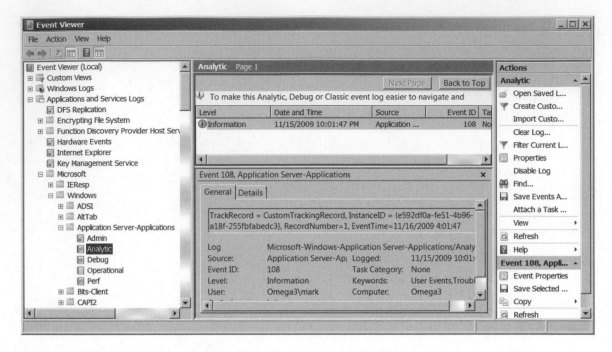

Figure 13-4. *The Event Viewer application*

■**Tip** You may need to enable this log. In the Actions window (refer to Figure 13-4), if there is a link to Enable Log, click it to allow entries into this log.

There should be a single event corresponding to the lead you just created. If you select this event and click the Details tab, you should see a more readable view of this data, as shown in Figure 13-5.

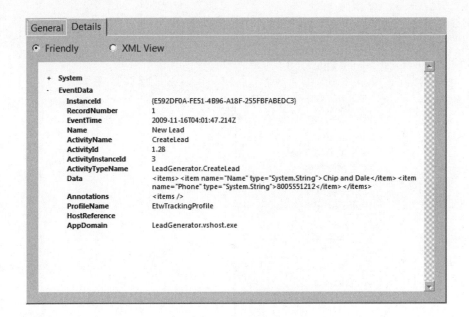

Figure 13-5. *The Friendly view from the Details tab*

Notice in the Data section that it includes the Name and Phone elements just like the
ListBoxTrackingParticipant did.

SqlTrackingParticipant

The last participant that you'll implement will write the events to a database. The tracking participant
will receive the track events based on the queries defined in the TrackingProfile. The tracking
participant is responsible for performing the database updates, which gives you complete control of how
this is stored.

Setting up the Database

The first step is to create the tables in the database. To store the four types of tracking events, you will
use the following tables:

- TrackInstance

- TrackBookmark

- TrackActivity

- TrackCustom

Run the Tracking.sql script in the Create Scripts folder and these four tables will be created.

Open the LeadData.dbml file, which should display the O/R Designer. In the Server Explorer, expand the Chapter13 data connection to get the list of tables in the database. (If the tracking tables are not listed, right-click the data connection and choose Refresh.) Drag these four tables to the O/R Designer. The diagram should look like the one shown in Figure 13-6.

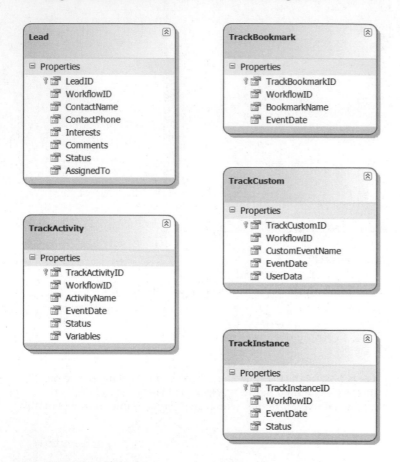

Figure 13-6. *The O/R DesignerO/R Designer*

■ **Note** You might get a warning telling you that the data connection you're using is different from the one initially used by the O/R Designer because you initially created the LeadData.dbml file in Chapter 11 and used the Chapter11 data connection. The warning asks if you want to update the connection used by the designer. You should choose Yes.

Implementing the SqlTrackingParticipant

In the Solution Explorer, right-click the Extensions folder and choose Add ➤ Class. For the class name, enter **SqlTrackingParticipant.cs**. The implementation for this class is shown in Listing 13-4.

Listing 13-4. Implementation of the SqlTrackingParticipant Class

```csharp
using System;
using System.Activities.Tracking;
using System.Collections.Generic;
using System.Text;
using System.Data.Linq;

namespace LeadGenerator
{
    public class SqlTrackingParticipant : TrackingParticipant
    {
        private string _connectionString { get; set; }
        private const String participantName = "SqlTrackingParticipant";

        public SqlTrackingParticipant(string connectionString)
        {
            _connectionString = connectionString;
        }

        protected override void Track(TrackingRecord record, TimeSpan timeout)
        {
            WorkflowInstanceRecord instanceTrackingRecord =
                record as WorkflowInstanceRecord;
            if (instanceTrackingRecord != null)
            {
                TrackInstance t = new TrackInstance();

                t.WorkflowID = instanceTrackingRecord.InstanceId;
                t.Status = instanceTrackingRecord.State;
                t.EventDate = DateTime.UtcNow;

                // Insert a record into the TrackInstance table
                LeadDataDataContext dc =
                    new LeadDataDataContext(_connectionString);
                dc.TrackInstances.InsertOnSubmit(t);
                dc.SubmitChanges();
            }

            BookmarkResumptionRecord bookTrackingRecord =
                record as BookmarkResumptionRecord;

            if (bookTrackingRecord != null)
            {
                TrackBookmark t = new TrackBookmark();
```

```
        t.WorkflowID = bookTrackingRecord.InstanceId;
        t.BookmarkName = bookTrackingRecord.BookmarkName;
        t.EventDate = DateTime.UtcNow;

        // Insert a record into the TrackBookmark table
        LeadDataDataContext dc =
            new LeadDataDataContext(_connectionString);
        dc.TrackBookmarks.InsertOnSubmit(t);
        dc.SubmitChanges();
    }

ActivityStateRecord activityStateRecord =
    record as ActivityStateRecord;
if (activityStateRecord != null)
{
    TrackActivity t = new TrackActivity();

    t.ActivityName = activityStateRecord.Activity.Name;
    t.WorkflowID = activityStateRecord.InstanceId;
    t.Status = activityStateRecord.State;
    t.EventDate = DateTime.UtcNow;

    // Concatenate all the variables into a string
    IDictionary<String, object> variables =
        activityStateRecord.Variables;
    StringBuilder s = new StringBuilder();

    if (variables.Count > 0)
    {
        foreach (KeyValuePair<string, object> v in variables)
        {
            s.AppendLine(String.Format("{0}: Value = [{1}]",
                v.Key, v.Value));
        }
    }

    // Store the variables string
    t.Variables = s.ToString();

    // Insert a record into the TrackActivity table
    LeadDataDataContext dc =
        new LeadDataDataContext(_connectionString);
    dc.TrackActivities.InsertOnSubmit(t);
    dc.SubmitChanges();
}

CustomTrackingRecord customTrackingRecord =
    record as CustomTrackingRecord;

if (customTrackingRecord != null)
{
```

```
        TrackCustom t = new TrackCustom();

        t.WorkflowID = customTrackingRecord.InstanceId;
        t.CustomEventName = customTrackingRecord.Name;
        t.EventDate = DateTime.UtcNow;

        // Concatenate all the user data into a string
        string s = "";
        if ((customTrackingRecord != null) &&
            (customTrackingRecord.Data.Count > 0))
        {
            foreach (string data in customTrackingRecord.Data.Keys)
            {
                if (s.Length > 1)
                    s += "\r\n";
                s += String.Format("{0}: Value = [{1}]", data,
                    customTrackingRecord.Data[data]);
            }
        }
        t.UserData = s;

        // Insert a record into the TrackUser table
        LeadDataDataContext dc =
            new LeadDataDataContext(_connectionString);
        dc.TrackCustoms.InsertOnSubmit(t);
        dc.SubmitChanges();
        }
      }
    }
}
```

As with the `ListBoxTrackingParticipant`, this class overrides the `Track()` method. A generic `TrackingRecord` is passed in to this method. It is then cast to the each of the four record types: `WorkflowInstanceRecord`, `BookmarkResumptionRecord`, `ActivityStateRecord`, and `CustomTrackingRecord`. If the cast succeeds, the subsequent code creates the corresponding LINQ class (`TrackInstance`, `TrackBookmark`, `TrackActivity`, or `TrackCustom`, respectively) that is then inserted into the database.

Configuring the Tracking Participant

Open the `AddLead.xaml.cs` file and add the following class member, which will hold a reference to the new tracking participant:

```
private SqlTrackingParticipant _sqlTracking;
```

Add the following code to the `Loaded` event handler. This calls the method that you will write to create and configure the `SqlTrackingParticipant`:

```
CreateSqlTrackingParticipant();
```

Now add the following code to the SetupInstance() method, which adds this extension to the workflow instance:

```
i.Extensions.Add(_sqlTracking);
```

Finally, add the CreateSqlTrackingParticipant() method using the code shown in Listing 13-5.

Listing 13-5. *Implementation of the CreateSqlTrackingParticipant() Method*

```
private void CreateSqlTrackingParticipant()
{
    _sqlTracking = new SqlTrackingParticipant(_connectionString)
    {
        TrackingProfile = new TrackingProfile()
        {
            Name = "SqlTrackingProfile",
            Queries =
            {
                new WorkflowInstanceQuery()
                {
                    States = { "*" },
                },

                new BookmarkResumptionQuery()
                {
                    Name = "*"
                },
                new ActivityStateQuery()
                {
                    // Subscribe for track records from all activities
                    // for all states
                    ActivityName = "*",
                    States = { "*" },
                },
                // For User data, track all events
                new CustomTrackingQuery()
                {
                    Name = "*",
                    ActivityName = "*"
                }
            }
        }
    };
}
```

This code should be familiar to you. It first creates the SqlTrackingParticipant class, passing the connection string to the constructor. It then creates a TrackingProfile and adds four queries to this profile.

■ **Caution** If you are using different tracking profiles in the same workflow instance (as you did in this project), it is important that you give them different values for the Name property. When an event occurs, the workflow instance will obtain the profile using the Name property. If there are two profiles with the same Name, it might not use the one you expected.

Running the Application

Press F5 to run the application. Create a lead and close the application. Press F5 to restart the application. Select this lead and assign it to an agent. Then close the application.

From the Server Explorer, right click the TrackInstance table and choose Show Table Data. The data should look similar to Figure 13-7.

TrackInstan...	WorkflowID	EventDate	Status
1	5b955e90-ec08-4c36-8c97-d8ba1f2ef689	9/12/2009...	Started
2	5b955e90-ec08-4c36-8c97-d8ba1f2ef689	9/12/2009...	Idle
3	5b955e90-ec08-4c36-8c97-d8ba1f2ef689	9/12/2009...	Unloaded
4	5b955e90-ec08-4c36-8c97-d8ba1f2ef689	9/12/2009...	Resumed
5	5b955e90-ec08-4c36-8c97-d8ba1f2ef689	9/12/2009...	Completed
6	5b955e90-ec08-4c36-8c97-d8ba1f2ef689	9/12/2009...	Deleted
NULL	NULL	NULL	NULL

Figure 13-7. *Contents of the TrackInstance table*

■ **Note** This is a good opportunity to explain the life cycle of a persisted workflow. The workflow instance was Started when the Add Lead button was clicked. It then started executing activities until it came to the WaitForInput activity. The instance then became Idle because the bookmark was blocking it. The PersistableIdle event handler instructed the workflow to be Unloaded from memory. Later, when an agent was assigned, the workflow was Resumed. The remaining activities were executed and the instance Completed. Because the instance was now complete, it was Deleted from the persistent store.

You should check the contents of the other tables as well. Also, there are scripts in the Change Scripts folder that you can use if you want to clear the database of existing instances. DeleteTracking.sql truncates all the tracking tables. Truncate.sql truncates the Lead table as well as the persistent store (the InstanceData table).

The complete implementation of AddLead.xaml.cs is shown in Listing 13-6.

Listing 13-6. *Complete Implementation of AddLead.xaml.cs*

```
using System;
using System.Collections.Generic;
using System.Linq;
using System.Text;
using System.Windows;
using System.Windows.Controls;
using System.Windows.Data;
using System.Windows.Documents;
using System.Windows.Input;
using System.Windows.Media;
using System.Windows.Media.Imaging;
using System.Windows.Navigation;
using System.Windows.Shapes;

using System.Activities;
using System.Activities.DurableInstancing;
using System.Runtime.DurableInstancing;
using System.Data.Linq;
using System.Configuration;
using System.Activities.Tracking;

namespace LeadGenerator
{
    /// <summary>
    /// Interaction logic for AddLead.xaml
    /// </summary>
    public partial class AddLead : Window
    {
        private string _connectionString = "";
        private InstanceStore _instanceStore;
        private DBExtension _dbExtension;
        private ListBoxTrackingParticipant _tracking;
        private EtwTrackingParticipant _etwTracking;
        private SqlTrackingParticipant _sqlTracking;

        public AddLead()
        {
            InitializeComponent();

            ApplicationInterface._app = this;
        }

        // Add a line of text to the Event Log
        private void AddEvent(string szText)
        {
            lstEvents.Items.Add(szText);
        }

        public ListBox GetEventListBox()
        {
```

```csharp
        return this.lstEvents;
}

private void Window_Loaded(object sender, RoutedEventArgs e)
{
    // Open the config file and get the connection string
    Configuration config =
        ConfigurationManager.OpenExeConfiguration
            (ConfigurationUserLevel.None);
    ConnectionStringsSection css =
        (ConnectionStringsSection)config.GetSection("connectionStrings");
    _connectionString =
        css.ConnectionStrings["LeadGenerator"].ConnectionString;

    _instanceStore = new SqlWorkflowInstanceStore(_connectionString);
    InstanceView view = _instanceStore.Execute
        (_instanceStore.CreateInstanceHandle(),
        new CreateWorkflowOwnerCommand(),
        TimeSpan.FromSeconds(30));
    _instanceStore.DefaultInstanceOwner = view.InstanceOwner;

    // Create the DBExtension
    _dbExtension = new DBExtension(_connectionString);

    // Set up the tracking participants
    CreateTrackingParticipant();
    CreateETWTrackingParticipant();
    CreateSqlTrackingParticipant();

    LoadExistingLeads();
}

private void btnAddLead_Click(object sender, RoutedEventArgs e)
{
    // Setup a dictionary object for passing parameters
    Dictionary<string, object> parameters =
        new Dictionary<string, object>();
    parameters.Add("ContactName", txtName.Text);
    parameters.Add("ContactPhone", txtPhone.Text);
    parameters.Add("Interests", txtInterest.Text);
    parameters.Add("Notes", txtNotes.Text);
    parameters.Add("Rating", int.Parse(txtRating.Text));
    parameters.Add("Writer", new ListBoxTextWriter(lstEvents));

    WorkflowApplication i = new WorkflowApplication
        (new EnterLead(), parameters);

    // Setup persistence
    SetupInstance(i);

    i.Run();
}
```

```
public void AddNewLead(Lead l)
{
    this.lstLeads.Dispatcher.BeginInvoke
        (new Action(() => this.lstLeads.Items.Add(l)));
}

private void lstLeads_SelectionChanged(object sender, RoutedEventArgs e)
{
    if (lstLeads.SelectedIndex >= 0)
    {
        Lead l = (Lead)lstLeads.Items[lstLeads.SelectedIndex];
        lblSelectedNotes.Content = l.Comments;
        lblSelectedNotes.Visibility = Visibility.Visible;
        if (l.Status == "Open")
        {
            lblAgent.Visibility = Visibility.Visible;
            txtAgent.Visibility = Visibility.Visible;
            btnAssign.Visibility = Visibility.Visible;
        }
        else
        {
            lblAgent.Visibility = Visibility.Hidden;
            txtAgent.Visibility = Visibility.Hidden;
            btnAssign.Visibility = Visibility.Hidden;
        }
    }
    else
    {
        lblSelectedNotes.Content = "";
        lblSelectedNotes.Visibility = Visibility.Hidden;
        lblAgent.Visibility = Visibility.Hidden;
        txtAgent.Visibility = Visibility.Hidden;
        btnAssign.Visibility = Visibility.Hidden;
    }
}

private void btnAssign_Click(object sender, RoutedEventArgs e)
{
    if (lstLeads.SelectedIndex >= 0)
    {
        Lead l = (Lead)lstLeads.Items[lstLeads.SelectedIndex];
        Guid id = l.WorkflowID;

        LeadDataDataContext dc = new LeadDataDataContext(_connectionString);
        dc.Refresh(RefreshMode.OverwriteCurrentValues, dc.Leads);
        l = dc.Leads.SingleOrDefault<Lead>(x => x.WorkflowID == id);
        if (l != null)
        {
            l.AssignedTo = txtAgent.Text;
            l.Status = "Assigned";
            dc.SubmitChanges();
```

```
            // Clear the input
            txtAgent.Text = "";
        }

        // Update the grid
        lstLeads.Items[lstLeads.SelectedIndex] = l;
        lstLeads.Items.Refresh();

        WorkflowApplication i = new WorkflowApplication(new EnterLead());

        SetupInstance(i);
        i.Load(id);

        try
        {
            i.ResumeBookmark("GetAssignment", l);
        }
        catch (Exception e2)
        {
            AddEvent(e2.Message);
        }
    }
}

private void LoadExistingLeads()
{
    LeadDataDataContext dc = new LeadDataDataContext(_connectionString);
    dc.Refresh(RefreshMode.OverwriteCurrentValues, dc.Leads);
    IEnumerable<Lead> q = dc.Leads
        .Where<Lead>(x => x.Status == "Open" || x.Status == "Assigned");
    foreach (Lead l in q)
    {
        AddNewLead(l);
    }
}

private void SetupInstance(WorkflowApplication i)
{
    // Setup the instance store
    i.InstanceStore = _instanceStore;

    // Setup the PersistableIdle event handler
    i.PersistableIdle = (waiea) => PersistableIdleAction.Unload;

    // Setup the connection string
    i.Extensions.Add(_dbExtension);

    // Display the accumulated comments
    i.Completed = (wacea) =>
    {
```

```
        // Get the CommentExtension
        IEnumerable<CommentExtension> q =
            wacea.GetInstanceExtensions<CommentExtension>();

        // Add the comments to the event log
        if (q.Count() > 0)
        {
            string comments = "Comments: \r\n" +
                q.First<CommentExtension>().Comments;
            this.lstEvents.Dispatcher.BeginInvoke
                (new Action(() => this.lstEvents.Items.Add(comments)));
        }

        this.lstEvents.Dispatcher.BeginInvoke
            (new Action(() => this.lstEvents.Items.Add
                ("\r\nThe workflow has completed")));
    };

    // Set up tracking
    i.Extensions.Add(_tracking);
    i.Extensions.Add(_etwTracking);
    i.Extensions.Add(_sqlTracking);
}

private void CreateTrackingParticipant()
{
    _tracking = new ListBoxTrackingParticipant(this.lstEvents)
    {
        TrackingProfile = new TrackingProfile()
        {
            Name = "ListBoxTrackingProfile",
            Queries =
            {
                // For instance data, only track the started and
                // completed events
                new WorkflowInstanceQuery()
                {
                    States = { WorkflowInstanceStates.Started,
                               WorkflowInstanceStates.Completed },
                },

                // For bookmark data, only track the GetAssignment event
                new BookmarkResumptionQuery()
                {
                    Name = "GetAssignment"
                },

                // For activity data, track all states of the InvokeMethod
                new ActivityStateQuery()
                {
```

```
                    ActivityName = "InvokeMethod",
                    States = { "*" },
                },

                // For User data, track all events
                new CustomTrackingQuery()
                {
                    Name = "*",
                    ActivityName = "*"
                }
            }
        }
    };
}

private void CreateETWTrackingParticipant()
{
    _etwTracking = new EtwTrackingParticipant()
    {
        TrackingProfile = new TrackingProfile()
        {
            Name = "EtwTrackingProfile",
            Queries =
            {
                new CustomTrackingQuery()
                {
                 Name = "*",
                 ActivityName = "*"
                }
            }
        }
    };
}

private void CreateSqlTrackingParticipant()
{
    _sqlTracking = new SqlTrackingParticipant(_connectionString)
    {
        TrackingProfile = new TrackingProfile()
        {
            Name = "SqlTrackingProfile",
            Queries =
            {
                new WorkflowInstanceQuery()
                {
                    States = { "*" },
                },

                new BookmarkResumptionQuery()
                {
```

```
                    Name = "*"
                },
                new ActivityStateQuery()
                {
                    // Subscribe for track records from all activities
                    // for all states
                    ActivityName = "*",
                    States = { "*" },
                },
                // For User data, track all events
                new CustomTrackingQuery()
                {

                    Name = "*",
                    ActivityName = "*"
                }
            }
        }
    };
            }
        }
}
```

CHAPTER 14

■ ■ ■

Transactions

In this chapter, you will learn how to enlist your workflow activities on the same database transaction to ensure that updates are performed in a consistent manner.

Setting Up the Solution

You will reuse the project that you developed in Chapter 13. Start by creating a blank solution as shown in Figure 14-1. For the solution name, enter **Chapter14**.

Figure 14-1. Creating a blank solution

From Windows Explorer, copy the LeadGenerator folder from the Chapter13 folder to the Chapter14 folder. Back in Visual Studio, from the Solution Explorer, right-click the Chapter14 solution and choose Add ➤ Existing Project. Select the LeadGenerator project that you just copied to the Chapter14 folder.

Create a Chapter14 database and run the following scripts to initialize the database schema:

- SqlWorkflowInstanceStoreSchema.sql

- SqlWorkflowInstanceStoreLogic.sql

- Lead.sql

- Tracking.sql

Open the app.config file and change the connectionString attribute to use the Chapter14 database. Right-click the LeadGenerator project and choose Add Reference. In the .NET tab, add the System.Transaction assembly.

Assignments

In the previous chapters, the user data consisted of a single table: Lead. When an agent was assigned to a lead, the AssignedTo column was populated with the agent's name. In this chapter you'll add an Assignment table so additional details about the assignment can be stored as well. The Lead.sql that you just executed created both the Lead and Assignment tables. It also set up a foreign key relationship between these two tables.

Adding the LINQ to SQL Class

Open the LeadData.dbml file, which should display the O/R Designer. In the Server Explorer, expand the Chapter14 data connection. Drag the Assignment table to the design surface. The designer should look like the one shown in Figure 14-2.

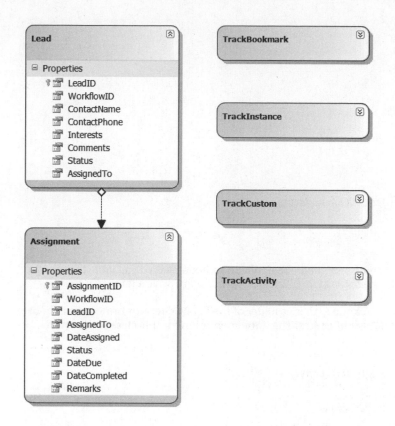

Figure 14-2. O/R Designer with the added Assignment table

The connection between the Assignment and Lead tables is because of the foreign key relationship that was set up in the database schema. By default, the O/R Designer creates a two-way association. The Assignment class will have a property to reference the associated Lead object. The Lead class will also have a property that is a collection of Assignment objects.

For this project you do not want the Lead class to have a collection of Assignment objects. Because the Lead class is used as a variable in the workflow definition, when the workflow is persisted, the Lead class will be serialized and written to the InstancesTable. The Assignment collection is not serializable, and this will generate errors.

To resolve it, click the association link in the O/R Designer. In the Properties window, select the Child Property and set its value to False, as shown in Figure 14-3.

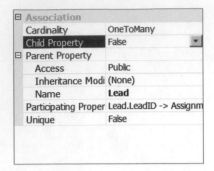

Figure 14-3. *The Properties window of a LINQ Association*

AssignLead Activity

In the current application, when an agent is assigned, the application updates the Lead table to store the agent's name. This is implemented in the btnAssign_Click event handler. Now you'll move it to a custom activity.

From the Solution Explorer, right-click the Activities folder of the LeadGenerator project and choose Add ➤ Class. For the class name, enter **AssignLead.cs**. The implementation for this class is shown in Listing 14-1.

Listing 14-1. *Implementation of the AssignLead activity*

```
using System;
using System.Activities;
using System.Configuration;
using System.Activities.Tracking;
using System.Linq;
using System.Data.Linq;
using System.Transactions;

namespace LeadGenerator
{
    /***************************************************/
    // This custom activity assigns Lead to the specified
    // person (AssignedTo parameter). The updated Lead is
    // returned in the output parameter.
    /***************************************************/
    public sealed class AssignLead : NativeActivity
    {
        public InArgument<string> AssignedTo { get; set; }
        public OutArgument<Lead> Lead { get; set; }

        protected override void Execute(NativeActivityContext context)
        {
```

```
        // Get the connection string
        DBExtension ext = context.GetExtension<DBExtension>();
        if (ext == null)
            throw new InvalidProgramException("No connection string available");

        // Query the Lead table
        LeadDataDataContext dc = new LeadDataDataContext(ext.ConnectionString);
        dc.Refresh(RefreshMode.OverwriteCurrentValues, dc.Leads);
        Lead l = dc.Leads.SingleOrDefault<Lead>
            (x => x.WorkflowID == context.WorkflowInstanceId);

        if (l == null)
            throw new InvalidProgramException
                ("The Lead was not found in the database");

        l.AssignedTo = AssignedTo.Get(context);
        l.Status = "Assigned";

        // Enlist on the current transaction
        RuntimeTransactionHandle rth = new RuntimeTransactionHandle();
        rth = context.Properties.Find(rth.ExecutionPropertyName)
            as RuntimeTransactionHandle;
        if (rth != null)
        {
            Transaction t = rth.GetCurrentTransaction(context);
            dc.Connection.EnlistTransaction(t);
        }

        dc.SubmitChanges();

        // Store the request in the OutArgument
        Lead.Set(context, l);
        }
    }
}
```

The AssignLead activity takes an input argument, AssignedTo that specifies the name of the agent being assigned. It provides an output argument, Lead, which is the updated Lead record.

The Execute() method uses the DBExtension to get the correct connection string (refer to Chapter 12 for an explanation). It then queries the Lead table to get the current record. Notice that there is no input argument to indicate which lead is being assigned. The query can obtain the correct record by using the WorkflowInstanceID that is provided in the NativeActivityContext class.

■ **Tip** LINQ to SQL has a tendency to cache database records for better performance. To ensure that you get the current data, the Refresh() method of the data context class is called.

The `AssignedTo` and `Status` properties are then updated, and the changes are written to the database.

RuntimeTransactionHandle

Before the changes are committed, however, the `Execute()` method checks to see whether there is a transaction defined in this context. It does this by using the `RuntimeTransactionHandle` class. The `Properties` property of the `NativeActivityContext` contains a collection of execution properties. If there is an ambient transaction defined for this context, it will be included in this collection.

The `ExecutionPropertyName` property of the `RuntimeTransactionHandle` class defines the name of the transaction handle. This is passed to the `Find()` method. The result from the `Find()` method is cast as a `RuntimeTransactionHandle`.

If the `RuntimeTransactionHandle` was found, the transaction is obtained and passed to the data context class using the `Enlist()` method. When this happens, the database changes are written to the database but not committed yet. They will be committed when all the updates in this transaction have completed. If there is a subsequent failure, the transaction, including these updates, will be rolled back.

CreateAssignment Activity

Now you'll create a custom activity to create an `Assignment` class. This will be similar to the `CreateLead` activity that you created in Chapter 11. In addition to creating the `Assignment` class, it will also insert a record in the `Assignment` table.

From the Solution Explorer, right-click the Activities folder and choose Add ➤ Class. For the class name, enter **CreateAssignment.cs**. The implementation for this activity is shown in Listing 14-2.

Listing 14-2. Implementation of the CreateAssignment Activity

```
using System;
using System.Activities;
using System.Activities.Tracking;
using System.Linq;
using System.Data.Linq;
using System.Transactions;

namespace LeadGenerator
{
    /***************************************************/
    // This custom activity creates an Assignment class
    // using the input parameters (LeadID and AsignedTo).
    /***************************************************/
    public sealed class CreateAssignment : NativeActivity
    {
        public InArgument<int> LeadID { get; set; }
        public InArgument<string> AssignedTo { get; set; }

        protected override void Execute(NativeActivityContext context)
        {
```

```
// Get the connection string
DBExtension ext = context.GetExtension<DBExtension>();
if (ext == null)
    throw new InvalidProgramException("No connection string available");

// Create a data context
LeadDataDataContext dc = new LeadDataDataContext(ext.ConnectionString);

// Enlist on the current transaction
RuntimeTransactionHandle rth = new RuntimeTransactionHandle();
rth = context.Properties.Find(rth.ExecutionPropertyName)
    as RuntimeTransactionHandle;
if (rth != null)
{
    Transaction t = rth.GetCurrentTransaction(context);

    // Open the connection, if necessary
    if (dc.Connection.State == System.Data.ConnectionState.Closed)
        dc.Connection.Open();

    dc.Connection.EnlistTransaction(t);
}

// Create an Assignment class and populate its properties
Assignment a = new Assignment();
dc.Assignments.InsertOnSubmit(a);

a.WorkflowID = context.WorkflowInstanceId;
a.LeadID = LeadID.Get(context);
a.DateAssigned = DateTime.Now;
a.AssignedTo = AssignedTo.Get(context);
a.Status = "Assigned";
a.DateDue = DateTime.Now + TimeSpan.FromDays(5);

dc.SubmitChanges();
        }
    }
}
```

The CreateAssignment activity takes two input arguments: LeadID, which defines the ID of the lead being assigned, and AssignedTo, which is the name of the agent it is being assigned to. The Execute() method gets the connection string from the DBExtension and creates a data context. It then enlists on the ambient transaction if there is one, just as you did with the AssignLead activity.

■ **Caution** Before you can enlist a data context, the connection to the database must be opened first. In the AssignLead activity, the Execute() method had to first query the database so the connection was already open. In this activity, you'll need to check and open the connection, if necessary, before calling the Enlist() method.

The `Execute()` method then creates an `Assignment` class, populates its properties, and submits the changes. Just like with the `AssignLead` activity, if there is a transaction in the context, these changes are not committed until the whole transaction has finished.

Application Changes

Now you'll need to make some adjustments to the application code to work correctly with this new design.

Updating the List of Leads

In the current application, when the Assign button is clicked, the application updates the list to indicate an agent has been assigned. Now you'll modify this so the form is not updated until the workflow indicates the changes have been committed.

Open the `AddLead.xaml.cs` file and add the `UpdateControls()` and `UpdateLead()` methods using the code shown in Listing 14-3.

Listing 14-3. *Implementation of the UpdateControls() and UpdateLead() Methods*

```
private void UpdateControls(Lead l)
{
    lblSelectedNotes.Content = l.Comments;
    lblSelectedNotes.Visibility = Visibility.Visible;
    if (l.Status == "Open")
    {
        lblAgent.Visibility = Visibility.Visible;
        txtAgent.Visibility = Visibility.Visible;
        btnAssign.Visibility = Visibility.Visible;
    }
    else
    {
        lblAgent.Visibility = Visibility.Hidden;
        txtAgent.Visibility = Visibility.Hidden;
        btnAssign.Visibility = Visibility.Hidden;
    }
}

public void UpdateLead(Lead lead)
{
    // Find the row that matches this record
    int nSelected = -1;
    for (int i = 0; i < lstLeads.Items.Count; i++)
    {
        Lead l = lstLeads.Items[i] as Lead;
        if (l.LeadID == lead.LeadID)
        {
            nSelected = i;
            break;
        }
    }
```

```
    // Update the grid
    if (nSelected >= 0)
    {
        lstLeads.Items[nSelected] = lead;
        lstLeads.Items.Refresh();

        UpdateControls(lead);
    }
}
```

The UpdateControls() method updates the controls to reflect the item in the ListView control that is being selected. The UpdateLead() method finds the associated entry in the lstLeads control and updates it using the Lead class passed in.

The lstLeast_SelectionChanged() event handler can be simplified by calling the new UpdateControls() method. Update this method using the following code:

```
private void lstLeads_SelectionChanged(object sender, RoutedEventArgs e)
{
    if (lstLeads.SelectedIndex >= 0)
    {
        Lead l = (Lead)lstLeads.Items[lstLeads.SelectedIndex];
        UpdateControls(l);
    }
    else
    {
        lblSelectedNotes.Content = "";
        lblSelectedNotes.Visibility = Visibility.Hidden;
        lblAgent.Visibility = Visibility.Hidden;
        txtAgent.Visibility = Visibility.Hidden;
        btnAssign.Visibility = Visibility.Hidden;
    }
}
```

Open the ApplicationInterface.cs file and add the following method, which will be used by the workflow to call the UpdateLead() method:

```
public static void UpdateLead(Lead l)
{
    if (_app != null)
        _app.lstLeads.Dispatcher.BeginInvoke(new Action(() => _app.UpdateLead(l)));
}
```

Removing Database Updates

Now you must remove some code from the btnAssign_Click() event handler in the AddLead.xaml.cs file. The final implementation of this method is shown in Listing 14-4. Remove all code not listed here. Also, the ResumeBookmark() method should now pass the agent's name instead of the Lead class.

Listing 14-4. *Final Implementation of btnAssign_Click*

```
private void btnAssign_Click(object sender, RoutedEventArgs e)
{
    if (lstLeads.SelectedIndex >= 0)
    {
        Lead l = (Lead)lstLeads.Items[lstLeads.SelectedIndex];
        Guid id = l.WorkflowID;

        WorkflowApplication i = new WorkflowApplication(new EnterLead());

        SetupInstance(i);
        i.Load(id);

        try
        {
            i.ResumeBookmark("GetAssignment", txtAgent.Text);
        }
        catch (Exception e2)
        {
            AddEvent( e2.Message);
        }
    }
}
```

Adding Workflow Event Handlers

Add the following code to the SetupInstance() method. It displays any exceptions that might be
generated by the workflow, which will help if you need to troubleshoot any issues.

```
// Display any unhandled exceptions
i.OnUnhandledException = (waueea) =>
{
    this.lstEvents.Dispatcher.BeginInvoke(new Action(() =>
        this.lstEvents.Items.Add(waueea.UnhandledException.Message)));
    return UnhandledExceptionAction.Terminate;
};

// Display an error when an instance is aborted
i.Aborted = (waaea) =>
{
    this.lstEvents.Dispatcher.BeginInvoke(new Action(() =>
        this.lstEvents.Items.Add("Aborted: " + waaea.Reason.Message + "\n" +
            waaea.Reason.InnerException.Message)));
};
```

The complete implementation of AddLead.xaml.cs is shown in Listing 14-5.

Listing 14-5. *Complete Implementation of AddLead.xaml.cs*

```csharp
using System;
using System.Collections.Generic;
using System.Linq;
using System.Text;
using System.Windows;
using System.Windows.Controls;
using System.Windows.Data;
using System.Windows.Documents;
using System.Windows.Input;
using System.Windows.Media;
using System.Windows.Media.Imaging;
using System.Windows.Navigation;
using System.Windows.Shapes;

using System.Activities;
using System.Activities.DurableInstancing;
using System.Runtime.DurableInstancing;
using System.Data.Linq;
using System.Configuration;
using System.Activities.Tracking;

namespace LeadGenerator
{
    /// <summary>
    /// Interaction logic for AddLead.xaml
    /// </summary>
    public partial class AddLead : Window
    {
        private string _connectionString = "";
        private InstanceStore _instanceStore;
        private DBExtension _dbExtension;
        private ListBoxTrackingParticipant _tracking;
        private EtwTrackingParticipant _etwTracking;
        private SqlTrackingParticipant _sqlTracking;

        public AddLead()
        {
            InitializeComponent();

            ApplicationInterface._app = this;
        }

        // Add a line of text to the Event Log
        private void AddEvent(string szText)
        {
            lstEvents.Items.Add(szText);
        }

        public ListBox GetEventListBox()
```

```
{
    return this.lstEvents;
}

private void Window_Loaded(object sender, RoutedEventArgs e)
{
    // Open the config file and get the connection string
    Configuration config =
        ConfigurationManager.OpenExeConfiguration
            (ConfigurationUserLevel.None);
    ConnectionStringsSection css =
        (ConnectionStringsSection)config.GetSection("connectionStrings");
    _connectionString
        = css.ConnectionStrings["LeadGenerator"].ConnectionString;

    _instanceStore = new SqlWorkflowInstanceStore(_connectionString);
    InstanceView view = _instanceStore.Execute
        (_instanceStore.CreateInstanceHandle(),
        new CreateWorkflowOwnerCommand(),
        TimeSpan.FromSeconds(30));
    _instanceStore.DefaultInstanceOwner = view.InstanceOwner;

    // Create the DBExtension
    _dbExtension = new DBExtension(_connectionString);

    // Set up the tracking participants
    CreateTrackingParticipant();
    CreateETWTrackingParticipant();
    CreateSqlTrackingParticipant();

    LoadExistingLeads();
}

private void btnAddLead_Click(object sender, RoutedEventArgs e)
{
    // Setup a dictionary object for passing parameters
    Dictionary<string, object> parameters =
        new Dictionary<string, object>();
    parameters.Add("ContactName", txtName.Text);
    parameters.Add("ContactPhone", txtPhone.Text);
    parameters.Add("Interests", txtInterest.Text);
    parameters.Add("Notes", txtNotes.Text);
    parameters.Add("Rating", int.Parse(txtRating.Text));
    parameters.Add("Writer", new ListBoxTextWriter(lstEvents));

    WorkflowApplication i = new WorkflowApplication
        (new EnterLead(), parameters);

    // Setup persistence
    SetupInstance(i);

    i.Run();
```

```csharp
    }
    public void AddNewLead(Lead l)
    {
        this.lstLeads.Dispatcher.BeginInvoke
            (new Action(() => this.lstLeads.Items.Add(l)));
    }

    private void lstLeads_SelectionChanged(object sender, RoutedEventArgs e)
    {
        if (lstLeads.SelectedIndex >= 0)
        {
            Lead l = (Lead)lstLeads.Items[lstLeads.SelectedIndex];
            UpdateControls(l);
        }
        else
        {
            lblSelectedNotes.Content = "";
            lblSelectedNotes.Visibility = Visibility.Hidden;
            lblAgent.Visibility = Visibility.Hidden;
            txtAgent.Visibility = Visibility.Hidden;
            btnAssign.Visibility = Visibility.Hidden;
        }
    }

    private void btnAssign_Click(object sender, RoutedEventArgs e)
    {
        if (lstLeads.SelectedIndex >= 0)
        {
            Lead l = (Lead)lstLeads.Items[lstLeads.SelectedIndex];
            Guid id = l.WorkflowID;

            WorkflowApplication i = new WorkflowApplication(new EnterLead());

            SetupInstance(i);
            i.Load(id);

            try
            {
                i.ResumeBookmark("GetAssignment", txtAgent.Text);
            }
            catch (Exception e2)
            {
                AddEvent(e2.Message);
            }
        }
    }

    private void LoadExistingLeads()
    {
        LeadDataDataContext dc = new LeadDataDataContext(_connectionString);
        dc.Refresh(RefreshMode.OverwriteCurrentValues, dc.Leads);
```

```
        IEnumerable<Lead> q = dc.Leads
            .Where<Lead>(x => x.Status == "Open" || x.Status == "Assigned");
        foreach (Lead l in q)
        {
            AddNewLead(l);
        }
    }

    private void SetupInstance(WorkflowApplication i)
    {
        // Setup the instance store
        i.InstanceStore = _instanceStore;

        // Setup the PersistableIdle event handler
        i.PersistableIdle = (waiea) => PersistableIdleAction.Unload;

        // Setup the connection string
        i.Extensions.Add(_dbExtension);

        // Display the accumulated comments
        i.Completed = (wacea) =>
        {
            // Get the CommentExtension
            IEnumerable<CommentExtension> q =
                wacea.GetInstanceExtensions<CommentExtension>();

            // Add the comments to the event log
            if (q.Count() > 0)
            {
                string comments = "Comments: \r\n" +
                    q.First<CommentExtension>().Comments;
                this.lstEvents.Dispatcher.BeginInvoke
                    (new Action(() => this.lstEvents.Items.Add(comments)));
            }

            this.lstEvents.Dispatcher.BeginInvoke
                (new Action(() => this.lstEvents.Items.Add
                    ("\r\nThe workflow has completed")));
        };

        // Display any unhandled exceptions
        i.OnUnhandledException = (waueea) =>
        {
            this.lstEvents.Dispatcher.BeginInvoke(new Action(() =>
                this.lstEvents.Items.Add(waueea.UnhandledException.Message)));
            return UnhandledExceptionAction.Terminate;
        };

        // Display an error when an instance is aborted
        i.Aborted = (waaea) =>
        {
```

```
            this.lstEvents.Dispatcher.BeginInvoke(new Action(() =>
                this.lstEvents.Items.Add("Aborted: " +
                    waaea.Reason.Message + "\n" +
                    waaea.Reason.InnerException.Message)));
    };

    // Set up tracking
    i.Extensions.Add(_tracking);
    i.Extensions.Add(_etwTracking);
    i.Extensions.Add(_sqlTracking);
}

private void UpdateControls(Lead l)
{
    lblSelectedNotes.Content = l.Comments;
    lblSelectedNotes.Visibility = Visibility.Visible;
    if (l.Status == "Open")
    {
        lblAgent.Visibility = Visibility.Visible;
        txtAgent.Visibility = Visibility.Visible;
        btnAssign.Visibility = Visibility.Visible;
    }
    else
    {
        lblAgent.Visibility = Visibility.Hidden;
        txtAgent.Visibility = Visibility.Hidden;
        btnAssign.Visibility = Visibility.Hidden;
    }
}

public void UpdateLead(Lead lead)
{
    // Find the row that matches this record
    int nSelected = -1;
    for (int i = 0; i < lstLeads.Items.Count; i++)
    {
        Lead l = lstLeads.Items[i] as Lead;
        if (l.LeadID == lead.LeadID)
        {
            nSelected = i;
            break;
        }
    }
    // Update the grid
    if (nSelected >= 0)
    {
        lstLeads.Items[nSelected] = lead;
        lstLeads.Items.Refresh();

        UpdateControls(lead);
    }
}
```

```
private void CreateTrackingParticipant()
{
    _tracking = new ListBoxTrackingParticipant(this.lstEvents)
    {
        TrackingProfile = new TrackingProfile()
        {
            Name = "ListBoxTrackingProfile",
            Queries =
            {
                // For instance data, only track the started
                // and completed events
                new WorkflowInstanceQuery()
                {
                    States = { WorkflowInstanceStates.Started,
                               WorkflowInstanceStates.Completed },
                },

                // For bookmark data, only track the GetAssignment event
                new BookmarkResumptionQuery()
                {
                    Name = "GetAssignment"
                },

                // For activity data, track all states of the InvokeMethod
                new ActivityStateQuery()
                {
                    ActivityName = "InvokeMethod",
                    States = { "*" },
                },

                // For User data, track all events
                new CustomTrackingQuery()
                {
                    Name = "*",
                    ActivityName = "*"
                }
            }
        }
    };
}

private void CreateETWTrackingParticipant()
{
    _etwTracking = new EtwTrackingParticipant()
    {
        TrackingProfile = new TrackingProfile()
        {
            Name = "EtwTrackingProfile",
            Queries =
            {
                new CustomTrackingQuery()
```

```csharp
            {
              Name = "*",
              ActivityName = "*"
            }
          }
        }
    };
}

private void CreateSqlTrackingParticipant()
{
    _sqlTracking = new SqlTrackingParticipant(_connectionString)
    {
        TrackingProfile = new TrackingProfile()
        {
            Name = "SqlTrackingProfile",
            Queries =
            {
                new WorkflowInstanceQuery()
                {
                    States = { "*" },
                },

                new BookmarkResumptionQuery()
                {
                    Name = "*"
                },
                new ActivityStateQuery()
                {
                    // Subscribe for track records from all activities
                    // for all states
                    ActivityName = "*",
                    States = { "*" },
                },
                // For User data, track all events
                new CustomTrackingQuery()
                {

                    Name = "*",
                    ActivityName = "*"
                }
            }
        }
    };
}
}
}
```

Workflow Changes

Now you'll modify the workflow to use the new `AssignLead` and `CreateAssignment` activities. Open the `LeadGeneratorWF.cs` file and add the following `Variable`. It should go at the beginning of the `EnterLead` constructor in which the other `Variable` objects are defined.

```
Variable<string> assignedTo = new Variable<string> { Name = "assignedTo" };
```

You will also need to add this to the variable list declared in the body of the workflow as demonstrated in the following code:

```
Variables = { lead, assignedTo },
```

Then replace the existing `WaitForInput` activity with the code shown in Listing 14-6.

Listing 14-6. *Additional Workflow Activities*

```
new WaitForInput<string>
{
    BookmarkName = "GetAssignment",
    Input = new OutArgument<string>(env => assignedTo.Get(env))
},
new TransactionScope
{
    Body = new Sequence
    {
        Activities =
        {
            new AssignLead
            {
                AssignedTo = new InArgument<string>(env => assignedTo.Get(env)),
                Lead = new OutArgument<Lead>(env => lead.Get(env)),
            },
            new Delay
            {
                Duration = TimeSpan.FromSeconds(20)
            },
            new CreateAssignment
            {
                AssignedTo = new InArgument<string>(env => assignedTo.Get(env)),
                LeadID = new InArgument<int>(env => lead.Get(env).LeadID),
            }
        }
    },
},
new InvokeMethod
{
    TargetType = typeof(ApplicationInterface),
    MethodName = "UpdateLead",
    Parameters =
```

```
    {
        new InArgument<Lead>(env => lead.Get(env))
    }
},
```

The WaitForInput activity was modified to expect the agent's name as a string instead of a Lead class. This was necessary because the application is no longer updating the Lead class. At the time the workflow is resumed, the Lead class does not have the AssignedTo property populated. Instead, the application will provide the agent's name and let the workflow update the Lead.

TransactionScope

The first activity you added was a TransactionScope. It has a single child activity that is a Sequence activity. The Sequence activity has three child activities: the AssignLead and CreateAssignment custom activities separated by a Delay activity.

A TransactionScope creates a database transaction that is stored in the NativeActivityContext so it is available to all the child activities. You already coded the AssignLead and CreateAssignment activities to use this transaction when making the database updates. The transaction is committed when all child activities have completed.

The Delay activity is added so you can verify that the first update (by AssignLead) is not committed until the insert (by CreateAssignment) is finished.

InvokeMethod

You have used the InvokeMethod activity before. This is how the workflow will inform that application that the lead has been updated. In this scenario, it calls the UpdateLead() method that you just implemented, passing in the updated Lead class.

The complete implementation of the LeadGeneratorWF class is shown in Listing 14-7

Listing 14-7. Final Implementation of the LeadGeneratorWF Class

```
using System;
using System.Activities;
using System.Activities.Statements;
using System.IO;

namespace LeadGenerator
{
    /**************************************************/
    // This file contains the definition of the EnterLead
    // workflow
    /**************************************************/
    public sealed class EnterLead : Activity
    {
        // Define the input and output arguments
        public InArgument<string> ContactName { get; set; }
        public InArgument<string> ContactPhone { get; set; }
        public InArgument<string> Interests { get; set; }
```

```csharp
public InArgument<string> Notes { get; set; }
public InArgument<int> Rating { get; set; }
public InArgument<TextWriter> Writer { get; set; }

public EnterLead()
{
    // Define the variables used by this workflow
    Variable<Lead> lead = new Variable<Lead> { Name = "lead" };
    Variable<string> assignedTo = new Variable<string>
        { Name = "assignedTo" };

    // Define the SendRequest workflow
    this.Implementation = () => new Sequence
    {
        DisplayName = "EnterLead",
        Variables = { lead, assignedTo },
        Activities =
        {
            new CreateLead
            {
                ContactName = new InArgument<string>
                    (env => ContactName.Get(env)),
                ContactPhone = new InArgument<string>
                    (env => ContactPhone.Get(env)),
                Interests = new InArgument<string>
                    (env => Interests.Get(env)),
                Notes = new InArgument<string>(env => Notes.Get(env)),
                Lead = new OutArgument<Lead>(env => lead.Get(env)),
            },
            new WriteLine
            {
                Text = new InArgument<string>
                    (env => "Lead received [" + Rating.Get(env).ToString()
                     + "]; waiting for assignment"),
                TextWriter = new InArgument<TextWriter>
                    (env => Writer.Get(env))
            },
            new InvokeMethod
            {
                TargetType = typeof(ApplicationInterface),
                MethodName = "NewLead",
                Parameters =
                {
                    new InArgument<Lead>(env => lead.Get(env))
                }
            },
            new AddComment
            {
                Comment = new InArgument<string>
                    (env => "Lead has been created")
            },
```

```
new WaitForInput<string>
{
    BookmarkName = "GetAssignment",
    Input = new OutArgument<string>(env => assignedTo.Get(env))
},
new TransactionScope
{
    Body = new Sequence
    {
        Activities =
        {
            new AssignLead
            {
                AssignedTo = new InArgument<string>
                    (env => assignedTo.Get(env)),
                Lead = new OutArgument<Lead>
                    (env => lead.Get(env)),
            },
            new Delay
            {
                Duration = TimeSpan.FromSeconds(20)
            },
            new CreateAssignment
            {
                AssignedTo = new InArgument<string>
                    (env => assignedTo.Get(env)),
                LeadID = new InArgument<int>
                    (env => lead.Get(env).LeadID),
            }
        }
    },
},
new InvokeMethod
{
    TargetType = typeof(ApplicationInterface),
    MethodName = "UpdateLead",
    Parameters =
    {
        new InArgument<Lead>(env => lead.Get(env))
    }
},
new AddComment
{
    Comment = new InArgument<string>
        (env => "Lead is being assigned")
},
new WriteLine
{
    Text = new InArgument<string>
        (env => "Lead assigned [" + Rating.Get(env).ToString()
        + "] to " + lead.Get(env).AssignedTo),
```

```
                    TextWriter = new InArgument<TextWriter>
                        (env => Writer.Get(env))

                }
            }
        };
    }
  }
}
```

Running the Application

Now you're ready to run the application. Other than the 20-second delay when you assign an agent, it should work just like the solution from Chapter 13. You can demonstrate that both updates are committed as an atomic unit by closing the application after you click the Assign button.

The Lead record is updated before the delay, but not committed until after the delay. If you close the application during the delay, this update should be rolled back. Look at the data in the Lead table and verify that the Status is still Open and the AssignedTo field is null. If you restart the application, you should be able to select this lead and assign an agent.

■ **Caution** When a workflow instance is created or loaded from the persistence store, it is locked to prevent other users from accessing it. Under normal circumstances, it is unlocked when the instance becomes idle (and is unloaded from memory). If you close the application when an activity is in progress, the normal unlock sequence is skipped. When you shut down the application and restart it, it might look like a different user to the workflow and when you try to reload it, you'll get an InstanceLockedException. The instance store will eventually release the lock; you might have to wait a minute or so.

■ ■ ■

CHAPTER 15

Transactions with Persistence

In this chapter, you will modify the application to coordinate the database updates with the workflow persistence so they are performed on the same database transaction. This will ensure that your application tables are consistent with the instance data. You will provide extensions that override the PersistenceParticipant class and update your application data when the workflow is persisted.

Setting Up the Solution

You will reuse the project that you developed in Chapter 14. Start by creating a blank solution, as shown in Figure 15-1. For the solution name, enter **Chapter15**.

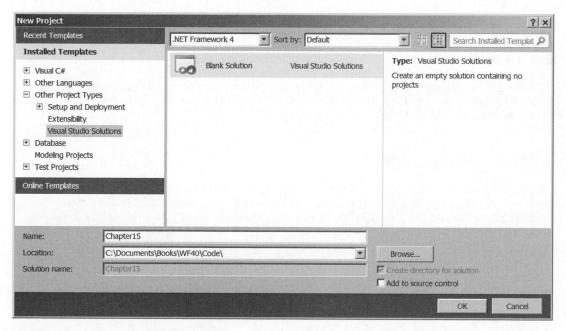

Figure 15-1. *Creating a blank solution*

From Windows Explorer, copy the LeadGenerator folder from the Chapter14 folder to the Chapter15 folder. Back in Visual Studio, from the Solution Explorer, right-click the Chapter15 solution and choose Add ➤ Existing Project. Select the LeadGenerator project that you just copied to the Chapter15 folder. Create a Chapter15 database and run the following scripts to initialize the database schema:

- SqlWorkflowInstanceStoreSchema.sql

- SqlWorkflowInstanceStoreLogic.sql

- Lead.sql

- Tracking.sql

Open the app.config file and change the connection string to use the Chapter15 database.

PersistenceParticipant

In Chapter 12, you created a CommentExtension that allowed you to append a comment string. The comment was persisted along with the workflow instance data by inheriting from the PersistenceParticipant class and overriding the CollectValues() and PublishValues() methods. You will now use a similar approach in this chapter, but first, let's review.

Persistence providers perform two basic operations:

- Save—when a workflow instance is persisted to a durable store

- Load—when a workflow instance is reloaded into memory

When one of these operations is being performed, the extensions included on the instance are enumerated. The corresponding methods are called in any extension that is derived from the PersistenceParticipant class.

The CollectValues() method in the CommentExtension returned the comment string to the persistence provider. This was then passed back to the CommentExtension when the PublishValues() method was called. Although this is a convenient way to persist custom data, the data is persisted as part of the workflow state data. Now I'll show you how this technique can be used to update application tables (such as the Lead and Assignment tables you're using).

PersistLead Extension

You will create a custom extension that will perform updates to the Lead table when the workflow is persisted. From the Solution Explorer, right-click the Extensions folder (under the LeadGenerator project) and choose Add ➤ Class. For the class name, enter **PersistLead.cs**. The implementation of this class is shown in Listing 15-1.

Listing 15-1. Implementation of PersistLead.cs

```csharp
using System;
using System.Activities.Persistence;
using System.Collections.Generic;
using System.Linq;
using System.Data.Linq;
using System.Transactions;
using System.Xml.Linq;

namespace LeadGenerator
{
    public class PersistLead : PersistenceParticipant
    {
        private string _connectionString;
        private IDictionary<Guid, Lead> _object;
        private IDictionary<Guid, string> _action;

        public PersistLead(string connectionString)
        {
            _connectionString = connectionString;

            _object = new Dictionary<Guid, Lead>();
            _action = new Dictionary<Guid, string>();
        }

        internal void AddLead(Lead l, string action)
        {
            _object.Remove(l.WorkflowID);
            _action.Remove(l.WorkflowID);

            _object.Add(l.WorkflowID, l);
            _action.Add(l.WorkflowID, action);
        }


        protected override void CollectValues
            (out IDictionary<XName, object> readWriteValues,
             out IDictionary<XName, object> writeOnlyValues)
        {
            // We're not actually providing data to the caller
            readWriteValues = null;
            writeOnlyValues = null;

            // See if there is any work to do...
            if (_object.Count > 0)
            {
                // Get the current transaction
                Transaction t = System.Transactions.Transaction.Current;

                // Setup the DataContext
```

```
        LeadDataDataContext dc = new LeadDataDataContext(_connectionString);

        // Open the connection, if necessary
        if (dc.Connection.State == System.Data.ConnectionState.Closed)
            dc.Connection.Open();

        if (t != null)
            dc.Connection.EnlistTransaction(t);

        // Process each object in our work queue
        foreach (KeyValuePair<Guid, Lead> kvp in _object)
        {
            Lead l = kvp.Value as Lead;
            string action = _action[l.WorkflowID];

            // Perform the insert
            if (action == "Insert")
            {
                dc.Leads.InsertOnSubmit(l);
            }

            // Perform the update
            if (action == "Update")
            {
                dc.Refresh(RefreshMode.OverwriteCurrentValues, dc.Leads);
                Lead lTmp = dc.Leads.SingleOrDefault<Lead>
                    (x => x.WorkflowID == l.WorkflowID);

                if (lTmp != null)
                {
                    lTmp.AssignedTo = l.AssignedTo;
                    lTmp.Status = l.Status;
                }
            }
        }

        // Submit all the changes to the database
        dc.SubmitChanges();

        // Remove all objects since the changes have been submitted
        _object.Clear();
        _action.Clear();
    }
  }
}
```

The PersistLead class has two Dictionary objects: the first stores the Lead objects that represent records that need to be persisted, and the second stores the action that is required (Insert, Update, or Delete). Both will use the same key, which is the workflow instance ID. These dictionaries represent the work that is needed to be done; we'll call this the *work queue*. The connection string is passed in to the constructor. The AddLead() method is used by the application or the workflow to place items in the work queue.

■ **Note** The AddLead() method first calls Remove() to make sure that there isn't a work item for this instance. A typical scenario might be that a Lead record was modified and the updated record was placed in the work queue. Then another update was made before the workflow was persisted. The second update supersedes the first update, so we need to remove the first one.

Connecting to the Database

The current transaction is obtained from the static Transaction class. This will be the transaction currently being used by the SqlWorkflowInstanceStore class. Then a DataContext class is created, which was generated by the O/R Designer in the previous chapter. The connection string is passed in to the constructor. The connection to the database is opened if it was not already open. Finally, if there is a current transaction, it is passed to the DataContext using the EnlistTransaction() method.

Performing the Updates

The CollectValues() method then iterates the items in the work queue, obtaining both the Lead object and the action to be taken. For Insert, the code simply passes the Lead object to the DataContext using the InsertOnSubmit() method. For updates, it has to first query the record from the database and then apply the updates from the Lead object in the work queue. In this project, once a Lead is inserted, the only changes that are allowed are to assign it, so the code updates only the Status and AssignedTo columns.

Once all the items in the work queue have been completed, the SubmitChanges() method is called to make the updates. They will not be committed, however, until the entire persistence operation has completed. The last step is to remove all the items from the work queue. Now that the work is done, they can be removed. You don't want to take action on them again the next time the instance is persisted.

■ **Tip** You are not actually returning any data items for the workflow to persist. The readWriteValues and writeOnlyValues are simply set to null. Also, notice that the PublishValues() method is not overridden here because we don't expect any data to be provided.

Using the PersistLead Extension

Now you'll need to change every place where the Lead table is being modified directly and use the PersistLead extension instead. There are two custom activities that will require modification: CreateLead and AssignLead.

Modifying the CreateLead Activity

Currently, the CreateLead activity inserts a Lead record into the database. Now, you'll modify this activity to use the PersistLead extension instead. Open the CreateLead.cs class in the Activities folder. The modified implementation is shown in Listing 15-2.

Listing 15-2. Modified Implementation of CreateLead.cs

```
using System;
using System.Activities;
using System.Activities.Tracking;

namespace LeadGenerator
{
    /****************************************************/
    // This custom activity creates a Lead class using
    // the input parameters (ContactName, ContactPhone,
    // Interests and Notes).  A Lead record is inserted
    // into the database and then this is returned in
    // the Lead output parameter.
    /****************************************************/
    public sealed class CreateLead : CodeActivity
    {
        public InArgument<string> ContactName { get; set; }
        public InArgument<string> ContactPhone { get; set; }
        public InArgument<string> Interests { get; set; }
        public InArgument<string> Notes { get; set; }
        public InArgument<string> ConnectionString { get; set; }
        public OutArgument<Lead> Lead { get; set; }

        protected override void Execute(CodeActivityContext context)
        {
            // Create a Lead class and populate it with the input arguments
            Lead l = new Lead();
            l.ContactName = ContactName.Get(context);
            l.ContactPhone = ContactPhone.Get(context);
            l.Interests = Interests.Get(context);
            l.Comments = Notes.Get(context);
            l.WorkflowID = context.WorkflowInstanceId;
            l.Status = "Open";

            // Add this to the work queue to be persisted later
            PersistLead persist = context.GetExtension<PersistLead>();
            persist.AddLead(l, "Insert");

            // Store the request in the OutArgument
            Lead.Set(context, l);

            // Add a custom track record
            CustomTrackingRecord userRecord = new CustomTrackingRecord("New Lead")
```

```
        {
            Data =
            {
                {"Name", l.ContactName},
                {"Phone", l.ContactPhone}
            }
        };

        // Emit the custom tracking record
        context.Track(userRecord);
    }
  }
}
```

The class is changed to remove all the code that performed the database update and replace it with the following code:

```
PersistLead persist = context.GetExtension<PersistLead>();
persist.AddLead(l, "Insert");
```

This code gets the `PersistLead` extension and calls its `AddLead()` method. This will place this `Lead` object on the work queue to be inserted when the instance is persisted.

Modifying the AssignLead Activity

Now make similar changes to the `AssignLead` activity. The modified implementation is shown in Listing 15-3.

Listing 15-3. *Modified Implementation of AssignLead.cs*

```
using System;
using System.Activities;

namespace LeadGenerator
{
    /*****************************************************/
    // This custom activity assigns a Lead to the specified
    // person (AssignedTo parameter). The updated Lead is
    // returned in the output parameter.
    /*****************************************************/
    public sealed class AssignLead : CodeActivity
    {
        public InArgument<string> AssignedTo { get; set; }
        public InOutArgument<Lead> Lead { get; set; }

        protected override void Execute(CodeActivityContext context)
        {
            Lead l = Lead.Get(context);
            l.AssignedTo = AssignedTo.Get(context);
```

```
                    l.Status = "Assigned";

                    PersistLead persist = context.GetExtension<PersistLead>();
                    persist.AddLead(l, "Update");

                    // Store the request in the OutArgument
                    Lead.Set(context, l);
                }
            }
        }
```

PersistAssignment Extension

Now you'll provide an extension for persisting the Assignment table. The implementation is very similar to PersistLead. From the Solution Explorer, right-click the Extensions folder and choose Add ➤ Class. For the class name, enter **PersistAssignment.cs**. The implementation is shown in Listing 15-4.

Listing 15-4. *Implementation of PersistAssignment.cs*

```
using System;
using System.Activities.Persistence;
using System.Collections.Generic;
using System.Linq;
using System.Data.Linq;
using System.Transactions;
using System.Xml.Linq;

namespace LeadGenerator
{
    public class PersistAssignment : PersistenceParticipant
    {
        private string _connectionString;
        private IDictionary<Guid, Assignment> _object;
        private IDictionary<Guid, string> _action;

        public PersistAssignment(string connectionString)
        {
            _connectionString = connectionString;

            _object = new Dictionary<Guid, Assignment>();
            _action = new Dictionary<Guid, string>();
        }

        internal void AddAssignment(Guid id, Assignment a, string action)
        {
            // Make sure there isn't one already here
            _object.Remove(id);
            _action.Remove(id);
```

```
        _object.Add(id, a);
        _action.Add(id, action);
}


protected override void CollectValues
        (out IDictionary<XName, object> readWriteValues,
         out IDictionary<XName, object> writeOnlyValues)
{
        // We're not actually providing data to the caller
        readWriteValues = null;
        writeOnlyValues = null;

        // See if there is any work to do...
        if (_object.Count > 0)
        {
            // Get the current transaction
            Transaction t = System.Transactions.Transaction.Current;

            // Setup the DataContext
            LeadDataDataContext dc = new LeadDataDataContext(_connectionString);

            // Open the connection, if necessary
            if (dc.Connection.State == System.Data.ConnectionState.Closed)
                dc.Connection.Open();

            if (t != null)
                dc.Connection.EnlistTransaction(t);

            // Process each object in our work queue
            foreach (KeyValuePair<Guid, Assignment> kvp in _object)
            {
                Assignment a = kvp.Value as Assignment;
                string action = _action[kvp.Key];

                // Perform the insert
                if (action == "Insert")
                {
                    dc.Assignments.InsertOnSubmit(a);
                }

                // Perform the update
                if (action == "Update")
                {
                    dc.Refresh(RefreshMode.OverwriteCurrentValues, dc.Leads);
                    Assignment aTmp = dc.Assignments
                        .SingleOrDefault<Assignment>
                            (x => x.WorkflowID == kvp.Key);

                    if (aTmp != null)
                    {
                        aTmp.DateCompleted = a.DateCompleted;
```

```
                            aTmp.Remarks = a.Remarks;
                            aTmp.Status = a.Status;
                        }
                    }
                }

                // Submit all the changes to the database
                dc.SubmitChanges();

                // Remove all objects since the changes have been submitted
                _object.Clear();
                _action.Clear();
            }
        }
    }
}
```

The only difference in the way this extension was implemented is that the workflow instance ID is passed in to the AddAssignment() method. This is necessary because the Assignment class does not store the workflow instance ID like the Lead class does.

Using the PersistAssignment Extension

Open the CreateAssignment.cs file (in the Activities folder). Make the same modifications to this file that you did for the CreateLead and AssignLead activities. The modified code is shown in Listing 15-5.

Listing 15-5. *Modified Implementation of CreateAssignment.cs*

```
using System;
using System.Activities;

namespace LeadGenerator
{
    /*****************************************************/
    // This custom activity creates an Assignment class
    // using the input parameters (LeadID and AsignedTo).
    /*****************************************************/
    public sealed class CreateAssignment : CodeActivity
    {
        public InArgument<int> LeadID { get; set; }
        public InArgument<string> AssignedTo { get; set; }

        protected override void Execute(CodeActivityContext context)
        {
            // Create an Assignment class and populate its properties
            Assignment a = new Assignment();

            a.WorkflowID = context.WorkflowInstanceId;
            a.LeadID = LeadID.Get(context);
            a.DateAssigned = DateTime.Now;
```

```
            a.AssignedTo = AssignedTo.Get(context);
            a.Status = "Assigned";
            a.DateDue = DateTime.Now + TimeSpan.FromDays(5);

            PersistAssignment persist = context.GetExtension<PersistAssignment>();
            persist.AddAssignment(context.WorkflowInstanceId, a, "Insert");
        }
    }
}
```

Application Changes

Open the AddLead.xaml.cs file and, in the SetupInstance() method, add the following code to assign these extensions to the workflow instances:

```
// Setup persistence
i.Extensions.Add(new PersistLead(_connectionString));
i.Extensions.Add(new PersistAssignment(_connectionString));
```

Open the LeadGeneratorWF.cs file. For the AssignLead activity, the Lead argument has been changed to an InOutArgment. Make the same change here as well.

Running the Application

Now you're ready to run the application. It should work just like the application from the previous chapter. There is one minor difference, however. There should be a 20-second delay between the AssignLead and CreateAssignment activities. In the implementation used in Chapter 14, the Lead table is updated before the delay but not committed until after. This means that the record is locked; if you try to query the table, the query will wait until the lock is released.

You can try this by starting Visual Studio and opening the Chapter14 solution and starting the application. Create a lead and assign it. During the 20-second delay, try running a query against the Lead table. The query will wait until the application has committed the update before returning the data.

Now try the same thing with the Chapter 15 implementation. You'll see that it returns right away; it doesn't reflect the assignment yet, but the record is not locked. This is because the database operation is not actually performed until the workflow is persisted, which isn't until after TransactionScopeActivity has completed.

The obvious advantage of using this approach is that the application updates are consistent with the workflow. This eliminates the possibility of the workflow marking an activity complete but the application data not actually being saved (or vice versa). Another advantage is that the application updates are all done at the same time. If there are multiple updates spread throughout the workflow, this could lock the database while waiting for the other updates to be completed. With this approach, the updates are queued up in the workflow and not actually applied until all processing has completed.

One aspect that is particularly nice about this approach is that all the database work is done in a separate class. The workflow activities such as CreateLead and AssignLead do not perform any database persistence. This allows you to focus on the business requirements when designing the workflow without being concerned about database updates. The database updates are now logically and physically attached to the process of persistence, rather than the workflow logic.

CHAPTER 16

WorkflowServiceHost

So far in this section, you built an application that is used to enter sales leads and assign them to a sales agent. For the final chapter in this section, you'll create a separate application that the agents can use to view and update their leads.

Setting Up the Solution

You will reuse the solution that you developed in Chapter 15. Start by creating a blank solution, as shown in Figure 16-1. For the solution name, enter **Chapter16**.

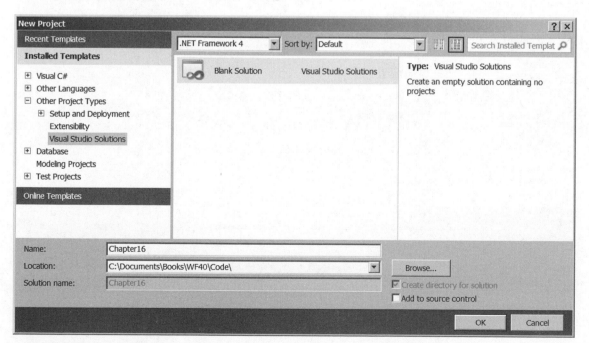

Figure 16-1. Creating a blank solution

From Windows Explorer, copy the LeadGenerator folder from the Chapter15 folder to the Chapter16 folder. In Visual Studio, from the Solution Explorer, right-click the Chapter16 solution and choose Add ➤ Existing Project. Select the LeadGenerator project that you just copied to the Chapter16 folder. Create a Chapter16 database and run the following scripts to initialize the database schema:

- SqlWorkflowInstanceStoreSchema.sql

- SqlWorkflowInstanceStoreLogic.sql

- Lead.sql

- Tracking.sql

Open the app.config file and change the connection string to use the Chapter16 database.

Adding LeadResponse

You'll start by creating the new application called LeadResponse. From the Solution Explorer, right-click the Chapter16 solution and choose Add ➤ New Project. In the Add New Project dialog, select the WPF Application template and enter **LeadResponse** for the Name, as shown in Figure 16-2.

Figure 16-2. *Adding the LeadResponse project*

Renaming the Window

The template will generate a window form named `MainWindow.xaml`. Rename this file to `FollowUpLead.xaml`. Open the `App.xaml` file and change the `StartupUri` attribute as follows:

```
StartupUri="FollowUpLead.xaml"
```

Then open the `FollowUpLead.xaml.cs` file and modify the class as follows (the modified lines are in bold):

```
namespace LeadResponse
{
    /// <summary>
    /// Interaction logic for FollowUpLead.xaml
    /// </summary>
    public partial class FollowUpLead : Window
    {
        public FollowUpLead()
        {
            InitializeComponent();
        }
    }
}
```

In the Solution Explorer, right-click the LeadResponse project and choose Add Reference. From the .NET tab, add the following references:

- `System.Activities`

- `System.Activities.DurableInstancing`

- `System.Configuration`

- `System.Data.Linq`

- `System.Runtime.DurableInstancing`

- `System.ServiceModel`

- `System.ServiceModel.Activities`

- `System.Transactions`

You'll also need to add a reference to the LeadGenerator project, which you'll find in the Projects tab.

Defining the Window Form

Open the `FollowUpLead.xaml` file. Double-click the XAML tab and enter the code shown in Listing 16-1.

Listing 16-1. *Implementation of FollowUpLead.xaml*

```
<Window x:Class="LeadResponse.FollowUpLead"
        xmlns="http://schemas.microsoft.com/winfx/2006/xaml/presentation"
        xmlns:x="http://schemas.microsoft.com/winfx/2006/xaml"
```

```xml
       Title="Lead Follow-Up" Height="518" Width="547"
       Loaded="Window_Loaded" Unloaded="Window_Unloaded">
  <Grid MinWidth="300" MinHeight="100" Width="514">
    <ListView x:Name="lstLeads" Margin="10,12,10,0" Height="145"
     VerticalAlignment="Top" ItemsSource="{Binding}"
     HorizontalContentAlignment="Center"
     SelectionChanged="lstLeads_SelectionChanged" >
        <ListView.View>
            <GridView>
                <GridViewColumn Header="Current Leads" Width="480">
                    <GridViewColumn.CellTemplate>
                        <DataTemplate>
                            <StackPanel Orientation="Horizontal">
                                <TextBlock Text="{Binding Lead.ContactName}"
                                 Width="110"/>
                                <TextBlock Text="{Binding Lead.ContactPhone}"
                                 Width="70"/>
                                <TextBlock Text="{Binding Lead.Interests}"
                                 Width="130"/>
                                <TextBlock Text="{Binding Status}"
                                 Width="70"/>
                                <TextBlock Text="{Binding AssignedTo}"
                                 Width="100"/>
                            </StackPanel>
                        </DataTemplate>
                    </GridViewColumn.CellTemplate>
                </GridViewColumn>
            </GridView>
        </ListView.View>
    </ListView>
    <Label Height="37" Margin="12,163,3,0"
     Name="lblSelectedNotes" VerticalAlignment="Top" Visibility="Hidden" />

    <Label Height="28" Margin="12,190,0,0" Width="60" Content="Assigned:"
     Name="lblAssigned" VerticalAlignment="Top"
     HorizontalAlignment="Left" HorizontalContentAlignment="Right" />
    <Label Height="28" Margin="12,220,0,0" Width="60" Content="Due:"
     Name="lblDue" VerticalAlignment="Top"
     HorizontalAlignment="Left" HorizontalContentAlignment="Right" />
    <Label Height="28" Margin="12,250,0,0" Width="60" Content="Complete:"
     Name="lblComplete" VerticalAlignment="Top"
     HorizontalAlignment="Left" HorizontalContentAlignment="Right" />

    <Label Height="28" Margin="82,190,0,0" Width="100"
     Name="lblDateAssigned" VerticalAlignment="Top"
     HorizontalAlignment="Left" />
    <Label Height="28" Margin="82,220,0,0" Width="100"
     Name="lblDateDue" VerticalAlignment="Top"
     HorizontalAlignment="Left" />
    <Label Height="28" Margin="82,250,0,0" Width="100"
     Name="lblDateCompleted" VerticalAlignment="Top"
     HorizontalAlignment="Left" />
```

```xml
            <Label Height="28" Margin="200,200,0,0" Width="60" Content="Remarks:"
             Name="lblRemarks" VerticalAlignment="Top" HorizontalAlignment="Left" />
            <TextBox Height="100" HorizontalAlignment="Stretch" Margin="200,220,10,0"
             Name="txtRemarks" VerticalAlignment="Top"  />
            <Button Height="25" Margin="100,290,0,0" Name="btnComplete"
             VerticalAlignment="Top" HorizontalAlignment="Left" Width="90"
             Click="btnComplete_Click" >Complete</Button>

            <Label Height="27" HorizontalAlignment="Left" Margin="10,0,0,140"
             Name="lblEvent" VerticalAlignment="Bottom" Width="76">Event Log</Label>
            <ListBox Margin="12,0,5,12" Name="lstEvents" Height="135"
             VerticalAlignment="Bottom" FontStretch="Condensed" FontSize="10"
             FontFamily="Tahoma" />
        </Grid>
</Window>
```

Click the Design tab; the form should look like the one shown in Figure 16-3.

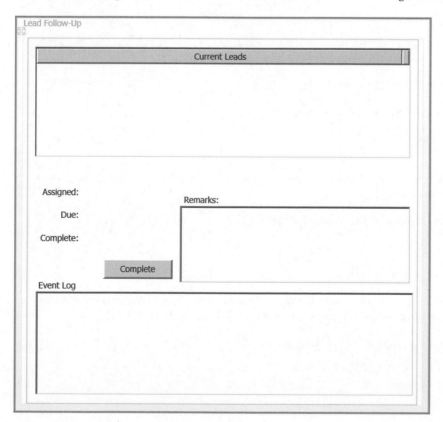

Figure 16-3. *FollowUpLead form layout*

Copying Classes from LeadGenerator

From Windows Explorer, copy the ListBoxTextWriter.cs file from the LeadGenerator folder to the LeadResponse folder. Because this class relies on static properties, each application will need its own copy. From the Solution Explorer, right-click the LeadResponse project and choose Add ➤ Existing Item. Select this file from the LeadResponse folder (make sure that you do not use the file in the LeadGenerator folder). Open the ListBoxTextWriter.cs file and change the Namespace to **LeadResponse**.

From Windows Explorer, move the CreateAssignment.cs file from the LeadGenerator\Activities folder to the LeadResponse folder. Also, move the PersistAssignment.cs class from the LeadGenerator\Extensions to the LeadResponse folder.

From the Solution Explorer, right-click the CreateAssignment.cs file in the Activities folder of the LeadGenerator project and choose Delete. Do the same for the PersistAssignment.cs file in the Extensions folder. Right-click the LeadResponse project and choose Add ➤ Existing Item. Then select the CreateAssignment.cs and PersistAssignment.cs files from the LeadResponse folder. Open both files and change the namespace from LeadGenerator to **LeadResponse**. Add the following namespace at the top of each file:

```
using LeadGenerator;
```

The CreateAssignment activity will also need an additional output argument so the Assignment class can be returned. Add the following code after the input arguments are defined:

```
public OutArgument<Assignment> Assignment { get; set; }
```

Then add the following code at the end of the Execute() method:

```
// Store the request in the OutArgument
Assignment.Set(context, a);
```

Open the AddLead.xaml.cs class on the LeadGenerator project. At the end of the SetupInstance() method, remove the following code:

```
i.Extensions.Add(new PersistAssignment(_connectionString));
```

Implementing the Application

Listing 16-2 shows the complete implementation of the FollowUpLead.xaml.cs class. This follows the same approach explained in the previous chapters, so I won't go into much detail.

Listing 16-2. *Implementation of FollowUpLead.xaml.cs*

```
using System;
using System.Collections.Generic;
using System.Linq;
using System.Text;
using System.Windows;
using System.Windows.Controls;
using System.Windows.Data;
```

```csharp
using System.Windows.Documents;
using System.Windows.Input;
using System.Windows.Media;
using System.Windows.Media.Imaging;
using System.Windows.Navigation;
using System.Windows.Shapes;

using System.Activities;
using System.Activities.DurableInstancing;
using System.Runtime.DurableInstancing;
using System.Data.Linq;
using System.Configuration;
using System.ServiceModel;
using System.ServiceModel.Activities;
using System.ServiceModel.Activities.Description;

using LeadGenerator;

namespace LeadResponse
{
    /// <summary>
    /// Interaction logic for FollowUpLead.xaml
    /// </summary>
    public partial class FollowUpLead : Window
    {
        private string _connectionString = "";
        private InstanceStore _instanceStore;
        private DBExtension _dbExtension;
        private System.ServiceModel.Activities.WorkflowServiceHost _wsh;

        public FollowUpLead()
        {
            InitializeComponent();

            LeadResponse.ApplicationInterface._app = this;
        }

        private void Window_Loaded(object sender, RoutedEventArgs e)
        {
            // Open the config file and get the connection string
            Configuration config =
                ConfigurationManager.OpenExeConfiguration
                    (ConfigurationUserLevel.None);
            ConnectionStringsSection css =
                (ConnectionStringsSection)config.GetSection("connectionStrings");
            _connectionString =
                css.ConnectionStrings["LeadResponse"].ConnectionString;

            _instanceStore = new SqlWorkflowInstanceStore(_connectionString);
            InstanceView view = _instanceStore.Execute
                (_instanceStore.CreateInstanceHandle(),
```

```
            new CreateWorkflowOwnerCommand(),
            TimeSpan.FromSeconds(30));
    _instanceStore.DefaultInstanceOwner = view.InstanceOwner;

    // Create the DBExtension
    _dbExtension = new DBExtension(_connectionString);

    // Create a service to handle incoming requests
    SetupHost();

    LoadExistingLeads();
}

private void SetupHost()
{
    WorkflowService service = new WorkflowService
    {
        Name = "LeadResponse",
        Body = new WorkAssignment(),
        Endpoints =
        {
            new Endpoint
            {
                ServiceContractName="CreateAssignment",
                AddressUri = new Uri("http://localhost/CreateAssignment"),
                Binding = new BasicHttpBinding(),
            }
        }
    };

    // Create a WorkflowServiceHost that listens for incoming messages
    _wsh = new System.ServiceModel.Activities.WorkflowServiceHost(service);

    SqlWorkflowInstanceStoreBehavior instanceStoreBehavior
        = new SqlWorkflowInstanceStoreBehavior(_connectionString);
    instanceStoreBehavior.InstanceCompletionAction
        = InstanceCompletionAction.DeleteAll;
    instanceStoreBehavior.InstanceLockedExceptionAction
        = InstanceLockedExceptionAction.AggressiveRetry;
    _wsh.Description.Behaviors.Add(instanceStoreBehavior);

    WorkflowIdleBehavior wib = new WorkflowIdleBehavior();
    wib.TimeToUnload = TimeSpan.FromMilliseconds(100);
    _wsh.Description.Behaviors.Add(wib);

    _wsh.Description.Behaviors.Add
        (new DBExtensionBehavior(_connectionString));
    _wsh.Description.Behaviors.Add
        (new PersistAssignmentBehavior(_connectionString));
```

```csharp
        // Open the service so it will listen for messages
        _wsh.Open();
    }

    private void Window_Unloaded(object sender, RoutedEventArgs e)
    {
        // Close the WorkflowServiceHost
        _wsh.Close();
    }

    private void LoadExistingLeads()
    {
        LeadDataDataContext dc = new LeadDataDataContext(_connectionString);
        dc.Refresh(RefreshMode.OverwriteCurrentValues, dc.Assignments);
        IEnumerable<Assignment> q = dc.Assignments
            .Where<Assignment>(x => x.Status == "Assigned" ||
                                    x.Status == "Completed");
        foreach (Assignment a in q)
        {
            AddAssignment(a);
        }
    }

    public void AddAssignment(Assignment a)
    {
        LeadDataDataContext dc = new LeadDataDataContext(_connectionString);

        dc.Refresh(RefreshMode.OverwriteCurrentValues, dc.Leads);
        Assignment aTmp = dc.Assignments
            .SingleOrDefault<Assignment>
                (x => x.AssignmentID == a.AssignmentID);

        if (aTmp != null)
            this.lstLeads.Items.Add(aTmp);
    }

    private void btnComplete_Click(object sender, RoutedEventArgs e)
    {
        if (lstLeads.SelectedIndex >= 0)
        {
            Assignment a
                = lstLeads.Items[lstLeads.SelectedIndex] as Assignment;
            a.Remarks = txtRemarks.Text;
            Guid id = a.WorkflowID;

            // Reload the workflow instance
            WorkflowApplication i
                = new WorkflowApplication(new WorkAssignment());

            SetupInstance(i);
            i.Load(id);
```

```
            // Resume the instance from the last bookmark
            try
            {
                i.ResumeBookmark("GetCompletion", a);
            }
            catch (Exception e2)
            {
                AddEvent(e2.Message);
            }
        }
    }

    private void lstLeads_SelectionChanged(object sender, RoutedEventArgs e)
    {
        if (lstLeads.SelectedIndex >= 0)
        {
            Assignment a
                = lstLeads.Items[lstLeads.SelectedIndex] as Assignment;
            UpdateControls(a);
        }
        else
        {
            lblSelectedNotes.Content = "";
            lblSelectedNotes.Visibility = Visibility.Hidden;
            btnComplete.Visibility = Visibility.Hidden;
            txtRemarks.Visibility = Visibility.Hidden;
        }
    }

    public void UpdateAssignment(Assignment assignment)
    {
        // Find the row that matches this record
        int nSelected = -1;
        for (int i = 0; i < lstLeads.Items.Count; i++)
        {
            Assignment a = lstLeads.Items[i] as Assignment;
            if (a.AssignmentID == assignment.AssignmentID)
            {
                nSelected = i;
                break;
            }
        }

        // Update the grid
        if (nSelected >= 0)
        {
            lstLeads.Items[nSelected] = assignment;
            lstLeads.Items.Refresh();

            UpdateControls(assignment);
        }
    }
```

```csharp
private void UpdateControls(Assignment a)
{
    lblSelectedNotes.Content = a.Lead.Comments;
    lblSelectedNotes.Visibility = Visibility.Visible;

    lblDateAssigned.Content = a.DateAssigned.ToShortDateString();

    if (a.DateDue.HasValue)
        lblDateDue.Content = a.DateDue.Value.ToShortDateString();
    else
        lblDateDue.Content = "";

    if (a.DateCompleted.HasValue)
        lblDateCompleted.Content
            = a.DateCompleted.Value.ToShortDateString();
    else
        lblDateCompleted.Content = "";

    txtRemarks.Visibility = Visibility.Visible;
    txtRemarks.Text = a.Remarks;

    if (a.Status == "Assigned")
    {
        btnComplete.Visibility = Visibility.Visible;
        txtRemarks.IsReadOnly = false;
    }
    else
    {
        btnComplete.Visibility = Visibility.Hidden;
        txtRemarks.IsReadOnly = true;
    }
}

private void SetupInstance(WorkflowApplication i)
{
    // Setup the instance store
    i.InstanceStore = _instanceStore;

    // Setup the PersistableIdle event handler
    i.PersistableIdle = (waiea) => PersistableIdleAction.Unload;

    // Setup the connection string
    i.Extensions.Add(_dbExtension);

    i.Aborted = (waaea) =>
    {
        this.lstEvents.Dispatcher.BeginInvoke
            (new Action(() => this.lstEvents.Items.Add
                ("Aborted: " + waaea.Reason.Message)));
    };
```

```
        i.OnUnhandledException = (waueea) =>
        {
            this.lstEvents.Dispatcher.BeginInvoke
                (new Action(() => this.lstEvents.Items.Add
                    (waueea.UnhandledException.Message)));
            return UnhandledExceptionAction.Terminate;
        };

        // Display the accumulated comments
        i.Completed = (wacea) =>
        {
            this.lstEvents.Dispatcher.BeginInvoke
                (new Action(() => this.lstEvents.Items.Add
                    ("\r\nThe workflow has completed")));
        };

        i.Unloaded = (waea) =>
        {
            this.lstEvents.Dispatcher.BeginInvoke
                (new Action(() => this.lstEvents.Items.Add
                    ("Workflow unloaded")));
        };

        i.Extensions.Add(new PersistAssignment(_connectionString));
    }

    // Add a line of text to the Event Log
    private void AddEvent(string szText)
    {
        lstEvents.Items.Add(szText);
    }

    public ListBox GetEventListBox()
    {
        return this.lstEvents;
    }
    }
}
```

WorkflowService

One part of this implementation is new: the SetupHost() method. The LeadResponse application will be receiving messages from the LeadGenerator application. A special type of ServiceHost (called a WorkflowServiceHost) is needed to listen for the WCF messages. When a message is received, a WorkflowServiceHost initiates a workflow instance by using a WorkflowService. The implementation of the WorkflowService should look familiar to you. The Body property specifies that the WorkAssignment workflow should be started. (You will implement this a little later.) The Endpoint property indicates the address, binding, and contract that define WCF endpoint.

■ **Note** The SetupInstance() method is still needed. When a lead is completed, the instance is loaded from the instance store and resumed, just like the LeadGenerator application. So both methods must be supported.

Behaviors

In Chapters 11–15, you created a WorkflowApplication, configured the necessary extensions such as the InstanceStore, and then started the workflow. With the LeadResponse application, the workflow instance will be created by the WorkflowServiceHost in response to incoming messages. This brings up an interesting question: how do you configure the extensions?

Fortunately, the answer is fairly simple. It is done by defining *behaviors* and adding them to the WorkflowServiceHost. You can think of a behavior as a sort of extension factory. When a new workflow instance is created, the WorkflowServiceHost goes through all its defined behaviors, generates and configures the associated extension, and then adds it to the WorkflowApplication before it is started.

The standard extensions such as SqlWorkflowInstanceStore will provide the behavior class—SqlWorkflowInstanceStoreBehavior in this case. Notice in the SetupHost() method, after the SqlWorkflowInstanceStoreBehavior class is created, several of its properties are configured. The behavior class should provide all the same configuration options as the extension itself.

You need to provide a behavior class for your custom extensions such as DBExtension and PersistAssignment. By convention, the name of the behavior class should be the same as the extension with the Behavior suffix added. The last part of the SetupHost() method is configuring behaviors for your custom extensions. You will create them now.

DBExtensionBehavior

Open the DBExtension.cs file in the Extensions folder of the LeadGenerator project. You will now add the behavior class. The complete implementation of this file is shown in Listing 16-3.

Listing 16-3. DBExtension and its Behavior Class

```
using System;
using System.ServiceModel;
using System.ServiceModel.Activities;
using System.ServiceModel.Channels;
using System.ServiceModel.Description;
using System.Collections.ObjectModel;

namespace LeadGenerator
{
    public class DBExtension
    {
        private string _connectionString = "";

        public DBExtension(string connectionString)
        {
            _connectionString = connectionString;
        }
```

```
        public string ConnectionString { get { return _connectionString; } }
    }

    public class DBExtensionBehavior : IServiceBehavior
    {
        private string _connectionString;

        public DBExtensionBehavior(string connectionString)
        {
            _connectionString = connectionString;
        }

        public virtual void ApplyDispatchBehavior
            (ServiceDescription serviceDescription, ServiceHostBase serviceHostBase)
        {
            WorkflowServiceHost workflowServiceHost
                = serviceHostBase as WorkflowServiceHost;
            if (null != workflowServiceHost)
            {
                DBExtension db = new DBExtension(_connectionString);
                workflowServiceHost.WorkflowExtensions.Add(db);
            }
        }

        public virtual void AddBindingParameters
            (ServiceDescription serviceDescription,
                ServiceHostBase serviceHostBase,
                Collection<ServiceEndpoint> endpoints,
                BindingParameterCollection bindingParameters)
        {
        }

        public virtual void Validate
            (ServiceDescription serviceDescription,
                ServiceHostBase serviceHostBase)
        {
        }
    }
}
```

The DBExtensionBehavior class implements the IServiceBehavior interface. It has three methods that must be provided: ApplyDispatchBehavior(), AddBindingParameters(), and Validate(). The only method we use in this scenario is ApplyDispatchBehavior(). (The other two are used for configuring and validating the WCF endpoint.)

You can provide additional properties and methods that can be used to configure the behavior. In this case, there is a _connectionString member that is passed in the constructor. When a DBExtension class is created, this _connectionString is passed into its constructor.

PersistAssignmentBehavior

Open the `PersistAssignment.cs` file from the LeadResponse project. Add the following namespaces:

```
using System.ServiceModel;
using System.ServiceModel.Activities;
using System.ServiceModel.Channels;
using System.ServiceModel.Description;
using System.Collections.ObjectModel;
```

Add the `PersistAssignmentBehavior` class to this file using the code shown in Listing 16-4.

Listing 16-4 *Implementation of the PersistAssignmentBehavior Class*

```
public class PersistAssignmentBehavior : IServiceBehavior
{
    private string _connectionString;

    public PersistAssignmentBehavior(string connectionString)
    {
        _connectionString = connectionString;
    }

    public virtual void ApplyDispatchBehavior
        (ServiceDescription serviceDescription,
            ServiceHostBase serviceHostBase)
    {
        WorkflowServiceHost workflowServiceHost
            = serviceHostBase as WorkflowServiceHost;
        if (null != workflowServiceHost)
        {
            PersistAssignment persist
                = new PersistAssignment(_connectionString);
            workflowServiceHost.WorkflowExtensions.Add(persist);
        }
    }

    public virtual void AddBindingParameters
        (ServiceDescription serviceDescription,
            ServiceHostBase serviceHostBase,
            Collection<ServiceEndpoint> endpoints,
            BindingParameterCollection bindingParameters)
    {
    }

    public virtual void Validate
        (ServiceDescription serviceDescription,
            ServiceHostBase serviceHostBase)
    {
    }
}
```

The PersistAssignmentBehavior class works just like the DBExtensionBehavior class. The only configurable property, the connection string, is passed in through the constructor.

Defining the Workflows

Next you will make some adjustments to the workflow to call the LeadResponse application. You will also design another workflow for this application.

CompleteAssignment

You will need an additional custom activity to update an assignment to mark it complete. From the Solution Explorer, right-click the LeadResponse project and choose Add ➤ Class. Enter the name as **CompleteAssignment.cs**. The implementation of this class is shown in Listing 16-5.

Listing 16-5. *Implementation of CompleteAssignment.cs*

```
using System;
using System.Activities;
using LeadGenerator;

namespace LeadResponse
{
    /***************************************************/
    // This custom activity completes an Assignment.
    /***************************************************/
    public sealed class CompleteAssignment : CodeActivity
    {
        public InOutArgument<Assignment> Assignment { get; set; }

        protected override void Execute(CodeActivityContext context)
        {
            Assignment a = Assignment.Get(context);
            a.Status = "Completed";
            a.DateCompleted = DateTime.Now;

            PersistAssignment persist = context.GetExtension<PersistAssignment>();
            persist.AddAssignment(context.WorkflowInstanceId, a, "Update");

            // Store the request in the OutArgument
            Assignment.Set(context, a);
        }
    }
}
```

This activity uses the PersistAssignment extension to perform the actual database update.

EnterLead Workflow Modifications

Open the LeadGeneratorWF.cs file in the LeadGenerator project. You will add activities this to send a message to the LeadResponse application. The modified implementation is shown in Listing 16-6; the new or modified lines are shown in bold.

Listing 16-6. Implementation of LeadGeneratorWF.cs

```
using System;
using System.Activities;
using System.Activities.Statements;
using System.IO;
using System.ServiceModel;
using System.ServiceModel.Activities;

namespace LeadGenerator
{
    /***************************************************/
    // This file contains the definition of the EnterLead
    // workflow
    /***************************************************/
    public sealed class EnterLead : Activity
    {
        // Define the input and output arguments
        public InArgument<string> ContactName { get; set; }
        public InArgument<string> ContactPhone { get; set; }
        public InArgument<string> Interests { get; set; }
        public InArgument<string> Notes { get; set; }
        public InArgument<int> Rating { get; set; }
        public InArgument<TextWriter> Writer { get; set; }

        public EnterLead()
        {
            // Define the variables used by this workflow
            Variable<Lead> lead = new Variable<Lead> { Name = "lead" };
            Variable<string> assignedTo = new Variable<string>
                { Name = "assignedTo" };

            Send send = new Send
            {
                OperationName = "Assign",
                ServiceContractName = "CreateAssignment",
                Content = new SendParametersContent
                {
                    Parameters =
                    {
                        {
                            "leadID",
                            new InArgument<int> (env => lead.Get(env).LeadID)
                        },
                        {
```

```
                    "assignedTo",
                    new InArgument<string>(env => assignedTo.Get(env))
            }
        }
    },
    EndpointAddress = new InArgument<Uri>
        (env => new Uri("http://localhost/CreateAssignment")),
    Endpoint = new Endpoint
    {
        Binding = new BasicHttpBinding()
    }
};

// Define the LeadGenerator workflow
this.Implementation = () => new Sequence
{
    DisplayName = "EnterLead",
    Variables = { lead, assignedTo },
    Activities =
    {
        new CreateLead
        {
            ContactName = new InArgument<string>
                (env => ContactName.Get(env)),
            ContactPhone = new InArgument<string>
                (env => ContactPhone.Get(env)),
            Interests = new InArgument<string>
                (env => Interests.Get(env)),
            Notes = new InArgument<string>(env => Notes.Get(env)),
            Lead = new OutArgument<Lead>(env => lead.Get(env)),
        },
        new WriteLine
        {
            Text = new InArgument<string>
                (env => "Lead received [" + Rating.Get(env).ToString()
                + "]; waiting for assignment"),
            TextWriter = new InArgument<TextWriter>
                (env => Writer.Get(env))
        },
        new InvokeMethod
        {
            TargetType = typeof(ApplicationInterface),
            MethodName = "NewLead",
            Parameters =
            {
                new InArgument<Lead>(env => lead.Get(env))
            }
        },
        new AddComment
        {
            Comment = new InArgument<string>
```

```
                        (env => "Lead has been created")
            },
            new WaitForInput<string>
            {
                BookmarkName = "GetAssignment",
                Input = new OutArgument<string>(env => assignedTo.Get(env))
            },
            new AssignLead
            {
                AssignedTo = new InArgument<string>
                    (env => assignedTo.Get(env)),
                Lead = new InOutArgument<Lead>(env => lead.Get(env)),
            },
            new CorrelationScope
            {
                Body = new Sequence
                {
                    Activities =
                    {
                        send,
                        new ReceiveReply
                        {
                            Request = send
                        }
                    }
                }
            },
            new InvokeMethod
            {
                TargetType = typeof(ApplicationInterface),
                MethodName = "UpdateLead",
                Parameters =
                {
                    new InArgument<Lead>(env => lead.Get(env))
                }
            },
            new AddComment
            {
                Comment = new InArgument<string>
                    (env => "Lead has been assigned")
            },
            new WriteLine
            {
                Text = new InArgument<string>
                    (env => "Lead assigned [" + Rating.Get(env).ToString()
                    + "] to " + lead.Get(env).AssignedTo),
                TextWriter = new InArgument<TextWriter>
                    (env => Writer.Get(env))
            }
        }
    }
};
```

```
        }
    }
}
```

The Send activity is defined as a named class so it can be referenced by the corresponding ReceiveReply activity. (You might want to refer to Chapter 8 for an explanation of Send and Receive activities.) It includes two parameters, leadID and assignedTo, that are needed to create the Assignment record.

In the previous chapter, the AssignLead and CreateAssignment activities were included in a TransactionScope activity. In this solution, the CreateAssignment activity will be performed by the LeadResponse application and was removed from this workflow. The Send and ReceiveReply activities are contained in a CorrelationScope activity (explained in Chapter 8).

■ **Note** The ReceiveReply activity has neither a Content nor a Parameters property. The purpose of this activity is to wait for acknowledgment that the message was received. It does not expect any data to be provided. You could remove this activity, and this workflow would complete without waiting for a response. Depending on your design, it might be an appropriate solution.

WorkAssignment Workflow

Now you will define the workflow used by the LeadResponse application. From the Solution Explorer, right-click the LeadResponse project and choose Add ➤ Class. For the Name, enter **AssignmentWF.cs**. The implementation of this workflow is shown in Listing 16-7.

Listing 16-7. *Implementation of AssignmentWF.cs*

```
using System;
using System.Activities;
using System.Activities.Statements;
using System.IO;
using System.ServiceModel.Activities;
using System.ServiceModel;

using LeadGenerator;

namespace LeadResponse
{
    /**************************************************/
    //
    /**************************************************/
    public sealed class WorkAssignment : Activity
    {
        public InArgument<TextWriter> Writer { get; set; }

        public WorkAssignment()
        {
```

```
// Define the variables used by this workflow
Variable<int> leadID = new Variable<int> { Name = "leadID" };
Variable<string> assignedTo = new Variable<string>
    { Name = "assignedTo" };
Variable<Assignment> assignment = new Variable<Assignment>
    { Name = "assignment" };

Receive receive = new Receive
{
    OperationName = "Assign",
    ServiceContractName = "CreateAssignment",
    CanCreateInstance = true,
    Content = new ReceiveParametersContent
    {
        Parameters =
        {
            { "leadID", new OutArgument<int>(leadID) },
            { "assignedTo", new OutArgument<string>(assignedTo) }
        }
    }
};

// Define the Assignment workflow
this.Implementation = () => new Sequence
{
    DisplayName = "WorkAssignment",
    Variables = { assignment, leadID, assignedTo },
    Activities =
    {
        receive,
        new Delay
        {
            Duration = TimeSpan.FromSeconds(5)
        },
        new CreateAssignment
        {
            LeadID = new InArgument<int>(env => leadID.Get(env)),
            AssignedTo = new InArgument<string>
                (env => assignedTo.Get(env)),
            Assignment = new OutArgument<Assignment>
                (env => assignment.Get(env)),
        },
        new SendReply
        {
            Request = receive
        },
        new Persist
        {
        },
        new WriteLine
        {
```

```
                Text = new InArgument<string>
                    (env => "Lead has been assigned to " +
                        assignment.Get(env).AssignedTo),
                TextWriter = new InArgument<TextWriter>
                    (env => Writer.Get(env))
            },
            new InvokeMethod
            {
                TargetType = typeof(ApplicationInterface),
                MethodName = "AddAssignment",
                Parameters =
                {
                    new InArgument<Assignment>(env => assignment.Get(env))
                }
            },
            new WaitForInput<Assignment>
            {
                BookmarkName = "GetCompletion",
                Input = new OutArgument<Assignment>
                    (env => assignment.Get(env))
            },
            new CompleteAssignment
            {
                Assignment = new InOutArgument<Assignment>
                    (env => assignment.Get(env))
            },
            new InvokeMethod
            {
                TargetType = typeof(ApplicationInterface),
                MethodName = "UpdateAssignment",
                Parameters =
                {
                    new InArgument<Assignment>(env => assignment.Get(env))
                }
            },
            new WriteLine
            {
                Text = new InArgument<string>
                    (env => "Assignment has been completed"),
                TextWriter = new InArgument<TextWriter>
                    (env => Writer.Get(env))
            },
        }
    };
        }
    }
}
```

The Receive activity is defined as a named class, so it can be referenced by the SendReply activity. As expected, it has the same two parameters that were defined in the Send activity from the previous workflow. The CanCreateInstance property is set to true; this is important because it allows the workflow to start a new instance when the message is received.

I added a five-second delay after the Receive activity so you can verify that the LeadGenerator application will wait for the response before completing. The CreateAssignment activity is then executed. This is the same activity that you used in Chapter 15, except now it is executed from the LeadResponse application. After the Assignment has been created, the reply is sent, and the first workflow can complete.

Persist

Next, the Persist activity is executed. Normally, the workflow is persisted when it becomes idle. However, you can also use the Persist activity to force persistence to occur at other points in the workflow. With this design, the application tables are updated only when the workflow is persisted. So the CreateAssignment activity doesn't actually insert into the Assignment table; the record won't exist until the workflow is persisted. The Persist activity is used here to ensure that the data is written to the database before the remaining activities are executed.

■ **Note** There are places in the workflow where the Persist activity is not allowed. For example, you can't use it inside of a TransactionScope activity. If you try to execute a Persist activity in one of these places, an exception will be thrown. Also, the NoPersistScope activity can be used to contain a sequence of activities. The workflow will prevent persistence until the scope has been completed. This is useful if you have several activities that need to be completed as a single unit and you don't want anything persisted until they all complete. Obviously, if you put a Persist activity inside a NoPersistScope activity, an exception will be thrown.

The remaining activities are similar to the approach used in the previous chapters. The InvokeMethod activity is used to update the form to show the new assignment and the WaitForInput activity waits for the agent to update it.

Final Application Changes

There are a few more changes that you'll need to make before the application is ready.

ApplicationInterface

You will now add a static ApplicationInterface class to the LeadResponse application, which will be similar to the one used in the LeadGenerator application. From the Solution Explorer, right-click the LeadResponse project and choose Add ➤ Class. For the Name, enter **ApplicationInterface.cs**. The implementation of this class is shown in Listing 16-8.

Listing 16-8. *Implementation of ApplicationInterface*

```csharp
using System;
using System.IO;
using System.Windows.Controls;
using System.Activities;

namespace LeadResponse
{
    public static class ApplicationInterface
    {
        public static FollowUpLead _app { get; set; }

        public static void AddAssignment(LeadGenerator.Assignment a)
        {
            if (_app != null)
                _app.lstLeads.Dispatcher.BeginInvoke
                    (new Action(() => _app.AddAssignment(a)));
        }

        public static void UpdateAssignment(LeadGenerator.Assignment a)
        {
            if (_app != null)
                _app.lstLeads.Dispatcher.BeginInvoke
                    (new Action(() => _app.UpdateAssignment(a)));
        }

        public static TextWriter GetStatusWriter()
        {
            if (_app != null)
                return new ListBoxTextWriter(_app.GetEventListBox());
            else
                return null;
        }

        public static void AddEvent(String status)
        {
            if (_app != null)
            {
                GetStatusWriter().WriteLine(status);
            }
        }
    }
}
```

Adding the app.config File

From the Solution Explorer, right-click the LeadResponse project and choose Add ➤ New Item. Select
the Application Configuration File template from the General category. Enter the name as **app.config**, as
shown in Figure 16-4.

Figure 16-4. *Adding the app.config file*

Enter the following code in this file:

```xml
<?xml version="1.0" encoding="utf-8" ?>
<configuration>
  <configSections>
  </configSections>
  <connectionStrings>
    <add name="LeadResponse"
      connectionString=
        "Data Source=localhost;Initial Catalog=Chapter16;Integrated Security=True"
      providerName="System.Data.SqlClient" />
  </connectionStrings>
</configuration>
```

LINQ Conflict

When a workflow is persisted, the arguments and variables are serialized and then they are deserialized when the workflow instance is loaded. The deserialization process can cause conflicts with the LINQ classes when there are associated classes. In this case, the Assignment class has an associated Lead object that is bound to the LeadID property. When the Assignment class is deserialized, an exception is thrown because there is already an associated Lead object.

313

The easiest way around this is to simply comment out the line of code that throws the exception. Open the `LeadData.Designer.cs` file in the LeadGenerator project. At the top of the code window, select the `LeadGenerator.Assignment` class and the `LeadID` property. Comment out the `throw` statement as shown in Figure 16-5.

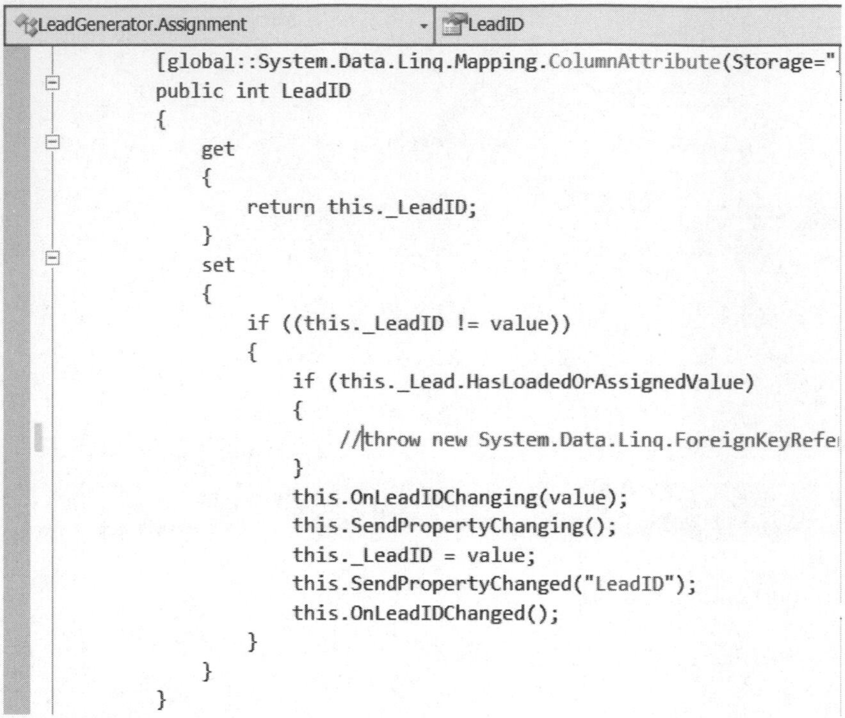
LeadGenerator.Assignment
LeadID
[global::System.Data.Linq.Mapping.ColumnAttribute(Storage="
public int LeadID
{
get
{
return this._LeadID;
}
set
{
if ((this._LeadID != value))
{
if (this._Lead.HasLoadedOrAssignedValue)
{
//throw new System.Data.Linq.ForeignKeyRefe
}
this.OnLeadIDChanging(value);
this.SendPropertyChanging();
this._LeadID = value;
this.SendPropertyChanged("LeadID");
this.OnLeadIDChanged();
}
}
}

Figure 16-5. *Modifying the LeadID property*

Running the Applications

From the Solution Explorer, right-click the Chapter16 solution and choose Set StartUp Projects. Select the Multiple startup projects radio button and set the `Action` for both the LeadGenerator and LeadResponse projects to be `Start`. Press F5 to start both applications.

In the LeadGenerator application, enter a lead and then assign it just as you did in the previous chapters. An entry should appear in the LeadResponse application, as shown in Figure 16-6.

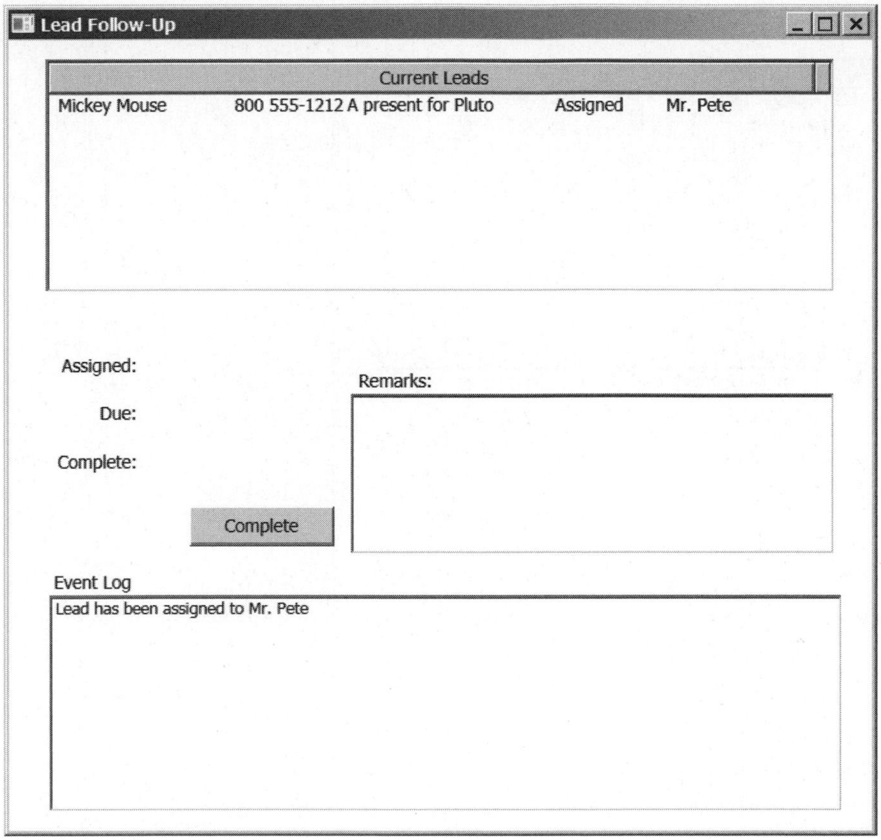

Figure 16-6. *A new entry display in LeadResponse*

Select this lead, and details such as the assigned and due dates will be displayed. Enter some notes in the Remarks section and click the Complete button. The lead will be marked complete, and the form should look like the one shown in Figure 16-7.

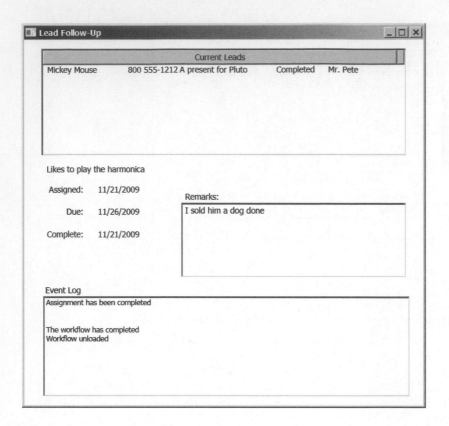

Figure 16-7. *Completed lead in LeadResponse*

In the Solution Explorer, expand the Chapter16Data project, right-click the `Assignment.dtq` query, and choose Open and Run. This should list the contents of the Assignment table, as shown in Figure 16-8.

AssignmentID	WorkflowID	LeadID	AssignedTo	Date...	Status	Date...	Date...	Remarks
1	a0e17bce-...	1	Mr. Pete	11/2...	Completed	11/26...	11/21...	I sold him a dog bone
NULL	*NULL*	*NULL*	*NULL*	*NULL*	*NULL*	*NULL*	*NULL*	*NULL*

Figure 16-8. *The contents of the Assignment table*

Review

In working through the projects in this section, you should have a good sense of how you can use workflow extensions. Extensions provide the operating environment in which the activities are executed in. Extensions can be created by the host application, the workflow activities, or (as you saw in this chapter) by the `WorkflowServiceHost`. They provide a mechanism for sharing data with all the activities, as was demonstrated by the `DBExtension` you developed in Chapter 12. Extensions usually provide the mechanics of persisting and tracking, freeing up the workflow activities to focus on the business process.

PART 5

■ ■ ■

Advanced Topics

In this section I'll demonstrate some advanced features of WF such as Compensation, Collections, and Policy. I will also show you how to use the Interop activity to execute activities and workflows developed in previous versions of WF. As with the other projects in this book, I'll show you step by step how to create the applications using the tools provided in Visual Studio 2010.

The implementation for some of these projects may seem a bit tedious because I wanted to provide a significant enough solution for you to see the usefulness and application of the feature. All the projects presented in this book are available for you to download by going to this book's page on http://www.apress.com. If you prefer, you can download the code instead of entering it yourself.

Either way, I encourage you to work through these sample projects. If you're like me, you may be thinking that you now have the basics down and you'll read these chapters later, when you have a specific need. I think you'll find them to be interesting and valuable for developing enterprise-class solutions. Understanding how these features work will help you design your next workflow-based solution.

CHAPTER 17

■ ■ ■

Compensation, Confirmation, and Cancellation

When working with long-running workflows that can take hours or even days to complete, you often need to handle the scenario in which something goes wrong and the workflow cannot be completed. The activities that have already executed may need to be "undone" in some fashion. As part of the workflow design, you should plan for these situations. In this chapter, you'll use the techniques provided by WF to incorporate the necessary cleanup activities into your workflow design.

The sample project will model the activities performed in planning a typical wedding such as scheduling the church, reserving the reception facility, and sending the invitations. When the wedding is called off, you'll also execute the appropriate activities depending on the current progress of the event. Open Visual Studio and create a new project, as shown in Figure 17-1. Use the Workflow Console Application template. For the project name, enter **Wedding**, and use **Chapter17** for the solution.

Figure 17-1. *Creating a new workflow project*

■ **Note** To save you some time, you can download a partial implementation of this solution from this book's page on the `http://www.apress.com` web site. Download the `Chapter17_Partial.zip` file, unzip it, and open the `Chapter17.sln` file. Then follow along with the first part of this chapter. I'll tell you where you'll need to add the remaining portions of this project.

Designing the Workflow

You'll start by defining the normal workflow activities and add the error-handling logic later.

Modifying the Application

Open the `Program.cs` file and replace the generated code with the implementation shown in Listing 17-1.

Listing 17-1. *Implementation of Program.cs*

```
using System;
using System.Activities;
```

```
using System.Threading;

namespace Wedding
{

    class Program
    {
        static void Main(string[] args)
        {
            AutoResetEvent syncEvent = new AutoResetEvent(false);

            WorkflowApplication i = new WorkflowApplication(new Workflow1());

            i.OnUnhandledException = (waueea) =>
            {
                Console.WriteLine("{0} - {1}", waueea.UnhandledException.GetType(),
                    waueea.UnhandledException.Message);
                return UnhandledExceptionAction.Cancel;
            };

            i.Completed = (wacea) => { syncEvent.Set(); };

            i.Run();

            syncEvent.WaitOne();

            Console.WriteLine("Press ENTER to exit");
            Console.ReadLine();
        }
    }

    public class CallItOffException : Exception
    {
        public CallItOffException()
            : base()
        {
        }

        public CallItOffException(string message)
            : base(message)
        {
        }
    }
}
```

The default action when an unhandled exception is thrown is to terminate the workflow. When this occurs, the cancellation or compensation handlers are not executed. For this project, you must return the Cancel action. This will stop the normal workflow processing, but will allow the cancellation and compensation handlers to perform their defined activities. The WorkflowInvoker class does not give you the ability to override the default action, so you must use the WorkflowApplication class. This file also defines the CallItOffException class that will be used later when the wedding is cancelled:

Configuring a TryCatch Activity

Open the Workflow1.xaml file in design view. Drag a TryCatch activity onto the sequence. The designer should look like the one shown in Figure 17-2. (You used the TryCatch activity in Chapter 6 if you want to refer to it for more information.)

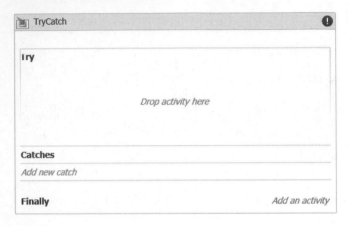

Figure 17-2. *An empty TryCatch activity*

Drag a Sequence activity to the Try section and set the DisplayName to **Wedding Preparations**. Click the link that says "*Add new catch*" and then select "Browse for types" in the drop-down list. In the dialog, expand the Wedding assembly and choose the CallItOffException class, as shown in Figure 17-3.

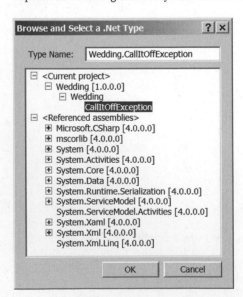

Figure 17-3. *Selecting the exception to be caught*

Drag a WriteLine activity to the Catches section where it says "Drop activity here". For the Text property, enter **"Catch: " + exception.Message**. The designer should look like the one shown in Figure 17-4.

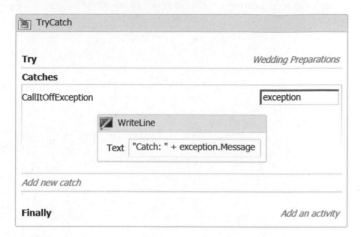

Figure 17-4. *Completed TryCatch activity*

■ **Tip** For the Text properties, you will begin the output text with a word that indicates where the activity was executed from. In this case, it was the Catch activity. The remainder of the WriteLine activities will indicate whether the activity was in the Body, Compensation, Confirmation, or Cancellation section. This will help you analyze the results because there are numerous messages being generated.

Using a Parallel Activity

Expand the "Wedding Preparations" activity and drag a Parallel activity onto it. Set its DisplayName property to **Planning Activities**. In this workflow, you'll design three sequences of activities that will execute simultaneously. Drag three CompensableActivity objects onto the Parallel activity and set their DisplayName property to **Wedding**, **Reception**, and **Invitation**. The designer should look like the one shown in Figure 17-5.

Figure 17-5. *A Parallel activity with three CompensableActivity objects*

CompensableActivity

Double-click the "Wedding" activity. You should have four sections, as shown in Figure 17-6.

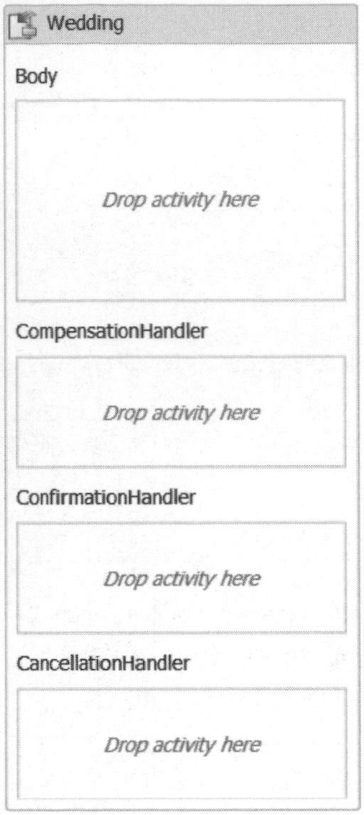

Figure 17-6. *An empty CompensableActivity*

As you can see from Figure 17-6, a CompensableActivity allows you to define handlers for *compensation*, *confirmation*, and *cancellation*. The Body section is the normal activity (or sequence of activities) that are executed. If the Body activity must be cancelled before it has completed, the activity in the Cancellation Handler section is executed. The activity in the Compensation Handler section is executed, if necessary, to undo the work of the Body section if the Body has completed. The Compensation Handler section is where you'll define the activity (or sequence of activities) that should be executed if subsequent workflow activities fail and the workflow is aborted. The activity in the Confirmation Handler section is executed when the activity has been confirmed. By default, confirmation happens automatically when the workflow instance has completed. You can place any finalization activities here.

The following set of rules may help you remember when these handlers are executed:

- An activity can be compensated only if it has completed; in-process activities cannot be compensated.

- The Cancellation Handler is automatically called if an activity must be cancelled before it has completed.

- Completed activities are confirmed automatically when the workflow completes.

- Once confirmed, an activity cannot be compensated.

Designing the Wedding Activity

Drag a Sequence activity onto the Body section. Drag a WriteLine activity onto the sequence. Set the DisplayName to **Reserve Church** and enter the Text property as **"Body: The church has been reserved"**. Drag a Delay activity below "Reserve Church" and set the Duration to **TimeSpan.FromSeconds(2)**. Next, drag a WriteLine activity and set the DisplayName to **Schedule Rehearsal** and the Text property to **"Body: The rehearsal has been scheduled"**. Drag a Delay activity below "Schedule Rehearsal" and set the Duration to **TimeSpan.FromSeconds(5)**. Finally, drag a WriteLine activity, set the DisplayName to **Order Flowers**, and set the Text property to **"Body: The flowers have been ordered"**. The sequence should look like the one shown in Figure 17-7.

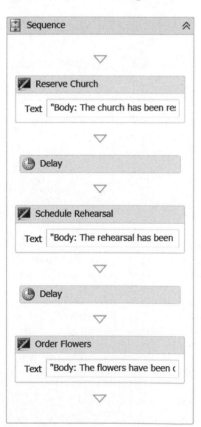

Figure 17-7. *Body sequence of the Wedding activity*

In workflows like this, in which the activities are nested, the navigation bar at the top of the designer is quite helpful. Your navigation bar should look similar to the one shown in Figure 17-8. Each of the activities listed is a link that will expand the selected activity.

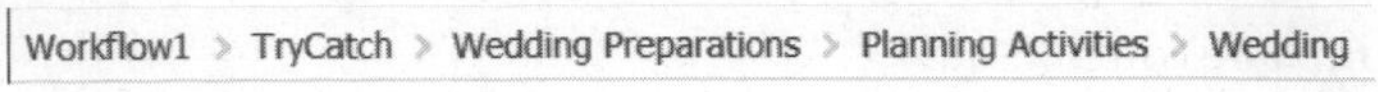

Workflow1 > TryCatch > Wedding Preparations > Planning Activities > Wedding

Figure 17-8. *Workflow designer navigation bar*

Collapse the Body section so you can see the overall `CompensableActivity`. So far, you have specified the sequence for the Body section. Now drag a `WriteLine` activity to the Confirmation Handler section. Set the `Text` property to **"Confirmation: The wedding plans have been confirmed"**. Drag a `WriteLine` activity to the Cancellation Section and set the `Text` property to **"Cancellation: The church reservation has been released"**. You'll implement the Compensation Handler section later. The "Wedding" activity should look like the one shown in Figure 17-9.

Figure 17-9. *Partially completed CompensableActivity*

Designing the Reception Activity

Click the "Planning Activities" activity on the navigation bar. Then double-click the "Reception" activity. You should see an empty `CompensableActivity`. Drag a `Sequence` activity to the Body section.

Drag a `WriteLine` activity onto the `Sequence`. Set the `DisplayName` to **Reserve Facility** and enter the Text property as **"Body: The reception facility has been reserved"**. Drag a `Delay` activity below "Reserve Facility" and set the `Duration` property to **TimeSpan.FromSeconds(3)**. Drag a `WriteLine` activity below this, set the `DisplayName` to **Menu**, and enter the Text property as **"Body: The menu has been decided"**. Drag another `Delay` activity below the "Menu" activity and set the `Duration` property to **TimeSpan.FromSeconds(1)**. Finally, drag a `WriteLine` activity below this, set the `DisplayName` to **Pay Deposit** and enter the Text property as **"Body: The reception deposit has been paid"**. The designer should look like the one shown in Figure 17-10.

Figure 17-10. *Body sequence of the Reception activity*

Designing Confirmation Activities

Collapse the Body section and drag a Sequence activity onto the Confirmation Handler section. Drag a WriteLine activity onto the Sequence, set the DisplayName to **Pay for Facility**, and enter the Text property as **"Confirmation: The reception facility has been paid for"**. Drag another WriteLine activity below "Pay for Facility", set the DisplayName to **Display Confirmation**, and enter the Text property as **"Confirmation: The reception activities have been confirmed"**. The designer should look like the one shown in Figure 17-11.

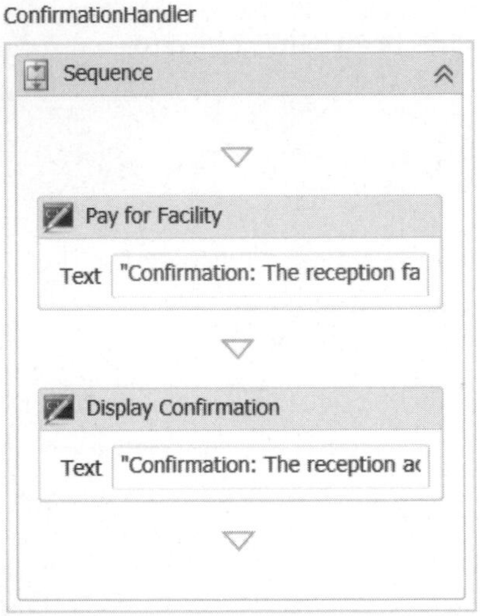

ConfirmationHandler

Figure 17-11. Confirmation sequence of the Reception activity

Notice in the "Reception" activity, you put a work item in the Confirmation Handler section ("Pay for Facility"). By putting this here, it will not be executed until the workflow has completed. Should something happen in the "Wedding" or "Invitations" activities and the workflow must be aborted, the facility will not be paid for. This will delay the execution of the activity until everything else has completed successfully and prevent paying for the facility when the event is called off.

Collapse the Confirmation section. Drag a WriteLine activity to the Cancellation Handler section and enter the Text property as **"Cancellation: The reception has been cancelled"**.

Designing the Invitations Activity

Click "Planning Activities" in the navigation bar, which should display the Parallel activity that contains the "Wedding", "Reception", and "Invitations" activities. Double-click the "Invitations" activity. Drag a Sequence activity onto the Body section.

Drag a Delay activity onto the Sequence and set the Duration property to **TimeSpan.FromSeconds(4)**. Drag a WriteLine activity below this, set the DisplayName as **Order Stationary**, and enter the Text property as **"Body: The stationary has been ordered"**. Drag another Delay activity and set the Duration property to **TimeSpan.FromSeconds(2)**. Drag a WriteLine activity below this, set the DisplayName as **Finalize List**, and enter the Text property as **"Body: The invite list has been agreed to"**. The designer should look like the one shown in Figure 17-12.

Figure 17-12. Body sequence of the Invitations activity

Designing the Confirmation Activities

Collapse the Body section and drag a Sequence activity to the Confirmation Handler section. Drag a WriteLine activity to the Sequence, set the DisplayName as **Mail Invitations**, and enter the Text property as **"Confirmation: The invitations have been sent"**. Drag another WriteLine activity below "Mail Invitations", set the DisplayName as **Display Confirmation**, and enter the Text property as **"Confirmation: The invitations activities have been confirmed"**.

Notice that the invitations are not actually mailed until the workflow completes. Like paying for the facility, you want to wait to mail the invitations until you know that the workflow activities have completed successfully.

Collapse the Confirmation section and drag a WriteLine activity to the Cancellation Handler section and enter the Text property as **"Cancellation: The invitation activity has been cancelled"**.

Click the "Wedding Preparations" activity in the navigation bar. This Sequence contains only the "Planning Activities" activity. Drag a WriteLine activity below it and enter the Text property as **"Main: Congratulations! The wedding preparations are complete."**. The designer should look like the one shown in Figure 17-13.

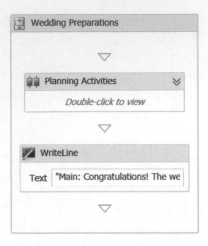

Figure 17-13. *The Wedding Preparation activity*

Running the Application

Press F5 to run the application. You should see results similar to the following:

Body: The reception facility has been reserved

Body: The church has been reserved

Body: The rehearsal has been scheduled

Body: The menu has been decided

Body: The reception deposit has been paid

Body: The stationary has been ordered

Body: The invite list has been agreed to

Body: The flowers have been ordered

Main: Congratulations! The wedding preparations are complete.

Confirmation: The wedding plans have been confirmed

Confirmation: The invitations have been sent

```
Confirmation: The invitation activities have been confirmed

Confirmation: The reception facility has been paid for

Confirmation: The reception activities have been confirmed

Press ENTER to exit
```

This represents the normal processing without any errors. Notice that the Body activities complete first, followed by the Congratulations line, which is the last of the regular activities to execute. The confirmation handlers are then executed.

■ **Note** If you started with the partial solution that is available from the website, you'll need to make the rest of the changes yourself.

Cancellation Handlers

Now, you'll make some changes to cause the workflow to fail and see how the handlers are executed. First, you'll exercise the cancellation handlers.

More on the Parallel Activity

The Parallel activity has a CompletionCondition property, as shown in Figure 17-14.

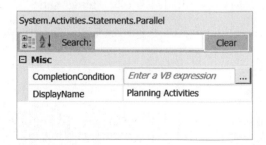

Figure 17-14. *The Properties window of a Parallel activity*

When a Parallel activity is executed, it starts all its child activities simultaneously. As each branch completes, it evaluates the CompletionCondition property, if specified. If it evaluates to True, all branches still executing are aborted. If they are a CompensableActivity, as in this case, the cancellation handler will be executed.

Click the "Wedding Preparations" activity in the navigation bar and select the "Planning Activities" activity. In the Properties window, set the `CompletionCondition` property to **True**. Press F5 to run the application. Your results should be similar to the following:

```
Body: The reception facility has been reserved

Body: The church has been reserved

Body: The rehearsal has been scheduled

Body: The menu has been decided

Body: The reception deposit has been paid

Cancellation: The church reservation has been released

Cancellation: The invitation activities have been cancelled

Main: Congratulations! The wedding preparations are complete.

Confirmation: The reception facility has been paid for

Confirmation: The reception activities have been confirmed

Press ENTER to exit
```

The "Reception" activity is the first to complete and the cancellation handler was executed for the "Wedding" and "Invitations" activities. This is not considered an error condition, however, and the workflow completed. Notice that the confirmation handler was NOT executed for the "Wedding" and "Invitations" activities because they did not complete.

This, obviously, is not how you want the workflow to function. Set the `CompletionCondition` property to **False** or just clear the property as it was originally.

Designing Compensation Handlers

Now you'll add the compensation handlers. Navigate to Workflow1 > Sequence > TryCatch > Wedding Preparations > Planning Activities > Wedding. The designer should display the `CompensableActivity`.

Designing the Wedding Compensation

Drag a Sequence activity to the Compensation Handler section. Drag three `WriteLine` activities onto this Sequence and set the `DisplayName` to **Starting**, **Church**, and **Flowers**. Enter the Text property for "Starting" as **"Compensation: The wedding compensation is starting"**. Enter the Text for the "Church" activity as **"Compensation: The church reservation was released"**. Set the Text property for "Flowers" to **"Compensation: The flowers have been cancelled"**. The designer should look like the one shown in Figure 17-15.

CompensationHandler

Figure 17-15. *Compensation sequence for the Wedding activity*

Recall that the compensation handler is called only if the activity has completed. When designing a compensation handler, you can therefore assume that the normal activities were executed. You should then decide what the appropriate actions are if the overall workflow is aborted after this activity has completed. In this case, you should cancel the flowers and let the church know so someone else can schedule for that date.

Designing the Reception Compensation

The appropriate actions to compensate for the "Reception" activity are to release the facility and to request a deposit refund. (It can't hurt to ask, right?)

Click "Planning Activities" on the navigation bar, which should display the Parallel activity. Double-click the "Reception" activity. Drag a Sequence activity to the Compensation Handler section. Drag three WriteLine activities onto this Sequence and set the DisplayName to **Starting**, **Facility**, and **Deposit**. Enter the Text property for "Starting" as **"Compensation: The reception compensation is starting"**. Enter the Text for the "Facility" activity as **"Compensation: The reception reservation was released"**. Set the Text property for "Deposit" to **"Compensation: A refund of the deposit was requested"**. The designer should look like the one shown in Figure 17-16.

CompensationHandler

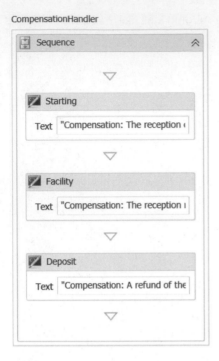

Figure 17-16. *Compensation sequence for the Reception activity*

Click "Planning Activities" on the navigation bar and double-click the "Invitations" activity. Drag a WriteLine activity to the Compensation Handler section and set the Text property as **"Compensation: The invitations compensation handler was called – nothing to do"**. Nothing needs to be done to compensate for the "Invitations" activity. The order was placed for stationary, but there's probably no recourse because they are usually fulfilled quickly. Fortunately, the invitations were not actually mailed because that activity is not done until the activity is confirmed.

Running the Application

Now you'll throw an exception to see the compensation handlers at work. Click the "Wedding Preparations" activity on the navigation bar. Drag a Throw activity below "Planning Activities". For the Exception property, enter **New Exception("Calling it off")**. Press F5 to run the application. Your results should be similar to these:

```
Body: The reception facility has been reserved

Body: The church has been reserved

Body: The rehearsal has been scheduled
```

```
Body: The menu has been decided

Body: The reception deposit has been paid

Body: The stationary has been ordered

Body: The invite list has been agreed to

Body: The flowers have been ordered

System.Exception - Calling it off

Compensation: The wedding compensation is starting

Compensation: The church reservation was released

Compensation: The flowers were cancelled

Compensation: The invitations compensation handler was called - nothing to do

Compensation: The reception compensation is starting

Compensation: The reception reservation was released

Compensation: A refund of the deposit was requested

Press ENTER to exit
```

After the Body activities were executed, the exception was displayed and then the compensation handlers were executed. Because the exception was thrown after all the activities were completed, all the compensation handlers were executed.

Now we'll try throwing the exception earlier in the workflow. Navigate to the "Wedding" branch of "Planning Activities" and expand the Body sequence. Drag a Throw activity after the "Schedule Rehearsal" activity. For the Exception property, enter **New Exception("The wedding is cancelled")**.

Press F5 to run the application. Your results should look like these:

```
Body: The reception facility has been reserved

Body: The church has been reserved

Body: The rehearsal has been scheduled

System.Exception - Wedding is cancelled
```

```
Cancellation: The reception has been cancelled

Cancellation: The invitation activities have been cancelled

Cancellation: The church reservation has been released

Press ENTER to exit
```

This time, the exception occurred before any of the activities had completed so, as expected, instead of executing the compensation handlers, the cancellation handlers were called. Now move the Throw activity to after the Delay activity (just before the "Order Flowers" activity). Press F5 to run the application. Your results should look like these:

```
Body: The reception facility has been reserved

Body: The church has been reserved

Body: The rehearsal has been scheduled

Body: The menu has been decided

Body: The reception deposit has been paid

Body: The stationary has been ordered

Body: The invite list has been agreed to

System.Exception - Wedding is cancelled

Cancellation: The church reservation has been released

Compensation: The invitations compensation handler was called - nothing to do

Compensation: The reception compensation is starting

Compensation: The reception reservation was released

Compensation: A refund of the deposit was requested

Press ENTER to exit
```

The "Wedding" activity did not complete, and its cancellation handler was called. The compensation handler was called for the other two activities ("Reception" and "Invitations"). Delete the Throw activity that you just created.

Customizing Compensation and Confirmation

So far, you have been using the default logic for executing the confirmation and compensation handlers. To summarize, confirmation handlers are called on completed activities when the workflow completes successfully, and compensation handlers are called when the workflow is cancelled. Now I'll show you how to manually call these handlers so you can customize when they are used.

Adding the Token Variables

In order to confirm or compensate an activity you'll need a handle to it, which is referred to as a *token*. Click the Variables link at the bottom left of the designer. You should see an empty collection of variables, as shown in Figure 17-17.

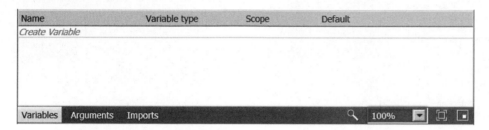

Figure 17-17. *An empty Variables collection*

Click the *Create variable* link and enter the Name as **weddingToken**. In the Variable type drop-down list, select "Browse for types". In the dialog that displays, expand the System.Activities assembly and select the CompensationToken class, as shown in Figure 17-18.

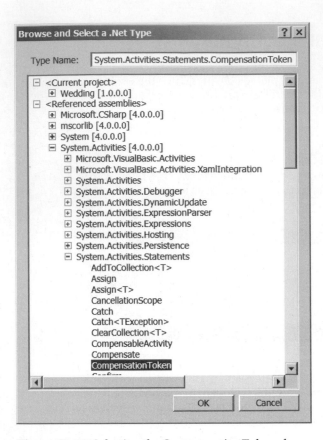

Figure 17-18. Selecting the CompensationToken class

The Scope should be the TryCatch activity. You can leave the Default property blank. Click the *Create variable* link again and enter the Name as **receptionToken**. The CompensationToken class should be in the Variable type drop-down list; select it and set the Scope property as TryCatch. In a similar fashion, create an invitationsToken variable. The Variables list should look like the one shown in Figure 17-19.

Name	Variable type	Scope	Default
invitationsToken	CompensationToken	TryCatch	*Enter a VB expression*
receptionToken	CompensationToken	TryCatch	*Enter a VB expression*
weddingToken	CompensationToken	TryCatch	*Enter a VB expression*
Create Variable			

| Variables | Arguments | Imports | | 🔍 | 100% ▾ | ▣ | ▪ |

Figure 17-19. The completed Variables collection

Setting the Result Property

Close the Variables window and navigate to "Planning Activities". Select the "Wedding" activity (you don't have to double-click to expand it; just click it to select it). In the Properties window, enter **weddingToken** for the Result property, as shown in Figure 17-20.

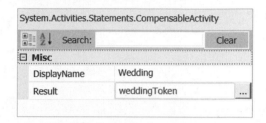

Figure 17-20. *Property window for a CompensableActivity*

The Result property is used to indicate the variable that will hold the token for this activity. The token is not set until the activity is completed. (Remember, you can't confirm or compensate an activity unless it has completed.) Now select the "Reception" activity and enter **receptionToken** for its Result property. Finally, select the "Invitations" activity and enter **invitationsToken** for the Result property. Now as each of these activities is completed, the appropriate token is set, which you can use to call its confirmation and compensation handlers.

Custom Confirmation

This workflow covers only the activities of planning a wedding. If you were to design one that included all the activities performed up to and including the actual wedding, the workflow would not complete until the wedding was over. It would not be appropriate to wait to send the invitation until then, for obvious reasons. So you'll need to confirm the Invitations activity manually, before the workflow completes. This could be triggered by the completion of some other activity, perhaps requiring a user input or based on a Delay activity.

Navigate to the "Wedding Preparations" activity. Drag a Confirm activity just before the Throw activity and set the DisplayName to **Confirm Invitations**. For the Target property, enter **invitationsToken**. The designer should look like the one shown in Figure 17-21.

Figure 17-21. *The main sequence including the Confirm activity*

Press F5 to run the application and your results should be like these:

```
Body: The reception facility has been reserved

Body: The church has been reserved

Body: The rehearsal has been scheduled

Body: The menu has been decided

Body: The reception deposit has been paid

Body: The stationary has been ordered

Body: The invite list has been agreed to

Body: The flowers have been ordered

Confirmation: The invitations have been sent
```

```
Confirmation: The invitation activities have been confirmed

System.Exception - Calling it off

Compensation: The wedding compensation is starting

Compensation: The church reservation was released

Compensation: The flowers were cancelled

Compensation: The reception compensation is starting

Compensation: The reception reservation was released

Compensation: A refund of the deposit was requested

Press ENTER to exit
```

Notice that the "Invitations" confirmation handler was executed before the exception was generated. Then because it had already been confirmed, it was not compensated.

Custom Compensation

The last thing I want to show you is how to manually control the compensation processing. In some situations, you might want to specify the order in which activities are compensated. Or perhaps you need to conditionally execute the compensation. To do that, you'll add logic to the exception handler in your workflow to perform the compensation logic.

First, navigate to the "Wedding Preparations" activity and select the Throw activity. Change the Exception property by entering the following code (it will use the new exception class that your TryCatch activity is configured to receive):

```
New Wedding.CallItOffException("The wedding has been cancelled")
```

Navigate to the TryCatch activity. Right-click the WriteLine activity in the Catches section and choose Cut. Drag a Sequence activity in its place; then double-click it to expand the Sequence. Right-click inside the Sequence and choose Paste. The WriteLine activity should now be included in the new Sequence.

Drag an If activity below the WriteLine activity and set the DisplayName as **Compensate Reception**. For the Condition property, enter **Not receptionToken Is Nothing**. Drag a Compensate activity to the Then section. For the Target property, enter **receptionToken**. Press F5 to run the application and you should see the following results:

```
Body: The reception facility has been reserved

Body: The church has been reserved
```

```
Body: The rehearsal has been scheduled

Body: The menu has been decided

Body: The facility deposit has been paid

Body: The stationary has been ordered

Body: The invite list has been agreed to

Body: The flowers have been ordered

Confirmation: The invitations have been sent

Confirmation: The invitation activities have been confirmed

Catch: The wedding has been cancelled

Compensation: The reception compensation is starting

Compensation: The reception reservation was released

Compensation: A refund of the deposit was requested

Confirmation: The wedding plans have been confirmed

Press ENTER to exit
```

After the exception was caught, the "Reception" was compensated as expected, but the "Wedding" activity was confirmed. You probably didn't expect that. Because your workflow handled the exception, the workflow could continue. Since the "Wedding" activity had completed, the workflow confirmed it.

Rethrow Activity

To resolve this, you will re-throw the exception. Go back to the Catch sequence and drag a Rethrow activity after the Compensate activity. The Rethrow activity doesn't have any properties; it simply rethrows the current exception. For this reason, a Rethrow activity can be used only in a Catch section of a TryCatch activity.

Press F5 to run the application. This time, the results should look like these:

```
Body: The reception facility has been reserved

Body: The church has been reserved
```

```
Body: The rehearsal has been scheduled

Body: The menu has been decided

Body: The facility deposit has been paid

Body: The stationary has been ordered

Body: The invite list has been agreed to

Body: The flowers have been ordered

Confirmation: The invitations have been sent

Confirmation: The invitation activities have been confirmed

Catch: The wedding has been cancelled

Compensation: The reception compensation is starting

Compensation: The reception reservation was released

Compensation: A refund of the deposit was requested

Wedding.CallItOffException - The wedding has been cancelled

Compensation: The wedding compensation is starting

Compensation: The church reservation was released

Compensation: The flowers were cancelled

Press ENTER to exit
```

Your exception handler compensated the "Reception" activity. The rethrown exception was caught by the application and the remaining activity ("Wedding") was also compensated. (Because the "Invitations" activity was explicitly confirmed previously, it was not compensated.)

■ **Caution** When using the `Confirm` or `Compensate` activities, you should include them in a `TryCatch` activity because they can throw exceptions. If you try to confirm an activity that has already been confirmed, for example, it will throw an exception. You can test for a non-null token, as we did in this project to verify that the activity has completed. However, you can't test to see whether it has already been confirmed or compensated. Because we had a controlled environment and were throwing the exception, you knew what the state of the activity would be. In a real scenario, you can't predict when an exception might be thrown. In more complicated workflows, it's not easy to know what other processing may have already confirmed or compensated the activity. So to be safe, always wrap the `Confirm` and `Compensate` activity in a `TryCatch` activity. You can usually ignore the exception; you just don't want it to terminate your workflow.

■■■

CHAPTER 18

Collections

WF 4.0 provides some built-in activities that enable you to manipulate a collection in your workflow. In this chapter, you'll build a console application that demonstrates these activities using a shopping list application.

Creating a Collection

Start by creating a console application project in Visual Studio. For the project name, use **ShoppingList**; for the solution name, enter **Chapter18**, as shown in Figure 18-1.

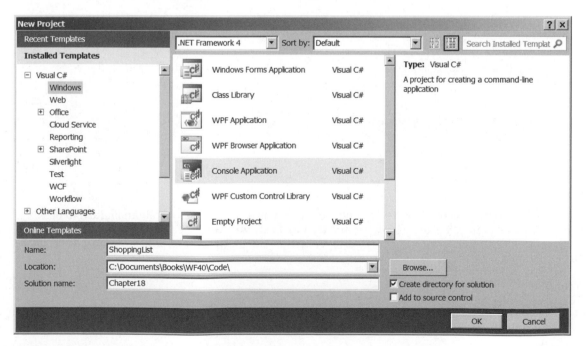

Figure 18-1. Creating a console application

From the Solution Explorer, right-click the ShoppingList project and choose Add Reference. From the .NET tab, add a reference to System.Activities.

Defining the Shopping List

First, you'll start by implementing the class that defines an item in your shopping list. Open the Program.cs file and add the ListItem class using the code in Listing 18-1.

Listing 18-1. *Implementation of the ListItem Class*

```
public class ListItem
{
    public string Description { get; set; }
    public int Quantity { get; set; }
    public decimal UnitPrice { get; set; }
    public int Priority { get; set; }
    public string Comments { get; set; }

    public ListItem(string description, int quantity, decimal unitPrice,
        int priority, string comments)
    {
        Description = description;
        Quantity = quantity;
        UnitPrice = unitPrice;
        Priority = priority;
        Comments = comments;
    }

    public ListItem(string description)
    {
        Description = description;
    }
}
```

The ListItem class contains a few public properties that store information about an item to be purchased. The Priority property will be used later to determine which items are most important. The class contains a couple of constructors. The first populates all the properties, while the second sets only the Description.

Initial Workflow

Add the following namespace to the Program.cs file:

```
using System.Activities.Expressions;
```

Add a CollectionWF() method to the Program class, which defines the initial workflow. The implementation is shown in Listing 18-2.

Listing 18-2. *Initial Workflow Definition*

```
private static WorkflowElement CollectionWF()
{
    // myList is a collection of ListItem objects
    Variable<ICollection<ListItem>> myList =
        new Variable<ICollection<ListItem>>()
    {
        Name = "MyList",
        Default = new LambdaValue<ICollection<ListItem>>
            (env => new List<ListItem>())
    };

    return new Sequence
    {
        Variables = { myList },
        Activities =
        {
            new WriteLine
            {
                Text = "Workflow starting..."
            },
            new AddToCollection<ListItem>
            {
                Collection = myList,
                Item = new LambdaValue<ListItem>
                    (env => new ListItem("Milk", 1, 3.99m, 2, ""))
            },
            new AddToCollection<ListItem>
            {
                Collection = myList,
                Item = new LambdaValue<ListItem>
                    (env => new ListItem("Bread", 2, 2.95m, 1,
                    "Get 100% Whole Wheat, if possible"))
            },
            new AddToCollection<ListItem>
            {
                Collection = myList,
                Item = new LambdaValue<ListItem>
                    (env => new ListItem("Cheese", 1, 1.75m, 4, ""))
            },
```

```
            new AddToCollection<ListItem>
            {
                Collection = myList,
                Item = new LambdaValue<ListItem>
                    (env => new ListItem("Ice Cream", 4, 5.75m, 5, ""))
            },
            new WriteLine
            {
                Text = "Workflow ended"
            }
        }
    };
}
```

■**Tip** You might have noticed some new syntax here. When passing in a value as an argment to an activity the value needs to be a workflow variable or argument or a literal value (such as "Workflow starting..."). Otherwise, you need to wrap it inside of a `LambdaValue<>` class. When passing in a `ListItem` or an `ICollection<ListItem>`, they are wrapped inside of a `LambdaValue<>` class. Notice that the `env` parameter is specified even though it is not used.

This workflow defines a variable that is a collection of `ListItem` classes. The variable can be any type of collection that supports the `ICollection` interface. That actual collection object is created by the `Default` property as a `List<ListItem>` class.

AddToCollection Activity

The workflow has four instances of the `AddToCollection` activity. Each one adds an object to the collection. This is a template class and you must declare the type of object that is stored in the collection. In this case, the `ListItem` data type is specified. The `AddToCollection` activity has two properties: `Collection` specifies the variable that holds the collection, and `Item` is the object that is to be added. For the `Item` property, it creates a new instance of the `ListItem` class using the constructor that populates all the class members.

Invoking a Workflow

Implement the `main()` method using the following code:

```
static void Main(string[] args)
{
```

```
WorkflowInvoker.Invoke(CollectionWF());

Console.WriteLine("Press ENTER to exit");
Console.ReadLine();
}
```

■ **Tip** This method illustrates just how easy it is to start a workflow. Just call the `Invoke()` method of the static `WorkflowInvoker` class, passing in a workflow definition.

Running the Application

Now you're ready to execute the application. Press F5 to run it. Your results should look like these:

```
Workflow starting...
Workflow ended
Press ENTER to exit
```

Printing and Sorting

So far, you have created a collection of items; now you'll create some custom activities that operate on this collection.

Printing the Collection

First, you will provide a way to display the contents of the shopping list. From the Solution Explorer, right-click the ShoppingList project and choose Add ➤ Class. For the class name, enter **PrintList.cs**. The implementation of this class is shown in Listing 18-3.

Listing 18-3. *Implementation of PrintList.cs*

```
using System;
using System.Activities;
using System.Collections.Generic;

namespace ShoppingList
{
    public sealed class PrintList : CodeActivity
    {
        public InArgument<ICollection<ListItem>> Collection { get; set; }
        public InArgument<decimal> Budget { get; set; }
```

```
        protected override void Execute(CodeActivityContext context)
        {
            ICollection<ListItem> list =
                this.Collection.Get<ICollection<ListItem>>(context);

            if (list.Count == 0)
            {
                Console.WriteLine("The list is empty");
            }
            else
            {
                decimal total = 0m;
                decimal budget = Budget.Get(context);

                foreach (ListItem l in list)
                {
                    // See if this item will put us over budget
                    if (budget > 0 && total + (l.Quantity * l.UnitPrice) > budget)
                        break;

                    total += l.Quantity * l.UnitPrice;

                    Console.WriteLine("{0}: {1}, {2} @ ${3} [{4}]",
                        l.Priority.ToString(), l.Description,
                        l.Quantity.ToString(), l.UnitPrice, l.Comments);
                }

                Console.WriteLine("Total cost: ${0}", total.ToString());
                Console.WriteLine();
            }
        }
    }
}
```

This custom activity receives the collection as an input argument. It expects a collection of `ListItem` classes. It also has a second input argument that specifies the budget amount. If a non-zero value is supplied for the budget argument, it will stop printing items after the budget has been reached.

Open the `Program.cs` file and add the following activity definition to the `CollectionWF()` method (add it just before the final `WriteLine` activity):

```
new PrintList()
{
    Budget = 15m,
    Collection = myList
},
```

Press F5 to run the application. Your results should look like these:

```
Workflow starting...
2: Milk, 1 @ $3.99 []
1: Bread, 2 @ $2.95 [Get 100% Whole Wheat, if possible]
4: Cheese, 1 @ $1.75 []
Total cost: $11.64

Workflow ended
Press ENTER to exit
```

Notice that the Ice Cream you added was not displayed. That's because 4 cartons at $5.75 each would have put you over your $15 budget. Change the Budget property to **0m** and re-run the application. This time, the Ice Cream will be displayed, and the order total should be $34.64.

Sorting the Collection

Next, you'll provide a custom activity that will sort the shopping list, putting the higher-priority items first. If you want to limit the items based on a budget, you'll want to make sure to get the most important items first.

From the Solution Explorer, right-click the ShoppingList project and choose Add ➤ Class. For the class name, enter **SortCollection.cs**. The implementation for this class is shown in Listing 18-4.

Listing 18-4. Implementation of SortCollection.cs

```csharp
using System;
using System.Activities;
using System.Collections.Generic;

namespace ShoppingList
{
    public sealed class SortCollection : CodeActivity
    {
        public InOutArgument<ICollection<ListItem>> Collection { get; set; }

        protected override void Execute(CodeActivityContext context)
        {
            ICollection<ListItem> tempList =
                this.Collection.Get<ICollection<ListItem>>(context);

            if (tempList.Count > 0)
            {

                List<ListItem> sortedList = new List<ListItem>(tempList);
```

```
                ItemComparer c = new ItemComparer();
                sortedList.Sort(c as IComparer<ListItem>);

                Collection.Set(context, sortedList as ICollection<ListItem>);
            }
        }
    }

    public class ItemComparer : IComparer<ListItem>
    {
        public int Compare(ListItem x, ListItem y)
        {
            // Handle null arguments
            if (x == null && y == null)
                return 0;
            if (x == null)
                return -1;
            if (y == null)
                return 1;

            // Perform comparison based on the priority
            if (x.Priority == y.Priority)
                return 0;
            if (x.Priority > y.Priority)
                return 1;
            else
                return -1;
        }
    }
}
```

The Execute() method of this activity takes a collection as both an input and output argument. A collection is passed in to the activity, and the collection is sorted and returned using the same argument. The collection is provided as an ICollection interface, so it must be copied to a List object.

The Sort() method of the List class is used to perform the sort, but you must supply a class that implements the IComparer interface because the standard implementation will not know how to sort ListItem objects. The IComparer interface provides a single method called Compare(), which receives two objects (x and y) as input parameters. It returns 0 if the two objects are equal, 1 if x is greater than y, and -1 if x is less than y.

Open the Program.cs file and add the following activities to the CollectionsWF() method just before the final WriteLine activity:

```
new SortCollection
{
    Collection = myList
```

```
},
new PrintList()
{
    Budget = 0m,
    Collection = myList
},
```

Press F5 to run the application. The output should look like this:

```
Workflow starting...
2: Milk, 1 @ $3.99 []
1: Bread, 2 @ $2.95 [Get 100% Whole Wheat, if possible]
4: Cheese, 1 @ $1.75 []
5: Ice Cream, 4 @ $5.75 []
Total cost: $34.64

1: Bread, 2 @ $2.95 [Get 100% Whole Wheat, if possible]
2: Milk, 1 @ $3.99 []
4: Cheese, 1 @ $1.75 []
5: Ice Cream, 4 @ $5.75 []
Total cost: $34.64

Workflow ended
Press ENTER to exit
```

Notice that when it is printed the second time, the items are in priority order.

Searching the Collection

Next, you'll use some built-in activities to find items in a collection and remove them.

Overriding the Equals() Method

For the remaining features that you'll add, the built-in activities must be able to find an item in the collection. They do this by iterating through the objects in the collection, calling their Equals() method until one returns True. The default implementation of the Equals() method in the base Object class compares the object references to determine equality. For our purposes, we want to consider two items equal if they have the same description.

Open the Program.cs file and add two methods shown in Listing 18-5 to the ListItem class.

Listing 18-5. Adding the Equals() Method

```
public override bool Equals(object obj)
{
    ListItem i = obj as ListItem;
```

353

```
        if (i == null)
            return false;
        else
        {
            if (i.Description == this.Description)
                return true;
            else
                return false;
        }
}

public override int GetHashCode()
{
    return base.GetHashCode();
}
```

The Equals() method cast the input object to a ListItem and returns True if the Description property matches. When overriding the Equals() method, the compiler expects you to also override the GetHashCode() method. This implementation simply calls the base method.

ExistsInCollection Activity

Add the following activities to the CollectionsWF() method just before the final WriteLine activity:

```
new If
{
    Condition = new ExistsInCollection<ListItem>()
    {
        Collection = myList,
        Item = new LambdaValue<ListItem>
            (env => new ListItem("Ice Cream"))
    },
    Then = new WriteLine
    {
        Text = "You don't really need Ice Cream?"
    }
},
```

This adds an If activity, and the Condition property is an ExistsInCollection activity. The ExistsInCollection activity expects two input arguments—the collection to be searched and the item you're looking for—and returns a Boolean to indicate whether the item was found. A new ListItem object is created and passed in. Notice, however, that only the Description is specified. This is because that's the only property used for making the comparison.

RemoveFromCollection Activity

Add the following activities just before the final WriteLine activity:

```
new WriteLine
{
    Text = "Removing Ice Cream..."
},
new RemoveFromCollection<ListItem>()
{
    Collection = myList,
    Item = new LambdaValue<ListItem>
        (env => new ListItem("Ice Cream"))
},
new PrintList()
{
    Budget = 0m,
    Collection = myList
},
```

The RemoveFromCollection activity removes the specified item from the collection, if found. If there is more than one activity in the collection that matches the specified item, only the first is removed. Again, only the Description property is specified since that is all that is needed.

ClearCollection Activity

Finally, to remove all items from your collection, add the following activities to your workflow:

```
new ClearCollection<ListItem>()
{
    Collection = myList
},
new PrintList()
{
    Budget = 0m,
    Collection = myList
}
```

Press F5 to run the application. Your results should look like these:

```
Workflow starting...
2: Milk, 1 @ $3.99 []
1: Bread, 2 @ $2.95 [Get 100% Whole Wheat, if possible]
```

```
4: Cheese, 1 @ $1.75 []
5: Ice Cream, 4 @ $5.75 []
Total cost: $34.64

1: Bread, 2 @ $2.95 [Get 100% Whole Wheat, if possible]
2: Milk, 1 @ $3.99 []
4: Cheese, 1 @ $1.75 []
5: Ice Cream, 4 @ $5.75 []
Total cost: $34.64

You don't really need Ice Cream?
Removing Ice Cream...
1: Bread, 2 @ $2.95 [Get 100% Whole Wheat, if possible]
2: Milk, 1 @ $3.99 []
4: Cheese, 1 @ $1.75 []
Total cost: $11.64

The list is empty
Workflow ended
Press ENTER to exit
```

The complete implementation of Program.cs is shown in Listing 18-6.

Listing 18-6. Implementation of Program.cs

```csharp
using System;
using System.Collections.Generic;
using System.Activities;
using System.Activities.Statements;
using System.Activities.Expressions;

namespace ShoppingList
{
    class Program
    {
        static void Main(string[] args)
        {
            WorkflowInvoker.Invoke(CollectionWF());

            Console.WriteLine("Press ENTER to exit");
            Console.ReadLine();
        }

        private static Activity CollectionWF()
        {
```

```
// myList is a collection of ListItem objects
Variable<ICollection<ListItem>> myList =
    new Variable<ICollection<ListItem>>()
{
    Name = "MyList",
    Default = new LambdaValue<ICollection<ListItem>>
        (env => new List<ListItem>())
};

return new Sequence
{
    Variables = { myList },
    Activities =
    {
        new WriteLine
        {
            Text = "Workflow starting..."
        },
        new AddToCollection<ListItem>
        {
            Collection = myList,
            Item = new LambdaValue<ListItem>
                (env => new ListItem("Milk", 1, 3.99m, 2, ""))
        },
        new AddToCollection<ListItem>
        {
            Collection = myList,
            Item = new LambdaValue<ListItem>
                (env => new ListItem("Bread", 2, 2.95m, 1,
                "Get 100% Whole Wheat, if possible"))
        },
        new AddToCollection<ListItem>
        {
            Collection = myList,
            Item = new LambdaValue<ListItem>
                (env => new ListItem("Cheese", 1, 1.75m, 4, ""))
        },
        new AddToCollection<ListItem>
        {
            Collection = myList,
            Item = new LambdaValue<ListItem>
                (env => new ListItem("Ice Cream", 4, 5.75m, 5, ""))
        },
```

```
new PrintList()
{
    Budget = 0m,
    Collection = myList
},
new SortCollection
{
    Collection = myList
},
new PrintList()
{
    Budget = 0m,
    Collection = myList
},
new If
{
    Condition = new ExistsInCollection<ListItem>()
    {
        Collection = myList,
        Item = new LambdaValue<ListItem>
            (env => new ListItem("Ice Cream"))
    },
    Then = new WriteLine
    {
        Text = "You don't really need Ice Cream?"
    }
},
new WriteLine
{
    Text = "Removing Ice Cream..."
},
new RemoveFromCollection<ListItem>()
{
    Collection = myList,
    Item = new LambdaValue<ListItem>
        (env => new ListItem("Ice Cream"))
},
new PrintList()
{
    Budget = 0m,
    Collection = myList
},
new ClearCollection<ListItem>()
```

```
            {
                Collection = new myList
            },
            new PrintList()
            {
                Budget = 0m,
                Collection = myList
            },
            new WriteLine
            {
                Text = "Workflow ended"
            }
        }
    };
}
}


//-------------------------------------------
// The ListItem class defines the items that
// are stored in the collection
//-------------------------------------------
public class ListItem
{
    public string Description { get; set; }
    public int Quantity { get; set; }
    public decimal UnitPrice { get; set; }
    public int Priority { get; set; }
    public string Comments { get; set; }

    public ListItem(string description, int quantity, decimal unitPrice,
        int priority, string comments)
    {
        Description = description;
        Quantity = quantity;
        UnitPrice = unitPrice;
        Priority = priority;
        Comments = comments;
    }

    public ListItem(string description)
    {
        Description = description;
    }
```

```csharp
        // The Equals() method must be overridden
        // to enable a search using the description
        public override bool Equals(object obj)
        {
            ListItem i = obj as ListItem;
            if (i == null)
                return false;
            else
            {
                if (i.Description == this.Description)
                    return true;
                else
                    return false;
            }
        }

        public override int GetHashCode()
        {
            return base.GetHashCode();
        }
    }
}
```

■ ■ ■

CHAPTER 19

Interoperability with Workflow 3.5

I stated in Chapter 1 that activities created in WF 4.0 are not interchangeable with WF 3.5 activities. However, as promised, I'll now show you how you can execute workflows and activities created in WF 3.5 from within a WF 4.0 workflow. This will allow you to do the following:

- Continue to use third-party activities that you cannot port to WF 4.0

- Delay porting parts of your solution to WF 4.0

- Use 3.0 and 3.5 activities not yet provided in WF 4.0

Creating a 4.0 Workflow

Start by creating a Workflow Console Application as shown in Figure 19-1. For the project name, enter **SampleInterop**, and for the solution use **Chapter19**.

Figure 19-1. *Creating a WF 4.0 application*

Drag a Sequence onto the workflow, drag a WriteLine activity onto this Sequence, and enter the Text property as **"Workflow has started..."**. Open the Program.cs file and add the following code at the end of the Main() method:

```
Console.WriteLine("Press ENTER to exit");
Console.ReadLine();
```

Creating a 3.5 Workflow

From the Solution Explorer, right-click the Chapter19 solution and choose Add ➤ New Project. In the Add New Project dialog, change the .NET version to 3.5. The list of available templates should change as shown in Figure 19-2. Select the Sequential Workflow Library template. For the project name, enter **Workflow35**.

Figure 19-2. *Creating a WF 3.5 project*

The 3.5 workflow designer should be displayed, which is shown in Figure 19-3.

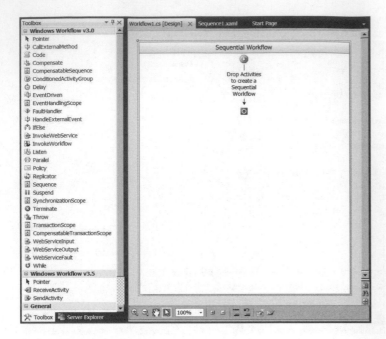

Figure 19-3. *The WF 3.5 designer*

Drag a `CodeActivity` to the workflow and then double-click it, which will open the code-behind file. Enter the following implementation:

```
Console.WriteLine("The 3.5 Workflow has started...");
```

Go back to the 3.5 designer and drag another `CodeActivity` to the workflow. Double-click it and enter the following implementation:

```
Console.WriteLine("The 3.5 Workflow has finished");
```

The completed workflow should look like the one shown in Figure 19-4.

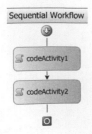

Figure 19-4. *The completed 3.5 workflow design*

From the Solution Explorer, right-click the SampleInterop project and choose Add Reference. From the Projects tab, select the Workflow35 project. Press F6 to rebuild the solution.

From the Solution Explorer, right-click the SampleInterop project and choose properties. The project's Property window will be displayed. Make sure that the target framework is the full .NET 4.0 version, not the client profile as shown in Figure 19-5. The Interop activity is not currently available in the client profile.

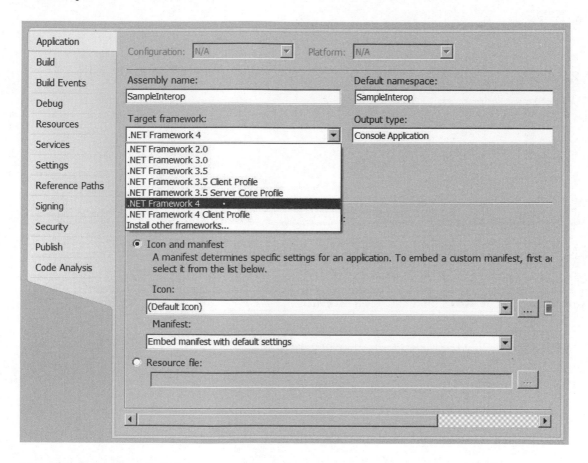

Figure 19-5. *Selecting the full .NET 4.0 profile*

You also need to add a reference to System.Workflow.ComponentModel assembly in the SampleInterop project.

Interop Activity

Open the 4.0 workflow (`Workflow1.xaml` file) and drag an `Interop` activity below the existing `WriteLine` activity. You should find the `Interop` activity in the Migration tab of the toolbox. The design should look like the one shown in Figure 19-6.

Figure 19-6. *An Interop activity in the workflow designer*

Click the link where it says "Click to browse". This will display the dialog shown in Figure 19-7. Expand the `Workflow35` assembly and select `Workflow1`.

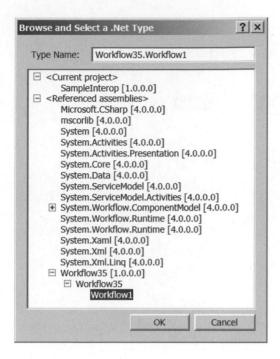

Figure 19-7. Selecting the workflow to execute

Drag a WriteLine activity below the Interop activity and enter the Text property as **"Workflow has finished"**.

Running the Application

Press F5 to run the application. Your results should look like this:

```
Workflow has started...
The 3.5 Workflow has started...
The 3.5 Workflow has finished
Workflow has finished.
Press ENTER to exit
```

Executing a Custom 3.5 Activity

The Interop activity can also be used to execute a single activity. You will now create a custom activity in the WF 3.5 project and execute it from the 4.0 workflow.

Creating a Custom Activity

From the Solution Explorer, right-click the Workflow35 project and choose Add ➤ New Item. This will display the Add New Item dialog shown in Figure 19-8.

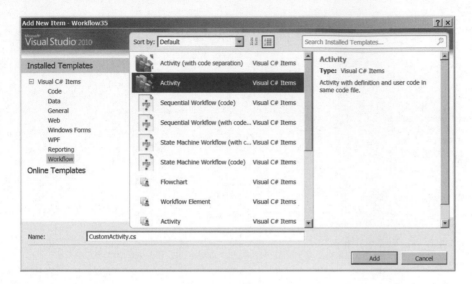

Figure 19-8. *Adding a custom activity (WF 3.5)*

Select the Activity template and enter the name as **CustomActivity.cs**. The activity designer shown in Figure 19-9 should be displayed.

Figure 19-9. *Custom activity designer (WF 3.5)*

Drag a CodeActivity onto this designer and double-click it which should display the code-behind file. Before entering the code for this activity, add the code shown in Listing 19-1 just after the class constructor.

Listing 19-1. *Adding a public property*

```
public static DependencyProperty MessageProperty =
    DependencyProperty.Register("Message", typeof(string), typeof(CustomActivity));

[DescriptionAttribute("Message")]
[BrowsableAttribute(true)]
[DesignerSerializationVisibilityAttribute(DesignerSerializationVisibility.Visible)]
public string Message
{
    get
    {
        return ((string)(base.GetValue(MessageProperty)));
    }
    set
    {
        base.SetValue(MessageProperty, value);
    }
}
```

This code defines a string property named Message, which can be accessed from outside the workflow. Now enter the following implementation for the CodeActivity to display the Message property:

```
Console.WriteLine(this.Message);
```

The complete implementation of CustomActivity.cs is shown in Listing 19-2.

Listing 19-2. *Implementation of CustomActivity.cs*

```
using System;
using System.ComponentModel;
using System.ComponentModel.Design;
using System.Collections;
using System.Drawing;
using System.Linq;
using System.Workflow.ComponentModel;
using System.Workflow.ComponentModel.Design;
using System.Workflow.ComponentModel.Compiler;
using System.Workflow.ComponentModel.Serialization;
using System.Workflow.Runtime;
using System.Workflow.Activities;
using System.Workflow.Activities.Rules;

namespace Workflow35
{
    public partial class CustomActivity : SequenceActivity
    {
        public CustomActivity()
        {
            InitializeComponent();
        }
```

```
public static DependencyProperty MessageProperty =
    DependencyProperty.Register("Message", typeof(string),
    typeof(CustomActivity));

[DescriptionAttribute("Message")]
[BrowsableAttribute(true)]
[DesignerSerializationVisibilityAttribute
    (DesignerSerializationVisibility.Visible)]
public string Message
{
    get
    {
        return ((string)(base.GetValue(MessageProperty)));
    }
    set
    {
        base.SetValue(MessageProperty, value);
    }
}

private void codeActivity1_ExecuteCode(object sender, EventArgs e)
{
    Console.WriteLine(this.Message);
}
    }
}
```

Throwing an Exception

Open the WF 3.5 designer (CustomActivity.cs[Design] tab) and drag a ThrowActivity below the CodeActivity. The Properties window for a ThrowActivity is shown in Figure 19-10.

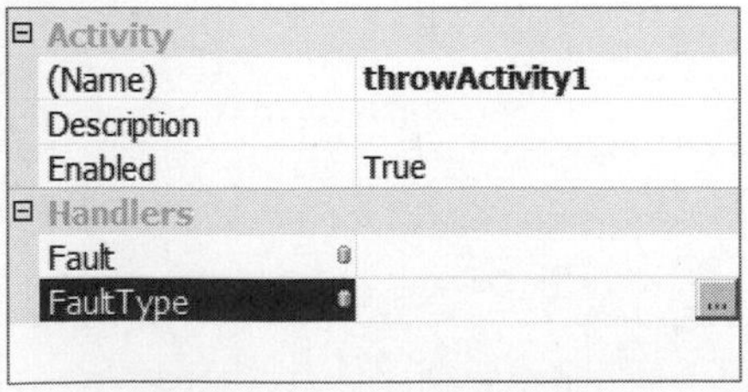

Figure 19-10. ThrowActivity Properties window

Select the FaultType property and click the ellipsis beside it. In the dialog that is displayed, expand the mscorlib assembly and select the System namespace. Then scroll down and select the InvalidProgramException, as shown in Figure 19-11.

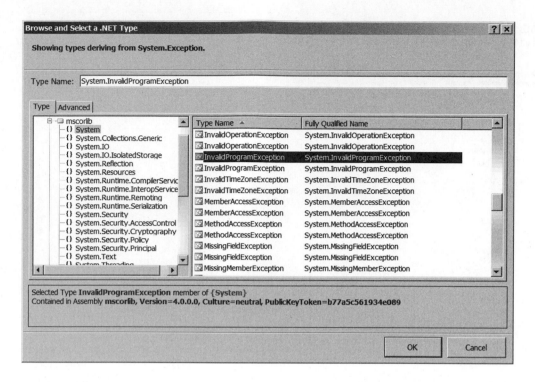

Figure 19-11. Select the exception to throw

The diagram of the custom activity should look like the one shown in Figure 19-12.

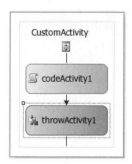

Figure 19-12. Final custom activity design

Invoking the Custom Activity

Press F6 to rebuild the solution. Go back to the WF 4.0 workflow (Workflow1.xaml). Drag a TryCatch activity onto the workflow just below the Interop activity. Drag an Interop activity to the Try section.

371

Click the link to browse for the workflow to be invoked. Expand the Workflow35 assembly and select the CustomActivity, as shown in Figure 19-13.

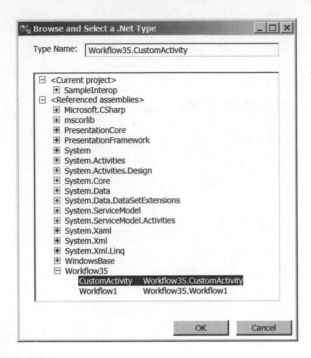

Figure 19-13. *Selecting the CustomActivity*

Notice that there is a Message property in the Properties window as well as a MessageOut property (see Figure 19-14). Because you created a public property in the custom activity, it is available to the WF 4.0 workflow.

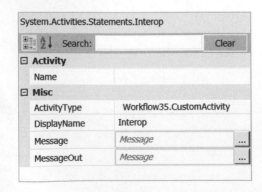

Figure 19-14. *Properties window showing the Message property*

You can bind the data passed in and the data returned to different variables. This will allow you to bind a literal string for input and store the resulting data in an argument or variable. For the Message property, enter **"Called from a 4.0 workflow"**. Leave the MessageOut property blank because you are not expecting returned data.

Click the *Add new catch* link and choose "Browse for types". Expand the mscorlib assembly and select the InvalidProgramException, as shown in Figure 19-15.

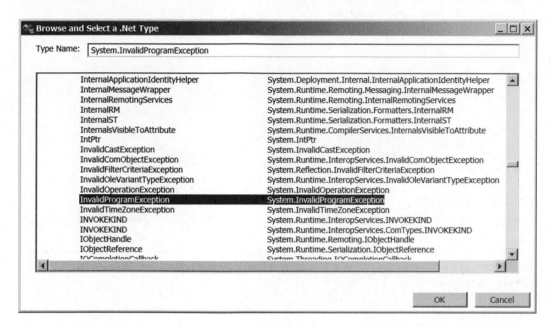

Figure 19-15. *Selecting the InvalidProgramException*

Drag a WriteLine activity onto the Catch section and enter the Text property as **"Custom 3.5 activity threw an exception"**. The completed TryCatch activity should look like the one shown in Figure 19-16.

373

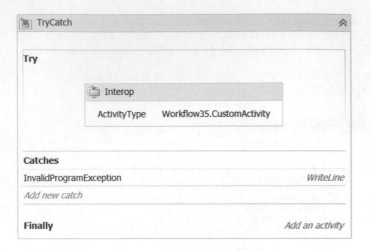

Figure 19-16. Completed TryCatch activity

Running the Application

Press F5 to run the application. Your results should look like this:

```
Workflow has started...
The 3.5 Workflow has started...
The 3.5 Workflow has finished
Called from a 4.0 workflow
Custom 3.5 activity threw an exception
Workflow has finished.
Press ENTER to exit
```

■ ■ ■

CHAPTER 20

Policy

In this chapter, you'll use a `PolicyActivity` to determine whether a particular workflow activity needs to be reviewed. Here's the scenario: a workflow has some type of data entry activity, and you want to perform a quality control review of the output from that step. It might be a call center taking an order over the phone or a request placed from the Web or from a self-service kiosk. You don't want to review that step every time, however. You might want to review only those orders that exceed a certain value or when the operator who performed that step is being evaluated for some reason. Maybe you just want to check every tenth transaction.

What I've just listed are *rules*; a rule specifies the appropriate action to a defined condition. A *policy* is a set of rules. As you might imagine, rules can overlap and even contradict each other, so a policy also specifies the priority of rules and allows for re-evaluation if one rule changes the conditions that affect other rules.

Creating a Custom Activity

The `PolicyActivity` is not currently available in WF 4.0, so you'll need to use version 3.5. Start by creating a workflow activity library using .NET 3.5, as shown in Figure 20-1.

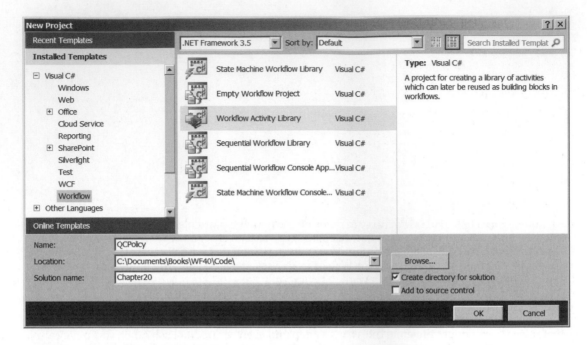

Figure 20-1. *Creating a Workflow Activity Library (in version 3.5)*

For the project name, enter **QCPolicy**; for the solution, enter **Chapter20**. The workflow designer should be displayed and look similar to Figure 20-2.

Figure 20-2. *Initial workflow designer*

Defining the Data Structures

The rules that you will define are based on properties of the operator, customer, transaction, and so on. So you'll first define the structure of the data elements that will be used. From the Solution Explorer, right-click the QCPolicy project and choose Add ➤ Class. For the name, enter **DataElements.cs**. The implementation of this file is shown in Listing 20-1.

Listing 20-1. *Implementation of DataElements.cs*

```csharp
using System;
using System.Collections.Generic;

namespace QCPolicy
{
    /***************************************************/
    // Configuration options for a specific activity
    /***************************************************/
    public class ActivityConfig
    {
        public decimal MinimumAmount { get; set; }
        public decimal ThresholdAmount { get; set; }
        public int Frequency { get; set; }
        public int NumberSinceLastEval { get; set; }

        public ActivityConfig (decimal min, decimal max, int freq)
        {
            this.MinimumAmount = min;
            this.ThresholdAmount = max;
            this.Frequency = freq;
            this.NumberSinceLastEval = 0;
        }

        public int IncrementEvalCount()
        {
            this.NumberSinceLastEval++;
            return this.NumberSinceLastEval;
        }

        public void ResetEval()
        {
            this.NumberSinceLastEval = 0;
        }
    }

    /***************************************************/
    // Details about the operator
    /***************************************************/
    public class OperatorConfig
    {
        public bool UnderEvaluation { get; set; }
        public int Frequency { get; set; }
        public int NumberSinceLastEval { get; set; }

        public OperatorConfig (bool eval, int freq)
        {
            this.UnderEvaluation = eval;
            this.Frequency = freq;
            this.NumberSinceLastEval = 0;
        }
```

```csharp
    public int IncrementEvalCount()
    {
        this.NumberSinceLastEval++;
        return this.NumberSinceLastEval;
    }

    public void ResetEval()
    {
        this.NumberSinceLastEval = 0;
    }
}

/***************************************************/
// Properties of the customer needed fot processing
/***************************************************/
public class CustomerConfig
{
    public string Category { get; set; }

    public CustomerConfig(string cat)
    {
        this.Category = cat;
    }
}

/***************************************************/
// Details needed to process a transaction
/***************************************************/
public class TransactionConfig
{
    public decimal Amount { get; set; }

    public TransactionConfig(decimal amt)
    {
        this.Amount = amt;
    }
}

/***************************************************/
// Contains a list of transaction to be processed
/***************************************************/
public class TransactionList
{
    public List<TransactionConfig> List { get; set; }

    public TransactionList()
    {
        this.List = new List<TransactionConfig>();
    }
}
}
```

These classes contain public properties that will be used when defining the rules. The ActivityConfig class contains a MinimumAmount property; transactions below this amount do not need to be reviewed. The ThresholdAmount defines the level at which all transactions must be reviewed. Frequency specifies how often the activity should be reviewed. The NumberSinceLastEval keeps track of how many instances were not reviewed so you'll know when a review is required.

The OperatorConfig class has a Boolean property named UnderEvaluation. This is set for operators that are being evaluated. The Frequency and NumberSinceLastEval are used just as they are for the ActivityConfig class. The CustomerConfig class has a Category property, which is used to indicate whether this is a major account or some other classification. The TransactionConfig class has an Amount property that specifies the total amount of the transaction. Finally, the TransactionList class holds a collection of TransactionConfig objects.

PolicyActivity

The project template created a custom activity file named Activity1. From the Solution Explorer, rename this file as **QCPolicy.cs**. Visual Studio will prompt you to ask whether you want all references to this class changed (see Figure 20-3); choose Yes.

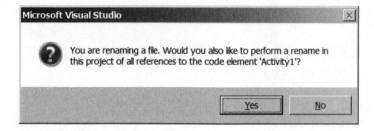

Figure 20-3. Modifying references to a renamed file

Now open the QCPolicy.cs file; it should open in design mode by default. Drag a PolicyActivity onto the QCPolicy activity. In the Properties window, change the name of this activity to **ReviewPolicy**. The designer should now look like the one shown in Figure 20-4. The red circle with an exclamation point indicates that the *ruleset* has not been defined yet. You'll take care of that now.

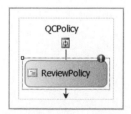

Figure 20-4. ReviewPolicy activity

Adding Dependency Properties

In WF 3.5 arguments and variables are implemented differently than they are in WF 4.0. Properties that are passed into or out of an activity are declared as a DependencyProperty. You'll need to define these so the input data (that the rules are based on) can be passed in and the policy result can be made available.

Right-click anywhere in the workflow designer and choose View Code. In the QCPolicy.cs class add the code shown in Listing 20-2 just after the constructor.

Listing 20-2. *Declaring the Dependency properties*

```
public static DependencyProperty ActivityDataProperty =
    DependencyProperty.Register("ActivityData", typeof(ActivityConfig),
        typeof(QCPolicy));

[DescriptionAttribute("ActivityData")]
[CategoryAttribute("Input Category")]
[BrowsableAttribute(true)]
[DesignerSerializationVisibilityAttribute(DesignerSerializationVisibility.Visible)]
public ActivityConfig ActivityData
{
    get
    {
        return ((ActivityConfig)(base.GetValue(QCPolicy.ActivityDataProperty)));
    }
    set
    {
        base.SetValue(QCPolicy.ActivityDataProperty, value);
    }
}

public static DependencyProperty OperatorDataProperty =
    DependencyProperty.Register("OperatorData", typeof(OperatorConfig),
        typeof(QCPolicy));

[DescriptionAttribute("OperatorData")]
[CategoryAttribute("Input Category")]
[BrowsableAttribute(true)]
[DesignerSerializationVisibilityAttribute(DesignerSerializationVisibility.Visible)]
public OperatorConfig OperatorData
{
    get
    {
        return ((OperatorConfig)(base.GetValue(QCPolicy.OperatorDataProperty)));
    }
    set
    {
        base.SetValue(QCPolicy.OperatorDataProperty, value);
    }
}
```

```csharp
public static DependencyProperty CustomerDataProperty =
    DependencyProperty.Register("CustomerData", typeof(CustomerConfig),
        typeof(QCPolicy));

[DescriptionAttribute("CustomerData")]
[CategoryAttribute("Input Category")]
[BrowsableAttribute(true)]
[DesignerSerializationVisibilityAttribute(DesignerSerializationVisibility.Visible)]
public CustomerConfig CustomerData
{
    get
    {
        return ((CustomerConfig)(base.GetValue(QCPolicy.CustomerDataProperty)));
    }
    set
    {
        base.SetValue(QCPolicy.CustomerDataProperty, value);
    }
}

public static DependencyProperty TransactionDataProperty =
    DependencyProperty.Register("TransactionData", typeof(TransactionConfig),
        typeof(QCPolicy));

[DescriptionAttribute("TransactionData")]
[CategoryAttribute("Input Category")]
[BrowsableAttribute(true)]
[DesignerSerializationVisibilityAttribute(DesignerSerializationVisibility.Visible)]
public TransactionConfig TransactionData
{
    get
    {
        return ((TransactionConfig)
            (base.GetValue(QCPolicy.TransactionDataProperty)));
    }
    set
    {
        base.SetValue(QCPolicy.TransactionDataProperty, value);
    }
}

public static DependencyProperty ReviewProperty =
    DependencyProperty.Register("Review", typeof(bool), typeof(QCPolicy));

[DescriptionAttribute("Review")]
[CategoryAttribute("Output Category")]
[BrowsableAttribute(true)]
[DesignerSerializationVisibilityAttribute(DesignerSerializationVisibility.Visible)]
public bool Review
{
```

```
    get
    {
        return ((bool)(base.GetValue(QCPolicy.ReviewProperty)));
    }
    set
    {
        base.SetValue(QCPolicy.ReviewProperty, value);
    }
}

public static DependencyProperty PriorityProperty =
    DependencyProperty.Register("Priority", typeof(string), typeof(QCPolicy));

[DescriptionAttribute("Priority")]
[CategoryAttribute("Output Category")]
[BrowsableAttribute(true)]
[DesignerSerializationVisibilityAttribute(DesignerSerializationVisibility.Visible)]
public string Priority
{
    get
    {
        return ((string)(base.GetValue(QCPolicy.PriorityProperty)));
    }
    set
    {
        base.SetValue(QCPolicy.PriorityProperty, value);
    }
}
```

After entering this code, right-click anywhere on the code file and choose View Designer. This will display the workflow designer. The Properties window of a PolicyActivity is shown in Figure 20-5.

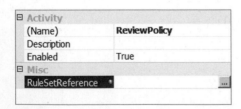

Figure 20-5. *Properties window of a PolicyActivity*

Creating a Rule Set

The RuleSetReference defines the set of rules (called a *ruleset*) for this policy, which is implemented by a RuleSet class. Select this property and click on the ellipses. The dialog shown in Figure 20-6 is displayed.

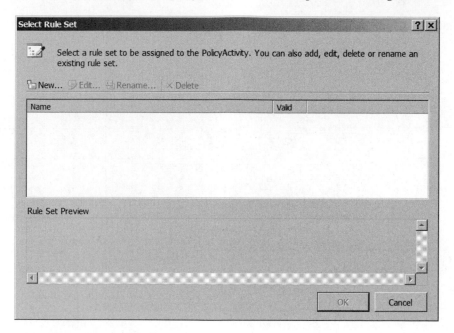

Figure 20-6. *Creating a new RuleSet*

There are no existing rulesets, so click the New link to create a new RuleSet. This will display the Rule Set Editor ((see Figure 20-7).

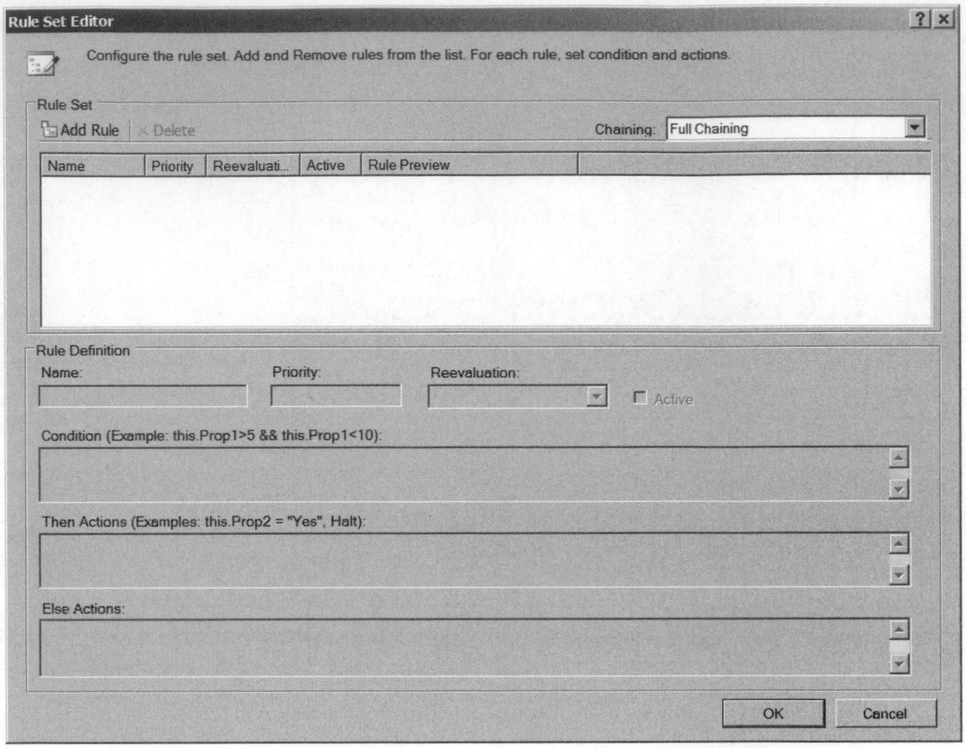

Figure 20-7. *An empty ruleset editor*

Defining the Rules

Let's start by entering a few rules and then I'll explain how the PolicyActivity uses them. For each Rule, you'll need to give it a Name (which is just used for display purposes), a Condition, and Then and Else actions (Else actions are optional).

Click the Add Rule link. Enter the Name as **Operator Eval**, the Priority as **6**, and the Condition as **this.OperatorData.UnderEvaluation**. Enter the following code for the Then action:

```
this.Review = True
Halt
```

This Rule states that if the operator is being evaluated, the activity should be reviewed. The Halt command indicates that no further rules need to be checked. Now define a Rule that says if the transaction is less than the minimum amount, no review is necessary. Click the Add Rule link. Enter the Name as **Minimum Amount**, the Priority as **5**, and the Condition as the following:

```
this.TransactionData.Amount < this.ActivityData.MinimumAmount
```

For the Then action, enter **this.Review = False**. The Halt command is not used because the activity might require a review for other reasons.

Now add a Rule to ensure that if the customer is coded as a Major account, the activity will be reviewed. Click the Add Rule link and enter the Name as **Major Account** and enter **4** for the Priority. Enter the following code for the Condition:

```
this.CustomerData.Category == "Major" &&
this.TransactionData.Amount >= this.ActivityData.MinimumAmount
```

For the Then action, enter the following code:

```
this.Review = True
Halt
```

This Rule was coded so transactions for Major accounts that are below the minimum amount do not need to be reviewed. Now add another Rule so activities over the threshold amount are reviewed. Click the Add Rule link. Enter the Name as **Over Limit**, the Priority as **3**, and the Condition as

```
this.TransactionData.Amount >= this.ActivityData.ThresholdAmount
```

Enter the following code for the Then action:

```
this.Review = True
Halt
```

The last two rules that you'll add are used to ensure that even if none of the previous rules require a review, the activity is still reviewed periodically. The properties that you created for both the activity and operator, include a Frequency property to specify how often a review is required. For example, if the Frequency is set to **10**, a review is performed at least every tenth time. These classes also have a NumberSinceLastEval property that keeps track of how many activities have been executed without a review. This is verified for both the operator and activity because if there are multiple operators performing the same activities, it's possible that while every tenth activity is reviewed, a particular operator might never have its work reviewed.

Click the Add Rule link. Enter the Name as **Operator Frequency**, the Priority as **2**, and the Condition as

```
this.OperatorData.NumberSinceLastEval >= this.OperatorData.Frequency
```

For the Then action, enter **this.Review = True**. Click the Add Rule link. Enter the Name as **Activity Frequency**, the Priority as **1**, and the Condition as

```
this.ActivityData.NumberSinceLastEval >= this.ActivityData.Frequency
```

For the Then action, enter **this.Review = True**. The completed RuleSet should look like the one shown in Figure 20-8.

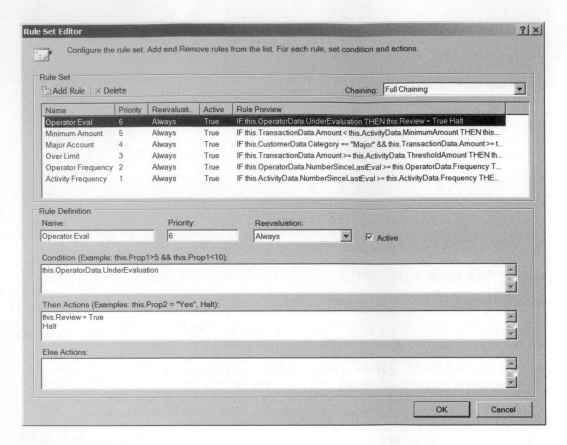

Figure 20-8. *The completed RuleSet*

Click OK. The Select Rule Set dialog will now show the new `RuleSet`. Click Rename and enter the Name as **Review Policy**. The dialog should look like the one shown in Figure 20-9.

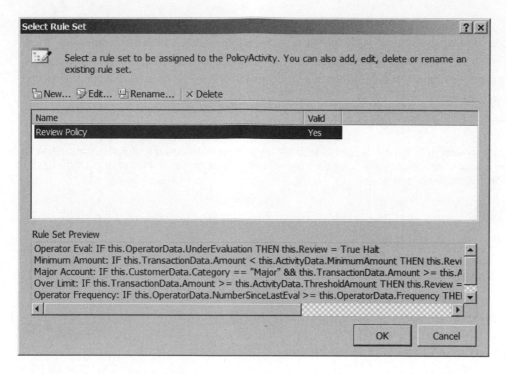

Figure 20-9. *Select Rule Set dialog with the new RuleSet*

Understanding Rule Sets

Now let's look into some of the details of how a RuleSet works.

Rules

As I already mentioned, the basic elements of a Rule are the Condition and the Then and Else actions. These work just like an if-then-else statement. In both the Condition and Then and Else actions, you can access the workflow class members and static members in referenced assemblies (such as DateTime.Now). You do not need to specify both Then and Else actions.

In the Then and Else actions, you can write code to do things such as the following:

- Update workflow members

- Call workflow methods

- Call static methods from referenced assemblies

- Execute a Halt or Update command (explained later)

387

■ **Caution** The conditions and actions are written in typical C# syntax except that there are no semi-colons at the end of each statement. This might seem strange because all the expressions you've written so far have been using Visual Basic syntax. In this chapter, you have been using WF 3.5 instead of 4.0. This is just one of the differences between the two versions.

Rule instances are executed in priority order with higher priorities executed first. Rule instances with the same priority are executed in alphabetical order based on the Name property. By default, a Rule has a priority of 0. Priorities can be negative.

Chaining

When a RuleSet is executed, each Rule is evaluated one by one, starting with the highest priority. It is possible that the Then or Else action of a Rule modifies a property used in a condition of a previous Rule. If that happens, the feature referred to as *chaining* means that the previous rules would be re-evaluated (and its Then or Else action executed as appropriate). Rule evaluations would then continue from where it left off.

Let me give you a scenario to help illustrate this. Suppose that we had the following rules in priority order:

1. `if nTotal > 10 && bSuccess Then nResult = 5 Else nResult = -1`

2. `if nTotal > 20 Then bSuccess = True`

3. `if nResult > 3 Then bSuccess = False`

4. `if nTotal > 20 Then bSuccess = False`

And the initial values of the properties are the following:

- `nTotal = 15`

- `bSuccess = True`

- `nResult = 0`

The rules will be executed as follows:

- Rule #1 will set nResult to 5.

- Rule #2 is executed but because the condition is false, no action is taken.

- Rule #3 will set bSuccess to False.

- Rule #1 will set nResult to -1 (#1 is re-executed because bSuccess was modified).

- Rule #2 is not re-executed because none of its dependencies changed.

- Rule #3 is re-executed because nResult was changed; however, its condition is false, so no action is taken.

- Rule #4 is executed, but no action is taken.

The final results will be the following:

- nTotal = 15
- bSuccess = False
- nResult = -1

For each Rule, the Reevaluation property can be set to either Always (the default value) or Never. Always doesn't actually mean always; it means to re-evaluate if a member in the condition is modified (as described previously). Never means the Rule is evaluated only once, even if a member has been changed. The Never option turns off chaining for that Rule.

The RuleSet has a Chaining property, which also controls if/how chaining is applied. The default value is Full Chaining, which re-evaluates rules as defined previously. The Sequential option turns off chaining. It is equivalent to setting the Reevaluate property to Never for all rules. The Explicit Update Only option performs re-evaluation only when specifically directed to with the Update action.

Halt and Update

In addition to setting properties and calling workflow methods, you can also use the Halt and Update commands in the Then and Else actions. The Halt command causes all rule evaluation to stop immediately, and the activity is completed. You used it on several of the Rule instances in the previous RuleSet.

If the Chaining option is set to Explicit Update Only, you must use the Update command to force any necessary rule re-evaluations. The Update command specifies a single property. Any previous rule that uses that property is re-evaluated. If you need to check for multiple properties, you can call the Update command multiple times. The property is generally specified using the this. notation. For example, the Update command could be this:

```
Update(this.Review)
```

This is also an acceptable form:

```
Update("this/Review")
```

Rules File

The actual Rule definition is stored in the QCPolicy.rules file. You can select this from the Solution Explorer, as shown in Figure 20-10.

Figure 20-10. *Selecting the rules file*

If you double-click this file, you can see the actual contents. It uses an XML structure to store the various parts of the RuleSet and each of the Rule objects.

Determining the Priority

If you determine that this activity should be reviewed, now you'll also decide what priority should be given to the review. For example, we might want higher value transactions to move to the top of the list.

Open the QCPolicy.cs file in design mode and drag an IfElseActivity below the ReviewPolicy activity. Click the left branch, and in the Properties window set the Name property to IfReview. For the Condition property, select **Declarative Rule Condition**. Expand the Condition property; for the ConditionName, enter **Review**; for the Expression property, click the ellipsis and enter **this.Review**. This branch will be executed only when the Review property is True. The Properties window should look like the one shown in Figure 20-11.

Activity	
(Name)	**ifReview**
Description	
Enabled	True
Conditions	
Condition	**Declarative Rule Condition**
ConditionName	**Review**
Expression	**this.Review**

Figure 20-11. *Properties windows of an IfElseBranch activity*

Drag a PolicyActivity onto the ifReview branch and set the Name property to PriorityPolicy. The workflow diagram should look like the one shown in Figure 20-12.

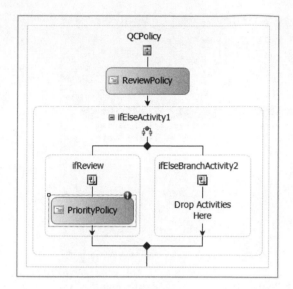

Figure 20-12. *Workflow diagram for the QCPolicy custom activity*

Entering the Priority Rules

Select the PriorityPolicy activity. In the Properties window, select the RuleSetReference property and click the ellipses. The Select Rule Set dialog should show the RuleSet that you just created. Click the New link to create a different RuleSet for this PolicyActivity.

Click the Add Rule link. Enter the Name as **Major Account**, the Priority as **3**, and the Condition as:

```
this.CustomerData.Category == "Major"
```

For the Then action, enter **this.Priority = "High"**; for the Else action, enter **this.Priority = "Normal"**. This will set the Priority to High for major accounts and Normal for everyone else.

Add another Rule to handle transactions that exceed the ThresholdAmount. Enter the Name as **Over Limit**, the Priority as **2**, and the Condition as:

```
this.TransactionData.Amount >= this.ActivityData.ThresholdAmount
```

For the Then action, enter **this.Priority = "High"**; there is no Else action. Add a final Rule named **Minimum**. For the Condition, enter:

```
this.TransactionData.Amount < this.ActivityData.MinimumAmount
```

For the Then action, enter **this.Priority = "Low"**. The completed RuleSet should look like the one shown in Figure 20-13.

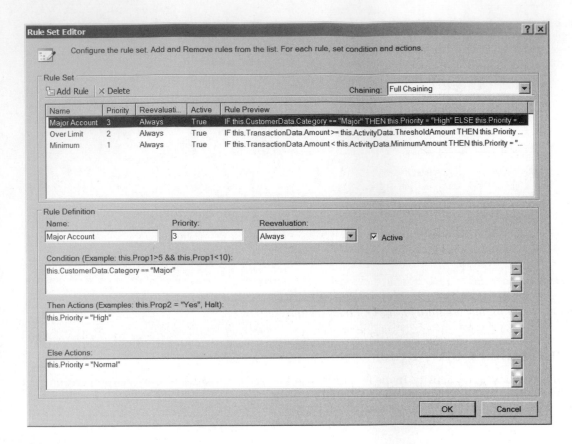

Figure 20-13. Completed RuleSet for PriorityPolicy

After clicking OK in the Rule Set Editor, rename the RuleSet to **Priority Policy**, as you did with the first RuleSet. You have completed the implementation of your custom policy activity. Press F6 to build the solution.

Creating a Workflow Application

Now you'll build a workflow that will use the new custom activity. From the Solution Explorer, right-click the Chapter20 solution and choose Add ➤ New Project. Make sure you change the .NET version to 4.0 and select the Workflow Console Application template, as shown in Figure 20-14. Enter the project name as **PolicySample**.

Figure 20-14. *Completed RuleSet for PriorityPolicy*

This application will need to use the QCPolicy activity as well as the data structures defined in DataElements.cs. From the Solution Explorer, right-click the PolicySample project and choose Add Reference. From the Projects tab, select QCPolicy and click OK. Press F6 to rebuild the solution. Right-click the PolicySample project and choose Set as Startup Project. When you're ready to run the application, you'll need to start this application, not the QCPolicy project.

From the Solution Explorer, right-click the PolicySample project and choose properties. The project's Property window will be displayed. Just as you did in the previous chapter, make sure that the target framework is the full .NET 4.0 version, not the client profile. Add a reference to the System.Workflow.ComponentModel assembly.

Creating a Custom Activity

Start by creating a custom activity that will perform the activity and then use the QCPolicy activity to determine whether this work needs to be reviewed. Right-click the PolicySample project and choose Add ➤ New Item. In the Add New Item dialog, select the Activity template in the Workflow category (see Figure 20-15). Enter the name as **MyActivity.xaml**.

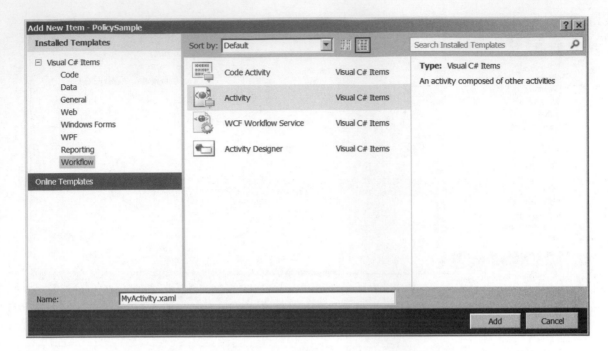

Figure 20-15. Adding a custom activity to the project

This will display a blank designer for the custom activity, as shown in Figure 20-16.

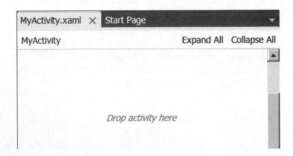

Figure 20-16. A blank custom activity designer

You will first need to define the arguments that will be passed in to this activity. These are the data structures for the operator, customer, activity, and transaction. Click the Arguments button at the bottom left of the designer. Click the *Create Argument* link and enter the Name as **customerData**. For the Argument type, select Browse for Types. In the dialog that is displayed, expand the QCPolicy assembly and select the CustomerConfig class.

Add another argument named **transactionData** and use the TransactionConfig class for the Argument type. Add two more arguments named **operatorData** and **activityData** using the

OperatorConfig and ActivityConfig classes, respectively. The list of arguments should look like the one shown in Figure 20-17.

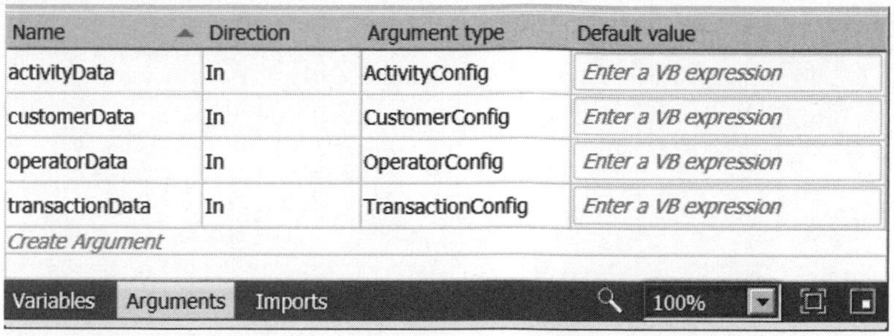

Name ▲	Direction	Argument type	Default value
activityData	In	ActivityConfig	*Enter a VB expression*
customerData	In	CustomerConfig	*Enter a VB expression*
operatorData	In	OperatorConfig	*Enter a VB expression*
transactionData	In	TransactionConfig	*Enter a VB expression*
Create Argument			

| Variables | **Arguments** | Imports | 🔍 | 100% ▼ | ⬚ | ▪ |

Figure 20-17. *Arguments defined for this activity*

You will also need a couple of variables. Click the Variable button and you'll notice that there are no variables defined yet and also no link to create a variable. That's because variables need be scoped to a specific activity, and so far there are no activities. Drag a Sequence activity to the designer. The *Create Variable* link should appear; click it, enter **review** for the Name property, and enter **Boolean** for the Variable type. Add another variable named **priority** and leave the Variable type as **String**. The variables should look like the ones shown in Figure 20-18.

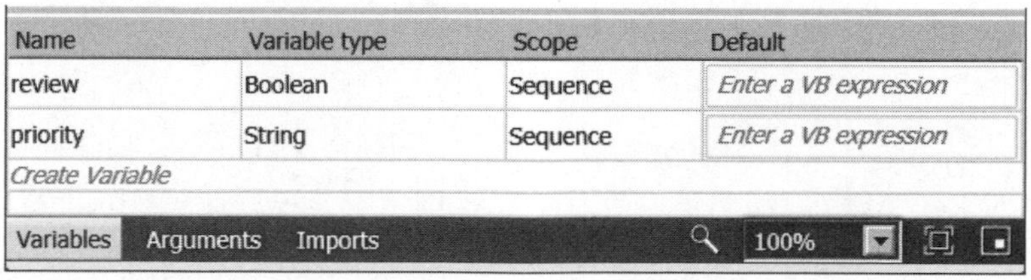

Name	Variable type	Scope	Default
review	Boolean	Sequence	*Enter a VB expression*
priority	String	Sequence	*Enter a VB expression*
Create Variable			

| **Variables** | Arguments | Imports | 🔍 | 100% ▼ | ⬚ | ▪ |

Figure 20-18. *Variables defined for this activity*

Close the variables section. Drag a WriteLine activity to the Sequence, enter the DisplayName as **Execute Activity**, and enter **"The activity is executing…"** for the Text property. This simulates the normal execution of the workflow activity. Drag another WriteLine activity to the Sequence; for the Text property; enter the following code, which displays some information about the transaction to help with debugging:

```
"Amount = $" + transactionData.Amount.ToString() +
", # since oper eval = " + operatorData.NumberSinceLastEval.ToString() +
", # since activity eval = " + activityData.NumberSinceLastEval.ToString()
```

Now you'll check to see if the activity needs to be reviewed. Drag an Interop activity to the Sequence and set the DisplayName to **QCPolicy**. For the Body property, select "Browse for types", expand the QCPolicy assembly, and select the QCPolicy activity. All the DependencyProperty objects that you defined for the QCPolicy activity should now show as properties of the Interop activity. There will also be an output property used for passing the updated data back. There is a corresponding argument or variable with the same name (except lowercase). Enter the appropriate argument or variable for each property. For the properties in the Output category, you will use the output properties. The Properties window should look like the one shown in Figure 20-19.

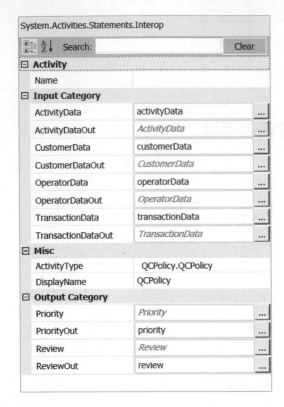

Figure 20-19. *Interop Properties window*

The QCPolicy is executed passing in the various data structures that contain the information used to determine whether a review is required. The review and priority variables are set by the QCPolicy activity and passed back through the output properties. Now you'll use those variables to execute a review step if appropriate.

Drag an If activity just below the QPolicy activity, and enter the Condition property as **review**. Double-click the If activity to expand it and drag a WriteLine to the Then section. Enter the Text property as

```
"Activity is being reviewed; priority is " + priority
```

Incrementing the Activity Counters

Two of the rules that you entered were based on the number of activities that have been executed since the last review. Both the OperatorConfig and ActivityConfig classes contain a NumberSinceLastEval property. You will need to either increment this property (if the activity is not reviewed) or reset it to zero (if the activity was reviewed). To do that, you'll need a custom activity.

From the Solution Explorer, right-click the PolicySample project and choose Add ➤ New Item. Select the Code Activity template, and enter the name as **UpdateCounter.cs**, as shown in Figure 20-20.

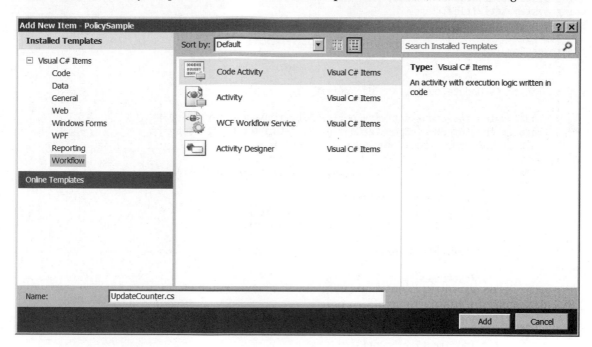

Figure 20-20. *Creating a custom activity*

■ **Tip** You created two types of custom activities in this WF 4.0 project. The first used the workflow designer, in which you could drag activities onto the new activity. This created a sequence of activities that is actually a mini-workflow. The template for this type is called `Activity`. The second type creates a code file in which you can override the `Execute()` method. This allows you to define a new activity, not a sequence of existing activities. The template for this is called `Code Activity`. To help you remember which to use, look at the default file extension when you select the template. The first creates a `.xaml` file while the second creates a `.cs` file. The `.xaml` file is used by the workflow designer, while the `.cs` file is a code file where you override the `Execute()` method.

The implementation of `UpdateCounters.cs` is shown in Listing 20-3.

Listing 20-3. UpdateCounter.cs implementation

```
using System;
using System.Collections.Generic;
using System.Activities;
using QCPolicy;

namespace SamplePolicy
{

    public class UpdateCounters : CodeActivity
    {
        public InOutArgument<ActivityConfig> ActivityData { get; set; }
        public InOutArgument<OperatorConfig> OperatorData { get; set; }
        public InArgument<bool> Review { get; set; }

        protected override void Execute(CodeActivityContext context)
        {
            // Get the current data structures
            ActivityConfig a = ActivityData.Get(context);
            OperatorConfig o = OperatorData.Get(context);

            if (Review.Get(context))
            {
                a.ResetEval();
                o.ResetEval();
            }
            else
            {
                a.IncrementEvalCount();
                o.IncrementEvalCount();
            }

            // Return the updated data
            ActivityData.Set(context, a);
            OperatorData.Set(context, o);
        }
    }
}
```

If the activity is being reviewed, this method calls the ResetEval() method of both the ActivityConfig and OperatorConfig classes. If not being reviewed, the IncrementEvalCount() method is called instead. Press F6 to rebuild the solution.

Open the MyActivity.xaml file (in design mode) and drag the UpdateCounters activity from the toolbox to below the If activity. For the ActivityData property, enter **activityData**; for the OperatorData property, enter **operatorData**; and for the Review property, enter **review**. The Properties window should look like the one shown in Figure 20-21.

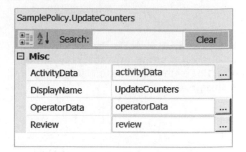

Figure 20-21. *Setting the properties of the UpdateCounters activities*

The custom activity is ready and the complete sequence of MyActivity should look like Figure 20-22. Press F6 to rebuild the solution.

Figure 20-22. *Completed MyActivity sequence*

Creating the Main Workflow

Now you're ready to create the main workflow that will use the custom activity, MyActivity, which you just implemented. The application will pass in the OperatorConfig, CustomerConfig, and ActivityConfig data structures along with a collection of TransactionConfig objects. For each transaction, MyActivity will be executed to perform the action as well as a QC step, if appropriate.

Configuring the Arguments

Open the Workflow1.xaml file (in design mode) and drag a Sequence activity to the workflow. Click the Argument button and then click the *Create Argument* link. For the Name, enter **customerData**; for the Argument type, use the CustomerConfig class. You will need to select Browse for Types, expand the QCPolicy assembly, and select the CustomerConfig class as you did before. Add another argument named **activityData** using the ActivityConfig class for the Argument type. Add a third argument named **operatorData** using the OperatorConfig class. For the final argument, use the TransactionList class; for the Name property, enter **transactionList**. The argument list should look like the one shown in Figure 20-23.

Name	Direction	Argument type	Default value
customerData	In	CustomerConfig	*Enter a VB expression*
transactionList	In	TransactionList	*Enter a VB expression*
activityData	In	ActivityConfig	*Enter a VB expression*
operatorData	In	OperatorConfig	*Enter a VB expression*
Create Argument			

| Variables | Arguments | Imports | | 🔍 | 100% | ▼ | 🗗 🗖 |

Figure 20-23. *Argument list*

Close the Arguments window and drag a WriteLine activity to the Sequence. For the Text property, enter **"The workflow is starting…"**.

Drag a ForEach activity below the WriteLine activity. Enter **Process Transactions** for the DisplayName property. For the TypeArgument property, select Browse for Types and choose the TransactionConfig class from the QCPolicy assembly. For the Values property, enter **transactionList.List**.

Drag a MyActivity from the toolbox to where it says "Drop activity here". In the Properties window, enter the appropriate argument for each input argument that MyActivity is expecting. For the transactionData argument, enter **item**. This is the name given to the element of the Values property of the ForEach activity. For the remaining arguments, enter the same name as the argument. The completed Property window should look like the one shown in Figure 20-24.

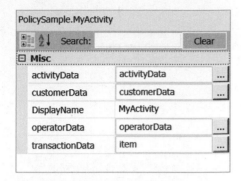

Figure 20-24. *MyActivity Properties window*

The final workflow should look like the one shown in Figure 20-25.

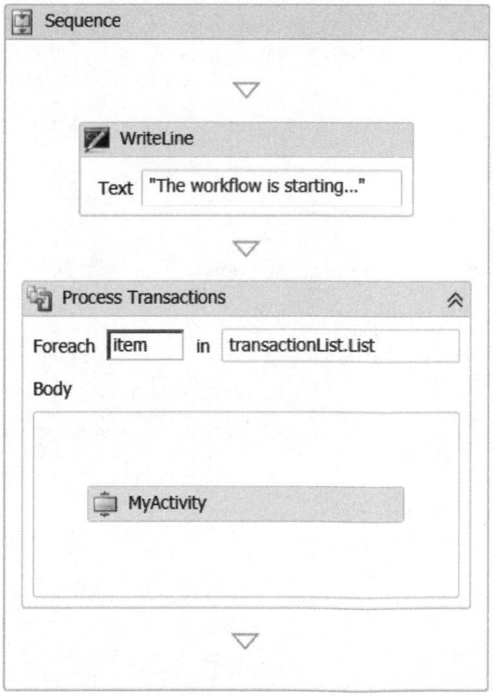

Figure 20-25. *Final application workflow*

Implementing the Console Application

Open the Program.cs file and replace the code that was generated for this file with the code shown in Listing 20-4.

Listing 20-4. Implementation of Program.cs

```
using System;
using System.Activities;
using System.Activities.Statements;
using System.Collections.Generic;
using QCPolicy;

namespace PolicySample
{
    class Program
    {
        static void Main(string[] args)
        {
            TransactionList l = new TransactionList();
            l.List.Add(new TransactionConfig(500.00m));
            l.List.Add(new TransactionConfig(300.00m));
            l.List.Add(new TransactionConfig(250.00m));
            l.List.Add(new TransactionConfig(1200.00m));
            l.List.Add(new TransactionConfig(2100.00m));
            l.List.Add(new TransactionConfig(1100.00m));

            IDictionary<string, object> input = new Dictionary<string, object>
            {
                { "operatorData", new OperatorConfig(false, 2) },
                { "customerData", new CustomerConfig("Prospect") },
                { "activityData", new ActivityConfig(800, 2000, 3) },
                { "transactionList", l }
            };

            IDictionary<string, object> output
                = WorkflowInvoker.Invoke(new Workflow1(), input);

            Console.WriteLine();
            Console.WriteLine("Press ENTER to exit");
            Console.ReadLine();
        }
    }
}
```

This creates a TransactionList class and adds a few TransactionConfig objects to it. It then creates a Dictionary object that contains the OperatorConfig, CustomerConfig, and ActivityConfig objects as well as the TransactionList object. Finally, it invokes the workflow passing in this Dictionary.

Running the Application

Press F5 to run the applications. The results should look like this:

```
The workflow is starting...
The activity is executing.
Amount = $500.00, # since oper eval = 0, # since activity eval = 0
The activity is executing.
Amount = $300.00, # since oper eval = 1, # since activity eval = 1
The activity is executing.
Amount = $250.00, # since oper eval = 2, # since activity eval = 2
Activity is being reviewed; priority is Low
The activity is executing.
Amount = $1200.00, # since oper eval = 0, # since activity eval = 0
The activity is executing.
Amount = $2100.00, # since oper eval = 1, # since activity eval = 1
Activity is being reviewed; priority is High
The activity is executing.
Amount = $1100.00, # since oper eval = 0, # since activity eval = 0

Press ENTER to exit
```

After two transactions that were not reviewed, the third one was because of the Frequency rule. Because the transaction was only $250, it was given a low priority in the QC review. The fifth transaction was reviewed because it had a total of $2,100. Try changing the configuration values by editing the Program.cs file, and verify that the results are as you would expect. For example, change the Category property of the CustomerConfig class to **"Major"** and you should see that all transactions are reviewed.

Review

The solution in this chapter is a good example of creating reusable building blocks. This is the recommended approach for designing workflows. The QCPolicy activity can be reused with any activity that might need a review process. Then MyActivity implements the activity and handles the review step, if appropriate, using QCPolicy to make that determination.

The main workflow then simply calls MyActivity. In a large workflow, this will greatly simplify the design. Each activity provides its own QC process. The activity designer would be responsible for designing the QC step as well. This is similar to the compensation model you implemented in Chapter 17. The compensation, confirmation, and cancellation actions were all implemented by the activity designer. The main workflow just adds the activity to the overall process and can assume that the activity itself knows how to handle these conditions.

This chapter also uses some of the concepts that you learned throughout this book. If you want to review some of these principles, you can refer to the appropriate chapter as follows:

- Passing Arguments: Chapter 4

- ForEach: Chapter 5

- Custom Activities: Chapter 7

- Interop: Chapter 19

A very brief description of using WF 3.5 was provided in both this chapter and Chapter 19. I was not able to adequately cover WF 3.5 in this book so if you will be using WF 3.5 for parts of your solution, you might want to read a book that provides more information about WF 3.5.

■ ■ ■

Sample Workflow Project

The sample project provided in the appendix is designed as a review of many of the concepts discussed in this book. It also demonstrates how the techniques you've learned can be combined to build a full-featured application. Instead of giving you step-by-step instructions for building the solution, the complete project is available for you to download from http://www.apress.com. As you'll see, this project is fairly extensive and this will save you quite a bit of time (and typing).

Project Overview

The application provides a web page in which end users can enter requests, comments, or questions. Based on the topic selected, the request is placed in one of several queues for individuals to view and respond to. A second web page is provided to show the contents of these queues. Once a queue is selected, items are presented to be worked. Each queue can be configured in one of two modes: either the oldest request is automatically presented to be worked or all requests are displayed for the user to select one.

After a request has been worked, it might require a QC review step based on rules defined in a Policy object. (The implementation is very similar to one you created in Chapter 20.) Requests can also be rerouted to a different queue if necessary. A tracking extension is used to record the various events (started, assigned, reviewed, rerouted, and so on) so you can see how a particular request made its way through the workflow.

All the workflow functionality is provided through a web service. The web site uses the native .Net membership services, which gives the site the capability to "log in." The operator information is provided to the workflow so it can track which users worked on each request. Finally, the generic workflow features and queue logic is provided by a set of workflow activities and extensions that are implemented in a separate library project. This allows you to reuse this code in other applications.

I'll explain the solution in more detail later, but first, let's run the application so you can see what it does. You'll need to download the Appendix.zip file and extract this to an appropriate location.

Configuring the Database

The AppendixData folder contains the scripts you'll need to set up the database schema. First, create a SQL Server database for this solution. Expand the Create Scripts folder and run the included scripts in the following order:

- SqlWorkflowInstanceStoreSchema.sql
- SqlWorkflowInstanceStoreLogic.sql
- Config.sql
- Request.sql
- Tracking.sql

The scripts used to create the membership tables and procedures assume that there is a database named aspnetdb on the server that the connection string is referencing. This is the default database that the ASP.Net services use. If you do not already have this setup, create a database called aspnetdb and then run the InstallCommon.sql and InstallMembership.sql scripts (in that order).

■ **Caution** If you need to modify the database connection for your environment, make sure that you make the change to the configuration files; there are two places. The web.config file in the root folder of the web site project defines the connection string for the aspnetdb database used by the .Net services. There is also a web.config file in the root folder of the ServiceLayer project. This is used to configure the workflow persistence store as well as the application data that your custom activities will use.

Running the Application

Once your database has been configured, from Visual Studio, press F5 to start the application. The initial page should look like the one shown in Figure A-1.

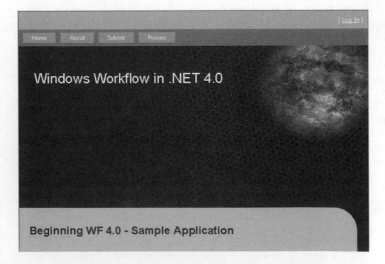

Figure A-1. Initial web page

Logging In

Click the Log In link at the top-right corner of the page. The first time you log in, you'll need to create a new account by clicking the register link. This will display the page shown in Figure A-2.

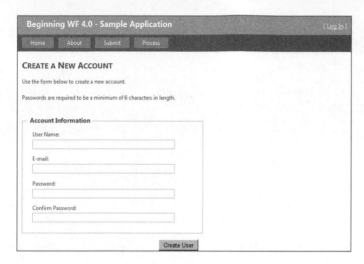

Figure A-2. Creating a new account

Enter your name, e-mail address, and a password (the e-mail address is not actually used to send e-mails so you can enter any text here that you want.) The next time you log in, you'll want to check the "Keep me logged in" check box, as shown in Figure A-3. If you do, you won't need to log in again even if you restart the application.

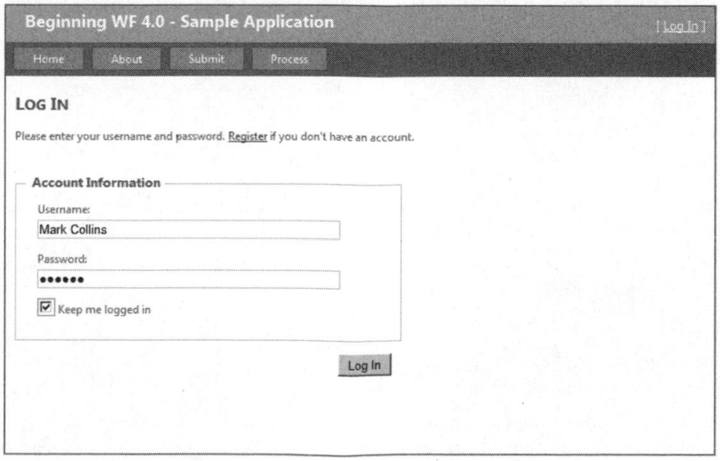

Figure A-3. Using the "Keep me logged in" option

Submitting a Request

Click the Submit link at the top of the page. This will display the page used for entering a new request/comment, which is shown in Figure A-4.

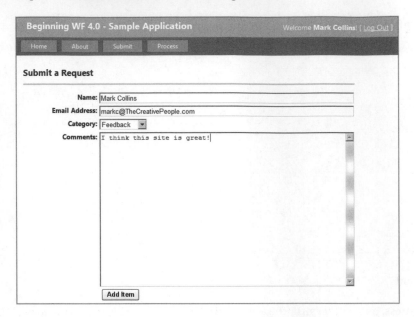

Figure A-4. Entering a new request

If you've logged in, the name and e-mail address will be filled in for you. Select the Feedback category and enter a comment. Then click the Add Item link. Figure A-5 shows a completed submit page. The comment field is cleared and the unique identifier assigned to this request is displayed at the top of the page. Enter a couple more requests using the same Feedback category.

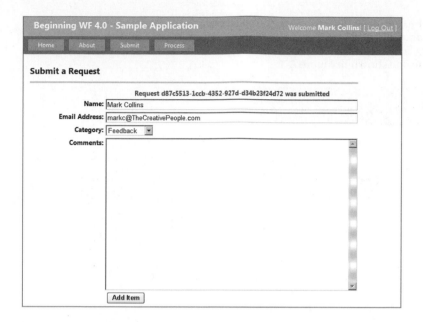

Figure A-5. The completed submit page

Processing Requests

Click the Process link at the top of the page. This will display the Process page that is shown in Figure A-6.

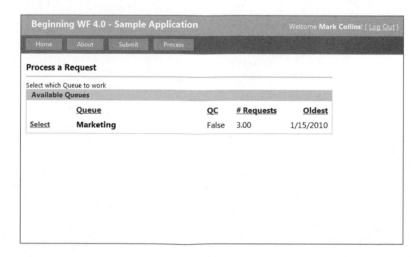

Figure A-6. Displaying the available queues

The grid on this page lists the queues that have requests that need to be responded to. The Feedback category was assigned to the Marketing queue so all the requests you entered are in this queue. This grid indicates how many requests are in this queue and the date of the oldest request. Click the Select link and the page should look like the one shown in Figure A-7.

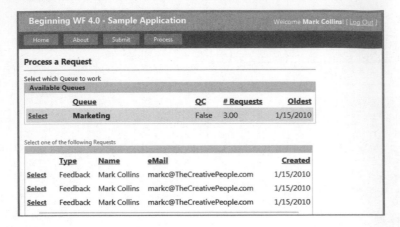

Figure A-7. Selecting a request

The Marketing queue is configured to allow selection. This means that instead of automatically assigning the oldest request in the queue, all the requests are listed, and you are allowed to select the one you want to work on. Click one of the Select links and the request will be displayed, as shown in Figure A-8.

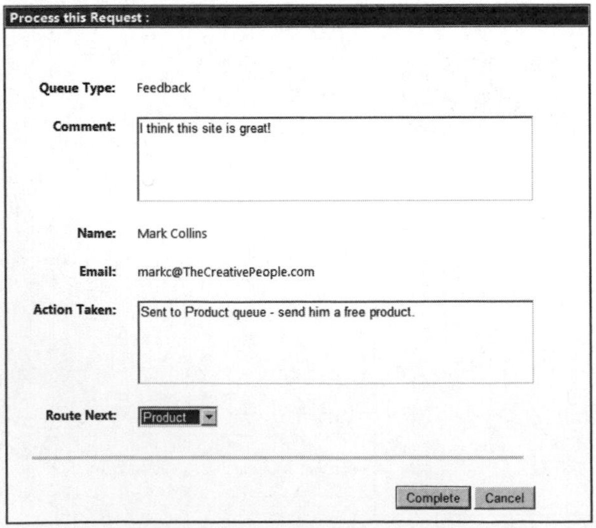

Figure A-8. Responding to a request

Below the request there is a place to enter the action that was taken. You can also select a queue to route this request to. You could click the Cancel button if you decided not to work on this request. That will unassign the request and put it back in the queue for someone else to work. Enter some notes in the Action Taken field, select the Product queue, and click the Complete button. The page should now look like the one shown in Figure A-9.

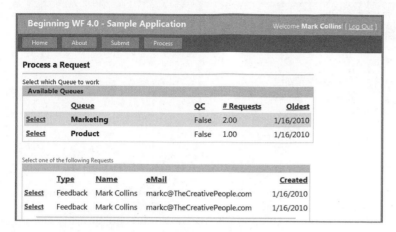

Figure A-9. The updated queue list

Notice that the Product queue is now displayed in the queue list, and there are only two requests to choose from in the Marketing queue. Click the Select link next to the Product queue. The page should look like the one shown in Figure A-10.

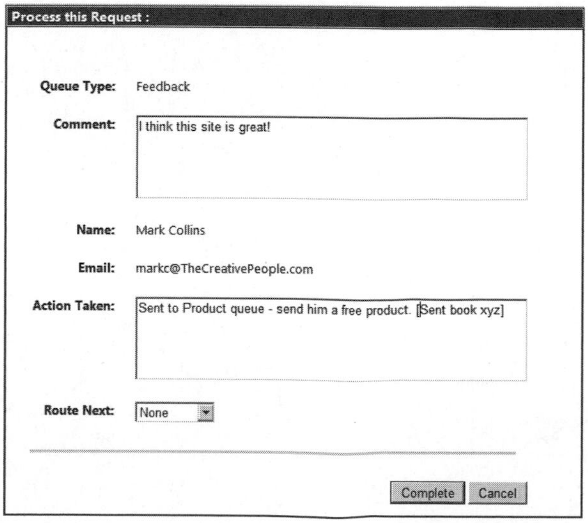

Figure A-10. Working the request in the Product queue

Because there is only one item in the Product queue, it was automatically assigned. You can edit or append to the Action Taken field. You can also reroute this request to another queue, if necessary. For this request, append a note to the Action Taken field and leave the Route Next field blank. Click the Complete button. The page should look like the one shown in Figure A-11.

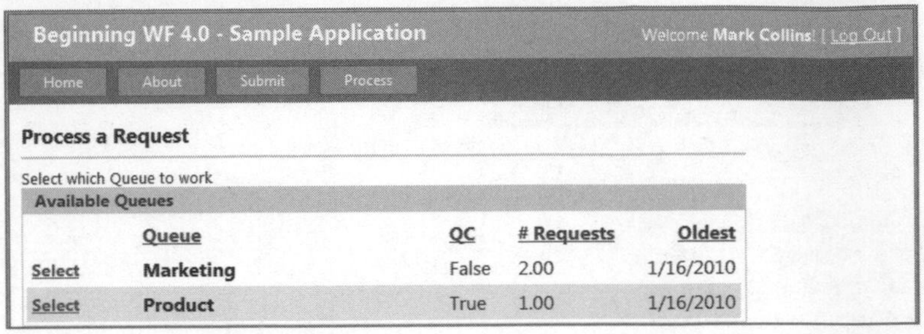

Figure A-11. Request moved to QC mode

Notice that this request is still in the Product queue, but the QC column shows "True". The Product queue is configured so that all requests in the Product queue must go through a QC review. Consequently, the request is put back into the queue in QC mode. Select the Product queue again and the request should be displayed; this time in QC mode, as shown in Figure A-12.

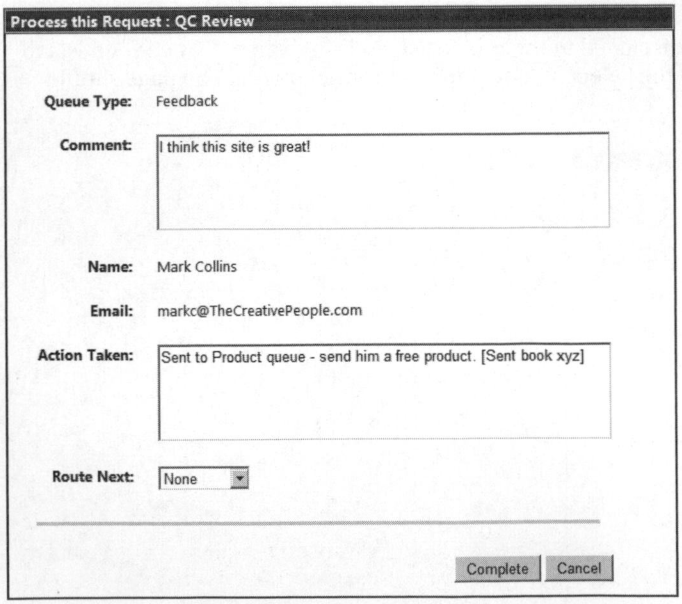

Figure A-12. Performing QC review

In QC review, you can view and modify the Action Taken. Edit this field and click the Complete button. The request is now complete. Figure A-13 shows the updated queue list with only the remaining items in the Marketing queue.

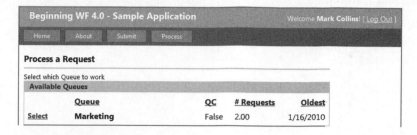

Figure A-13. Updated queue list

Tracking the Workflow

Close the web application and go back to Visual Studio. From the Server Explorer, open the contents of the QueueTrack table. The results should be similar to those shown in Figure A-14.

QueueName	SubQueueN...	QueueInsta...	EventType	QC	OperatorKey	EventDate
Request	Marketing	efcbab4c-4b...	Start	False	NULL	1/9/2010 5:...
Request	Marketing	efcbab4c-4b...	Assign	False	b4a8b43c-e...	1/9/2010 5:...
Request	Product	efcbab4c-4b...	Route	False	NULL	1/9/2010 5:...
Request	Product	efcbab4c-4b...	Assign	False	b4a8b43c-e...	1/9/2010 5:...
Request	Product	efcbab4c-4b...	QC	False	NULL	1/9/2010 5:...
Request	Product	efcbab4c-4b...	Assign	True	b4a8b43c-e...	1/9/2010 5:...
Request	Marketing	3c97677a-c...	Start	False	NULL	1/9/2010 5:...
Request	Marketing	4c41ce42-f8...	Start	False	NULL	1/9/2010 5:...

Figure A-14. Showing the tracking results

The QueueTrack table records the various events that occurred on each of the requests: Started, Assigned, Route, QC, and so on. The request that you just worked was started in the Marketing queue. It was then assigned to an operator and then routed to the Product queue. It was again assigned to the same operator and then put into QC mode. Finally, it was assigned to the operator for a third time□this time in QC mode.

Generic Queue Logic

Using queues for managing human tasks is a common practice that can be used in many applications. I designed this solution to encapsulate the generic activities in a separate project called UserTasks. This should help you to reuse this logic more easily in your own applications.

Database Design

Figure A-15 shows the tables used by the UserTasks project. You can also view this diagram by opening the UserTasks.dbml file in the UserTasks project.

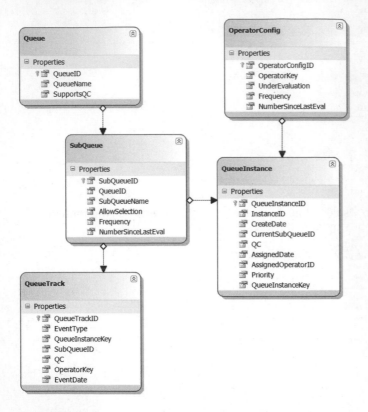

Figure A-15. Database design for the UserTasks project

The database contains both a Queue and a SubQueue table. The queues that you used, such as Marketing and Product, are really subqueues, and this solution uses a single queue called Request. This approach allows you to reuse the same tables (and workflow activities) for any number of human-centric workflow tasks.

The Queue and SubQueue tables provide configuration options such as SupportsQC (at the queue level) and AllowSelection (at the subqueue level). The SubQueue table includes the Frequency column, which defines how often requests in this subqueue need to be reviewed. The NumberSinceLastEval is used to keep track of this to know when it's time to force another review. The OperatorConfig table provides other QC-related options (see Chapter 20 for more details.)

The QueueInstance table is the main table that drives the queue logic. A record is created for every request. It keeps track of what subqueue the request is currently in, whether it's in QC mode, and who it is currently assigned to. The QueueTrack table is populated by the tracking extension in response to user-defined tracking events.

Activities

The UserTasks project is an activity library project that provides activities that can be dropped onto other workflows. The included activities are listed in Table A-1.

Table A-1. Activities provided in the UserTasks project

Activity Name	Description
AssignQueue	Moves a QueueInstance to the specified subqueue.
AssignQueueInstance	Assigns a QueueInstance to the specified operator.
CompleteInstance	Provides QC and rerouting logic.
CreateQueueInstance	Creates a new QueueInstance record.
GetQueueInstances	Returns the available QueueInstance records in the specified subqueue (if allow selection is turned off, it returns only the oldest record).
LoadQueueInstance	Loads the specified QueueInstance.
LookupQueueStats	Returns the number of records in each queue/subqueue.
RequestQC	Moves the specified QueueInstance into QC mode.
UnAssignQueueInstance	Unassigns the current operator and makes this QueueInstance available to be assigned to another operator.

All these activities, with the exception of CompleteInstance, are implemented as coded activities. I won't take the time to list all the source code here; you can browse the code in Visual Studio. They use a DBConnection extension to obtain the connections string (see Chapter 12) and use a PersistQueueInstance extension to save the changes as part of the workflow persistence (see Chapter 15). As with all the other projects in this book, they use LINQ to SQL to access the database tables.

CompleteInstance

The CompleteInstance activity is provides as a designed activity. The workflow design for it is shown in Figure A-16.

Figure A-16. Design of the CompleteInstance activity

After loading the QueueInstance record, it then checks to see whether this queue supports QC or whether the QueueInstance is already in QC mode. If not, it invokes the QCPolicy activity, which determines whether this record should be QC'ed. If QC is required, the RequestQC activity is executed to update the QueueInstance. The Complete output argument is passed back to the calling workflow to indicate whether the QueueInstance was actually completed or whether it requires a QC step.

QCPolicy

The QCPolicy activity is an Interop activity that invokes a QCPolicy activity, which is implemented in .Net 3.5. (You might want to refer to Chapter 20 for more details on using the Policy activity.) The design of the QCPolicy activity is shown in Figure A-17.

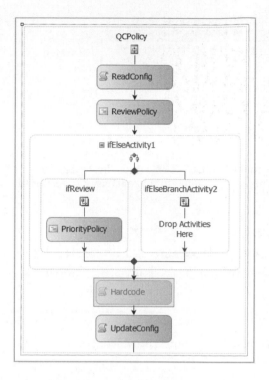

Figure A-17. QCPolicy Design (.Net 3.5)

Unlike the implementation in Chapter 20, this QCPolicy activity reads and updates the configuration data from the database. Because the Policy activity uses the .Net 3.5 version of workflow, it cannot access the DBConnection extension. Instead, the connection string is passed in as a DependencyProperty.

The ReviewPolicy activity is a Policy that determines whether the QueueInstance needs to be reviewed. The rule set used is shown in Figure A-18.

Name	Priority	Reeval...	Active	Rule Preview
No Configuration	5	Always	True	IF this._queue == null THEN this.Review = False Halt
ActivityFrequency	4	Always	True	IF this._queue.NumberSinceLastEval >= this._queue.Frequency THEN this.Review = True...
No Operator	3	Always	True	IF this._operator == null THEN this.Review = False Halt
Under Evaluation	2	Always	True	IF this._operator.UnderEvaluation == True THEN this.Review = True Halt
Operator Frequency	1	Always	True	IF this._operator.NumberSinceLastEval >= this._operator.Frequency THEN this.Review = ...

Figure A-18. ReviewPolicy rule set

If QC is needed, the PriorityPolicy is executed to determine what priority it should be given. Its rule set is shown in Figure A-19.

417

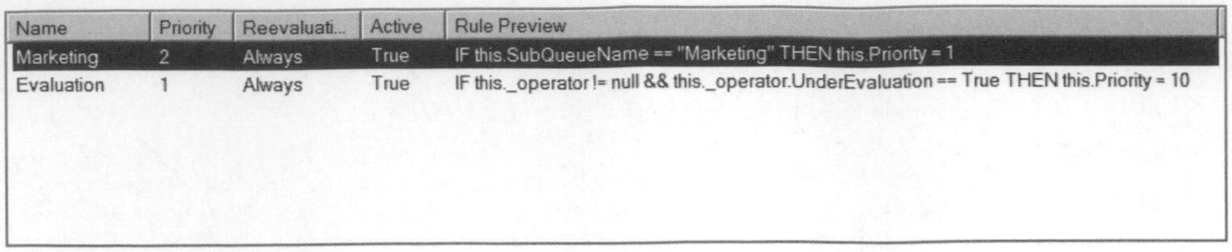

Name	Priority	Reevaluati...	Active	Rule Preview
Marketing	2	Always	True	IF this.SubQueueName == "Marketing" THEN this.Priority = 1
Evaluation	1	Always	True	IF this._operator != null && this._operator.UnderEvaluation == True THEN this.Priority = 10

Figure A-19. PriorityPolicy rule set

The Hardcode activity is used for testing only and is normally disabled. It overrides the Review and Priority properties that were set by the Policy activities. This was provided to make it easier to test both QC and non-QC scenarios.

■ **Note** WF 3.0/3.5 provided the ability to disable an activity. When the workflow is executed, disabled activities are ignored. This feature had limited usefulness and is *not* provided in WF 4.0. This particular scenario was one of the useful applications of this feature.

To test the actual Policy implementation, a separate TestQC application is provided. This is a simple workflow application with the QCPolicy activity dropped onto it.

Tracking

The ability to track workflow events was described in Chapter 13. This project relies on custom tracking events. The following code (or something similar) is included in several of the custom activities:

```
CustomTrackingRecord userRecord = new CustomTrackingRecord("Route")
{
    Data =
    {
        {"QueueInstanceKey", qi.QueueInstanceKey},
        {"SubQueueID", qi.CurrentSubQueueID}
    }
};

// Emit the custom tracking record
context.Track(userRecord);
```

This causes a custom tracking event to be generated, which is received and processed by the QueueTracking extension. The implementation of the Track method of this extension is shown in Listing A-1.

Listing A-1. Implementation of the Track Method

```
protected override void Track(TrackingRecord record, TimeSpan timeout)
{
    CustomTrackingRecord customTrackingRecord =
        record as CustomTrackingRecord;

    if (customTrackingRecord != null)
    {
        if (customTrackingRecord.Name == "Start"    ||
            customTrackingRecord.Name == "Route"    ||
            customTrackingRecord.Name == "Assign"   ||
            customTrackingRecord.Name == "UnAssign" ||
            customTrackingRecord.Name == "QC")
        {
            QueueTrack t = new QueueTrack();

            // Extract all the user data
            if ((customTrackingRecord != null) &&
                (customTrackingRecord.Data.Count > 0))
            {
                foreach (string key in customTrackingRecord.Data.Keys)
                {
                    switch (key)
                    {
                        case "QueueInstanceKey":
                            if (customTrackingRecord.Data[key] != null)
                                t.QueueInstanceKey =
                                    (Guid)customTrackingRecord.Data[key];
                            break;
                        case "SubQueueID":
                            if (customTrackingRecord.Data[key] != null)
                                t.SubQueueID = (int)customTrackingRecord.Data[key];
                            break;
                        case "QC":
                            if (customTrackingRecord.Data[key] != null)
                                t.QC = (bool)customTrackingRecord.Data[key];
                            break;
                        case "OperatorKey":
                            if (customTrackingRecord.Data[key] != null)
                                t.OperatorKey =
                                    (Guid)customTrackingRecord.Data[key];
                            break;
                    }
                }
            }

            if (t.SubQueueID != null && t.QC == null)
                t.QC = false;
```

```
        t.EventType = customTrackingRecord.Name;
        t.EventDate = DateTime.UtcNow;

        // Insert a record into the TrackUser table
        UserTasksDataContext dc =
            new UserTasksDataContext(_connectionString);
        dc.QueueTracks.InsertOnSubmit(t);
        dc.SubmitChanges();
    }
  }
}
```

This first checks to see whether this is one of the events that should be processed. Specifically, it is looking for the following:

- Start: A new QueueInstance is created.

- Route: A QueueInstance is placed in a queue.

- Assign: The QueueInstance is assigned to a specific operator.

- UnAssign: The QueueInstance is unassigned.

- QC: The QueueInstance is placed to QC mode.

■ **Note** As I demonstrated in Chapter 13, the events that should be tracked can be configured instead of written in code. This is the preferred approach. However, this tracking extension is writing to a database table specifically designed for these events. It doesn't know how to track other events. In this case, it is appropriate to put the filter in code. This still allows you to configure the events that are actually tracked within this set of supported events.

The various data records are extracted from the event to populate the corresponding columns in the table.

Service Layer

As I mentioned previously, all the workflow functionality is provided by a web service. You created a fairly simple web service in Chapter 10. This implementation is significantly more complex.

Service Contract

In Chapter 10, you used both the traditional method of defining a service contract and a declarative style provided by WF. In this project, I used the later method exclusively. On each of the Receive activities, the OperationName and appropriate input parameters are defined. Similarly, on the SendReply activities the output parameters are defined.

Also, on the Receive activities, the interface name is specified. You don't have to define this interface; just specify the name to use when one is created for you. If you want all the methods on the same interface, use the same interface name on all the Receive activities. You can also use different names, which will result in multiple interfaces. For this project, I used IProcessRequest for all the methods. Figure A-20 shows the methods that are implemented in the IProcessRequest interface.

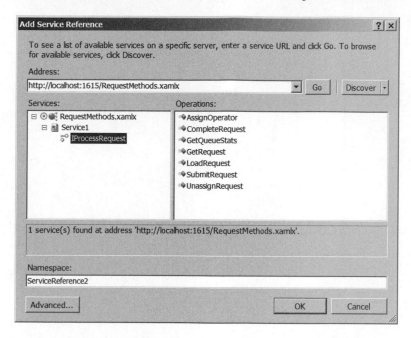

Figure A-20. Web service methods

When a service reference is added to the web application, all the necessary web service details are generated for you, including the Web Service Definition Language (.wsdl) file that explicitly defines the web service and the methods provided. You can open Service1.wsdl and see what this looks like. It's a little cryptic for the human reader. It also generates several .xsd files that define the data types and data contracts that are used in the input and output messages. Figure A-21 shows one of these files displayed in the XML Schema Explorer.

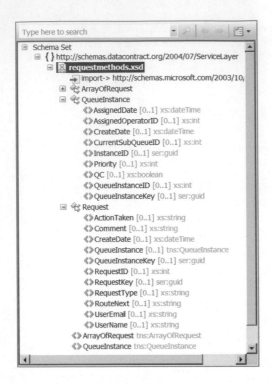

Figure A-21. XML Schema Explorer

Database Design

Because the queue logic is provided by the UserTasks project, the service layer can focus on request-specific design elements. Consequently, the data model is quite simple, as shown in Figure A-22.

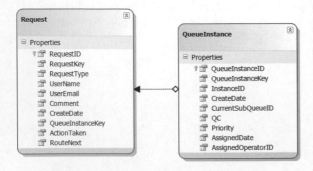

Figure A-22. Service layer data model

The Request table contains the data, such as name, e-mail, and comment, entered by the user who submitted the request. It also records the action taken, which is entered by the operator who worked the request. It has a reference to a QueueInstance record. The QueueInstance record handles all the queue details such as the current queue, to whom it's assigned, and so on. This design keeps the Request table clear of all these "plumbing" details.

Activities

The ServiceLayer project implements some custom activities, which are listed in Table A-2.

Table A-2. Activities provided in the ServiceLayer project

Activity Name	Description
BuildRequestList	Maps the data returned by GetQueueInstances into a list of Request objects.
CreateRequest	Creates a new Request record.
LoadRequest	Load the specified Request from the database.
UpdateRequest	Updates a Request.

The CreateRequest and UpdateRequest use the PersistRequest extension to perform the database update when the workflow is persisted. The BuildRequestList activity is the only one that is particularly interesting. The GetQueueInstances activity (provided in the UserTasks project) handles all the logic to determine which records are available to be worked, but it knows nothing about requests. It uses only the QueueInstance table as well as the Queue and SubQueue setup tables. BuildRequestList takes the list of QueueInstance objects returned by GetQueueInstances and maps them to a list of Request objects. The implementation is shown in Listing A-2.

Listing A-2. BuildRequestList Implementation

```
using System;
using System.Collections.Generic;
using System.Linq;
using System.Activities;
using UserTasks;
using UserTasks.Extensions;

namespace ServiceLayer.Activities
{

    public sealed class BuildRequestList : CodeActivity
    {
```

```csharp
public InArgument<UserTasks.QueueInstance[]> QueueInstanceList { get; set;}
public OutArgument<Request[]> RequestList { get; set; }

protected override void Execute(CodeActivityContext context)
{
    // Get the connection string
    DBConnection ext = context.GetExtension<DBConnection>();
    if (ext == null)
        throw new InvalidProgramException("No connection string available");

    RequestDataContext dc = new RequestDataContext(ext.ConnectionString);

    // Get the list of QueueInstances
    UserTasks.QueueInstance[] qiList = QueueInstanceList.Get(context);
    if (qiList != null && qiList.Count() > 0)
    {
        // Build a list of Request objects
        Request[] rList = new Request[qiList.Count()];
        int i = 0;
        foreach (UserTasks.QueueInstance qi in
            QueueInstanceList.Get(context))
        {
            Request r = dc.Requests.SingleOrDefault
                (x => x.QueueInstanceKey == qi.QueueInstanceKey);
            rList[i++] = r;
        }

        RequestList.Set(context, rList);
    }
}
```

Workflow Design

This web service is implemented using the workflow designer, which produces an .xamlx file. Figure A-23 shows the overall design with some of the activities collapsed to fit the diagram on a page.

Figure A-23. Overall workflow design

The workflow uses the Pick activity that was introduced in Chapter 10. To review, a Pick activity contains one or more PickBranch activities, in which each contains a Trigger activity and an Action sequence. When the Trigger is executed, the associated Action sequence is started, and all other PickBranch activities are cancelled. In this case there are four branches; the Trigger for each one contains a Receive activity that waits for a specific web service method.

The four methods are as follows:

- SubmitRequest: Initiates a new request.

- GetQueueStats: Gets the number of request in each queue.

- GetRequest: Gets the available request(s) from the specified queue.

- LoadRequest: Returns the request details of the specified request.

The last three are fairly straightforward. They perform a database operation and return the appropriate results back to the caller using a SendReply activity. When the application wants to get the current statistics about the queues, it calls the GetQueueStats() method of the web service. This will create a new workflow instance that is completed as soon as the response is sent back to the application. This workflow is very short-lived. The instance store is configured to remove the record from the InstancesTable when the workflow is completed. So using a workflow instance to perform a simple task does not leave any artifacts behind.

SubmitRequest

When SubmitRequest is called, it first determines the correct subqueue using a Switch activity (see Chapter 4 for details). It then creates a QueueInstance record and a Request record and returns data back

425

to the caller using SendReply. So far, this is similar to the other branches. However, the workflow continues after the SendReply activity. It is followed by a While activity; the design of this is shown in Figure A-24.

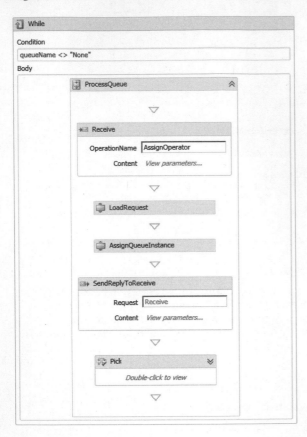

Figure A-24. While activity

The Condition on the While activity is as follows:

queueName <> "None"

This means that the While activity will continue to execute as long as the request is assigned to a queue. When the request is completed, without forwarding the request to another queue, the queueName is set to "None", causing the While activity to complete. The logic inside the While activity starts with a Receive activity that waits for the AssignOperator method. A request must be assigned to an operator before it can be worked. This helps ensure that two people are not working on the same request.

Processing a Request

When the `AssignOperator()` method is called, the `QueueInstance` associated with that request is updated to record the assignment and the response is sent back. The workflow then continues with another `Pick` activity that is shown in Figure A-25.

Figure A-25. The final Pick activity

When a request has been assigned to an operator, one of three things can happen:

- The request is completed.

- The page is cancelled forcing the request to be unassigned.

- Neither.

The three branches represent these scenarios. The first branch completes the request, and the second branch unassigns the request so someone else can work it. The third branch uses a `Delay` activity to wait for five minutes. If nothing has been done within that time, the request is automatically unassigned. If an operator has a request assigned to them and they decide to leave for the day and simply close their browser, the request would be left assigned to them. This means that no one else could work that request. This third branch was added to take care of that scenario.

If the `CompleteRequest()` method is called, the first branch updates the request with the data provided. It then executes the `CompleteInstance` activity that was described earlier. This activity determines whether the item in the queue needs to be reviewed in QC mode. It outputs a `Complete` argument to indicate whether the item is complete or whether it needs to be reviewed. Figure A-26 shows the sequence that is executed if the request is complete.

Figure A-26. *The sequence for completed requests*

■ **Note** When I say the request is complete, I'm referring to that particular task for that request is complete. The request might need to be worked in other queues before the workflow is completed.

The `routeNext` variable is specified in the `CompleteRequest()` method; it is determined by the operator working the request. This is copied to the `queueName` variable. If no queue was selected, this will signal that the workflow is done, and the `While` activity will complete. The `AssignQueue` activity is called to update the current subqueue for the `QueueInstance`. The `UpdateRequest` activity will clear the `RouteNext` field.

Correlation

The concept of correlation was introduced briefly in Chapter 8. A typical workflow will have hundreds, perhaps thousands, of workflow instances executing simultaneously. When a workflow design includes sending messages to (and between) instances, correlation provides the mechanism to ensure that messages are sent to the correct instance. There are three types of correlation provided by WF 4.0.

The first (and probably easiest) correlation is called request reply correlation. It is used when you have a two-way communication between workflow activities. For example, you send a request and wait for the response. You used this in Chapter 8 (and others). By placing the `Send` and `ReceiveReply` activities within a `CorrelationScope` activity, the workflow took care of the details for you. In this case, correlation was accomplished through the communication channel that was established between the sender and the receiver.

The other two types support more complex scenarios in which there are multiple messages between the workflows. The first is referred to as context correlation. In this case, the client sends a request, and the server includes a context ID with the response. This context ID must be included with all subsequent messages from the client. This is used by the server to associate the same instance that responded to the first message. This approach requires logic on both the client and server. This approach also requires that the first message be a two-way message; the server has to send back a response that includes the context ID.

The last approach, query correlation, is accomplished on the server side only. In a sense, this is actually very similar to context correlation. There is some sort of key that is included with each request that identifies the corresponding workflow instance. With context correlation, this key is generated by the server on the initial request. However, with query correlation, this key is based on data included in the message.

This project uses query correlation and the common key is the RequestKey, which is a Guid generated by the application. The RequestKey is provided as one of the parameters on every call to the service. When the first message is received, the RequestKey is mapped to that workflow instance. This is done through a correlation initializer, which sets up the mapping between the RequestKey and the associated workflow instance. On subsequent calls, this is extracted (queried) from the data in the incoming message and the mapping is used to determine the workflow instance.

Query correlation is accomplished through the Receive activity. There are three properties on the Receive activity that support correlation, as shown in Figure A-27.

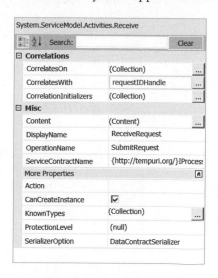

Figure A-27. Properties of a Receive activity

The CorrelatesWith property defines the handle, which is specified as a CorrelationHandle type. This is a workflow variable that is persisted with the workflow. A CorrelationInitializer is then added to the first Receive activity, as shown in Figure A-28.

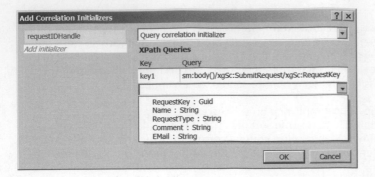

Figure A-28. A correlation initializer

The XPath query might seem a little cryptic, but don't worry; the Visual Studio takes care of this for you. You only need to select the appropriate property from the drop-down menu. The drop-down menu lists all the parameters in the incoming message. When the RequestKey is chosen, the query is generated automatically.

On subsequent Receive activities, instead of setting the CorrelationInitializer, the CorrelatedOn property is set. This is done by selecting the correct parameter; a query is then generated for you, as shown in Figure A-29.

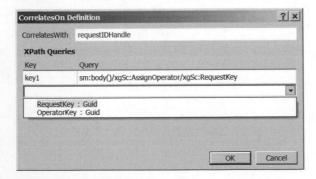

Figure A-29. The CorrelatesOn property

Using WorkflowServiceHost

This project uses several workflow extensions that were introduced in previous chapters (persistence in Chapter 11, sharing configuration data in Chapter 12, tracking in Chapter 13, and custom persistence in Chapter 14). In those projects there was a console or WPF application that configured these extensions and added them to the workflow instances as they were created. In this project, this is done by the WorkflowServiceHost.

Writing Extensions

To add extensions when using the WorkflowServiceHost, they must be configured in the web.config or app.config file. This requires some extra steps when writing the extensions. The modified implementation of DBConnection.cs is shown in Listing A-3.

Listing A-3. Implementation of the DBConnection Extension

```
using System;
using System.Collections.Generic;
using System.Collections.ObjectModel;
using System.Collections.Specialized;
using System.Configuration;
using System.Web.Configuration;
using System.ServiceModel;
using System.ServiceModel.Activities;
using System.ServiceModel.Channels;
using System.ServiceModel.Configuration;
using System.ServiceModel.Description;

namespace UserTasks.Extensions
{
    /****************************************************/
    // The extension class is used to define the behavior
    /****************************************************/
    public class DBConnectionExtension : BehaviorExtensionElement
    {
        public DBConnectionExtension()
        {
            Console.WriteLine("Behavior extension started");
        }

        [ConfigurationProperty("connectionStringName", DefaultValue = "",
            IsKey = false, IsRequired = true)]
        public string ConnectionStringName
        {
            get { return (string)this["connectionStringName"]; }
            set { this["connectionStringName"] = value; }
        }

        public string ConnectionString
        {
            get
            {
                ConnectionStringSettingsCollection connectionStrings =
                    WebConfigurationManager.ConnectionStrings;
                if (connectionStrings == null) return null;
                string connectionString = null;
                if (connectionStrings[ConnectionStringName] != null)
                {
```

```
                    connectionString =
                        connectionStrings[ConnectionStringName].ConnectionString;
            }
            if (connectionString == null)
            {
                throw new ConfigurationErrorsException
                    ("Connection string is required");
            }
            return connectionString;
        }
    }

    public override Type BehaviorType
    {
        get { return typeof(DBConnectionBehavior); }
    }
    protected override object CreateBehavior()
    {
        return new DBConnectionBehavior(ConnectionString);
    }
}

/****************************************************/
// The behavior class is used to create an extension
// for each new instance
/****************************************************/
public class DBConnectionBehavior : IServiceBehavior
{
    string _connectionString;

    public DBConnectionBehavior(string connectionString)
    {
        this._connectionString = connectionString;
    }

    public virtual void ApplyDispatchBehavior
        (ServiceDescription serviceDescription, ServiceHostBase serviceHostBase)
    {
        WorkflowServiceHost workflowServiceHost
            = serviceHostBase as WorkflowServiceHost;
        if (null != workflowServiceHost)
        {
            string workflowDisplayName
                = workflowServiceHost.Activity.DisplayName;

            workflowServiceHost.WorkflowExtensions.Add(()
                    => new DBConnection(_connectionString));
        }
    }

    public virtual void AddBindingParameters
```

```
        (ServiceDescription serviceDescription,
         ServiceHostBase serviceHostBase,
         Collection<ServiceEndpoint> endpoints,
         BindingParameterCollection bindingParameters)
    {
    }

    public virtual void Validate
        (ServiceDescription serviceDescription,
         ServiceHostBase serviceHostBase)
    {
    }
}


/***************************************************/
// This is the actual extension class
/***************************************************/
public class DBConnection
{
    private string _connectionString = "";

    public DBConnection(string connectionString)
    {
        _connectionString = connectionString;
    }

    public string ConnectionString { get { return _connectionString; } }
}
```

There are three classes implemented in this file:

- DBConnectionExtension

- DBConnectionBehavior

- DBConnection

DBConnectionExtension is derived from the BehaviorExtensionElement class. It specifies the configuration values that are supported. In this case, there is only one: connectionStringName. It also provides a ConnectionString() method that obtains the connection string from the configuration file using the connsctionStringName parameter. Finally, it overrides the CreateBehavior() method, which creates a DBConnectionBehavior object passing in the connection string to the constructor.

The DBConnectionBehavior class implements the IServiceBehavior interface. This interface defines an ApplyDispatchBehavior() method that creates an extension and adds it to a workflow instance. This is roughly equivalent to the SetupInstance() method you wrote in Chapter 12. When the WorkflowServiceHost is started, it looks for all the configured extensions and obtains an IServiceBehavior interface for each. As each workflow instance is created, it calls the ApplyDispatchBehavior() method on each of the IServiceBehavior interfaces. The ApplyDispatchBehavior() method creates a DBConnection class, passing in the connection string to the constructor and then adds it to the WorkflowExtensions collection.

The DBConnection class in same implementation you created in Chapter 12. It provides a ConnectionString property that supplies the connection string to any activity that needs it.

Configuring Extensions

A subset of the web.config file is shown in Listing A-4.

Listing A-4. A Portion of the web.config file

```
<configuration>
  <connectionStrings>
    <add name="Request" connectionString=
      "Data Source=localhost;Initial Catalog=Appendix;Integrated Security=True"
      providerName="System.Data.SqlClient" />
  </connectionStrings>
  <system.serviceModel>
    <extensions>
      <behaviorExtensions>
        <add name="dbConnection"
          type="UserTasks.Extensions.DBConnectionExtension, UserTasks,
                Version=1.0.0.0, Culture=neutral, PublicKeyToken=null" />
      </behaviorExtensions>
    </extensions>
    <behaviors>
      <serviceBehaviors>
        <behavior>
          <dbConnection connectionStringName="Request"/>
        </behavior>
      </serviceBehaviors>
    </behaviors>
  </system.serviceModel>
</configuration>
```

First, a connection string named "Request" is defined in the connectionStrings section. This allows you to reference it by name in various places in the web.config file. The advantage to this approach is that the actual connection string is specified only once. If you need to modify it later, you have to change it in only one place.

Next, an extension named "dbExtension" is added to the behaviorExtensions section. Note that the actual class that is referenced is the DBConnectionExtension class, not the DBConnectionBehavior or DBConnection classes. This extension is then configured in the behaviors section. The extension is specified by name, dbConnection, and its configuration values are defined. There is only one, connectionStringName and it is set to "Request" to use the connection string defined earlier.

Configuring Persistence

The persistence extension, SqlWorkflowInstanceStore, is configured in the behavior section as well. You do not need to add anything to the behaviorExtensions section. The subset of the web.config file is shown in Listing A-5.

Listing A-5. Configuring Persistence

```
<behaviors>
  <serviceBehaviors>
    <behavior>
      <sqlWorkflowInstanceStore
        connectionStringName="Request"
        instanceCompletionAction="DeleteAll"
        instanceLockedExceptionAction="NoRetry"
        instanceEncodingOption="GZip"
        hostLockRenewalPeriod="00:00:30" />
      <workflowIdle
        timeToUnload="00:00:10"
        timeToPersist="00:00:05" />
    </behavior>
  </serviceBehaviors>
</behaviors>
```

Notice that is uses the same connectionStringName. The code in Listing A-5 also configures the workflowIdle behavior. The timeToUnload property is set to 10 seconds. This will keep the instance in memory for 10 seconds after it has entered the Idle state.

Configuring Tracking

To add the tracking extension QueueTracking, the entries are added to extensions and behavior sections just as it was for the DBExtension discussed previously. In addition, a tracking section is added to specify queries used to define the tracking events that are to be included. Refer to Chapter 13 for more information about tracking queries. The web.config entries are shown in Listing A-6.

Listing A-6. Configuring Tracking

```
<configuration>
  <system.serviceModel>
    <extensions>
      <behaviorExtensions>
        <add name="tracking"
          type="UserTasks.Extensions.QueueTrackingExtension, UserTasks,
            Version=1.0.0.0, Culture=neutral, PublicKeyToken=null" />
      </behaviorExtensions>
    </extensions>
    <behaviors>
      <serviceBehaviors>
        <behavior>
          <tracking connectionStringName="Request"/>
        </behavior>
      </serviceBehaviors>
    </behaviors>
    <tracking>
      <profiles>
```

```
        <trackingProfile name="Queue_Tracking">
          <workflow>
            <customTrackingQueries>
              <customTrackingQuery name="*" activityName="*" />
            </customTrackingQueries>
          </workflow>
        </trackingProfile>
      </profiles>
    </tracking>
  </system.serviceModel>
</configuration>
```

The complete web.config file is shown in Listing A-7.

Listing A-7. Complete web.config File

```
<?xml version="1.0" encoding="utf-8" ?>
<configuration>
  <connectionStrings>
    <add name="Request" connectionString=
      "Data Source=localhost;Initial Catalog=Appendix;Integrated Security=True"
      providerName="System.Data.SqlClient" />
  </connectionStrings>
  <system.web>
    <compilation debug="true" targetFramework="4.0" />
  </system.web>
  <system.serviceModel>
    <extensions>
      <behaviorExtensions>
        <add name="persistRequest"
          type="ServiceLayer.Extensions.PersistRequestExtension, ServiceLayer,
            Version=1.0.0.0, Culture=neutral, PublicKeyToken=null" />
        <add name="persistQueueInstance"
          type="UserTasks.Extensions.PersistQueueInstanceExtension, UserTasks,
            Version=1.0.0.0, Culture=neutral, PublicKeyToken=null" />
        <add name="dbConnection"
          type="UserTasks.Extensions.DBConnectionExtension, UserTasks,
            Version=1.0.0.0, Culture=neutral, PublicKeyToken=null" />
        <add name="tracking"
          type="UserTasks.Extensions.QueueTrackingExtension, UserTasks,
            Version=1.0.0.0, Culture=neutral, PublicKeyToken=null" />
      </behaviorExtensions>
    </extensions>
    <behaviors>
      <serviceBehaviors>
        <behavior>
          <!-- To avoid disclosing metadata information, set the value below to
               false and remove the metadata endpoint above before deployment -->
          <serviceMetadata httpGetEnabled="True"/>
          <!-- To receive exception details in faults for debugging purposes,
               set the value below to true.  Set to false before deployment to
```

```
            avoid disclosing exception information -->
        <serviceDebug includeExceptionDetailInFaults="True"/>
        <!-- This line configures the persistence service -->
        <sqlWorkflowInstanceStore
          connectionStringName="Request"
          instanceCompletionAction="DeleteAll"
          instanceLockedExceptionAction="NoRetry"
          instanceEncodingOption="GZip"
          hostLockRenewalPeriod="00:00:30" />
        <workflowIdle
          timeToUnload="00:30:00"
          timeToPersist="00:00:05" />
        <!-- Configure the connection string for the persistence extensions-->
        <dbConnection connectionStringName="Request"/>
        <persistRequest connectionStringName="Request"/>
        <persistQueueInstance connectionStringName="Request"/>
        <tracking connectionStringName="Request"/>
      </behavior>
    </serviceBehaviors>
  </behaviors>
  <tracking>
    <profiles>
      <trackingProfile name="Queue_Tracking">
        <workflow>
          <customTrackingQueries>
            <customTrackingQuery name="*" activityName="*" />
          </customTrackingQueries>
        </workflow>
      </trackingProfile>
    </profiles>
  </tracking>
</system.serviceModel>
<system.webServer>
  <modules runAllManagedModulesForAllRequests="true"/>
</system.webServer>
</configuration>
```

Summary

This sample project is just one way workflow can be used to implement a solution. There are other approaches, such as the one described in Chapter 7 in which workflow was used to organize a processing algorithm. My goal throughout this book was to give you a variety of applications. Hopefully one or more of these will resemble a project you are currently working on.

You now have the tools to use the capabilities provided by Workflow Foundation. I wish you great success as you add this to your repertoire of software design patterns.

Index

M

You Need the Companion eBook

Your purchase of this book entitles you to buy the companion PDF-version eBook for only $10. Take the weightless companion with you anywhere.

We believe this Apress title will prove so indispensable that you'll want to carry it with you everywhere, which is why we are offering the companion eBook (in PDF format) for $10 to customers who purchase this book now. Convenient and fully searchable, the PDF version of any content-rich, page-heavy Apress book makes a valuable addition to your programming library. You can easily find and copy code—or perform examples by quickly toggling between instructions and the application. Even simultaneously tackling a donut, diet soda, and complex code becomes simplified with hands-free eBooks!

Once you purchase your book, getting the $10 companion eBook is simple:

❶ Visit **www.apress.com/promo/tendollars/**.

❷ Complete a basic registration form to receive a randomly generated question about this title.

❸ Answer the question correctly in 60 seconds, and you will receive a promotional code to redeem for the $10.00 eBook.

THE EXPERT'S VOICE™

233 Spring Street, New York, NY 10013

Offer valid through 8/10.